Against the
Vietnam War

Against the Vietnam War

Writings by Activists

EDITED BY MARY SUSANNAH ROBBINS

Syracuse University Press

Permission to initially publish or reprint from the following sources is gratefully acknowledged:
David Harris, "The Need to Remember," *Stanford Magazine,* Dec. 1993, 28–29, reprinted by
permission of *Stanford Magazine;* Howard Zinn, "The Impossible Victory: Vietnam," pp.
460–92, from *A People's History of the United States,* by Howard Zinn, copyright © 1980 by
Howard Zinn, reprinted by permission of HarperCollins Publishers, Inc.; Robert Malecki, *Ha
Ha Ha McNamara,* chapters 5 and 7, available on the Internet, published here by permission
of Robert Malecki; Noam Chomsky, "The Responsibility of Intellectuals," *The New York
Review of Books,* Feb. 23, 1967, pp. 16–26, copyright © Noam Chomsky, reprinted by permis-
sion of Noam Chomsky; Martin Luther King, Jr., "Declaration of Independence from the War
in Vietnam," reprinted by arragement with the Heirs to the Estate of Martin Luther King, Jr.,
c/o Writers House, Inc., agent for the proprietors, copyright © 1963 by Martin Luther King,
Jr., copyright © renewed 1991 by Coretta Scott King; Daniel Berrigan, S.J., from *Night Flight to
Hanoi:* "Night Flight to Hanoi," "Song," "Children in the Shelter," "Alert," "Bombardment."
Copyright © 1968 by Daniel Berrigan, S.J., reprinted by permission of Daniel Berrigan, S.J.;
Carl Oglesby, "Chicago 1968: Streetfightin' Man" from *Ravens on the Wing: A Memoir of the
Movement Against the Vietnam War,* copyright © 1995 by Carl Oglesby, published here by per-
mission of Carl Oglesby; Joan Baez, "Where Are You Now, My Son?" from *And a Voice to Sing
With: A Memoir* by Joan Baez, reprinted with the permission of Simon and Schuster, copy-
right © 1987 by Joan Baez; Joan Baez's song, "Where Are You Now, My Son?" copyright ©
1973 by Chandos Music, reprinted by permission of Joan Baez; James Fallows, "What Did
You Do in the Class War, Daddy?" reprinted by permission of *The Washington Monthly,* copy-
right by The Washington Monthly Company, 1611 Connecticut Avenue, N.W., Washington,
D.C. 20009; H. Bruce Franklin, "Burning Illusions: The Napalm Campaign," copyright ©
1997 by H. Bruce Franklin, all rights reserved; Eugene J. McCarthy, "Consequences of the
Vietnam War and Government Policies of the Seventies," from *Required Reading: A Decade of
Political Wit and Wisdom,* copyright © 1977 by Harcourt Brace Jovanovich, by permission of
Harcourt Brace and Company, New York.

The paper used in this publication meets the minimum repuirements of American National
Standard for Information Sciences—Permanence of paper for Printed Library Materials,
ANSI Z39.48-1984. ∞

Library of Congress Cataloging-in-Publication Data

Against the Vietnam War : writings by activists / edited by Mary Susannah Robbins.
      p.   cm.
     Includes index.
     ISBN 0-8156-2796-3 (cloth : alk. paper). — ISBN 0-8156-2797-1 (pbk. : alk. paper)
      1. Vietnamese Conflict, 1961–1975—Protest movements—United States. 2. United
    States—Politics and government—1963–1969. 3. United States—Politics and govern-
ment—
    1969–1974. I. Robbins, Mary Susannah.
    DS559.62.U6A35   1999   98-45027
    959.704'31—dc21

To my mother and father,
without whose love this
book would not have
been possible

Mary Susannah Robbins graduated from Radcliffe in 1967 and received a Ph.D. in English literature from Boston College in 1973. She has taught literature and writing at Boston College and at Vassar. Currently, she runs her own editorial service. She has published a book of poems and etchings, Amelie, and poems, stories, and prints in magazines. Her prints are represented in several American museums.

Contents

PART THREE
Soldiers Against the War

PART FOUR
Consequences

PART FIVE
Conclusions

Acknowledgments

THIS BOOK HAS been a collective endeavor. I would like to thank, first, its contributors, not only for their works and time, but for leading me to one another. I would also like to thank them for help with other matters concerning the book. And I would like to thank them for being.

Especially I would like to thank Staughton Lynd, for much labor and for his wise judgment in many matters.

Thanks to Howard Zinn for his interest, patience and help.

Thanks to H. Bruce Franklin for his time and sound editorial advice.

Thanks to my family and friends for their love and support. The title of the book came out of a discussion with my father, Herbert Robbins; my mother, Mary D. Robbins, provided much helpful advice and my sister, Marcia Robbins, many encouraging conversations.

Thanks to the director of Syracuse University Press, Robert A. Mandel, and its executive editor, Cynthia Maude-Gembler, for believing in this book.

I would like to remember Mitchell Goodman, who died while he was working on an essay for this collection.

And thanks to the many people not in the book who were active against the Vietnam War and who contributed to this story.

Introduction

MARY SUSANNAH ROBBINS

AT MY HARVARD twenty-fifth reunion in 1992, there was a symposium entitled "Vietnam: The Choices We Made." As the panelists spoke, some people wept in silence. It was like a memorial service. After the panelists had spoken, lines of people stood at the microphones placed around the room, waiting in silence to tell their own stories. Each person struggled to bear witness to a long nightmare, hitherto unspoken, unshared. The shaking backs of friends and strangers signified what they held—and held in—in common. "We never talked about it," some said afterward.

In Harvard Square it seemed that the sidewalk was glass, that below it lay the rubble of the Vietnam War on which American society was built, and that no one was looking down.

So, I would look down. I would not deny it any longer. I would look at the war and the antiwar movement, so inextricable.

My closest friends had led the 1968 strike at Harvard in which the students took over University Hall. I remember the police in riot gear in Harvard Square. I went to demonstrations in Washington and in Boston. I worked for Eugene McCarthy's presidential campaign. I wrote letters. I signed petitions. Like most of the people in the antiwar movement, I never went to jail, and I was not a leader. My own life was complex, and it was in large part a desire to go back to what lay behind all that happened to me during that time that inspired this book. When I talked to contributors and read their articles, it was as though the screen of my personal life

The untitled poem by Mary Susannah Robbins concluding the introduction was originally published in *Karamu* 13, no. 2 (Spring 1993), 94–95. Reprinted by permission of the poet.

lifted, and I saw the depths that lay behind it, the sorrow and passion of Vietnam. From the personal to the political, as the saying goes. Not only Vietnam, but the violence and assassinations in this country affected all our lives and made us what we are. It was not until I was teaching at Vassar in the early seventies that I was actively radicalized, and that was over issues of race and class. Vietnam swept me along, and in some way I wanted to go back and know and control it, to mourn. I knew that in one way or another everything I had done since, as well as everything that had happened politically in this country, was because of the Vietnam War. It seemed very important to go back to those roots.

I lived with a Vietnam vet for several years. He had been a sergeant in the army and had received a dishonorable discharge because he refused to send his men into a village for the third time after most of them had been killed the first two times. He came home and joined Vietnam Veterans Against the War. We felt that we had everything in common. We had both suffered from the violence of the war. He had shrapnel scars; mine were invisible. We were on the same side now. In the war lay the roots of our adult lives.

What I did not know was the complexity, the many facets of the anti-war movement, the shades of opinion. Putting this book together brought the issues to life—a varied, vivid, complicated life. I was made aware that it was a peace movement for some, and a "war against the war," to quote David Cortright, for others. I learned how individual an experience the antiwar movement had been.

The antiwar movement is almost as controversial today as it was then. H. Bruce Franklin suggests this series of questions that point out how unsure we are today of what the movement was:

> "Was it a futile, ineffective gesture, or did it actually prevent a US military victory? Was it the outburst of a vocal minority, or did it express the deepest convictions of a majority of Americans? Was it mainly an activity of affluent youths on college campuses, or did it appear in its most militant forms among poor and working class people in urban slums and within the army itself? Was the protest tantamount to treason, or did it represent the noblest traditions of American history? Did it divert from or reinforce the movement of black and other non-white people for equality? Did the revitalization of the movement for women's equality grow from the antiwar movement or develop as a reaction against male

domination within it? Was the movement's cultural thrust coopted, nullified, even reversed by diffusion into designer jeans, disco, and cocaine, or did it profoundly advance the values of post–Vietnam War America? Did the movement disappear with the war, or did it continue to evolve into movements for social change in the ensuing decades?"[1]

No book will answer all these questions, but they are questions that need to be considered if the proper place and meaning of the antiwar movement are to be found.

The authors of these articles are among the luminaries of the antiwar movement. Intellectuals, activists, working-class veterans, and teachers of the history of the war come together here to tell their own stories in their own ways. The themes are rich and heterogeneous. Some of the pieces are new, and some were published in the sixties and have become historical documents and classics. The latter provide a framework, a historical context for the book.

The book has five parts. The first is introductory. The second contains essays on the civilian antiwar movement; the third, essays on resistance and the military; the fourth, essays on the consequences of the war; and the fifth, concluding essays.

The book opens with David Harris's cogent and moving essay, "The Need to Remember," which is followed by Howard Zinn's "The Impossible Victory: Vietnam," a history of the war that forms a background to the rest of the book.

The section entitled "The War at Home" begins with a chapter from a book by Robert Malecki, who is now in exile in Sweden, about working-class young men and the military. Jane Bond Moore's "My Vietnam" discusses the many roles an African American woman—wife, mother, political activist, now lawyer—in the intertwined personal and political lives of the movement in the South. H. Bruce Franklin writes about community organizing around an effort to stop napalm production in a California town. Using the events in Vietnam as a focus for his views in "The Responsibilty of Intellectuals," Noam Chomsky argues that intellectuals have greater access to the truth than other people and therefore more responsibility to it. There follows the Reverend Martin Luther King, Jr.'s historic speech, given in 1967 at Riverside Church in New York, in which he linked the civil rights movement and the antiwar movement and came out against the war in Vietnam. Michael Ferber's essay, "Why I Joined the

Resistance," tells of his becoming a conscientious objector and standing trial, and I have included the speech, "A Time to Say No," he made at Arlington Church in 1967 in which he explores the meaning of the radical tradition. Daniel Berrigan's poems, written on a trip to Hanoi, express in very powerful images the meaning of this war. The chapter from Carl Oglesby's book on the movement tells of the demonstration and police violence at the Democratic Convention in 1968 in Chicago. Jeff Jones, who was with the Weather Underground, writes of his meeting with Kim Phuc—who, in the well-known photograph, was the child running down the road in Vietnam, her skin and clothes burned by napalm—and of his development from a peaceful activist to a revolutionary. Eugenia Kaledin writes of the arrest of demonstrating Vietnam veterans on the green in Lexington, Massachusetts, on Memorial Day 1971. The chapter from Joan Baez's book, *And A Voice To Sing With,* describes her stay in Hanoi during the Christmas bombing, her terror in the shelters, and her solidarity with the Vietnamese people.

In the section "Soldiers Against the War," James Fallows's essay "What Did You Do in the Class War, Daddy?" states that the difference between who went to Vietnam and who didn't was a matter of class, and that if ten thousand Harvard boys had been killed in Vietnam, the war would have stopped immediately. George Swiers's piece is about losing a buddy in Vietnam and never forgetting. In his essay, "American War Crimes and Vietnam Veterans," Tod Ensign recounts his participation in setting up citizens commissions to expose the atrocities committed by Americans in Vietnam after the events at My Lai were uncovered and describes the willingness of veterans to testify at these hearings which so discredited the war. David Cortright describes his own experience in the resistance within the army.

In the section entitled "Consequences," Eugene McCarthy's essay speaks of government deceit stemming from the war. Jerold Starr writes of a life in the movement and of his current work teaching the lessons of Vietnam. In a piece taken from her talk at our Harvard twenty-fifth reunion symposium, Arlene Ash writes of her "consciousness raising," her involvement in the antiwar movement, and her subsequent trips to Vietnam. David Dellinger's essay, "Chicago 1996: Despite Corporate Media Silence Many Powerful Protests," describes the protests in which he participated at the 1996 convention and connects them to both 1968 and the generation now growing up.

In "Conclusions," Jane Sass Collins's "What I Got Out of the War" tells of how the antiwar movement and the countercultural movement changed her life totally, and speaks of her hope that the fragmented movements that now exist will come together. William Ayers's essay, "Cherishing Vistas, Embracing Human Beings: Toward Peace and Freedom," speaks of his belief that teaching is the most radical activity, of his participation in the Weather Underground, and of his conviction that the struggle for participatory democracy and all it stands for continues and must continue. In his "Conclusion: Déjà Vu All Over Again," Staughton Lynd lays out the path from the civil rights movement to the Vietnam antiwar movement to activism against the Gulf War and states that what we valued in the 1960s is as true today as it was then—that it must, will come again.

Putting these essays together, I saw that the issues still lived, perhaps in a new perspective, but lived as they had always lived, as the coming of age of a generation, as a force that still divides the country. In these pages, they live with a freshness born of the movement's significance, classical documents and new essays side by side. The roots of the antiwar movement were complex, but it was a strong people's movement from which today's youth can perhaps learn something about democracy, about freedom of speech, and about the right to dissent.

This book will present itself differently to different people. To some who lived through the war, it will bring up things half forgotten. Some of it will be familiar to antiwar activists. To others, it will present a movement that they knew only in stereotype. To the youth of today, who evince a great interest in the period, it will be an introduction to some of the best writing on the subject by some of the leaders of the movement. Combining historical documents and new essays, it will show the living nature of a continued controversy.

There is in the United States today a new interest in the Vietnam War. Some of the contributors to this book—H. Bruce Franklin, David Harris, Carl Oglesby—are coming out with or have recently come out with new books of their own on the subject. The United States has established full relations with Vietnam. Classes on the war are taught in many high schools and colleges.

Now let these varied, living articles, these documents of the past and the present, speak for themselves.

love me occasionally
not in euphoria
only the heart
remembers at all
heroes are killed
each day in Pretoria
we stand beside them
we watch them fall
touch me kindly
not in euphoria
only the flesh
remembers at all

touch me kindly
not in euphoria
the sick are dying
or getting well
Rockefeller's in
the Waldorf Astoria
we're in Vietnam
and Vietnam is in hell
love me occasionally
not in euphoria
only the flesh
remembers who fell

only the heart
remembers the bitterness
only the flesh
remembers the pain
love me occasionally
not in euphoria
touch me kindly
and touch me again
heroes are killed
for less than this kindness
in Haiphong harbor
the mines are rain

teach me occasionally
over and over
how to love
and how not to die
to remember and
how to remember
how to ask why and
to ask why
teach me over
the noise of the bombers
that blacken out
the clear blue sky

Contributors

ARLENE ASH quantitatively examines social issues from power plant hazards to equity in teacher's pay. She is a research professor at Boston University at the School of Medicine and the School of Public Health. Her work focuses on protecting sick people and their providers. She supports her vibrant, quirky urban neighborhood as a board member of the Fenway Community Development Corporation.

WILLIAM AYERS is a school reform activist and professor of education at the University of Illinois at Chicago, where he teaches courses in interpretive research, urban school change, education for justice and democracy, youth and the modern predicament, and the cultural contexts of teaching. He is codirector of the Small Schools Workshop and cofounder of the Annenberg Challenge in Chicago. A graduate of Bank Street College of Education and Teachers College, Columbia University, he has written extensively about the importance of creating progressive educational opportunities in urban public schools. His interests focus on the political and social contexts of schooling, and on the meaning and ethical purposes of teachers, students, and families. His articles have appeared in many journals, including the *Harvard Educational Review,* the *Journal of Teacher Education, Teachers College Record,* the *Nation,* and the *Cambridge Journal of Education.* His books include *The Good Preschool Teacher* (1989) and *To Teach: The Journey of a Teacher* (1993), which was named Book of the Year in 1993 by Kappa Delta Pi and won the Witten Award for Distinguished Work in Biography and Autobiography in 1995. Recent edited books are *To Become a Teacher: Making a Difference in Children's Lives* (1995) and (with Pat Ford) *City Kids/City Teachers: Reports from the Front Row* (1996). His latest book is *A Kind and Just Parent: The Children of Juvenile Court* (1997).

JOAN BAEZ, in addition to making many records and films, has been active in the civil rights movement and the movement against the Vietnam War, as well as in such organizations as Amnesty International and Humanities International Human Rights Committee, which she founded. She has supported a nuclear freeze and has given concerts and done human rights work in many countries—including Russia, Greece, Czechoslovakia, and Vietnam.

DANIEL BERRIGAN, S. J., and his brother Philip were the leaders of the U.S.-based Catholic resistance to the Vietnam War. He is a writer, teacher, and political activist. In 1965, he helped to found Clergy and Layman Concerned. In 1968, he was one of the Catonsville Nine sentenced for draft resistance work. He is the author of *Night Flight to Hanoi,* a war diary, and of many books of poetry.

NOAM CHOMSKY has been on the MIT faculty since 1955. Apart from his professional work, he writes and speaks widely on a variety of social and political issues. He has helped to organize and has supported resistance and other activities of peace and justice movements.

JANE SASS COLLINS will write for food.

DAVID CORTRIGHT has served as president of the Fourth Freedom Forum since 1992. He is also a visiting fellow at the Joan B. Kroc Institute for International Peace Studies at the University of Notre Dame and assistant professor in the Department of Peace Studies at Goshen College. He is the recipient of a Research and Writing Award for peace and international cooperation from the John D. and Catherine T. McArthur Foundation. He was the executive director of SANE, the largest peace organization in the United States, from 1977 to 1987. Under his direction, the organization grew from four thousand to one hundred fifty thousand members. In 1987, he initiated the merger between SANE and the Nuclear Weapons Freeze Campaign, and for a time served as codirector of the merged organization. He is the author of *Soldiers in Revolt* (1975), *Left Face* (1991), and *Peace Works: The Citizen's Role in Ending the Cold War* (1993), as well as coeditor of *Economic Sanctions: Panacea or Peacebuilding in a Post–Cold War World* (1995) and of *India and the Bomb: Public Opinion and Nuclear Options* (1996). His articles have appeared in *The Fletcher Forum, The Bulletin of the*

Atomic Scientists, Peace and Change, The New York Times, Chicago Tribune, San Francisco Chronicle, and numerous other journals and newspapers.

DAVID DELLINGER is the author of *From Yale to Jail: A Memoir; Vietnam Revisited: Covert Action to Invasion to Reconstruction; Beyond Survival: New Directions for the Disarmament Movement* with Michael Albert; *More Power Than We Know: The People's Movement Toward Democracy; Revolutionary Nonviolence;* and *Cuba: America's Lost Plantations.* He spent three years in Danbury, Conn., Federal Correctional Institution (1940–41) and Lewisburg, Pa., Federal Penitentiary (1943–45) for refusal to register for the draft, although he was militarily exempt as a divinity student. He has had occasional refresher courses at other jails.

TOD ENSIGN, a lawyer, is director of Citizen Soldier, a nonprofit GI/veterans rights advocacy organization established in New York City in 1969. In addition to his involvement in public education and advocacy on behalf of the civil rights and liberties of GIs and veterans, Ensign has published extensively in magazines and newspapers such as *Radical America, The Progressive, Covert Action, The Pathologist, WIN, Africa Report, The Guardian,* and *In These Times.* Ensign is author of *Military Life: The Insider's Guide* (1990) and coauthor, of *GI Guinea Pigs: How the Pentagon Exposed Our Troops to Hazards Deadlier Than War* (1980). He also contributed a chapter on resistance to military service to *Collateral Damage,* edited by C. Peters (1992).

JAMES FALLOWS is the editor of *U.S. News & World Report.* He has written award-winning books and articles about a wide variety of topics, from military policy and international relations to immigration, mental testing, and the rise of the computer industry. Fallows joined *U.S. News* in September 1996. Previously, he spent seventeen years as Washington editor of the *Atlantic Monthly.* He was also chief speechwriter for President Jimmy Carter and an editor of the *Washington Monthly* and *Texas Monthly* magazines. Fallows has done regular weekly commentaries for National Public Radio since 1987. For four years during the late 1980s, Fallows lived with his wife and children in Japan and Malaysia. Since that time, he has worked and traveled in almost every country of East Asia. This reporting is the basis of his book *Looking at the Sun,* published in 1994. Previous books include *More Like Us* (1989) and *National Defense* (1981), which won the American Book

Award for nonfiction. His latest book is *Breaking the News: How the Media Undermine American Democracy* (1996). His articles on politics, foreign affairs, and technological developments in the United States have been published in many magazines, including the *New York Review of Books, Esquire, Fortune,* the *Smithsonian,* and the *New York Times Book Review.* Fallows was raised in Redlands, California, where he attended public schools. He studied U.S. history and literature at Harvard, where he was president of the Harvard *Crimson.* Between 1970 and 1972, he studied economics at Queen's College, Oxford, as a Rhodes scholar. He holds numerous honorary degrees. Fallows has testified frequently before Congress in discussions of economics, politics, and U.S.-Asian relations, and has spoken extensively at universities and to civic groups across the country. He lives in Washington, D.C., with his wife Deborah and their two sons.

MICHAEL FERBER was born in Buffalo, New York, in 1944. He attended Swarthmore College, where he was active in the civil rights movement in nearby Chester, Pennsylvania, and majored in Ancient Greek; received his M.A. and Ph.D. from Harvard in English Literature, during which time he took part in a movement called the Resistance; was an assistant professor at Yale, then a lobbyist for nuclear disarmament in Washington D.C.; and is now a professor of English and humanities at the University of New Hampshire. He is married and has a young daughter. He has written five books—one on the history of draft resistance in the sixties, *The Resistance* (1971, with Staughton Lynd), two on William Blake, one on Shelley, and one on literary symbolism.

H. BRUCE FRANKLIN, a leading humanist scholar and authority on the Vietnam War, is the author or editor of seventeen books and more than 150 articles on culture and history. Before his academic career, he served three years as a navigator and intelligence officer in the U.S. Air Force. In 1966, he resigned his commission as a captain in the U.S. Air Force Reserves in protest against the Vietnam War and became a prominent antiwar activist. He is currently the John Cotton Dana Professor of English and American Studies at Rutgers University in Newark.

DAVID HARRIS attended Stanford University and was elected student body president in 1966. During his undergraduate years, he was active in the civil rights movement in Mississippi and gained recognition as a national leader of the opposition to the Vietnam War. In 1968, he resisted the draft, and upon his conviction for violating the Selective Service Act, he spent nearly two years in federal prisons. After the Paris Peace Agreements were signed in 1973, he began a career in journalism, which he has pursued ever since, except during the time he spent standing as the Democratic Party's unsuccessful nomination for Congress in California's Twelfth Congressional District in 1976.

JEFF JONES joined the antiwar movement at Antioch College in October 1965. He worked with the Dayton Area Coordinating Committee to End the Vietnam War, the National Mobilization Committee to End the Vietnam War, and Students for a Democratic Society (SDS). In April 1967, he left college to work full-time for SDS as the organization's New York City regional coordinator. In November 1967, Jones traveled to Cambodia with an SDS delegation for meetings with representatives of the National Liberation Front and the North Vietnamese. In June 1969, he was elected SDS interorganizational secretary. The following March, he failed to show up for trial on federal conspiracy charges—crossing state lines to incite a riot—and remained a fugitive until his arrest in October 1981. In 1985, Jones went to Nicaragua to help in the coffee harvest and edited *Brigadista: Harvest and War in Nicaragua,* about the experiences of North American volunteers working in Nicaragua during the Reagan administration's Contra war. He returned to Southeast Asia in 1986, visiting Vietnam for three weeks. He became a reporter, covering New York State politics and policy for several publications. Jones currently works as an environmental lobbyist in Albany, New York.

EUGENIA KALEDIN is an independent scholar with two degrees from Harvard and a Ph.D. from Boston University. She has taught in schools as varied as Northeastern University, Goddard College, the University of Pennsylvania, and Yale. As a Fulbright professor, she also taught in Beijing and in Czechoslovakia. Her writing includes *Mothers and More: American Women in the 1950s* (1984) and *The Education of Mrs. Henry Adams* (1995).

THE REVEREND MARTIN LUTHER KING, JR., was born on January 15, 1929. He led the bus boycott in Selma and Montgomery in 1955–56, thus becoming the leader of the civil rights movement. In 1957, he became the head of the Southern Christian Leadership Conference. In 1963, he led another crucial march in Birmingham. He received the Nobel Prize for Peace in 1964. He was assassinated by James Earl Ray on April 4, 1968.

STAUGHTON LYND'S draft board, during the Korean War era, granted him 1-A-O a status that calls for entering the military but not carrying a weapon. He went through basic training to become a noncombatant in the United States Army Medical Corps. Thereafter, he was investigated as a security risk and received an undesirable discharge, which was later changed to an honorable discharge by court order. In the 1960s, Lynd taught at Spelman College (1961–64) and Yale University (1964–67). He helped to organize the Assembly of Unrepresented People in August 1965 and was arrested as the group attempted to declare peace with the people of Vietnam on the steps of the Capitol. In December 1965, he traveled to North Vietnam with Tom Hayden and Herbert Aptheker in an effort to determine on what terms the Vietnamese would end the war. As a result of this trip, Lynd was blacklisted as a history teacher, and his passport was confiscated by the government. He recovered it as a result of a lawsuit filed by the American Civil Liberties Union.

ROBERT MALECKI is a working-class veteran who in 1969 took public responsibility for the destruction of draft files and the Dow Chemical computer system, and was subsequently jailed for these acts. While in jail, he was charged with conspiracy. He went underground while pending trial and found asylum in Sweden, where he now lives.

EUGENE MCCARTHY was born in 1916. He holds degrees from St. John's and the University of Minnesota. He served in the House of Representatives from 1949 to 1959 and as a senator from Minnesota from 1959 to 1971. He was a leading Democratic candidate for president in 1968. His candidacy consolidated the opposition to the Vietnam War and helped convince Lyndon Johnson not to run for president again.

JANE BOND MOORE was born in Nashville, Tennessee. Her father worked at Fisk University. His life work was as an administrator in what are now known as historically Black colleges. Her mother, Julia Washington Bond, was a housewife until she became a librarian and is the coauthor with Moore's father of a book about a lynching in Mississippi, *Star Creek Papers*. Moore's brother, Julian, was active in the Student Nonviolent

Coordinating Committee and later in Atlanta politics. In her essay, Moore discusses his experience with the Georgia legislature. Moore graduated from Spelman College in Atlanta in 1959. Howard Zinn was a professor there and a friend. After college she attended graduate school at various places and in various subjects. She married Howard Moore Jr., a civil rights attorney. The Moores moved to California around 1970, when Howard Moore worked on the Angela Davis case. They stayed in California, and Jane Moore attended and graduated from the law school at the University of California at Berkeley in 1975. She is now an attorney for the Oakland Unified School District, a job that never ceases to interest and stimulate her. She and Howard have three children: Grace, Constance, and Kojo.

CARL OGLESBY is best known as a leader of the movement against the Vietnam War and as a president of Students for a Democratic Society. He has published four books and hundreds of articles on political themes. He has also recorded two LPs of original songs and written four full-length plays, which have been professionally produced. He is now writing his autobiography.

JEROLD M. STARR is professor of sociology at West Virginia University and director of the Center for Social Studies Education in Pittsburgh. He has been a Fulbright and National Endowment for the Humanities fellow and is author of *Lessons of the Vietnam War*.

GEORGE SWIERS was born in the upstate New York village of Chatham, where he enlisted in the Marine Corps after his high school graduation. Following service in Vietnam, where he was decorated for valor and wounded in action, he began a career in New York State government in the field of equal employment opportunity. A frequent lecturer at a number of state colleges utilizing a Vietnam curriculum, he also writes bimonthly political commentaries for the *Schenectady Daily Gazette*. He resides in Saratoga, New York.

HOWARD ZINN taught history and political science at Spelman College in Atlanta, Georgia, and then at Boston University. He was active in the civil rights movement in the South and then in the movement against the war in Vietnam. He is probably best known for his book *A People's History of the United States*.

Against the
Vietnam War

PART ONE

Beginnings

The Need to Remember

DAVID HARRIS

THERE IS, OF COURSE, no escaping those years for me. The time was too intense, and I was in far too deep for that to ever be an option. For nearly ten years, from Quitman County, Mississippi, in 1964 to the signing of the Paris Accords in 1973, the movement was everything to me. I gave it all my time, most of my passion and all of my mind. And I am still quite pleased to have done so.

At the time, most of my explanations for behaving that way was that I wanted to be able to look back after twenty years and feel at least comfortable, at best proud. And I do. But even were I looking to shed that history and my own incarnation in it, I doubt if I would be allowed. I suspect the phrases "Stanford's radical student body president" and "imprisoned for refusing to submit to the military draft" are now indelibly scribbled across my karma, if for no other reason than their endless repetition about me over that decade and the almost two since.

Having given of myself the way I did shaped me enormously, in both profound and petty ways, all of which still rattle around in my character. I am suspicious of power and have never managed to regain much respect for the use of force. I am haunted by the knowledge that there is much more here than meets the eye: that seemingly fine, bright, upstanding people will, with little compunction, lie, defile, and physically abuse in the most horrible and "unthinkable" of ways. All that these model citizens require is an accepted social role, a little intellectual theory, and a parking lot full of emotional avoidance.

Originally published in *Stanford Magazine*, Dec. 1993, 28–29.

The residue of those years has also left me constitutionally unable to accept bullshit as the currency of the modern age. I still believe that nothing but good can come from making decisions about what kind of person you are and acting accordingly, whatever the price. And I am still convinced that all any of us gets is the result of what we do. Our lives carry weight. Our professions of how we live or how we intend to live do not.

When I pace nervously, I walk in a nine-foot circle, the length of the maximum security cell I lived in during my imprisonment. I have had occasion to move in high social circles since my days in the movement, but there is still always part of me that looks around the tuxedoed room and wonders how in the world they ever let me in. I can still remember when the *only* option for a young American male was whether to be John Wayne in the *Sands of Iwo Jima* or John Wayne in *The Fighting Seabees*. To this day, I continue to wonder if someone is going to arrest me whenever I visit the Federal Building in San Francisco, and I have not yet accepted Lee Harvey Oswald as the lone assassin. I still think the Gulf of Tonkin incident never happened. I am devoted to the notion that democracy is only as good as the hearts of its citizens, only as real as their willingness to act democratically. I continue to regret that they never sent John Mitchell, Nixon's attorney general, to live on my cell block.

And those are only a few of the echoes that cling to me. No one who has lived through what we know shorthand as "the sixties" is without their own version of the same list.

Which is appropriate. Both during and because of those years, our collective life turned a corner, after which nothing was the same as before. We need to know what happened to us. Without knowing about that sharp and sudden bend in our collective and individual past, it may be impossible to know ourselves, and it is certainly impossible to understand our present. And our greatest asset in that task is our own remembered and considered experience.

Perhaps the longest-running tragedy of that era is how much that asset has been abused. Twenty years after the Vietnam War ended we are only marginally closer to any genuine communal consideration of what happened to us. Years ago, when we were making this history, it was easy to assume that, after the fact, the remembrance would somehow take care of itself, handled by a kind of automatic sorting process in which the truth would out. Needless to say, I am no longer nearly so sanguine. Several developments disturb me.

First, in what little public discussion there is of the era and the war that framed it, the weight of authority is still accorded to the architects of the disaster and the assumption of disbelief is still accorded to their opposition. The classic example of this fallacy occurred in the recent presidential campaign when Bill Clinton, who criticized the war, was grilled endlessly over his behavior and George Bush, who supported it, was never asked to explain or justify his. The assumption here is that avoiding conscription should disqualify someone for high office and sending young men off to die needlessly should not. The concept of The Emperor Has No Clothes is what kept us in that mess, and, unfortunately, it still holds sway.

Second, the entertainment media—the principal architect and custodian of our collective sense of self—has been unable or unwilling to treat the issue as anything more than an opportunity for special effects. Hence, with a scattering of exceptions, we are shown our years in Vietnam simply as Rambo and his clones, precisely the kind of testosterone fantasy that, in real life, sent hundreds of thousands of young Americans off to the rice paddies to senselessly blow the place and themselves to bits. We are given the decade's extracted adrenaline and shielded from its dilemmas. Entertaining ourselves that way is essentially a collective effort to deny the pain that was the everyday stuff of that policy and to pretend that what actually happened never happened at all.

Finally, we as a people seem to be rapidly losing our capacity to engage in serious consideration of anything, much less the kind of moral doubt and examination that waited around every one of the sixties' twists and turns. We are now a nation of instant gratification and galvanic response, demanding that whatever we consume make our palms sweat upon immediate exposure or otherwise be abandoned as boring. We are not nearly as serious as our own past. Hence, remembering, in many ways, is beyond us.

And we need very badly to remember. Whether or not those times affected us in lasting ways is not an issue. Of course they did. They couldn't have done otherwise. The real issue is how to use that experience today to make us both a better people and better persons. We still deserve no less.

2

The Impossible Victory: Vietnam

HOWARD ZINN

FROM 1964 TO 1972, the wealthiest and most powerful nation in the history of the world made a maximum military effort, with everything short of atomic bombs, to defeat a nationalist revolutionary movement in a tiny peasant country—and failed. When the United States fought in Vietnam, it was organized modern technology versus organized human beings, and the human beings won.

In the course of that war, there developed in the United States the greatest antiwar movement the nation had ever experienced, a movement that played a critical part in bringing the war to an end.

It was another startling fact of the sixties.

In the fall of 1945, Japan, defeated, was forced to leave Indochina, the former French colony it had occupied at the start of the war. In the meantime, a revolutionary movement had grown there, determined to end colonial control and to achieve a new life for the peasants of Indochina. Led by a communist named Ho Chi Minh, the revolutionists fought against the Japanese and, when they were gone, held a spectacular celebration in Hanoi in late 1945, with a million people in the streets, and issued a Declaration of Independence. It borrowed from the Declaration of the Rights of Man and the Citizen, in the French Revolution, and from the American Declaration of Independence, and began: "All men are created equal. They are endowed by their Creator with certain inalienable rights;

Originally published in Howard Zinn, *A People's History of the United States* (New York: Harper Collins, 1980), 460–92.

among these are Life, Liberty, and the pursuit of Happiness." Just as the Americans in 1776 had listed their grievances against the English king, the Vietnamese listed their complaints against French rule:

They have enforced inhuman laws. . . . They have built more prisons than schools. They have mercilessly slain our patriots, they have drowned uprisings in rivers of blood. They have fettered public opinion. . . . They have robbed us of our rice fields, our mines, our forests, and our raw materials. . . .

They have invented numerous unjustifiable taxes and reduced our people, especially our peasantry, to a state of extreme poverty. . . . [F]rom the end of last year, to the beginning of this year . . . more than two million of our fellow-citizens died of starvation. . . .

The whole Vietnamese people, animated by a common purpose, are determined to fight to the bitter end against any attempt by the French colonialists to reconquer their country.

The U.S. Defense Department study of the Vietnam War, intended to be "top secret" but released to the public by Daniel Ellsberg and Anthony Russo in the famous *Pentagon Papers* case, described Ho Chi Minh's work:

Ho had built the Viet Minh into the only Vietnam-wide political organization capable of effective resistance to either the Japanese or the French. He was the only Vietnamese wartime leader with a national following, and he assured himself wider fealty among the Vietnamese people when in August–September, 1945, he overthrew the Japanese . . . established the Democratic Republic of Vietnam, and staged receptions for in-coming allied occupation forces. . . . For a few weeks in September, 1945 Vietnam was—for the first and only time in its modern history—free of foreign domination, and united from north to south under Ho Chi Minh.

The Western powers were already at work to change this. England occupied the southern part of Indochina and then turned it back to the French. Nationalist China (this was under Chiang Kai-shek, before the communist revolution) occupied the northern part of Indochina, and the United States persuaded it to turn that back to the French. As Ho Chi Minh told an American journalist: "We apparently stand quite alone. . . . We shall have to depend on ourselves."

Between October 1945 and February 1946, Ho Chi Minh wrote eight letters to President Truman, reminding him of the self-determination promises of the Atlantic Charter. One of the letters was sent both to Truman and to the United Nations:

> I wish to invite attention of your Excellency for strict humanitarian reasons to following matter. Two million Vietnamese died of starvation during winter of 1944 and spring 1945 because of starvation policy of French who seized and stored until it rotted all available rice. . . . Three-fourths of cultivated land was flooded in summer 1945, which was followed by a severe drought; of normal harvest five-sixths was lost. . . . Many people are starving. . . . Unless great world powers and international relief organizations bring us immediate assistance we face imminent catastrophe.

Truman never replied.

In October of 1946, the French bombarded Haiphong, a port in northern Vietnam, and there began the eight-year war between the Viet Minh movement and the French over who would rule Vietnam. After the communist victory in China in 1949 and the Korean War the following year, the United States began giving large amounts of military aid to the French. By 1954, the United States had given three hundred thousand small arms and machine guns, enough to equip the entire French army in Indochina, and $1 billion; altogether, the U.S. was financing 80 percent of the French war effort.

Why was the United States doing this? To the public, the word was that the United States was helping to stop communism in Asia, but there was not much public discussion. In the secret memoranda of the National Security Council (which advised the president on foreign policy), there was talk in 1950 of what came to be known as the "domino theory"—that, like a row of dominoes, if one country fell to communism, the next one would do the same and so on. It was important, therefore, to keep the first one from falling.

A secret memo of the National Security Council in June 1952 also pointed to the chain of U.S. military bases along the coast of China, the Philippines, Taiwan, Japan, South Korea:

> Communist control of all of Southeast Asia would render the U.S. position in the Pacific offshore island chain precarious and would seriously jeopardize fundamental U.S. security interests in the Far East.

And:

> Southeast Asia, especially Malaya and Indonesia, is the principal world
> source of natural rubber and tin, and a producer of petroleum and other
> strategically important commodities.

It was also noted that Japan depended on the rice of Southeast Asia, and
communist victory there would "make it extremely difficult to prevent
Japan's eventual accommodation to communism."

In 1953, a congressional study mission reported: "The area of Indochina
is immensely wealthy in rice, rubber, coal and iron ore. Its position makes
it a strategic key to the rest of Southeast Asia." That year, a State Department
memorandum said that the French were losing the war in Indochina, had
failed "to win a sufficient native support," feared that a negotiated settlement
"would mean the eventual loss to Communism not only of Indo-China
but of the whole Southeast Asia," and concluded: "If the French actually
decided to withdraw, the U.S. would have to consider most seriously whether
to take over in this area."

In 1954, the French, having been unable to win Vietnamese popular
support, which was overwhelmingly behind Ho Chi Minh and the revolutionary movement, had to withdraw.

An international assemblage at Geneva presided over the peace agreement
between the French and the Vietminh. It was agreed that the French would
temporarily withdraw into the southern part of Vietnam, that the Vietminh
would remain in the north, and that an election would take place in two
years in a unified Vietnam to enable the Vietnamese to choose their own
government.

The United States moved quickly to prevent the unification and to
establish South Vietnam as an American sphere. It set up in Saigon as head
of the government a former Vietnamese official named Ngo Dinh Diem,
who had recently been living in New Jersey, and encouraged him not to
hold the scheduled elections for unification. A memo in early 1945 of the
Joint Chiefs of Staff said that intelligence estimates showed "a settlement
based on free election would be attended by almost certain loss of the
Associated States [Laos Cambodia, and Vietnam—the three parts of Indochina
created by the Geneva Conference] to Communist control." Diem again
and again blocked the elections requested by the Vietminh, and with
American money and arms, his government became more and more firmly

established. As the *Pentagon Papers* put it: "South Vietnam was essentially the creation of the United States."

The Diem regime became increasingly unpopular. Diem was a Catholic, and most Vietnamese were Buddhists; Diem was close to the landlords, and this was a country of peasants. His pretenses at land reform left things basically as they were. He replaced locally selected provincial chiefs with his own men, appointed in Saigon; by 1962, 88 percent of these provincial chiefs were military men. Diem imprisoned more and more Vietnamese who criticized the regime for corruption, for the lack of reform.

Opposition grew quickly in the countryside, where Diem's apparatus could not reach well, and around 1958 guerrilla activities began against the regime. The communist regime in Hanoi gave aid, encouragement, and sent people south—most of them southerners who had gone north after the Geneva Accords—to support the guerrilla movement. In 1960, the National Liberation Front was formed in the south. It united the various strands of opposition to the regime; its strength came from South Vietnamese peasants, who saw it as a way of changing their daily lives. A U.S. government analyst named Douglas Pike, in his book *Viet Cong,* based on interviews with rebels and captured documents, tried to give a realistic assessment of what the United States faced:

In the 2,561 villages of South Vietnam, the National Liberation Front created a host of nation-wide socio-political organizations in a country where mass organizations . . . were virtually nonexistent. . . . Aside from the NLF there had never been a truly mass-based political party in South Vietnam.

Pike wrote: "The Communists have brought to the villages of South Vietnam significant social change and have done so largely by means of the communication process." That is, they were organizers much more than they were warriors. "What struck me most forcibly about the NLF was its totality as a social revolution first and as a war second." Pike was impressed with the mass involvement of the peasants in the movement. "The rural Vietnamese was not regarded simply as a pawn in a power struggle but as the active element in the thrust. He was the thrust." Pike wrote:

The purpose of this vast organizational effort was . . . to restructure the social order of the village and train the villages to control themselves.

This was the NFL's one undeviating thrust from the start. Not the killing of ARVN (Saigon) soldiers, not the occupation of real estate, not the preparation for some great pitched battle . . . but organization in depth of the rural population through the instrument of self-control.

Pike estimated that the NLF membership by early 1962 stood at around three hundred thousand. The *Pentagon Papers* said of this period: "Only the Viet Cong had any real support and influence on a broad base in the countryside."

When Kennedy took office in early 1961, he continued the policies of Truman and Eisenhower in Southeast Asia. Almost immediately, he approved a secret plan for various military actions in Vietnam and Laos, including the "dispatch of agents to North Vietnam" to engage in "sabotage and light harassment," according to the *Pentagon Papers*. Back in 1956, he had spoken of "the amazing success of President Diem" and said of Diem's Vietnam: "Her political liberty is an inspiration."

One day in June 1963, a Buddhist monk sat down in the public square in Saigon and set himself afire. More Buddhist monks began committing suicide by fire to dramatize their opposition to the Diem regime. Diem's police raided the Buddhist pagodas and temples, wounded thirty monks, arrested fourteen hundred people, and closed down the pagodas. There were demonstrations in the city. The police fired, killing nine people. Then, in Hué, the ancient capital, ten thousand demonstrated in protest.

Under the Geneva Accords, the United States was permitted to have 685 military advisers in southern Vietnam. Eisenhower secretly sent several thousand. Under Kennedy, the figure rose to sixteen thousand, and some of them began to take part in combat operations. Diem was losing. Most of the South Vietnam countryside was now controlled by local villagers organized by the NLF.

Diem was becoming an embarrassment, an obstacle to effective control over Vietnam. Some Vietnamese generals began plotting to overthrow his regime, staying in touch with a CIA man named Lucien Conein. Conein met secretly with American Ambassador Henry Cabot Lodge, who was enthusiastically for the coup. Lodge reported to Kennedy's assistant, McGeorge Bundy, on October 25 *(Pentagon Papers):* "I have personally approved each meeting between General Tran Van Don and Conein who has carried out my orders in each instance explicitly." Kennedy seemed hesitant, but no move was made to warn Diem. Indeed, just before the coup and just after he had been in touch through Conein with the plotters, Lodge spent a weekend with Diem at a seaside resort. When on November 1, 1963, the generals attacked the presidential palace, Diem phoned Ambassador Lodge, and the conversation went as follows:

> Diem: Some units have made a rebellion, and I want to know what is the attitude of the United States?
> Lodge: I do not feel well enough informed to be able to tell you. I have heard the shooting, but am not acquainted with all the facts. Also it is 4:30 A.M. in Washington and the U.S. government cannot possibly have a view.
> Diem: But you must have some general ideas . . .

Lodge told Diem to phone him if he could do anything for his physical safety.

That was the last conversation any American had with Diem. He fled the palace, but he and his brother were apprehended by the plotters, taken out in a truck, and executed.

Earlier in 1963, Kennedy's undersecretary of state, U. Alexis Johnson, was speaking before the Economic Club of Detroit:

> What is the attraction that Southeast Asia has exerted for centuries on the great powers flanking it on all sides? Why is it desirable, and why is it important? First, it provides a lush climate, fertile soil, rich natural resources, a relatively sparse population in most areas, and room to expand. The countries of Southeast Asia produce rich exportable surpluses such as rice, rubber, teak, corn, tin, spices, and many others.

This is not the language used by President Kennedy in his explanations to the American public. He talked of communism and freedom. In a news conference February 14, 1962, he said: "Yes, as you know, the U.S. for more than a decade has been assisting the government, the people of Vietnam, to maintain their independence."

Three weeks after the execution of Diem, Kennedy himself was assassinated, and his vice president, Lyndon Johnson, took office.

The generals who succeeded Diem could not suppress the National Liberation Front. Again and again, American leaders expressed their bewilderment at the popularity of the NLF, at the high morale of its soldiers.

The Pentagon historians wrote that when Eisenhower met with President-elect Kennedy in January 1961, he "wondered aloud why, in interventions of this kind, we always seemed to find that the morale of the Communist forces was better than that of the democratic forces." And General Maxwell Taylor reported in late 1964:

> The ability of the Viet-Cong continuously to rebuild their units and to make good their losses is one of the mysteries of the guerrilla war. . . . Not only do the Viet-Cong units have the recuperative powers of the phoenix, but they have an amazing ability to maintain morale. Only in rare cases have we found evidences of bad morale among Viet-Cong prisoners or recorded in captured Viet-Cong documents.

In early August 1964, President Johnson used a murky set of events in the Gulf of Tonkin, off the coast of North Vietnam, to launch full-scale war on Vietnam. Johnson and Secretary of Defense Robert McNamara told the American public there was an attack by North Vietnamese torpedo boats on American destroyers. "While on routine patrol on international waters," McNamara said, "the U.S. destroyer *Maddox* underwent an unprovoked attack." It later turned out that the Gulf of Tonkin episode was a fake, that the highest American officials had lied to the public—just as they had in the invasion of Cuba under Kennedy. In fact, the CIA had engaged in a secret operation attacking North Vietnamese coastal installations—so if there had been an attack, it would not have been "unprovoked." It was not a "routine patrol" because the *Maddox* was on a special electronic spying mission. And it was not in international waters but in Vietnamese territorial waters. It turned out that no torpedoes were fired at the *Maddox,* as McNamara said. Another reported attack on another destroyer, two nights later, which Johnson called "open aggression on the high seas," seems also to have been an invention.

At the time of the incident, Secretary of State Rusk was questioned on NBC television:

> Reporter: What explanation, then, can you come up with for this unprovoked attack?
> Rusk: Well, I haven't been able, quite frankly, to come to a fully satisfactory explanation. There is a great gulf of understanding, between that world and our world, ideological in character. They see what we think

of as the real world in wholly different terms. Their very processes of logic are different. So that it's very difficult to enter into each other's minds across that great ideological gulf.

The Tonkin "attack" brought a congressional resolution, which passed unanimously in the House and, with only two dissenting votes in the Senate, gave Johnson the power to take military action as he saw fit in Southeast Asia.

Two months before the Gulf of Tonkin incident, U.S. government leaders met in Honolulu and discussed such a resolution. Rusk said, in this meeting, according to the *Pentagon Papers*, that "public opinion on our Southeast Asia policy was badly divided in the United States at the moment and that, therefore, the President needed an affirmation of support."

The Tonkin Resolution gave the president the power to initiate hostilities without the declaration of war by Congress that the Constitution required. The Supreme Court, supposed to be the watchdog of the Constitution, was asked by a number of petitioners in the course of the Vietnam War to declare the war unconstitutional. Again and again, it refused even to consider the issue.

Immediately after the Tonkin affair, American warplanes began bombarding North Vietnam. During 1965, over two hundred thousand American soldiers were sent to South Vietnam, and in 1966, two hundred thousand more. By early 1968, there were more than five hundred thousand American troops there, and the U.S. Air Force was dropping bombs at a rate unequaled in history. Tiny glimmerings of the massive human suffering under this bombardment came to the outside world. On June 5, 1965, the *New York Times* carried a dispatch from Saigon:

As the Communists withdrew from Quangngai last Monday, United States jet bombers pounded the hills into which they were headed. Many Vietnamese—one estimate is as high as 500—were killed by the strikes. The American contention is that they were Vietcong soldiers. But three out of four patients seeking treatment in a Vietnamese hospital afterward for burns from napalm, or jellied gasoline, were village women.

On September 6, another press dispatch from Saigon:

In Bein Hoa province south of Saigon on August 15 United States aircraft accidentally bombed a Buddhist pagoda and a Catholic church. . . . it was the third time their pagoda had been bombed in 1965. A temple of the Cao Dai religious sect in the same area had been bombed twice this year.

In another delta province there is a woman who has both arms burned off by napalm and her eyelids so badly burned that she cannot close them. When it was time for her to sleep her family puts a blanket over her head. The woman had two of her children killed in the air strike that maimed her.

Few Americans appreciate what their nation is doing in South Vietnam with airpower. . . . innocent civilians are dying every day in South Vietnam.

Large areas of South Vietnam were declared "free fire zones," which meant that all persons remaining within them—civilians, old people, children—were considered an enemy, and bombs were dropped at will. Villages suspected of harboring Viet Cong were subject to "search and destroy" missions—men of military age in the villages were killed, the homes were burned, the women, children, and old people were sent off to refugee camps. Jonathan Schell, in his book *The Village of Ben Suc,* describes such an operation: a village surrounded, attacked, a man riding on a bicycle shot down, three people picnicking by the river shot to death, the houses destroyed, the women, children, old people herded together, taken away from their ancestral homes.

The CIA in Vietnam, in a program called "Operation Phoenix," secretly, without trial, executed at least twenty thousand civilians in South Vietnam who were suspected of being members of the communist underground. A pro-administration analyst wrote in the journal *Foreign Affairs* in January 1975: "Although the Phoenix program did undoubtedly kill or incarcerate many innocent civilians, it did also eliminate many members of the Communist infrastructure."

After the war, the release of records of the International Red Cross showed that in South Vietnamese prison camps, where at the height of the war sixty-five thousand to seventy thousand people were held and often beaten and tortured, American advisers observed and sometimes participated. The Red Cross observers found continuing, systematic brutality at the two principal Vietnamese POW camps—at Phu Quoc and Qui Nhon, where American advisers were stationed.

By the end of the Vietnam war, seven million tons of bombs had been dropped on Vietnam, more than twice the bombs dropped on Europe and Asia in World War II—almost one five-hundred-pound bomb for every human being in Vietnam. It was estimated that there were twenty million bomb craters in the country. In addition, poisonous sprays were dropped by planes to destroy trees and any kind of growth—an area the size of the state of Massachusetts was covered with such poison. Vietnamese mothers reported birth defects in their children. Yale biologists, using the same poison (2,4,5,T) on mice, reported defective mice born and said they had no reason to believe the effect on humans was different.

On March 16, 1968, a company of American soldiers went into the hamlet of My Lai 4, in Quang Ngai province. They rounded up the inhabitants, including old people and women with infants in their arms. These people were ordered into a ditch, where they were methodically shot to death by American soldiers. The testimony of James Dursi, a rifleman, at the later trial of Lieutenant William Calley, was reported in the *New York Times:*

> "Lieutenant Calley and a weeping rifleman named Paul D. Meadlo—the same soldier who had fed candy to the children before shooting them—pushed the prisoners into the ditch. . . .
>
> "There was an order to shoot by Lieutenant Calley. I can't remember the exact words—it was something like 'Start firing.'
>
> "Meadlo turned to me and said: 'Shoot, why don't you shoot?'
>
> "He was crying.
>
> "I said, 'I can't. I won't.'
>
> "Then Lieutenant Calley and Meadlo pointed their rifles into the ditch and fired.
>
> "People were diving on top of each other; mothers were trying to protect their children."

Journalist Seymour Hersh, in his book *My Lai 4,* writes:

> When Army investigators reached the barren area in November, 1969, in connection with the My Lai probe in the United States, they found mass graves at three sites, as well as a ditch full of bodies. It was estimated that between 450 and 500 people—most of them women, children and old men—had been slain and buried there.

The army tried to cover up what happened. But a letter began circulating from a GI named Ron Ridenhour, who had heard about the massacre. There were photos taken of the killing by an army photographer, Ralph

Haeberle. Seymour Hersh, then working for an antiwar news agency in Southeast Asia called Dispatch News Service, wrote about it. The story of the massacre had appeared in May 1968 in two French publications, one called *Sud Vietnam en Lutte,* and another published by the North Vietnamese delegation to the peace talks in Paris—but the American press did not pay any attention.

Several of the officers in the My Lai massacre were put on trial, but only Lieutenant William Calley was found guilty. He was sentenced to life imprisonment, but his sentence was reduced twice; he served three years—Nixon ordered that he be under house arrest rather than a regular prison—and then was paroled. Thousands of Americans came to his defense. Part of it was in patriotic justification of his action as necessary against the "communists." Part of it seems to have been a feeling that he was singled out in a war with many similar atrocities. Colonel Oran Henderson, who had been charged with covering up the My Lai killings, told reporters in early 1971: "Every unit of brigade size has its My Lai hidden someplace."

Indeed, My Lai was unique only in its details. Hersh reported a letter sent by a GI to his family and published in a local newspaper:

Dear Mom and Dad:

Today we went on a mission and I am not very proud of myself, my friends, or my country. We burned every hut in sight!

It was a small rural network of villages and the people were incredibly poor. My unit burned and plundered their meager possessions. Let me try to explain the situation to you.

The huts here are thatched palm leaves. Each one has a dried mud bunker inside. These bunkers are to protect the families. Kind of like air raid shelters.

My unit commanders, however, chose to think that these bunkers are offensive. So every hut we find that has a bunker we are ordered to burn to the ground.

When the ten helicopters landed this morning, in the midst of these huts, and six men jumped out of each 'chopper,' we were firing the moment we hit the ground. We fired into all the huts we could. . . .

It is then that we burned these huts. . . .

Everyone is crying, begging and praying that we don't separate them and take their husbands and fathers, sons and grandfathers. The women wail and moan.

Then they watch in terror as we burn their homes, personal possessions and food. Yes, we burn all rice and shoot all their livestock.

The more unpopular became the Saigon government, the more desperate the military effort became to make up for this. A secret congressional report of late 1967 said the Viet Cong were distributing about five times more land to the peasants than the South Vietnamese government, whose land distribution program had come "to a virtual stand-still." The report said: "The Viet Cong have eliminated landlord domination and reallocated lands owned by absentee landlords and the G.V.N. [Government of Vietnam] to the landless and others who cooperate with Viet Cong authorities."

The unpopularity of the Saigon government explains the success of the National Liberation Front in infiltrating Saigon and other government-held towns in early 1968, without the people there warning the government. The NLF thus launched a surprise offensive (it was the time of "Tet," their New Year holiday) that carried them into the heart of Saigon, immobilized Tan San Nhut airfield, even occupied the American embassy briefly. The offensive was beaten back, but it demonstrated that all the enormous fire-power delivered on Vietnam by the United States had not destroyed the NLF, its morale, its popular support, its will to fight. It caused a reassessment in the American government, more doubts among the American people.

The massacre at My Lai by a company of ordinary soldiers was a small event compared with the plans of high-level military and civilian leaders to visit massive destruction on the civilian population of Vietnam. Assistant Secretary of Defense John McNaughton in early 1966, seeing that large-scale bombing of North Vietnam villages was not producing the desired result, suggested a different strategy. The air strikes on villages, he said, would "create a counterproductive wave of revulsion abroad and at home." He suggests instead: "Destruction of locks and dams, however—if handled right—might . . . offer promise. It should be studied. Such destruction doesn't kill or drown people. By shallow-flooding the rice, it leads after a time to widespread starvation (more than a million?) unless food is provided—which we could offer to do 'at the conference table.'"

The heavy bombings were intended to destroy the will of ordinary Vietnamese to resist, as in the bombings of German and Japanese population centers in World War II—despite President Johnson's public insistence that only "military targets" were being bombed. The government was using language like "one more turn of the screw" to describe bombing. The CIA at one point in 1966 recommended a "bombing program of greater intensity," according to the *Pentagon Papers,* directed against, in the CIA's words, "the will of the regime as a target system."

Meanwhile, just across the border of Vietnam, in a neighboring country, Laos, where a right-wing government installed by the CIA faced a rebellion, one of the most beautiful areas in the world, the Plain of Jars, was being destroyed by bombing. This was not reported by the government or the press, but an American who lived in Laos, Fred Branfman, told the story in his book *Voices from the Plain of Jars:* "Over 25,000 attack sorties were flown against the Plain of Jars from May, 1964, through September, 1969; over 75,000 tons of bombs were dropped on it; on the ground, thousands were killed and wounded, tens of thousands driven underground, and the entire aboveground society leveled."

Branfman, who spoke the Laotian language and lived in the village with a Laotian family, interviewed hundreds of refugees from the bombing who poured into the capital city of Vientiane. He recorded their statements and preserved their drawings. A twenty-six-year-old nurse from Xieng Khouang told of her life in her village:

> I was at one with the earth, the air, the upland fields, the paddy and the seedbeds of my village. Each day and night in the light of the moon I and my friends from the village would wander, calling out and singing, through forest and field, amidst the cries of the birds. During the harvesting and planting season, we would sweat and labor together, under the sun and the rain, contending with poverty and miserable conditions, continuing the farmer's life which has been the profession of our ancestors.
>
> But in 1964 and 1965 I could feel the trembling of the earth and the shock from the sounds of arms exploding around my village. I began to hear the noise of airplanes, circling about the heavens. One of them would stick its head down and, plunging earthward, loose a loud roar, shocking the heart as light and smoke covered everything so that one could not see anything at all. Each day we would exchange news with the neighboring villagers of the bombings that had occurred: the damaged houses, the injured and the dead. . . .
>
> The holes! The holes! During that time we needed holes to save our lives. We who were young took our sweat and our strength, which should have been spent raising food in the ricefields and forests to sustain our lives, and squandered it digging holes to protect ourselves. . . .

One young woman explained why the revolutionary movement in Laos, the Neo Lao, attracted her and so many of her friends:

> As a young girl, I had found that the past had not been very good, for men had mistreated and made fun of women as the weaker sex. But after the Neo Lao party began to administer the region . . . it became very different. . . . [U]nder the Neo Lao things changed psychologically, such as their teaching that women should be as brave as men. For example: although I had gone to school before, my elders advised me not to. They had said that it would not be useful for me as I could not hope to be a high ranking official after graduation, that only the children of the elite or rich could expect that.
>
> But the Neo Lao said that women should have the same education as men, and they gave us equal privileges and did not allow anyone to make fun of us. . . .
>
> And the old associations were changed into new ones. For example, most of the new teachers and doctors trained were women. And they changed the lives of the very poor . . . for they shared the land of those who had many rice fields with those who had none.

A seventeen-year-old boy told about the Pathet Lao revolutionary army coming to his village:

> Some people were afraid, mostly those with money. They offered cows to the Pathet Lao soldiers to eat, but the soldiers refused to take them. If they did take them, they paid a suitable price. The truth is that they led the people not to be afraid of anything.
>
> Then they organized the election of village and canton chief, and the people were the ones who chose them.

In September 1973, a former government official in Laos, Jerome Doolittle, wrote in the *New York Times:*

> The Pentagon's most recent lies about bombing Cambodia bring back a question that often occurred to me when I was press attaché at the American Embassy in Vientiane, Laos.
>
> Why did we bother to lie?
>
> When I first arrived in Laos, I was instructed to answer all press ques-

tions about our massive and merciless bombing campaign in that tiny country with: "At the request of the Royal Laotian Government, the United States is conducting unarmed reconnaissance flights accompanied by armed escorts who have the right to return if fired upon."

This was a lie. Every reporter to whom I told it knew it was a lie. Hanoi knew it was a lie. The International Control Commission knew it was a lie. Every interested Congressman and newspaper reader knew it was a lie. . . .

After all, the lies did serve to keep something from somebody, and the somebody was us.

By early 1968, the cruelty of the war began touching the conscience of many Americans. For many others, the problem was that the United States was unable to win the war, while 40,000 American soldiers were dead at this time, 250,000 wounded, with no end in sight. (The Vietnam casualties were many times this number.)

Lyndon Johnson had escalated a brutal war and failed to win it. His popularity was at an all-time low; he could not appear publicly without a demonstration against him and the war. The chant "LBJ, LBJ, how many kids did you kill today?" was heard in demonstrations throughout the country. In the spring of 1968, Johnson announced he would not run again for president and that negotiations for peace would begin with the Vietnamese in Paris.

In the fall of 1968, Richard Nixon, pledging that he would get the United States out of Vietnam, was elected president. He began to withdraw troops; by February 1972, less then 150,000 were left. But the bombing continued. Nixon's policy was "Vietnamization": the Saigon government, with Vietnamese ground troops, using American money and air power, would carry on the war. Nixon was not ending the war; he was ending the most unpopular aspect of it, the involvement of American soldiers on the soil of a faraway country.

In the spring of 1970, Nixon and Secretary of State Henry Kissinger launched an invasion of Cambodia, after a long bombardment that the government never disclosed to the public. The invasion not only led to an outcry of protest in the United States, but it was also a military failure, and Congress resolved that Nixon could not use American troops in extending the war without congressional approval. The following year, without American troops, the United States supported a South Vietnamese invasion of Laos. This too failed. In 1971, eight hundred thousand tons of bombs were dropped by the United States on Laos, Cambodia, Vietnam. Meantime, the Saigon military regime, headed by President Nguyen Van Thieu, the last of a long succession of Saigon chiefs of state, was keeping thousands of opponents in jail.

Some of the first signs of opposition in the United States to the Vietnam War came out of the civil rights movement—perhaps because the experience of black people with the government led them to distrust any claim that it was fighting for freedom. On the very day that Lyndon Johnson was telling the nation in early August 1964 about the Gulf of Tonkin incident and announcing the bombing of North Vietnam, Black and White activists were gathering near Philadelphia, Mississippi, at a memorial service for the three civil rights workers killed there that summer. One of the speakers pointed bitterly to Johnson's use of force in Asia, comparing it with the violence used against Blacks in Mississippi.

In mid-1965, in McComb, Mississippi, young blacks who had just learned that a classmate of theirs was killed in Vietnam distributed a leaflet:

> No Mississippi Negroes should be fighting in Viet Nam for the White man's freedom, until all the Negro People are free in Mississippi.
>
> Negro boys should not honor the draft here in Mississippi. Mothers should encourage their sons not to go. . . .
>
> No one has the right to ask us to risk our lives and kill other Colored People in Santo Domingo and Viet Nam, so that the White American can get richer.

When Secretary of Defense Robert McNamara visited Mississippi and praised Senator John Stennis, a prominent racist, as a "man of very genuine greatness," White and Black students marched in protest with placards saying, "In Memory of the Burned Children of Vietnam."

The Student Nonviolent Coordinating Committee (SNCC) declared in early 1966 that "the United States is pursuing an aggressive policy in violation of international law" and called for withdrawal from Vietnam. That summer, six members of SNCC were arrested for an invasion of an induction center in Atlanta. They were convicted and sentenced to several years in prison. Around the same time, Julian Bond, a SNCC activist who had just been elected to the Georgia House of Representatives, spoke out against the war and the draft, and the House voted that he not be seated because his statements violated the Selective Service Act and "tend to bring discredit to the House." The Supreme Court restored Bond to his seat, saying he had the right to free expression under the First Amendment.

One of the great sports figures of the nation, Muhammad Ali, the Black boxer and heavyweight champion, refused to serve in what he called a "White man's war"; boxing authorities took away his title as champion. Martin Luther King, Jr., spoke out in 1967 at Riverside Church in New York:

> Somehow this madness must cease. We must stop now. I speak as a child of God and brother to the suffering poor of Vietnam. I speak for those whose land is being laid waste, whose homes are being destroyed, whose culture is being subverted. I speak for the poor of America who are paying the double price of smashed hopes at home and death and corruption in Vietnam. I speak as a citizen of the world, for the world as it stands aghast at the path we have taken. I speak as an American to the leaders of my own nation. The great initiative in this war is ours. The initiative to stop it must be ours.

Young men began to refuse to register for the draft, refused to be inducted if called. As early as May 1964, the slogan "We Won't Go" was widely publicized. Some who had registered began publicly burning their draft cards to protest the war. One, David O'Brien, burned his draft card in South Boston; he was convicted, and the Supreme Court overruled his argument that his act was a protected form of free expression. In October of 1967, there were organized draft card "turn-ins" all over the country; in San Francisco alone, three hundred draft cards were returned to the government. Just before a huge demonstration at the Pentagon that month, a sack of collected draft cards was presented to the Justice Department.

By mid-1965, 380 prosecutions were begun against men refusing to be inducted; by mid-1968 that figure was up to 3,305. At the end of 1969, there were 33,960 delinquents nationwide.

In May 1969, the Oakland induction center, where draftees reported from all of northern California, reported that of 4,400 men ordered to report for induction, 2,400 did not show up. In the first quarter of 1970, the Selective Service system, for the first time, could not meet its quota.

A Boston University graduate student in history, Philip Supina, wrote on May 1, 1968, to his draft board in Tucson, Arizona: "I am enclosing the order for me to report for my pre-induction physical exam for the armed forces. I have absolutely no intention to report for that exam, or for induction, or to aid in any way the American war effort against the people of Vietnam."

He ended his letter by quoting the Spanish philosopher Miguel Unamuno, who during the Spanish civil war said: "Sometimes to be Silent is to Lie." Supina was convicted and sentenced to four years in prison.

Early in the war, there had been two separate incidents, barely noticed by most Americans. On November 2, 1965, in front of the Pentagon in Washington, as thousands of employees were streaming out of the building in the late afternoon, Norman Morrison, a thirty-two-year-old pacifist, father of three, stood below the third-floor windows of Secretary of Defense Robert McNamara, doused himself with kerosene, and set himself afire, giving up his life in protest against the war. Also that year, in Detroit, an eighty-two-year-old woman named Alice Herz burned herself to death to make a statement against the horrors of Indochina.

A remarkable change in sentiment took place. In early 1965, when the bombing of North Vietnam began, a hundred people gathered on the Boston Common to voice their indignation. On October 15, 1969, the number of people assembled on the Boston Common to protest the war was one hundred thousand. Perhaps two million people across the nation gathered that day in towns and villages that had never seen an antiwar meeting.

In the summer of 1965, a few hundred people had gathered in Washington to march in protest against the war: the first in line—historian Staughton Lynd, SNCC organizer Bob Moses, and longtime pacifist David Dellinger— were splattered with red paint by hecklers. But by 1970, the Washington peace rallies were drawing hundreds of thousands of people. In 1970, twenty thousand came to Washington to commit civil disobedience, trying to tie up Washington traffic to express their revulsion against the killing still going on in Vietnam. Fourteen thousand of them were arrested, the largest mass arrest in American history.

Hundreds of volunteers in the Peace Corps spoke out against the war. In Chile, ninety-two volunteers defied the Peace Corps director and issued a circular denouncing the war. Eight hundred former members of the corps issued a statement of protest against what was happening in Vietnam.

The poet Robert Lowell, invited to a White House function, refused to come. Arthur Miller, also invited, sent a telegram to the White House: "When the guns boom, the arts die." Singer Eartha Kitt was invited to a luncheon on the White House lawn and shocked all those present by speaking out, in the presence of the president's wife, against the war. A teenager, called to the White House to accept a prize, came and criticized the war. In

Hollywood, local artists erected the sixty-foot Tower of Protest on Sunset Boulevard. At the National Book Award ceremonies in New York, fifty authors and publishers walked out on a speech by Vice President Humphrey in a display of anger at his role in the war.

In London, two young Americans gate-crashed the American ambassador's elegant Fourth of July reception and called out a toast: "To all the dead and dying in Vietnam." They were carried out by guards. In the Pacific Ocean, two young American seamen hijacked an American munitions ship to divert its load of bombs from airbases in Thailand. For four days they took command of the ship and its crew, taking amphetamine pills to stay awake until the ship reached Cambodian waters. The Associated Press reported in late 1972, from York, Pennsylvania: "Five antiwar activists were arrested by the state police today for allegedly sabotaging railroad equipment near a factory that makes bomb casings used in the Vietnam war."

Middle-class and professional people unaccustomed to activism began to speak up. In May 1970, the *New York Times* reported from Washington: "1000 'ESTABLISHMENT' LAWYERS JOIN WAR PROTEST." Corporations began to wonder whether the war was going to hurt their long-range business interests; the *Wall Street Journal* began criticizing the continuation of the war.

As the war became more and more unpopular, people in or close to the government began to break out of the circle of assent. The most dramatic instance was the case of Daniel Ellsberg.

Ellsberg was a Harvard-trained economist, a former marine officer, employed by the RAND Corporation, which did special, often secret research for the U.S. government. Ellsberg helped write the Department of Defense history of the war in Vietnam and then decided to make the top secret document public with the aid of his friend, Anthony Russo, a former RAND Corporation man. The two had met in Saigon, where both had been affected, in different experiences, by direct sight of the war and had become powerfully indignant at what the United States was doing to the people of Vietnam.

Ellsberg and Russo spent night after night, after hours, at a friend's advertising agency, duplicating the seven-thousand-page document. Then Ellsberg gave copies to various congressmen and to the *New York Times*. In June 1971, the *Times* began printing selections from what came to be known as the *Pentagon Papers*. It created a national sensation.

The Nixon administration tried to get the Supreme Court to stop further publication, but the Court said this was "prior restraint" of freedom of the press and thus unconstitutional. The government then indicted Ellsberg and Russo for violating the Espionage Act by releasing classified documents to unauthorized people; they faced long terms in prison if convicted. The judge, however, called off the trial during the jury deliberations because the Watergate events unfolding at the time revealed unfair practices by the prosecution.

Ellsberg, by his bold act, had broken with the usual tactic of dissidents inside the government who bided their time and kept their opinions to themselves, hoping for small changes in policy. A colleague urged him not to leave the government because there he had "access," saying, "Don't cut yourself off. Don't cut your throat." Ellsberg replied: "Life exists outside the Executive Branch."

The antiwar movement, early in its growth, found a strange, new constituency: priests and nuns of the Catholic Church. Some of them had been aroused by the civil rights movement, others by their experiences in Latin America, where they saw poverty and injustice under governments supported by the United States. In the fall of 1967, Father Philip Berrigan (a Josephite priest who was a veteran of World War II), joined by artist Tom Lewis and friends David Eberhardt and James Mengel, went to the office of a draft board in Baltimore, Maryland, drenched the draft records with blood, and waited to be arrested. They were put on trial and sentenced to prison terms of two to six years.

The following May, Philip Berrigan—out on bail in the Baltimore case—was joined in a second action by his brother Daniel, a Jesuit priest who had visited North Vietnam and seen the effects of U.S. bombing. They and seven other people went into a draft board office in Catonsville, Maryland, removed records, and set them afire outside in the presence of reporters and onlookers. They were convicted and sentenced to prison, and became famous as the "Catonsville Nine." Dan Berrigan wrote a "Meditation" at the time of the Catonsville incident:

> Our apologies, good friends, for the fracture of good order, the burning of paper instead of children, the angering of the orderlies in the front parlor of the charnel house. We could not, so help us God, do otherwise. . . . We say: killing is disorder, life and gentleness and community and unselfishness is the only order we recognize. For the sake of that order, we risk our liberty, our good name. The time is past when good men can remain silent, when obedience can segregate men from public risk, when the poor can die without defense.

When his appeals had been exhausted, and he was supposed to go to prison, Daniel Berrigan disappeared. While the FBI searched for him, he showed up at an Easter festival at Cornell University, where he had been teaching. With dozens of FBI men looking for him in the crowd, he suddenly appeared on stage. The lights went out; he hid inside a giant figure of the Bread and Puppet Theatre which was on stage, was carried out to a truck, and escaped to a nearby farmhouse. He stayed underground for four months—writing poems, issuing statements, giving secret interviews, appearing suddenly in a Philadelphia church to give a sermon and then disappearing again, baffling the FBI, until an informer's interception of a letter disclosed his whereabouts and he was captured and imprisoned.

The one woman among the Catonsville Nine, Mary Moylan, a former nun, also refused to surrender to the FBI. She was never found. Writing from underground, she reflected on her experience and how she came to it:

> We had all known we were going to jail, so we all had our toothbrushes. I was just exhausted. I took my little box of clothes and stuck it under the cot and climbed into bed. Now all the women in the Baltimore County jail were black—I think there was only one white. The women were waking me up and saying, "Aren't you going to cry?" I said, "What about?" They said, "You're in jail." And I said, "Yeah, I knew I'd be here.". . .
>
> I was sleeping between two of these women, and every morning I'd wake up and they'd be leaning on their elbows watching me. They'd say, "You slept all night." And they couldn't believe it. They were good. We had good times. . . .
>
> I suppose the political turning point in my life came while I was in Uganda. I was there when American planes were bombing the Congo, and we were very close to the Congo border. The planes came over and bombed two villages in Uganda. . . . Where the hell did the American planes come in?
>
> Later I was in Dar Es Salaam and Chou En-lai came to town. The American Embassy sent out letters saying that no Americans were to be on the street, because this was a dirty Communist leader; but I decided this was a man who was making history and I wanted to see him. . . .
>
> When I came home from Africa I moved to Washington, and had to deal with the scene there and the insanity and the brutality of the cops and the type of life that was led by most of the citizens of that city—70 percent black. . . .

And then Vietnam, and the napalm and the defoliants, and the bombings . . .

I got involved with the women's movement about a year ago. . . .

At the time of Catonsville, going to jail made sense to me, partially because of the black scene—so many blacks forever filling the jails. . . . I don't think it's a valid tactic anymore. . . . I don't want to see people marching off to jail with smiles on their faces. I just don't want them going. The Seventies are going to be very difficult, and I don't want to waste the sisters and brothers we have by marching them off to jail and having mystical experiences or whatever they're going to have.

The effects of the war and of the bold action of some priests and nuns was to crack the traditional conservatism of the Catholic community. On Moratorium Day 1969, at the Newton College of the Sacred Heart near Boston, a sanctuary of bucolic quiet and political silence, the great front door of the college displayed a huge painted red fist. At Boston College, a Catholic institution, six thousand people gathered that evening in the gymnasium to denounce the war.

Students were heavily involved in the early protests against the war. A survey by the Urban Research Corporation, for the first six months of 1969 only, and for only 232 of the nation's two thousand institutions of higher education, showed that at least 215,000 students had participated in campus protests, that 3,652 had been arrested, that 956 had been suspended or expelled. Even in the high schools in the late sixties, there were five hundred underground newspapers. At the Brown University commencement in 1969, two-thirds of the graduating class turned their backs when Henry Kissinger stood up to address them.

The climax of protest came in the spring of 1970 when President Nixon ordered the invasion of Cambodia. At Kent State University in Ohio, on May 4, when students gathered to demonstrate against the war, National Guardsmen fired into the crowd. Four students were killed. One was paralyzed for life. Students at four hundred colleges and universities went on strike in protest. It was the first general student strike in the history of the United States. During that school year of 1969–70, the FBI listed 1,785 student demonstrations, including the occupation of 313 buildings.

The commencement day ceremonies after the Kent State killings were unlike any the nation had ever seen. From Amherst, Massachusetts, came this newspaper report:

The 100th Commencement of the University of Massachusetts yesterday was a protest, a call for peace.

The roll of the funeral drum set the beat for 2600 young men and women marching "in fear, in despair and in frustration."

Red fists of protest, white peace symbols, and blue doves were stenciled on black academic gowns, and nearly every other senior wore an armband representing a plea for peace.

Student protests against the ROTC (Reserve Officers Training Corps) resulted in the canceling of those programs in over forty colleges and universities. In 1966, 191,749 college students enrolled in ROTC. By 1973, the number was 72,459. The ROTC was depended on to supply half the officers in Vietnam. In September 1973, for the sixth straight month, the ROTC could not fulfill its quota. One army official said: "I just hope we don't get into another war, because if we do, I doubt we could fight it."

The publicity given to the student protests created the impression that the opposition to the war came mostly from middle-class intellectuals. When some construction workers in New York attacked student demonstrators, the news was played up in the national media. However, a number of elections in American cities, including those where mostly blue-collar workers lived, showed that antiwar sentiment was strong in the working class. For instance, in Dearborn, Michigan, an automobile-manufacturing town, a poll as early as 1967 showed 41 percent of the population favored withdrawal from the Vietnam War. In 1970, in two counties in California where petitioners placed the issue on the ballot—San Francisco County and Marin County—referenda asking withdrawal of the U.S. forces from Vietnam received a majority vote.

In late 1970, when a Gallup poll presented the statement, "The United States should withdraw all troops from Vietnam by the end of next year," 65 percent of those questioned said, "Yes." In Madison, Wisconsin, in the spring of 1971, a resolution calling for an immediate withdrawal of U.S. forces from Southeast Asia won by thirty-one thousand to sixteen thousand (in 1968 such a resolution had lost).

But the most surprising data were in a survey made by the University of Michigan. This showed that, throughout the Vietnam War, Americans with only a grade school education were much stronger for withdrawal from the war than Americans with a college education. In June 1966, of people with a college education, 27 percent were for immediate withdrawal from

Vietnam; of people with only a grade school education, 41 percent were for immediate withdrawal. By September 1970, both groups were more antiwar: 47 percent of the college educated were for withdrawal, and 61 percent of grade school graduates.

There is more evidence of the same kind. In an article in the *American Sociological Review* (June 1968), Richard F. Hamilton found in his survey of public opinion: "Preferences for 'tough' policy alternatives are most frequent among the following groups, the highly educated, high status occupations, those with high incomes, younger persons, and those paying much attention to newspapers and magazines." And a political scientist, Harlan Hahn, doing a study of various city referenda on Vietnam, found support for withdrawal from Vietnam highest in groups of lower socioeconomic status. He also found that the regular polls, based on samplings, underestimated the opposition to the war among lower-class people.

All this was part of a general change in the entire population of the country. In August of 1965, 61 percent of the population thought the American involvement in Vietnam was not wrong. By May 1971, it was exactly reversed: 61 percent thought our involvement *was* wrong. Bruce Andrews, a Harvard student of public opinion, found that the people most opposed to the war were people over fifty, blacks, and women. He also noted that a study in the spring of 1964, when Vietnam was a minor issue in the newspapers, showed that 53 percent of college-educated people were willing to send troops to Vietnam, but only 33 percent of grade school–educated people were so willing.

It seems that the media, themselves controlled by higher-education, higher-income people who were more aggressive in foreign policy, tended to give the erroneous impression that working-class people were super-patriots for the war. Lewis Lipsitz, in a mid-1968 survey of poor Blacks and Whites in the South, paraphrased an attitude he found typical: "The only way to help the poor man is to get out of that war in Vietnam. . . . These taxes—high taxes—it's going over yonder to kill people with and I don't see no cause in it."

The capacity for independent judgment among ordinary Americans is probably best shown by the swift development of antiwar feeling among American GIs—volunteers and draftees who came mostly from lower-income groups. There had been, earlier in American history, instances of soldiers' disaffection from the war: isolated mutinies in the Revolutionary War, refusal of reenlistment in the midst of hostilities in the Mexican War, desertion and conscientious objection in World War I and World War II. But Vietnam produced opposition by soldiers and veterans on a scale, and with a fervor, never seen before.

It began with isolated protests. As early as June 1965, Richard Steinke, a West Point graduate in Vietnam, refused to board an aircraft taking him to a remote Vietnamese village. "The Vietnamese war," he said, "is not worth a single American life." Steinke was court-martialed and dismissed from the service. The following year, three army privates, one Black, one Puerto Rican, one Lithuanian Italian—all poor—refused to embark for Vietnam, denouncing the war as "immoral, illegal, and unjust." They were court-martialed and imprisoned.

In early 1967, Captain Howard Levy, an army doctor at Fort Jackson, South Carolina, refused to teach Green Berets, a Special Forces elite in the military. He said they were "murderers of women and children" and "killers of peasants." He was court-martialed on the grounds that he was trying to promote disaffection among enlisted men by his statements. The colonel who presided at the trial said: "The truth of the statements is not an issue in this case." Levy was convicted and sentenced to prison.

The individual acts multiplied: A Black private in Oakland refused to board a troop plane to Vietnam, although he faced eleven years at hard labor. A navy nurse, Lieutenant Susan Schnall, was court-martialed for marching in a peace demonstration while in uniform and for dropping antiwar leaflets from a plane on navy installations. In Norfolk, Virginia, a sailor refused to train fighter pilots because he said the war was immoral. An army lieutenant was arrested in Washington, D.C., in early 1968 for picketing the White House with a sign that said: "120,000 American Casualties—Why?" Two Black marines, George Daniels and William Harvey, were given long-term prison sentences (Daniels, six years, Harvey, ten years, both later reduced) for talking to other Black marines against the war.

As the war went on, desertions from the armed forces mounted. Thousands went to Western Europe—France, Sweden, Holland. Most deserters crossed into Canada; some estimates were fifty thousand, others one hundred thousand. Some stayed in the United States. A few openly defied the military authorities by taking "sanctuary" in churches, where, surrounded by antiwar friends and sympathizers, they waited for capture and court-martial. At Boston University, a thousand students kept vigil for five days and nights in the chapel, supporting an eighteen-year-old deserter, Ray Kroll.

Kroll's story was a common one. He had been inveigled into joining the army; he came from a poor family, was brought into court, charged with drunkenness, and given the choice of prison or enlistment. He enlisted. And then he began to think about the nature of the war.

On a Sunday morning, federal agents showed up at the Boston University chapel, stomped their way through aisles clogged with students, smashed down doors, and took Kroll away. From the stockade, he wrote to friends: "I ain't gonna kill; it's against my will." A friend he had made at the chapel brought him books, and he noted a saying he had found in one of them: "What we have done will not be lost to all Eternity. Everything ripens at its time and becomes fruit at its hour."

The GI antiwar movement became more organized. Near Fort Jackson, South Carolina, the first "GI coffeehouse" was set up, a place where soldiers could get coffee and doughnuts, find antiwar literature, and talk freely with others. It was called the UFO and lasted for several years before it was declared a "public nuisance" and closed by court action. But other GI coffee-houses sprang up in half a dozen other places across the country. An antiwar "bookstore" was opened near Fort Devens, Massachusetts, and another one at the Newport, Rhode Island, naval base.

Underground newspapers sprang up at military bases across the country; by 1970, more than fifty were circulating. Among them were: *About Face* in Los Angeles; *Fed Up!* in Tacoma, Washington; *Short Times* at Fort Jackson; *Vietnam GI* in Chicago; *Graffiti* in Heidelberg, Germany; *Bragg Briefs* in North Carolina; *Last Harass* at Fort Gordon, Georgia; *Helping Hand* at Mountain Home Air Base, Idaho. These newspapers printed antiwar articles, gave news about the harassment of GIs and practical advice on the legal rights of servicemen, told how to resist military domination.

Mixed with feeling against the war was resentment at the cruelty, the dehumanization, of military life. In the army prisons, the stockades, this was especially true. In 1968, at the Presidio stockade in California, a guard shot to death an emotionally disturbed prisoner for walking away from a work detail. Twenty-seven prisoners then sat down and refused to work, singing "We Shall Overcome." They were court-martialed, found guilty of mutiny, and sentenced to terms of up to fourteen years, later reduced after much public attention and protest.

The dissidence spread to the war front itself. When the great Moratorium Day demonstrations were taking place in October 1969 in the United States, some GIs in Vietnam wore black armbands to show their support. A news photographer reported that in a platoon on patrol near Da Nang, about half of the men were wearing black armbands. One soldier stationed at Cu Chi wrote to a friend on October 26, 1970, that separate companies had been set up for men refusing to go into the field to fight. "It's no big thing here anymore to refuse to go." The French newspaper *Le Monde* reported that in four months, 109 soldiers of the first air cavalry division were charged with refusal to fight. "A common sight," the correspondent for *Le Monde* wrote, "is the black soldier, with his left fist clenched in defiance of a war he has never considered his own."

Wallace Terry, a Black American reporter for *Time* magazine, taped conversations with hundreds of Black soldiers; he found bitterness against army racism, disgust with the war, generally low morale. More and more cases of "fragging" were reported in Vietnam —incidents in which servicemen rolled fragmentation bombs under tents of officers who were ordering them into combat or against whom they had other grievances. The Pentagon reported 209 fraggings in Vietnam in 1970 alone.

Veterans back from Vietnam formed a group called Vietnam Veterans Against the War. In December 1970, hundreds of them went to Detroit to what were called the "Winter Soldier" investigations to testify publicly about atrocities they had participated in or seen in Vietnam, committed by Americans against Vietnamese. In April 1971, more than a thousand of them went to Washington, D.C., to demonstrate against the war. One by one, they went up to a wire fence around the Capitol, threw over the fence the medals they had won in Vietnam, and made brief statements about the war, sometimes emotionally, sometimes in icy, bitter calm.

In the summer of 1970, twenty-eight commissioned officers of the military, including some veterans of Vietnam, saying they represented about 250 other officers, announced formation of the Concerned Officers Movement against the war. During the fierce bombings of Hanoi and Haiphong, around Christmas 1972, came the first defiance of B-52 pilots who refused to fly those missions.

On June 3, 1973, the *New York Times* reported dropouts among West Point cadets. Officials there, the reporter wrote, "linked the rate to an affluent, less disciplined, skeptical, and questioning generation and to the anti-military mood that a small radical minority and the Vietnam war had created."

But most of the antiwar action came from ordinary GIs, and most of these came from lower-income groups—White, Black, Native American, Chinese.

A twenty-year-old New York City Chinese American named Sam Choy enlisted at seventeen in the army, was sent to Vietnam, was made a cook, and found himself the target of abuse by fellow GIs, who called him "Chink" and "gook" (the term for the Vietnamese) and said he looked like the enemy. One day he took a rifle and fired warning shots at his tormentors. "By this time I was near the perimeter of the base and was thinking of joining the Viet Cong; at least they would trust me."

Choy was taken by military police, beaten, court-martialed, sentenced to eighteen months of hard labor at Fort Leavenworth. "They beat me up every day, like a time clock." He ended his interview with a New York Chinatown newspaper by saying, "One thing: I want to tell all the Chinese kids the army made me sick. They made me so sick that I can't stand it."

A dispatch from Phu Bai in April 1972 said that 50 GIs out of 142 men in the company refused to go on patrol, crying: "This isn't our war!" The *New York Times* on July 14, 1973, reported that American prisoners of war in Vietnam, ordered by officers in the POW camp to stop cooperating with the enemy, shouted back: "Who's the enemy?" They formed a peace committee in the camp, and a sergeant on the committee later recalled his march from capture to the POW camp: "Until we got to the first camp, we didn't see a village intact; they were all destroyed. I sat down and put myself in the middle and asked myself: Is this right or wrong? Is it right to destroy villages? Is it right to kill people en masse? After a while it just got to me."

Pentagon officials in Washington and navy spokesmen in San Diego announced after the United States withdrew its troops from Vietnam in 1973, that the navy was going to purge itself of "undesirables"—and that these included as many as six thousand men in the Pacific fleet, "a substantial proportion of them black." Altogether, about 700,000 GIs had received less than honorable discharges. In the year 1973, one of every five discharges was "less than honorable," indicating something less than dutiful obedience to the military. By 1971, 177 of every 1,000 American soldiers were listed as "absent without leave," some of them three or four times. Deserters doubled from 47,000 in 1967 to 89,000 in 1971.

One of those who stayed, fought, but then turned against the war was Ron Kovic. His father worked in a supermarket on Long Island. In 1963, at the age of seventeen, he enlisted in the marines. Two years later, in Vietnam at the age of nineteen, his spine was shattered by shellfire. Paralyzed from the waist down, he was put in a wheelchair. Back in the States, he observed the brutal treatment of wounded veterans in the veterans' hospitals, thought more and more about the war, and joined the Vietnam Veterans Against the War. He went to demonstrations to speak against the war. One evening he heard actor Donald Sutherland read from the post–World War I novel by Dalton Trumbo, *Johnny Got His Gun,* about a soldier whose limbs and face were shot away by gunfire, a thinking torso who invented a way of communicating with the outside world and then beat out a message so powerful it could not be heard without trembling. "Sutherland began to read the passage and something I will never forget swept over me. It was as if someone was speaking for everything I ever went through in the hospital. . . . I began to shake and I remember there were tears in my eyes."

Kovic demonstrated against the war and was arrested. He tells his story in *Born on the Fourth of July:*

> They help me back in the chair and take me to another part of the prison building to be booked.
> "What's your name?" the officer behind the desk says.
> "Ron Kovic," I say. "Occupation, Vietnam veteran against the war."
> "What?" he says sarcastically, looking down at me.
> "I'm a Vietnam veteran against the war," I almost shout back.
> "You should have died over there," he says. He turns to his assistant. "I'd like to take this guy and throw him off the roof."
> They fingerprint me and take my picture and put me in a cell. I have begun to wet my pants like a little baby. The tube has slipped out during my examination by the doctor. I try to fall asleep but even though I am exhausted, the anger is alive in me like a huge hot stone in my chest. I lean my head up against the wall and listen to the toilets flush again and again.

Kovic and the other veterans drove to Miami to the Republican National Convention in 1972, went into the Convention Hall, wheeled themselves down the aisles, and as Nixon began his acceptance speech, shouted, "Stop the bombing! Stop the war!" Delegates cursed them: "Traitor!" and Secret Service men hustled them out of the hall.

In the fall of 1973, with no victory in sight and North Vietnamese troops entrenched in various parts of the south, the United States agreed to accept a settlement that would withdraw American troops and leave the revolutionary troops where they were, until a new, elected government would be set up including communist and noncommunist elements. But the Saigon government refused to agree, and the United States decided to make one final attempt to bludgeon the North Vietnamese into submission. It sent waves of B-52s over Hanoi and Haiphong, destroying homes and hospitals, killing unknown numbers of civilians. The attack did not work. Many of the B-52s were shot down, there was angry protest all over the world—and Kissinger went back to Paris and signed very much the same peace agreement that had been agreed on before.

The United States withdrew its forces, continuing to give aid to the Saigon government, but when the North Vietnamese launched attacks in early 1975 against the major cities in South Vietnam, the government collapsed. In late April 1975, North Vietnamese troops entered Saigon. The American embassy staff fled, along with many Vietnamese who feared communist rule, and the long war in Vietnam was over. Saigon was renamed Ho Chi Minh City, and both parts of Vietnam were unified as the Democratic Republic of Vietnam.

Traditional history portrays the end of wars as coming from the initiatives of leaders—negotiations in Paris or Brussels or Geneva or Versailles—just as it often finds the coming of war a response to the demand of "the people." The Vietnam War gave clear evidence that at least for that war (making one wonder about the others) the political leaders were the last to take steps to end the war—"the people" were far ahead. The president was always far behind. The Supreme Court silently turned away from cases challenging the constitutionality of the war. Congress was years behind public opinion.

In the spring of 1971, syndicated columnists Rowland Evans and Robert Novak, two firm supporters of the war, wrote regretfully of a "sudden outbreak of anti-war emotionalism" in the House of Representatives, and said: "The anti-war animosities now suddenly so pervasive among the House Democrats are viewed by Administration backers as less anti-Nixon than as a response to constituent pressures."

It was only after the intervention in Cambodia ended, and only after the nationwide campus uproar over that invasion, that Congress passed a resolution declaring that American troops should not be sent into Cambodia without its approval. And it was not until late 1973, when American troops had finally been removed from Vietnam, that Congress passed a bill limiting the power of the president to make war without congressional consent; even there, in that "War Powers Resolution," the President could make war for sixty days on his own without a congressional declaration.

The administration tried to persuade the American people that the war was ending because of its decision to negotiate a peace—not because it was losing the war, not because of the powerful antiwar movement in the United States. But the government's own secret memoranda all through the war testify to its sensitivity at each stage about "public opinion" in the United States and abroad. The data is in the *Pentagon Papers*.

In June of 1964, top American military and State Department officials, including Ambassador Henry Cabot Lodge, met in Honolulu. "Rusk stated that public opinion on our SEA [Southeast Asia] policy was badly divided and that, therefore, the President needed an affirmation of support." Diem had been replaced by a general named Khanh. The Pentagon historians write: "upon his return to Saigon on June 5 Ambassador Lodge went straight from the airport to call on General Khanh. . . . [T]he main thrust of his talk with Khanh was to hint that the United States Government would in the immediate future be preparing U.S. public opinion for actions against North Vietnam." Two months later came the Gulf of Tonkin affair.

On April 2, 1965, a memo from CIA director John McCone suggested that the bombing of North Vietnam be increased because it was "not sufficiently severe" to change North Vietnam's policy. "On the other hand . . . we can expect increasing pressure to stop the bombing . . . from various elements of the American public, from the press, the United States and world opinion." The United States should try for a fast knockout before this opinion could build up, McCone said.

Assistant Secretary of Defense John McNaughton's memo of early 1966 suggested destruction of locks and dams to create mass starvation because "strikes at population targets" would "create a counterproductive wave of revulsion abroad and at home." In May 1967, the Pentagon historians write: "McNaughton was also very concerned about the breadth and intensity of public unrest and dissatisfaction with the war . . . especially with young people, the underprivileged, the intelligentsia and the women." McNaughton worried: "Will the move to call up 20,000 Reserves . . . polarize opinion to the extent that the 'doves' in the United States will get out of hand—massive refusals to serve, or to fight, or to cooperate, or worse?" He warned:

> There may be a limit beyond which many Americans and much of the world will not permit the United States to go. The picture of the world's greatest superpower killing or seriously injuring 1000 non-combatants a week, while trying to pound a tiny backward nation into submission, on an issue whose merits are hotly disputed, is not a pretty one. It could conceivably produce a costly distortion in the American national consciousness.

That "costly distortion" seems to have taken place by the spring of 1968, when, with the sudden and scary Tet offensive of the National Liberation Front, Westmoreland asked President Johnson to send him 200,000 more troops on top of the 525,000 already there. Johnson asked a small group of "action officers" in the Pentagon to advise him on this. They studied the situation and concluded that 200,000 troops would totally Americanize the war and would not strengthen the Saigon government because "the Saigon leadership shows no signs of a willingness—let alone an ability—to attract the necessary loyalty or support of the people." Furthermore, the report said, sending troops would mean mobilizing reserves, increasing the military budget. There would be more U.S. casualties, more taxes. And: "This growing disaffection accompanied as it certainly will be, by increased defiance of the draft and growing unrest in the cities because of the belief that we are neglecting domestic problems, runs great risks of provoking a domestic crisis of unprecedented proportions." The "growing unrest in the cities" must have been a reference to the Black uprisings that had taken place in 1967 and showed the link—whether Blacks deliberately made it or not—between the war abroad and poverty at home.

The evidence from the *Pentagon Papers* is clear—Johnson's decision in the spring of 1968 to turn down Westmoreland's request, to slow down for the first time the escalation of the war, to diminish the bombing, to go to the conference table was influenced to a great extent by the actions Americans had taken in demonstrating their opposition to the war.

When Nixon took office, he too tried to persuade the public that protest would not affect him. But he almost went berserk when one lone pacifist picketed the White House. The frenzy of Nixon's actions against dissidents—plans for burglaries, wiretapping, mail openings—suggests the importance of the antiwar movement in the minds of national leaders.

One sign that the ideas of the antiwar movement had taken hold in the American public was that juries became more reluctant to convict antiwar protesters, and local judges too were treating them differently. In Washington by 1971, judges were dismissing charges against demonstrators in cases where two years before they almost certainly would have been sent to jail. The antiwar groups who had raided draft boards—the Baltimore Four, the Catonsville Nine, the Milwaukee Fourteen, the Boston Five, and more—were receiving lighter sentences for the same crimes.

The last group of draft board raiders, the "Camden 28," were priests, nuns, and laypeople who raided a draft board in Camden, New Jersey, in

August 1971. It was essentially what the Baltimore Four had done four years earlier, when all were convicted and Phil Berrigan got six years in prison. But in this instance, the Camden defendants were acquitted by the jury on all counts. When the verdict was in, one of the jurors, a fifty-three-year-old Black taxi driver from Atlantic City named Samuel Braithwaite, who had spent eleven years in the army, left a letter for the defendants:

To you, the clerical physicians with your God-given talents, I say, well done. Well done for trying to heal the sick irresponsible men, men who were chosen by the people to govern and lead them. These men, who failed the people, by raining death and destruction on a hapless country. . . . You went out to do your part while your brothers remained in their ivory towers watching . . . [A]nd hopefully some day in the near future, peace and harmony may reign to people of all nations.

That was in May of 1973. The American troops were leaving Vietnam. C. L. Sulzberger, the *New York Times* correspondent (a man close to the government), wrote: "The U.S. emerges as the big loser and history books must admit this. . . . We lost the war in the Mississippi valley, not the Mekong valley. Successive American governments were never able to muster the necessary mass support at home."

In fact, the United States had lost the war in both the Mekong Valley and the Mississippi Valley. It was the first clear defeat to the global American empire formed after World War II. It was administered by revolutionary peasants abroad and by an astonishing movement of protest at home.

Back on September 26, 1969, President Richard Nixon, noting the growing antiwar activity all over the country, announced that "under no circumstance will I be affected whatever by it." But nine years later, in his *Memoirs*, he admitted that the antiwar movement caused him to drop plans for intensification of the war: "Although publicly I continued to ignore the raging antiwar controversy . . . I knew, however, that after all the protests and the Moratorium, American public opinion would be seriously divided by any military escalation of the war." It was a rare presidential admission of the power of public protest.

From a long-range viewpoint, something perhaps even more important had happened. The rebellion at home was spreading beyond the issue of war in Vietnam.

PART TWO

The War at Home

From Ha Ha Ha McNamara

ROBERT MALECKI

Chapter 5
Pavlov and Me: A Story About Atomic Bomb Drills in the Fifties!

MY RAZOR THINKS this story is depressing. It's probably jealous!

Pavlov was the guy who did experiments with the dogs, making them react to various forms of stimulation. There is a big word, *behaviourism*—gee, that almost sounds like communism. Behaviourism is a theory that if you give a living organism a certain stimulation it will react in a certain way.

Who am I? My name is Bob. Yeah, just Bob. I mean, telling you my last name certainly would not tell you anything about my mother's side of history. Her name was McGruder, and she raised me because my father died in 1942, the same year I was born. For some reason I got his last name. I mean, I never even met the guy. Who the fuck is he anyway? Oh, I almost forgot—that is another story.

Anyway, Bob is living in exile in Sweden, in a place called Robertsfors, which lies fairly near the polar circle. If I were to draw a straight line around the globe, I would find myself on the same level as such places as Fairbanks, Alaska, or Zyryanka, which is some fucking place in Siberia. Here we have a winter that lasts about six months. It is cold and dark here in the winter. When I say dark, I mean dark twenty-four hours a day! However, summer is light and just the opposite. The reason I am living here in exile goes back to the war in Vietnam. If I were to return to the United States, I could be

Chapters 5 and 6 from Robert Malecki, *Ha Ha Ha McNamara* are availabel on the Internet.

put away for a very long time because of my activities in opposition to the war in Vietnam. However, that is also another story. Christ! Stop ego tripping, Bob, and get down to the story about atomic bomb drills in the fifties. . . .

In the fifties the newspapers were writing about how the American soldiers captured by the Chinese communists in Korea were being brainwashed into making all kinds of weird confessions about American imperialist aggression. The Chinese communists were using the old dripping water torture trick. They made a soldier lie on a bench and let water drip on his head until he confessed to his crime of being a tool of American aggression and all that, according to newspaper reports based on leaks from high government sources and the CIA.

This was the McCarthy era. By the way, Richard Nixon was a torpedo lawyer for Joe McCarthy. They were trying to get all of the "pinkos" to confess and, having confessed, to jump out of the nearest window. The main question of the time was: "Have you ever been a member or sympathizer of a communist organization?" Even the liberals were terrified of getting the red stamp on their foreheads. Joe McCarthy and his freedom fighters, like the lawyer Nixon, had just about everybody scared shitless about being a part of a gigantic communist conspiracy. These commie creeps could come in the middle of the night and rape your mother, your sisters, if you didn't watch out!

Even Robert McNamara, who recently wrote his book about Vietnam, was a victim of these times. At least that is the feeling one gets when hearing about his confession twenty-five years later about the war being "all wrong." In my opinion, Bob McNamara is a political coward and is responsible for sending a lot of American working-class kids to their deaths, not to mention the suffering of the Vietnamese. Meanwhile, people like me who really and actively opposed that war are still living in exile, unable to return to the United States! If McNamara wants to do something besides make a lot of money on his book, he should try helping the victims of his mistakes. People like me who still can't go home. Or the GIs who are crippled, or the Vietnamese who suffered enormously. . . . Oops! There I go again. Ranting on about something that has nothing to do with the story. Sorry about that!

I was just a kid during those times. I was living on Staten Island in New York City. That was before they built the bridges and the Staten Island ferry cost only a nickel. I think the street I was living on was Lockwood Avenue. My house was right across the street from the Bethlehem steel plant. I remember the grey walls, the grey men with their lunch boxes, and the smoke and noise coming from across the street. I did not know that the McCarthy era was at its peak, nor did I know that I was part of the gigantic Pavlovian experiment of the times. In fact, most of the time, if I wasn't in school, I was playing with my friends in the streets or playing with my prick on the rooftops! Little did I know that I was being set up as future cannon fodder, in future wars, a future victim so that corporate creeps could make profits. No, not at all. I was just a kid who did not know his ass from a hole in the ground.

I was going to school. Public school! You know, the place where there are forty kids in a class. They've got numbers on them like P.S. 8 or P.S. 45. School for me at this time was made up of seasons. There was the spitball season, the paper clip season, the water balloon season, peashooter season, baseball card season, and so on. The other important part of school life in the fifties was the atomic air raid drills that went on about once a week in my public school and probably in many other public schools at the time. Little did I know that these drills were of the higher Pavlovian school of behaviorism. Little did I know that these drills were created to make little kids like me begin foaming at the mouth every time I heard the word *Russian* or *communist.* Nor did I know that, even today, I would get chills up and down my spine on hearing the national anthem. I was just a poor kid in a neighborhood with other poor kids trying to make the best out of what life had to give. The truth, in fact, was I was just trying to survive circumstances over which I had no control.

The atomic air raid drills started with sirens. Sirens on the school roof, sirens everywhere. Our teacher would inform us that it was a drill by screaming "the Russians are coming, the Russians are coming, take cover." Before taking cover, some of the kids in the class were assigned the duty of pulling down the dark shades over the windows. Then the actual detonation of a bomb was suppose to take place. The teacher began screaming, "FLASH," which meant that we were to cover our eyes with our hands. After that, the teacher screamed "BLAST," which meant that we kids were to cover our ears. Then the teacher screamed, "SHOCKWAVE," which meant that we kids were to roll up in a little ball under our desks. Finally, the sirens would start again, and the teacher would scream, "ALL CLEAR." Then we would all sing the national anthem! If you, the reader, had been there, I believe that you would have been scared too. Not only would the Russians rape your mother and your sisters, but they would drop atomic bombs on your fucking head too. This stuff pulled on little innocent kids like me prepared us to foam at the mouth when we heard the words *communist* or *Russian*. Not only that, for working-class kids who survived in New York City until the age necessary to go out and fight for "our country," it was the mental training ground to prepare us as the pieces of meat to be used by those in power for future wars. It is not the rich guy who goes out and dies for his country; he is too busy making money for that. No, it is poor creeps like us living in the ghettos who always get the shitty end of the stick—our main choice in life usually either to go be a soldier or go to jail!

These atomic air raid drills made an enormous impression on one. For many years, it affected my life and the lives of my family. My sister Judy is a good example. She came to visit me here in Sweden in the seventies, as a grown woman; she had a fur coat, a diamond ring, two sweet little girls she was sending to Catholic school. Christ, this sounds like the American dream in a nutshell. Anyway, we got drunk one night and talked. So she said to me, "Bobby, you remember how poor we were when we were little? Well, I am never going back to that," and she also said, "Bobby, you are my brother, and I love you, but I think you're a communist, and if you come back, I hope they put you away!" That really convinced me that my sister had also been brainwashed during the fifties. She was convinced that my actions protesting the war in Vietnam were a plot, a gigantic communist conspiracy, and I had been duped by communist propaganda! Wow, my very own sister, who did not have a pot to piss in when she was little. My sister—convinced I was a part of a gigantic conspiracy. But she had also said to me, "Bobby, you remember how poor we were when we were little? Well, I am never going back to that." So this was her way of climbing out of the pot, a bit selfish, but for my sister a way out. HMMM! I wonder how she is doing today. Maybe she is on unemployment. Maybe her husband, a jockey, dumped her. Who knows? The point being that my sister was also a victim of the times.

I found another good example during my stay in the Lewisburg Federal Penitentiary. I was imprisoned there for twenty-seven months for some of my activities against the Vietnam War. I met a "Russian" spy named R. G. Just meeting him sent shivers up my spine. Here I was face to face with a guy who people had told me from the time I was little would drop atomic bombs on my head and rape my mom and my sisters! Well, it turned out different. R. G. was not even a Russian, but a German. Not only that, he was one of the few people I have met in my life who turned out to be a very kind, thoughtful, and intelligent person. But that is another story. My feelings for him the first time I met him, though, belong to the atomic air raid drills, my teacher, and her "the Russians are coming" screaming bullshit of the McCarthy era.

So what kind of conclusions should you draw from this story? You could of course go out and shoot the first Russian you meet! However, the Russians have their own problems these days. Of course, you could say that the author of these lines is fucking sick in the head and probably should be shot on sight. My own conclusion is that my children and my grandchildren—whom I have not had the privilege of meeting yet because the U.S. government is still pissed off about my activities during the Vietnam War—should read these lines and perhaps think about what it is the rich and powerful people in the United States are using today in order to prepare the future generations of cannon fodder to fight their enemies! Anyone else can decide to do what he or she thinks best. I will be fifty-three years old soon and who cares what I am thinking about. Just an old bullshit artist.

Chapter 7: How I Got into the Military and, More Important, How I Got out of the Military!

If you're a poor kid living in New York City, military life can be a real opportunity! I mean, a lot of kids growing up in the city are usually faced with a choice early in life: join up with the army, navy, marines, or go to reform school or jail. Obviously, the military is a great opportunity!

I was seventeen and had quit school. My mom told me that I was going to wind up in reform school or jail. I said that I was going to join the United States Navy and see the world, if she would sign the papers. My mom willingly sent me off to become a man.

I will have to admit that for the first three and a half years or so, I just loved the navy. I was stationed in a place called Williamsburg, Virginia. The organization I belonged to was called CHB I. It was attached to the Seabees, and our main duty during wartime was to go in behind the Marine Corps and establish a beachhead after an invasion. During peacetime, we were being sent all over the world on various jobs—like to Antarctica to build a base there, or to the Mediterranean to supply the fleet. Life was great. I had gotten some tattoos on my arms, which proved my manhood, and I was beginning to get some peach fuzz on my face.

Things got serious, I think, in 1961 during the Cuban missile crisis, or was it the Bay of Pigs? I don't remember which, but I was sent to the big

U.S. base on Cuba during the crisis. We were flown in as the wives of the people stationed there were being flown out. The marines were mining the whole fucking base perimeter, expecting to do a last stand–type Corregidor or something. I got to stand guard duty with a 30-calibre rifle, left over from the Second World War! I was not stupid, though. I did not walk up and down like a nut waiting to be shot. I found a nice dark place so that if the shit started to hit the fan, my ass at least would have a chance to survive because when it came down to the cookie jar, that was about the only thing I wanted to think about, saving my ass and not going home in a box. That, my friends, is the bottom line for most working-class kids sent off to war: staying alive! That has always been the bottom line. It's not patriotism; it's not the John Wayne planting the stars and stripes on Iwo Jima Hollywood shit. It's not I'm singing in the rain with Gene Kelly, either. When the bullets start flying, it's my ass or his ass.

Of course, looking at it today I realize that the government certainly would have liked to have had a sort of mini Pearl Harbor at the Guantanamo base in Cuba. Had the Cubans attacked us and wiped us out, the U.S. government would have had an excuse to wipe Cuba off the face of the map. That certainly would not helped the guys who were there! We would have been dead!!

The problem with Cuba was also an ideological problem for me. Yeah, it was I, with my eighth-grade education, who had a real ideological problem with Cuba. The problem was very, very simple. All of my friends, my brother, and his friends were supporting the Cubans! Yeah, can you believe that? Most of the poor kids that I knew in New York City were on the Cuban side. Their reasons for holding this opinion varied, but they were usually quite clear and to the point.

Tony, a friend and small-time gangster, supported the Cuban revolution, mainly because of the money. He would say things like, "Man, the pot [marijuana] in Cuba is just fantastic, and if we join up with Fidel, maybe we can get a franchise." But Tony also had ideological convictions. He was Italian and knew people in the Mafia who hated the people who were running the casinos in Cuba before Batista's fall. The guys in Cuba were also Mafia people, but they had never worked on the docks or in the unions! Tony hated the companies in Cuba because he knew the dockworkers who unloaded the bananas in New York City.

There was Eddie, an Irishman who was running guns to the Cubans because he supported the IRA. He hated the English and "the fucking rats who ran the sugar companies and banana companies" in Cuba during the time of Batista. Eddie knew what the English were doing to the Irish. He knew that what the Americans wanted to do in Cuba was basically the same thing.

Then there were my Puerto Rican friends, who supported their brothers and sisters in Cuba.

There were my Black friends, who said, "Man, if I was livin' dar, det would be me who was loaden dem fucking bananas."

There was my brother, who had his room filled with Russian and Cuban flags and was studying Russian. He had a more ideological belief in the guerilla movement that came to power after leading the struggle from the mountains.

Then there was another friend, Zeke. He had even fought with the guerillas in Cuba during the early years. After the Cubans got rid of the Batista regime, Zeke was caught trying to smuggle lots of marijuana from Cuba. He was deported from Cuba, but he got to keep a medal he had received during the fighting. Zeke was pissed off at the Cubans for awhile, but he was still on their side.

And into all this I walked after three and one-half years in the navy. In fact, I had just enlisted for six more years! However, it was not to be. I came home to New York City for thirty days' leave. Little did I know that at this point my entire life would change course. It would be my first fumbling steps to political consciousness, my first encounters with the U.S. government and its naval intelligence, my first encounter with the fact that poor people who join the military are slaughtered so that the rich people can make a lot of money, and with the fact that if a poor person becomes aware of this, he is considered extremely dangerous and has to be stopped one way or another.

So I had just reenlisted for six more years of the navy. I had gotten a whole bunch of money for doing that. I had also been informed at my base that I was going to be transferred. Transferred to a little fucking oil tanker based in Savannah, Georgia! I was upset about it because I had no idea why I was being transferred all of a sudden.

It was not until many years later that I realized that my childhood friend and my brother and his friends and their activities were behind this sudden transfer. I was fucking naïve, stupid, idiotic—yeah, just a complete asshole. I will get back to this later. But already in 1963 the U.S. government was on my ass. They thought I was running an operation for the Cubans, perhaps smuggling guns or smuggling information about all the secret shit that went on underground in Williamsburg and was used later on to support the Bay of

Pigs! Well, the government wasted a lot of fucking money because at this time I did not know my ass from a hole in the ground. Back to this later on.

So after three years I came home to New York City. I had not been in touch with my brother or my friends during this time. Most of my friends were doing the Village scene at this particular time in history. The Village scene was different things to different people, usually depending on where they were coming from. There was the jazz scene, the coffee houses, the West Village scene, the East Village scene, and the general street scene. There were a lot of kids coming into the village from the suburbs, mostly middle-class and upper-middle-class kids. On the east side, there were lots of Black people and lots of "junk," mostly heroin, going on there. On the west side, there was lots of marijuana, and a lot of junk on the jazz scene. And finally there was also Timothy Leary, a Harvard chemist who was on everybody's lips because of LSD. Not to forget the speakeasies, where people like Lenny Bruce were appearing.

My friends—most of them dealing pot, hash, and LSD or selling paintings to the middle-class kids from the suburbs—would sleep all day and go into the city at night. They did not look like hippies or junkies but were usually well dressed with a Manchester jacket, jeans, shirt, and tie. Others had disguises and dressed up like hippies in order to sell paintings. Some of the women I knew were into a lot of speed and being witches. Yeah, that's right, witches. I was swept into this world of my childhood friends and immediately decided that my career in the navy had to end as quickly as possible. I would love to tell you about some of the incredible events going on at this time in the village; these people are probably alive today, though, and I feel it would be better to avoid mentioning anything that might endanger them, especially because the government has always been interested in one way or another!

I would like to take up here the questions of morality and intellectual snobbery. Many times in my life, I have met people who because of circumstances have had better educations, better morals, better everything if one were to believe all their bullshit. Some of these people have stood on the side of poor and working-class people at various times in history, but the majority of them were and are bullshit artists. You would think that they would treat people like me and my friends as equals at least, but that is never so. They are always trying to twist and turn our heads in all kinds of directions. All the *isms*—communism, capitalism, fascism—were introduced to poor and working-class people by people who came from another world.

These ideologies were introduced into the workers' movement, and the workers and poor people were tricked into walking under one flag or the other, which usually had devastating effects for the workers themselves.

One thing these people have in common is that they think that working people and poor people have to be enlightened, educated, and brought into the light by some sort of ideology in order to lead a better life. It reminds me of the missionaries who went out into the bush in Africa to teach the natives how to be civilized, or the white Europeans who ripped off America from the Indians by making deals like buying Manhattan for twenty-four dollars in trinkets.

In reality, these people imposed their lifestyles on the Africans and enslaved them. They killed off most of the American Indians, and more recently they have been using working-class people and the poor as bodies to be killed off by the latest ideological whim. They are so self-serving and smart. They think that poor and working-class people can't think, and therefore are always trying to stuff more bullshit down our throats!

Well, many of us certainly cannot express our thoughts in terms acceptable to these circles—nor even put forks and knives on the right side when setting the table. Yeah, the rich even have rules for this kind of stuff. But we have one thing that they do not understand at all, and that is historical experience. I mean, poor and working-class people have the experience of suffering because of whatever ideas are presently popular in upper-class circles. We are beginning to understand that when these people start pointing their finger at the enemy and scream, "kill," we had better watch our asses because usually the poor and working class wind up killing each other. Historically, every time the rich have become convinced of one particular theory or another, poor and working-class people have died in the millions. During the Second World War, there was imperialism, Nazism, feudalism, and Stalinism. All those little ideological trips cost the poor and working class millions and millions of lives.

Earlier in this book I took up the subject of a little Vietnamese girl running down a highway in Vietnam, napalm burning holes in her body. Well, that little girl, who was running for her very life, had something very much in common with me and my childhood friends. We were and are running for our lives, just as she was. We were running from the enemy. For this little girl, the enemy came from the sky; the ideology was the domino theory. Nick was and is still running for his life; he was a small-time gangster and the theory was capitalism—that is, rich people exploiting poor people like

Nick's dad on the docks so that they could drive Cadillacs. Eddie was running away too. His experience was with the English attempt to colonize Northern Ireland. Eddie's relatives were trying to stop it by building the IRA. Bob was running too. When I was a kid, I was running from my stepdad Harry, who was being destroyed down on the docks by the rich people. He was a union man, and the rich were trying to destroy the unions. The problem with Harry was that he was pointing the gun at his own stepkids instead of at the fat cats. We were all running from something that rich people and their intellectual lackeys were trying to push off on us. Our experience is a common one. Our history is a pyramid of skulls, our skulls! A lot of the people who come from this other world are always trying to get us killed in one way or another. Even when I read the letters of solidarity with my fight for amnesty, I find that they are permeated with ideological advice. This advice, if taken, would be devastating to poor and working-class people like me. For many years now, people have been trying to convince me of the rightness of one ideology or another. However, I have no trust in any one of them because every time I turn around, the Nicks, the Eddies, the Bobs, the Indians, the Blacks, the little Vietnamese girls are the ones running for their lives. It is pretty easy for these people with their nice cars and nice houses to come down into the streets of New York or into the African jungles or the Vietnamese countryside in order to convince us of the latest theory in their circles. But people like me are the ones who form the pyramid of skulls throughout history.

What I am trying to say here is, there is nothing these people want to give us. In fact, most of the rules they make up in society are to protect their interests and not the Nicks and Eddies or the little Vietnamese girl who was running for her life. Take the latest round of death sentences being handed down. Fifteen- and sixteen-year-old kids who rob a store for twenty dollars and shoot somebody in the process are to be executed by the state. When was the last time the state executed a rich person for robbing millions from working-class people? When was the last time the state executed somebody for sending working-class and poor kids off to a war that it started with the domino theory? How about the mining company officials on Bougainville today who are responsible for a genocidal war against the people on the island in order to open the copper mine for the profits they can make? No, the death penalty is not for rich people. They invented the death penalty to keep poor people in line.

Remember how they screamed when a couple of times in history that "rule" got turned around? The French Revolution for the people and the guillotine for the rich! Christ, they are still talking today about the Bolsheviks putting the czar against the wall. On the other hand, what about all the Vietnamese who were turned into dust for the domino theory? Or the fifty-five thousand GIs who came back in body bags?

The GIs got a black stone in Washington, D.C. (Ideologically, that stone is being used to prepare the next generation for a new war.) In the United States, nobody ever talks about the millions of Vietnamese turned into dust by the bombings. The people controlling things are only interested in making rules to put down anybody Vietnamese or American who gets in the way.

NO, THE RICH PEOPLE MAKE THE RULES AND THE IDEOLOGIES TO KEEP POOR AND WORKING-CLASS PEOPLE IN PLACE.

Don't pass any moral or ideological judgments on the Nicks and Eddies and Bobs in this story. These guys are certainly not angels. We are at least honest in saying that we were born into a system that has never given nor will ever give us a fucking chance. It is a system that is built up by oppressing the poor and working-class people. Your nice houses and cars and the rest—yes, your standard of living—are kept up by exploiting people like us everywhere on this fucking planet. So don't start telling us how we should try and survive a death sentence imposed on us by the rich from the very day we were born so that you can continue your bourgeois historical domination. Go fuck yourselves. I don't like rich people or their lackeys. I will never trust you because, oh, it is so fucking simple! I don't like you because I have been a victim, just as the little Vietnamese girl was a victim. We are on the same side. You rich people are on the other side. Until the historical inequalities built into this system are erased, we are deadly enemies! So long as there are rich and the poor, we are deadly enemies. When you talk about Black mothers on welfare or dope addicts or criminals, you're talking about people who never had a chance in this fucking society. They are victims, just as the little Vietnamese girl was a victim.

And listen to the talk about morals! Nick and Eddie and many other poor kids made their living by selling drugs to middle-class kids and rich kids coming in from the suburbs. I remember the moral outrage about this stuff. Why, there were articles in the newspaper every day about this stuff: our kids are being destroyed. I even remember seeing articles that claimed middle-class kids running down to the village to buy pot or LSD was a fucking communist conspiracy! We thought that it was great to see kids from the suburbs come slumming into our part of town. Later on, they would protest against the race riots and the war in Vietnam. Well, it was people like Nick and Eddie, Zeke and Clem, who got these kids to let their hair down, who let these kids know that their shit stinks just like our shit. The Nicks and the Eddies got all these kids pointed in a direction that led to the biggest military defeat in history that the American bourgeoisie have suffered. The pot and LSD that the Nicks and Eddies were selling to these kids formed the motor that made these kids drop out a short period of time in history. That dropout saved just as many Vietnamese lives as the political organizations did. I personally would like to thank the Nicks and Eddies of the world. They were small-time gangsters trying to survive in a world they never understood, but they turned the youth of America on and got them in a critical moment of history to turn their backs on their bourgeois parents. And to think those college kids still today think that they were solely responsible for helping the Vietnamese win the war! That is just a crock of bullshit.

We were watching these kids long before they even became aware of it. These kids were digging the music of Black people whose forefathers were slaves. These kids were buying drugs like pot and LSD from the Eddies and Nicks of the world, and that money was financing the IRA and the Cuban revolutionaries. These kids were buying paintings and lots of other shit in the Village, and that money was feeding workers on the picket lines. This stuff was going on before these kids even knew what race riots were. These kids helped finance the civil rights movement. The Blacks who dealt drugs were sending money to Martin Luther King, Jr. Even today these kids probably think that the struggle against inequality started on campus around 1968. But in 1917, the Bolsheviks had the hookers working in the party. The Bolsheviks understood poor and oppressed people in 1917, and it worked. The point being that through very special skills (sometimes skills the bourgeoisie consider criminal), poor and working-class kids have had an enormous effect on the outcome of historical struggles. The hookers in the Bolshevik Party are one example. The Nicks and the Eddies of the sixties are another example. So I hope the reader of these lines does not raise any bourgeois moral arguments or political arguments that condemn my childhood friends. Their role in history at this particular time saved a lot of people's lives, especially in Vietnam, where in 1963 the American bourgeoisie decided to take over the role of the French colonialists after they were militarily defeated. These street kids turned on a whole generation. The music came from Black slaves; the drugs came from Cuban, Mexican, and Vietnamese peasants. LSD came from Harvard, but peyote came from the Indians. In fact, the only thing the rich and middle-class kids had at this time was money, which they usually got from their parents! So no moral crap, OK?

In winding up this stuff on morals and intellectual snobbery, I would like to quote the words of a very old and wonderful Black man, Willie. Willie used to sit on the steps with us kids in the neighborhood. Willie was always there. This very old Black man. And I remember to this very day the words he often said to us on the hot, humid summer nights of New York City. Willie would say: "Watchit, boy. This nigger ain't got nothing never from rich white man!" Oh Willie, you wonderful old man—how right you were. All those years we sat with you on the steps, and that was what you were trying to hammer into our heads. Willie, how fucking right you were. I think Willie deserves a statue right next to old Abe Lincoln because he knew the bottom line in the fight between the haves and the have-nots, as he used to call it. Willie, with those few words, knew more about class struggle than all the fucking liberals alive today. Hats off to Willie, a great old Black man!

I was on a thirty-day leave from the navy. These thirty days turned into sixty days when I went AWOL (absent without leave), which meant that I would be court-martialed on returning to the navy. Going AWOL usually means spending a period of time in the brig, stockade, jail, or whatever to pay for the crime. I had not committed any crime. In fact, I was getting my head together for the first time in my life. I was beginning to get a primitive class consciousness. Learning and choosing which side of the fence to be on—the haves' or the have-nots'. Unfortunately, the navy had realized this also.

My friends and I discussed the question of getting out of this six-year reenlistment for which I had just signed up. There were a number of good suggestions. I think Eddie came with the idea of wearing a dress when I returned to ship. That would not work, though, because I'd been in the navy for three and one-half years already. Another suggestion was "just don't go back"—also not such a good idea because it could mean that people would start looking for me and find my friends. Finally, I decided on a suggestion that one of my friends had: to let them find out that I was using some kind of heavy drugs—opium, heroin, or something like that.

So I returned to the oil tanker and was put on court-martial. I was found guilty and sentenced to thirty days in the stockade in Charlotte, North Carolina. The stockade there is run by the marines. It was a real torture chamber then. To teach people like me not to break the rules they had a program to remind us who the boss was. One of the more interesting methods was to take prisoners out in the evening and making them lie at attention in the grass. When the mosquitoes started eating them alive, they could not move a muscle because the marine guard beat their asses if they moved. Fortunately, I did not have to go through this torture. I stayed in the brig in Charleston for forty-five minutes, probably a record.

The morning I was to be sent off to the stockade I put my plan into action. I went to the lifeboats on the ship. In the lifeboats there are medical kits. In these kits are syrettes (a needle with a tube on the end) filled with drugs such as morphine and atropine. I took a number of them and put some holes in my arms. Then I took two sugar cubes with LSD and off I went to the stockade.

On arriving, I was beginning to feel the effects of the chemicals. A guard came and took me to be registered as a prisoner. They took me into a shower room and told me to get undressed. By this time I was really high. I stood there hallucinating, just looking at all the things that were moving around the room. The marine whom I realized was my guard stood looking at me with his mouth hanging down to his ankles. He was a southern boy, probably never confronted with somebody with holes in his arms and wiped out of his mind. He got really fucking nervous and told me to sit down and gave me a cigarette. He went to get his superior, and I put on a really convincing scene. They took me into a room, put some clothes on me. Soon after, I was transferred to the Charleston Naval Hospital, Section Eight—the nut ward!

TO BE CONTINUED IN CHAPTER 9

My razor is getting edgy about this stuff. My cat Sputnik has disappeared now for four days. I'll be back to you soon. . . .

My Vietnam

JANE BOND MOORE

WRITING ABOUT MY EXPERIENCES during the Vietnam War is an act of personal revelation, not a discussion of the political currents that ran behind the war and the antiwar movement. Yet, as the women's movement told us in the sixties, the personal is political. Gloria Steinem reminded us in "Revolution from Within" that the political is also personal. My Vietnam story twists together politics and the personal. I cannot tell about one without the other. The two countries with three governments, the war, my marriage, my children, and my brother wind together with Atlanta, the civil rights movement, and the South.

Julian Bond's Vietnam story is the beginning of my Vietnam story. Julian Bond is my younger brother. On June 15, 1965, he was elected to the Georgia House of Representatives. He represented the 136th House District, a district of sixty-five thousand voters, six thousand of whom were African American, or, as we were known then, Negro. Julian's district covered the Atlanta University complex, which had four undergraduate colleges and a graduate school. A small number of the voters were faculty members and students. A larger number lived in projects. The majority were homeowners working as secretaries, maids, small business owners, laborers, and teachers. They lived in small, one-story wood houses around the colleges and Hunter Street. Then, Hunter Street, now M. L. King Jr. Drive was a center of Atlanta's Black businesses. There was the bank, a small hospital, Paschal's and other restaurants, a drug store, churches, a movie theater, and offices such as my husband's law offices. Now most of those businesses are gone, victims to desegregation. There is no need for a Black business district when we have so thoroughly desegregated Atlanta. Even the projects have changed. One of the projects was completely emptied and the buildings demolished because of the Olympics, my mother told me.

The June 1965 election was the second statewide Georgia election since Reconstruction in which Blacks ran for state legislative office. I was not too involved with Julian's first election. My first child was born in 1964, and I was occupied with her and learning to be a mother. We had also moved into our first home, and I was busy with it and my children. I was trying to live what I call the "women's magazines" life that America sold to women coming of age in the '50s. My role was to keep a neat, attractive home and children, and to support my husband. He, in turn, would work nine to five and spend the evening fixing the plumbing. Real life was very different from these bizarre fantasies. Howard, my husband, worked from six in the morning till ten at night, at a minimum, and did not know or care about plumbing. I was discovering that I am perhaps constitutionally unable to be neat, no matter how hard I try. I adored my babies, their looks and smells, but was slowly growing ever more depressed at the thought that this role was it for my life.

On January 6, 1966, before the House seated Julian, the Student Nonviolent Coordinating Committee (SNCC) issued a statement on American policy in Vietnam. The statement began: The Student Nonviolent Coordinating Committee has a right and a responsibility to dissent with United States foreign policy on an issue when it sees fit. SNCC itemized its disagreement with the country's Vietnam policy. Our government was as "deceptive" in its claimed concern for the freedom of the Vietnamese as it was for the freedom of colored people in such other countries as the Dominican Republic, the Congo, South Africa, Rhodesia and in the United States itself. SNCC declared violence against civil rights workers in the South to be similar to the violence of the U.S. forces in Vietnam. The ability and desire of the U.S. government to hold free elections either at home or abroad were questioned. The statement ended with these sentences:

> We recoil with horror at the inconsistency of a supposedly "free" society where responsibility to freedom is equated with the responsibility to lend oneself to military aggression. We take note of the fact that 16 per cent of the draftees from this country are Negroes called on to stifle the liberation of Vietnam, to preserve a "democracy" which does not exist for them at home.

We ask, where is the draft for the freedom fight in the United States?

We therefore encourage those Americans who prefer to use their energy in building democratic forms within this country. We believe that work in the civil rights movement and with other human relations organizations is a valid alternative to the draft. We urge all Americans to seek this alternative, knowing full well that it may cost them lives—as painfully as in Vietnam.

All hell broke loose when SNCC released that statement. A local radio station interviewed Julian, as director of communications for SNCC. He endorsed the SNCC statement because he was a pacifist. Julian felt that maintaining that the U.S. government was fighting for liberty in other places was hypocritical. The government could not guarantee life and liberty even to citizens inside the continental United States.

Howard came home with Julian in the middle of the day. They told me about the SNCC statement and the turmoil it had caused in the news and legislature. Julian said he could lose his seat. He asked me if he should apologize. Some thread of reality was still hanging in my women's magazine mind. I said no. I knew that an apology could not gain a seat for Julian and would only result in disgrace and failure for him.

Seventy-five White members of the house filed a petition challenging Julian's right to be seated. The petition claimed that Julian's statements gave aid and comfort to the enemies of the United States and Georgia, violated the Selective Service laws, and brought discredit and disrespect on the Georgia House.

Four days later, on January 10, when Julian went to the House to be sworn in, the clerk refused. The House had a hearing. Julian argued that he could take the oath, that the challenge was a deprivation of his First Amendment rights and was racially motivated. The hearings concluded, as we all knew they would, with a finding that Julian did not and would not support the constitutions of the United States and Georgia and that he adhered to the enemies of the State of Georgia. A case then began its way through the federal court system, first to the District Court for the Northern District of Georgia. When the three-judge panel decided against him, he went directly to the U.S. Supreme Court.

During all this time there were three elections: a special election in February, the regular 1966 election, and the September 1966 Democratic primary. Julian won all three of these elections. I played a large part in the outcome.

People whom the Georgia legislature would seat right away were running against Julian in those elections. My job, given to me by Howard and Leonard Boudin, his lawyers, was to call voters, remind them of the issues, and get them out to vote for Julian. I was glad to do it, not only for Julian and Howard, but because it gave me a chance to do something other than housework. I worked at Julian's district office. It was a scruffy, dusty room that overlooked Hunter Street. Other people must have helped me, but I only remember Freddie Greene and Faye Bellamy, two friends from SNCC who took time off to call. Freddie was sweet and soothing; Faye was caustic and efficient.

Constance is a central part of my Vietnam story, too. She was born on June 4, 1966. I could never be far from her during her first months as she was breast feeding. She was the baby I brought to the district office. In one arm I held her while she nursed, with the other arm I held the phone, and I talked to voters in Julian's precinct. Where was Grace—my three-year-old daughter? Probably at my mother's house, or was she there with me? I can't remember. Doing the work with one baby on a breast and a three-year-old child running around the room would have been impossible.

Meanwhile, the war was advancing fiercely. In 1965, there were 50,000 American troops; by January 1966, there were 190,000. A large percentage was Black. Hanoi was bombed by the United States, which also used search and destroy missions in South Vietnam. During dinner, every home in America saw the war on television in living color, courtesy of the network news.

The draftees were eighteen-, nineteen-, and twenty-year-old boys. Some came back in body bags. Others came back alive but with their legs or arms or both blown off and their minds blown up by what they had seen and experienced. Black draftees did not know about conscientious objector status. They didn't know where to get information on physical exemptions. Think of the number of Black men who were exempt due to physical problems, but whom the U.S. government drafted because no medical record was available. Think of the number of those men who were killed. Black draftees had no knowledge of their rights. They were too poor to have detailed medical records, and not many White physicians would provide the documentation to keep them out of Nam.

That war, the Vietnam War, was to the United States and the Black community what the First World War was to England. Many of the truly best and brightest were killed or maimed and mentally and emotionally wounded. No wonder our political and economic life is presently at its nadir. The best were blown away in Vietnam, and women are not allowed to do the job.

Yet, back at home, when I wasn't in the office calling voters or typing up Howard's briefs, I was still trying to put together this women's magazine life. I loved to watch my children, but how long could I watch babies? The endless, repetitive housework overcame me. Clean it up. It gets dirty; clean it up. It gets dirty. The lack of thought or analysis also weighed on me. Yes, the work was important, but why did I have to do it?

My husband's life, in contrast, was at a professional peak. Besides *Julian Bond versus James "Sloppy" Floyd,* he had other cases, many of them landmark civil rights cases. Howard was working as a cooperating attorney with the Inc. Fund, once the legal branch of the NAACP—the Legal Aid and Defense Fund—but now a separate organization. Most of the important civil rights cases of the 1960s and 1970s were handled by the Inc. Fund. Howard was working with the top legal minds of his profession; Derrick Bell, Leroy Clark, Marion Wright Edelman, Jack Greenberg, and others.

What was my role? Typing briefs, cooking interminable meals for the lawyers, sitting at meals unable to take part in their case and precedent discussions. All were men except Mrs. Motley and Marion Wright Edelman. Marion, who was just Marion Wright then, was a friend, a former college classmate with whom I could laugh and joke. Mrs. Motley was austere and intimidating, and had no conversation except the law.

The South went on about us also. Living in the South of that time was immediate and in your face. People talked to you, and you talked back. My neighbors sat on their porches while I pushed the baby carriage around and commented on how I dressed or didn't dress the children—never mean or hurtful, just warm, interested comments on what they saw and thought. It was a sharing of information between older Black women and a younger one. I got to know my neighbors that way.

The sounds were different, too. The kid next door was a James Brown freak and often played the same song ten to twenty times. One day, after listening to "Poppa's Got A Lickin Stick" for an hour, I could not stand it and told him to turn it down. He did, for an hour or so.

When I remember Atlanta and the South, it's always summer. The tastes are all from the summer—peaches, watermelon, fried corn, and iced tea. The colors are summer colors—yellow, beige, bronze, gold, and red. There were red tomatoes in vinegar, oil and sugar and green beans. There was a distinct sweet smell in Atlanta during the summer, as if everyone were cooking a peach cobbler or barbecuing. Then, when we left our neighborhood and went downtown, there was the distinctive southern accent of White southerners—their red faces and necks next to the black, brown, golden, beige, and pink of us. Men wore seersucker suits, and women wore dresses with wide skirts, lots of flowers, high heels, and crinolines.

In contrast to the summer heat I remember, it's winter in my next Vietnam scene. I went to Paris in March 1971 with a group sponsored by Concerned Clergy for Peace. Snow was on the ground when we arrived. I had left my newest baby, Kojo, at home with Howard. He had just turned one. I felt guilty about leaving him but went anyway. My group spoke to many different sides in the war—the South Vietnamese, the North Vietnamese, Bhuddists, and Americans. The trip was intended to gather more information to educate more people in the United States about the details of the war.

When I returned, I worked with others to start a draft-counseling program in the Black community. The American Friends Service Committee trained us. Howard and I had moved to a much bigger house by then, one with an upstairs and a large backyard with a built-in barbecue. We gave a party to raise money for our draft-counseling program. We had black doctors who were willing to give exams to inductees.

Then we moved to California. Howard was one of Angela Davis's lawyers. I did not want to go, as the draft-counseling program was just about to get going. Another part of me had always wanted to move and live somewhere else. I agreed to go and drove out in a two-car caravan with the girls, two friends, and my youngest brother. Howard flew to California with Kojo. Once in Berkeley, I needed to get the kids in school and see that they had a life despite the Angela Davis trial. When we got to our California home, though, law students and lawyers were already living there and working on the case. Everyone believed I could do nothing finer with my life than dedicate it to them because they were dedicating their lives to freeing Angela. No one, even the most dedicated communist party members, ever once asked me if they could babysit while I went to the trial.

I tried to connect to the East Bay draft-counseling community but found them extraordinarily cold and uninterested in draft counseling in the Black community. Maybe the Panthers had the market sewn up, but by that time they and SNCC had come to a bitter separation, and I was not at all inclined to look them up.

After the trial, we stayed in California, although I was (and still am) homesick for the South. Pushed by desire to get out of the house, I went to law school. Howard encouraged me because of his love of the law and his sure knowledge that law school is the answer to depression, homesickness, and whatever ails you. I was in my federal courts class when someone announced that the war was over. The class stopped, and we looked at each other. I had a hard, solid sense of satisfaction and accomplishment. I had helped to do that. My struggle with the Georgia legislature and the Selective Service System, added to everyone else's work, had changed U.S. foreign policy and history. My struggle with the women's magazine life led to law school. It's been more than twenty years since I graduated from law school and more than nineteen years since I passed the bar. All those sayings are correct: dare to struggle, dare to win. The personal is political, and the political is personal. That is my Vietnam story.

Burning Illusions: The Napalm Campaign

H. BRUCE FRANKLIN

IT WAS EARLY 1966. A woman in the suburban town of Redwood City, California, answered her doorbell. She was asked to sign a petition against the local production of napalm. "Napalm? No thank you," she responded. "I'm not interested. I always use Tide."

She represented the majority, for in early 1966 most Americans had never heard of napalm. By the end of that year, a national and global campaign had been launched against its use. Started by a handful of people in and around Stanford University in January 1966, that campaign was a turning point in the lives of many people, including mine.

Napalm is a highly flammable sticky jelly originally made by adding to aviation gas a chemical compound of aluminum naphthenates and palmitates. The Chemical Warfare Service developed napalm in 1944–45 for two purposes. First, because it sticks to clothing and flesh and continues to burn into the bone, it was an effective weapon on the battlefield. Its second usage in World War II was against the populations of cities. Under contract to the Chemical Warfare Service, university professors and other scientists supervised the construction of replicas of the working-class districts of Japanese industrial cities, including the homes made of paper and wood. Their goal was to develop an incendiary weapon that would leave flaming materials in contact with structures long enough to generate an urban firestorm so intense that the winds it created would make it self-sustaining and inextinguishable.

Other incendiary bombs were used, primarily by the British Royal Air Force, against a number of German cities, the most notorious example of course being the firebomb raid on Dresden. Napalm as a strategic weapon was to be reserved for nonwhite people. It was designed to be used against the Japanese, and the thousand-plane napalm raids on Japanese cities caused even more devastation than the Dresden inferno. In fact, one raid on Tokyo killed more people and destroyed more property than either the Hiroshima or Nagasaki atomic bombs. The overall effect was described by Major General Aden H. Waitt, chief of Chemical Warfare Service during World War II: "Sixty-six of Nippon's war centers with . . . 20 million population received more than 100,000 tons of incendiaries in 15,000 sorties. More than 100 square miles were burned out in five major cities, while incendiary destruction amounted to about 40% in the urban areas involved." Napalm was used again in the Korean War, so effectively that in vast areas almost all life was destroyed. Decades after the war, Koreans in the northern half of the country would show visitors a lone tree that survived the holocausts, referring to it as a "prewar tree."

But U.S. weapons technology never stands still. In early January 1966, a worker from a local corporation, United Technology Center (UTC) secretly communicated to a few of us antiwar activists the news that his company had just received a subcontract from Dow Chemical to develop a new, improved kind of napalm. The contract, we discovered, was for the development of Napalm-B, a thicker jelly that would stick more tenaciously, ignite more reliably, and burn more intensely.

Napalm-B consisted of 25 percent gasoline, 25 percent benzene, and 50 percent polystyrene, the marvelous new thickener, which was to be manufactured in quantity especially for napalm by Dow Chemical at Torrance, California. If UTC could successfully complete the research and development, production was scheduled to reach mammoth proportions. Our original research was later verified in *Chemical and Engineering News* (March 1966), which reported that the forthcoming use of polystyrene in Napalm-B would amount to twenty-five million pounds per month, so much that the normal industrial supplies would be severely overstrained. According to this figure, the production of Napalm-B was to reach five hundred million pounds each year, three times the total dropped on Japan during World War II.

The antiwar movement at Stanford was then embodied by the Stanford Committee for Peace in Vietnam (SCPV), accurately described by its vague, innocuous name. SCPV consisted of about two dozen students, faculty members, and people from the surrounding suburbs, each more or less fitfully active against the war. It included a few people who called themselves pacifists, two who called themselves Marxists, and many who no longer knew what to call themselves.

My wife Jane and I fitted into that last category. Sometime after I had gotten out of the Strategic Air Command in 1959, where I had flown as a navigator and squadron intelligence officer, we had inclined toward pacifism. We still didn't allow our two-and-one-half-year-old son to play with toy guns, and we were in favor of "militant, nonviolent protest." But we no longer considered ourselves pacifists, and our opposition to "violent" protest was not philosophical but tactical (it might "alienate" people). We were opposed to aggressive anticommunism, but deeply suspicious of communists. We avoided political ideology, particularly Marxism, about which we knew virtually nothing except that it was a musty old nineteenth-century dogma of little relevance to the modern world, especially to an advanced industrial society such as the United States. We were in favor of anything that would work to stop the war.

SCPV as a whole expressed a similar outlook. This was about a year after opposition to the Vietnam War had taken shape as an organized national movement, dedicated principally to convincing the government and the American people that U.S. involvement in the war was a "mistake." Each weekly SCPV meeting was spent mainly debating proposals for actions to take the following week. We were looking for the one spectacular action that would quickly educate the American people, bring the government to its senses, and end the "senseless killing" in Vietnam. We felt this action was urgent because we believed that the Vietnamese would soon be destroyed as a people. SCPV had no interest in any long-term programs to change American society.

When SCPV got the word about the local contract to develop Napalm-B, we thought we could at last do something concrete—stop this local production. And practically everybody saw a great potential for some kind of mass campaign that would swiftly educate people about the "immoral" nature of the war and the illusions of our government. Only two members disagreed.

One of the two, a self-declared Marxist, argued, "A campaign against napalm would only build false consciousness. It would suggest that the Vietnam War would be fine if it were fought with conventional weapons. Who would this kind of campaign appeal to? Only middle-class liberals. In fact, it will alienate working-class people because they want to use whatever weapons are necessary to support our troops. We must focus all our efforts on demanding immediate withdrawal of all our troops. That's the only demand that working-class people can support."

The other naysayer—whose identity I could not possibly recall—took a position that seemed almost the precise opposite: "There's only one way to deal with a napalm plant, and that's to deal with it. Anybody who is interested, see me after this bullshit meeting is over."

These two seemingly opposite positions in fact had much in common, for both were based on the assumption that we could not build effective mass opposition to napalm. I do not believe either of these alternate courses of action was wrong. We did have an obligation to build a mass movement calling for withdrawal of the troops. Also, at some point, the napalm plant should have been sabotaged. Many other things should have been done as well. But a mass movement against napalm, as it turned out, was certainly not a diversion from any of these goals.

One person, possibly only one in our little group, understood all that back then—Keith Lowe, a doctoral candidate in Stanford's English department. Evidently Keith saw both the potential and the limitations of the situation. He also had the patience to lead some of the rest of us step by step through a process of political and personal development that produced not only a mass antinapalm campaign spreading from the San Francisco Peninsula across the country and around the world, but also a number of people, including Jane and me, who saw the problem finally not as napalm or the war, but as the entire system responsible for the Vietnam War.

Keith was an unintimidating, modest, affectionate Jamaican, whose features seemed a mixture of the European, Asian, and African peoples who had mingled on that island. He responded to other human beings as though he were a stranger to none of them. He was later appropriately rewarded by the government of the United States and the administration of Stanford University, which worked together closely on his case. In 1969, Keith, then a highly regarded assistant professor of English at the University of California, San Diego, was denied a visa to reenter the United States from Jamaica. The main evidence against him in his immigration file consisted of statements from the administration of Stanford identifying him as a "subversive."

Keith's response to the news of the napalm contract was something unheard of—at least to most of us—at that time. He proposed that we carry the issue right to the people in the napalm company. Most of the members of SCPV were excited by this proposal, but held two contradictory views of how to apply it. Some thought the proposal meant we should go directly to the workers and try to persuade them not to help develop and produce the new form of napalm. Others thought that only the management had the power to pull the company out of the napalm business, so we should go to them. Most groups of activists I have seen would then have plunged into endless debate. One side would have argued that it was hopelessly impractical to go to the workers. The other side would have attacked this argument and those who put it forth as anti–working class. They in turn would have been attacked as dogmatists. If any action had come out of the debate, it would have been crippled by the divisive struggle that had brought it forth. What Keith apparently understood was that none of us had ever verified our arguments in experience and that most of us would use the debate, if we could, as an excuse to avoid the arena of practical struggle. He did not discount the importance of theory, but he pointed out that theories may often seem persuasive until they are tested and modified in practice. So we soon found ourselves testing both ideas. Because we ourselves were so naïve, we applied each in a somewhat ridiculous manner. We leafleted the workers as if a leaflet could convince them to quit their "immoral" jobs, and we sat down with the top management to convince them that they should cease being war profiteers.

The main office of United Technology was in Sunnyvale, about ten miles south of Stanford. In 1950, Sunnyvale had been a sleepy little town with a population of 9,800. The aerospace and electronics complex developed by Stanford had changed all that, transforming Sunnyvale into a boomtown. By 1960, its population was almost 53,000; in 1966, it reached 100,000. Five delegates were selected to visit the ultramodern office complex of UTC, strung out amid the similarly well-landscaped offices of the other corporate, manufacturing, and banking centers of Sunnyvale. Our mission: to meet with UTC's president and convince him, through rational dialogue, that the development and manufacture of napalm were immoral, so his company should refuse the contract. Off we went on January 25, 1966, all neatly attired in conservative jackets and dresses.

After some last-minute dickering, we were admitted into the office of Barnet Adelman, the president. He was flanked by three other officers—two retired generals and one retired admiral. We then had our rational dialogue about the Vietnam War and Napalm-B.

Mr. Adelman seemed a pleasant, mild-mannered Jewish scientist. He had gotten his master's degree in chemical engineering from Columbia in 1948 and then worked in rocketry for the Jet Propulsion Lab at Cal Tech, the rocket-fuels division of Phillips Petroleum, and RamoWooldridge. He belonged to the American Ordnance Association and the American Rocket Society. He assured us that he was just as interested as we were in having the Vietnam War end quickly.

"After all," he said, "our business has suffered a great deal from the war. Our main work is in long-range, liquid-fueled space rockets. These have no immediate military application. The Defense Department has taken away all our funds for these rockets because of Vietnam. So we have no choice. Even if we didn't want to work on napalm, we would have to just to stay in business."

"So you would do anything just for money?" asked an Asian American Stanford student who was part of our delegation.

"Napalm will help shorten the war," responded President Adelman. "Isn't that what we all want? Besides, whatever our government asks us to do is right."

Elena Greene, who had visited China and Vietnam with her husband, Felix Greene, brought up Nuremberg and pointed out that one of the main defenses of the war criminals tried there was that their government had ordered them to do it.

"But that was not a legally elected government," said Mr. Adelman.

Someone appealed to Mr. Adelman directly as a person whose own people had been the victim of war crimes. He responded, "That was Germany. This is America."

Because of my Air Force experience, I had been assigned to do much of the research for our meeting, so now I went into some of the history of Dow Chemical itself and its connections with Nazi war crimes, professorially reading from my research notes:

"In the 1930s, Dow Chemical and the giant German chemical corporation I. G. Farben formed an international cartel. They agreed to restrain U.S. production of magnesium and allow Germany to take world leadership in this element. So when World War II began, Germany was producing five times as much magnesium as we were.

"During the war, it was the Farben subsidiary, Badische Anilin and Soda-Fabrik, that developed and manufactured Zyklon-B, the poison gas used at Auschwitz and Dachau. Actually, Dow maintained secret ties with Badische throughout the war. As soon as the war was over, they formally renewed their prewar connection with Farben by going directly through Badische. Right now, Dow Chemical and Badische are in partnership in a giant chemical plant in Freeport, Texas, called the Dow-Badische Company."

My little speech had no visible effect on Mr. Adelman, not to mention his three colleagues. Finally, one of the other delegates asked if we could have an opportunity to discuss the issue with the employees.

"I am the employees of UTC," said Mr. Adelman. He then informed us he had to "take care of other business," and our discussion was "terminated."

So we next went to the workers, taking with us a leaflet asking, "Is Barnet Adelman the employees of UTC?"

UTC's napalm test site was located on a rambling old ranch off a dirt road several miles from the rural crossroads community of Coyote, south of San Jose. A few hundred yards back from the little dirt road were several mysterious-looking low buildings, a small tower, and some large chemical storage tanks. Along the road ran a barbed wire fence, and the property stretched as far back as the eye could see into the hills.

We were nervous the first day, especially because, according to the media, all the workers in America staunchly supported the war. We stood at the gate in the barbed wire fence and tried to hand leaflets to the workers as they drove through. That first day, most of them stopped to take the leaflet. Some went out of their way to be friendly. A few tried to run us down. On the second day, the company posted plainclothes security guards and a photographer at the gate. Almost every worker driving through that day pretended we didn't exist, except for a few who again tried to run us down. It looked as though the workers were as reactionary as the media claimed. Then two of our people began leafleting back down the road where it met U.S. Highway 101, three miles away from the company guards and photographer. Here the response was even friendlier than it was on the first day. Some workers got out of their cars to talk. They told us that the management was very nervous and had posted plainclothes security guards inside the plant to keep an eye on them. Most people, they explained, were very fearful of losing their jobs if they showed any sympathy for our position.

One of our leaflets asked the workers, of all things, to quit their jobs in protest. Two or three actually did and were quickly blacklisted from all employment in the area.

In the first week of February, we had an open meeting at Stanford to get people together for a caravan to Coyote, where we would hold a rally as the workers were leaving the day shift. At the Stanford meeting, one of the speakers was a young Black man from the Student Nonviolent Coordinating Committee (SNCC). He was tall, thin, unsmiling, and so tense he looked as if he might explode. Speaking in a soft voice, filled with barely restrained anger, he told us about a new political party he had helped organize in Alabama. It had split off from the regular Democratic Party of Alabama in order to conduct voter registration and run candidates in predominantly Black Lowndes County. Because the symbol of the Alabama Democratic Party was a snowy white rooster, they had chosen a black panther as their symbol. The speaker, Stokely Carmichael, then said he had just received his draft induction notice. He spoke of draft resistance. "I intend to walk right into that draft office and tell them," he said so quietly we had to cock our heads to hear, "'I don't belong to you, so you have no power over me.'" I heard his statement then as an existentialist affirmation, as well as an act in the individualist tradition of Thoreau. I realize now that I missed altogether the significance of what Carmichael was saying because I knew nothing about revolutionary Black nationalism. I heard Carmichael projecting himself as a representative of every individual human being. In reality, he was defying the draft as a representative of the African-American people. He was disputing the power of the draft board to claim ownership not so much of his own human essence, but of the lives of a people kidnapped from Africa.

At the Coyote rally, Carmichael spoke again. Standing at a microphone directly facing the gate in the barbed wire fence across the dirt road and covered with the dust churned up by the workers' cars, he spoke about the Vietnam War itself, his voice now loud, his words ringing out toward the napalm test site and the rolling hills beyond. Afterward, I walked up in my sports jacket, white shirt, and tie, and was introduced. I enthusiastically put out my hand and said, "That was a wonderful speech." Carmichael limply put his hand in mine for a second, glanced at me, stared past my head toward the chemical storage tanks, and mumbled something like, "Yeah?"

Several weeks later, SNCC held a national conference at which Stokely Carmichael was elected chairman. It was this conference that issued the historic paper entitled "The Basis of Black Power," a modest statement demanding self-determination for Blacks and asking "progressive Whites" to organize in the white communities. The mass media suddenly barraged the country with the name of Stokely Carmichael, depicting him as a "Black racist," a "disciple of hatred and race war," a "fiery inciter of passions." These phrases obviously didn't describe the man who had come to help in our campaign against napalm. It never occurred to me then that Carmichael had stuck his neck out to try to ally the Black movement with the antiwar movement and that we ought to be thinking about what we could do to further that alliance. I was too busy working to stop napalm.

About this time, both Jane and I began to notice cars following us and mysterious things happening on our phone. Jane was then often using the telephone to turn the San Francisco call-in shows into discussions of the war. Once, after dialing and before the phone was picked up at the other end, she heard a man's voice say, "Oh, she's just calling one of those damned shows again." One afternoon, one of the workers who had quit UTC telephoned and asked me to come to his home in Santa Clara. After supper, I drove to his moderately prosperous suburban community and, wary enough already to try to conceal our meeting, parked a few blocks away. He was still in contact with some UTC workers who said that many of the workers there were privately opposed to making napalm but that the plant had been turned into a virtual police state. Their casual conversations were being spied on, and even their personal reading matter was being inspected surreptitiously. On my way home, I thought I was being followed on the freeway. When I got to Palo Alto, I drove to a gas station and went to a telephone to call Jane to find out where SCPV was meeting that night. Suddenly, a car pulled in and rolled right up to the phone booth, blocking the door and fixing me in its headlights. I could barely make out the silhouettes of two men sitting in the front seat, wearing what seemed to be felt hats and business suits. I quickly told Jane what was happening. I could see the front license plate, so I made it obvious to the men in the car that I was reading its numbers into the phone. I continued facing the car and kept talking to Jane. After what seemed like a very long time, but probably only a few minutes, the car backed up and sped off, burning rubber.

By the middle of March, UTC had completed its contract for the development of Napalm-B. They received their reward: a large contract for the production of actual napalm bombs. They selected as the site for this production an unused Standard Oil storage facility in the port of Redwood City, at the end of a causeway sticking two miles out into San Francisco Bay. This site was on publicly owned tidal land. Therefore, all leases and uses of it were under the jurisdiction of the Redwood City Port Commission, and its rulings were legally subject to override by the citizens of Redwood City.

On March 21, the Port Commission convened in an old frame building amid the unused petroleum storage tanks Standard Oil was asking to sublease to UTC. About fifty protesters showed up. Some were members of Concerned Citizens, a Palo Alto peace organization. Others came from a Unitarian congregation in Redwood City. Most of us wore jackets and dresses. The most casually dressed were a few Stanford students. The room where the commissioners met could hold about only a dozen of us, so we presented them with our formal written protest and asked them to move to a larger facility. After much arguing, they agreed to adjourn to an auditorium in the county office building in downtown Redwood City.

By the time the meeting reconvened, almost two hundred people had gathered. The middle-aged white gentlemen on the commission set up ground rules for public participation, specifically ruling out of order "the moral question" and "the federal policy of war in Vietnam." Speaker after speaker rose to reason with the commissioners: a local minister, several Redwood City housewives, workers, students. Olive Mayer, an engineer from Redwood City who had inspected the gas ovens of Belsen, calmly stated: "As a professional engineer, I knew that other members of my profession planned and engineered these ovens as execution chambers. The manufacturer's name was proudly displayed over the door of the ovens. Engineers had to calculate the number of victims to be accommodated, means of ingress and egress, how many to be executed at one time, etc. Local government and professional people had to be involved in providing for locations for the manufacture of these ovens, just as you commissioners are now called upon to make a decision concerning a napalm factory."

I rose, intending to speak about the specific qualities of napalm, based on my Air Force experience and recent research. I got as far as my name. The chairman turned bright red and burst out angrily, "We know who you are and what you have to say, and we don't want to hear it. Sit down!" I couldn't believe my ears. I tried to ask why I shouldn't be allowed my opportunity to speak. The chairman yelled to the police at the back of the room, "Get that man out of here! Right now!" Two cops rushed up, twisted one of my arms behind my back, and started dragging me backward down the aisle. My seven-year-old daughter burst into tears. The people in the audience were all staring in shocked disbelief at the scene in the aisle. By the time the police got me to the rear door, I noticed that the commissioners were packing their briefcases and starting to leave. I broke loose, ran back down the aisle, and demanded, "What are you doing?" People began calling out: "What's going on?" "Why are you leaving?" "Aren't you going to discuss it?" "Aren't you even going to bother to vote?" The chairman looked over his shoulder, laughed, bent down to a microphone, and said: "We just did vote to grant the sublease. We also voted to adjourn. You probably couldn't hear because of all the commotion you were making."

During the next few days, we investigated the legal options open to us. We discovered that the vote of the commission could be overturned in a referendum called by an initiative petition signed by 10 percent of the registered voters of Redwood City. When our lawyer went for help in preparing the papers, the city attorney gave him false information that cheated us out of thirteen days of the thirty we were supposed to have. So we had only seventeen days to find volunteers, build an organization, and get the signatures of 10 percent of the voters. And we had to do this during a period when, according to the media and their polls, everybody but a handful of "dissidents" supported the war.

Signatures could be solicited only by registered voters of Redwood City. Redwood City was a suburban bedroom community of about fifty thousand, almost 100 percent white, mostly middle-income working-class, small business, and professional people. The city boundaries had been drawn to exclude the sizable population of Chicano, Black, and poorer white working-class people, mostly concentrated in the unincorporated area known informally as East Redwood City. Redwood City had no history of radical politics and no liberal political organizations. On top of all these obstacles, the local press launched a campaign to block the petition. The influential *Palo Alto Times* tacitly encouraged violence against us and then in two revealing editorials explained that if the people were allowed to vote on such matters, the country would be unable to wage war and the national government would be shattered:

> There is no question that considerable pressure is being brought by a small but vocal minority that objects to our use of napalm in the Vietnam war. It is the same minority that objects to our involvement in the war at all. . . . The voters of Redwood City do not have the right to preempt these decisions for themselves, to make the decisions for the rest of the country. . . . [T]o place on a municipal ballot decisions on military and foreign policy is to invite chaos. If all cities in the United States were to decide for themselves whether to permit the manufacture of military aircraft, bombs, rifles, grenades, rockets, torpedoes and other war material, they would wreck our armed forces. If all of them were to arrogate to themselves decisions on foreign policy, they would wreck the national government. (April 16, 1966)

While there may be some question about the use of napalm in warfare, it is not a question to be decided by the voters of Redwood City or any other municipality. . . . It is easy to see what would happen if every city were to be allowed to make its own decision as to what war material is acceptable to its citizens.

The people of Sunnyvale could vote on whether Polaris missiles should be manufactured by Lockheed. The people of Palo Alto could vote on whether electronics equipment for guided missiles should be built in the city. The citizens of San Francisco or Oakland could vote on whether their municipal port facilities should be permitted to load materials of war, such as napalm and atomic weapons, onto ships headed for the war.

The result would be chaos. (April 20, 1966)

In a few days, however, we had our volunteers and an organization. One hundred ten citizens of Redwood City, most of them working people, were out actively soliciting signatures. The regional local of the International Longshoremen and Warehousemen's Union (ILWU) sent a telegram of support, a small donation, and three volunteers. Thirty-four local clergymen signed a statement of support. Although the *Redwood City Tribune* had at first called us "treasonous," it began editorializing about the people's right to vote. The Huntley-Brinkley show covered the campaign, reporting that the attitudes of the people of Redwood City ranged from indifferent to hostile. On the seventeenth day, we stayed up all night verifying and counting the signatures on the petitions. Fifteen percent of the registered voters of Redwood City had signed.

Anyone who has done petition work knows this figure represents overwhelming support. In a petition campaign, it's good work just to see 15 percent of the registered voters in thirty days. On April 20, as we officially filed the petitions, we were confident we were going to win the election, and we knew this would have national and international significance.

Meanwhile, UTC had started production of napalm bombs. As we drove out along the causeway to the napalm facility, we now passed acres of stacked crates of 500-pound and 750-pound bombs. We could even stand at the high chain-link fence to watch as the empty bomb casings were swung over to a raised platform and pumped full of napalm. On May 1, a barge partly loaded with napalm bombs mysteriously developed two holes in its hull and began to sink. A vigil began across from the plant. On May 16 and 17, a Palo Alto psychiatrist, two students from Stanford, and a

Chicano jazz musician named Aaron Manganiello were arrested for lying down in front of some trucks bringing empty bomb shells to be filled.

The signatures on the petitions still remained uncounted in the city clerk's office. The city attorney had been using one legal maneuver after another to block the election. On May 20, Superior Court Judge Melvin Cohn ruled that the petition was invalid because it had attacked the original sublease from Standard Oil to UTC. He disclosed that on April 26, six days after we had filed the petition, Standard Oil, UTC, and the port commission had secretly scrapped the old sublease and arranged a new one. Judge Cohn informed us that in order to be valid a petition would have to attack this new lease. Because this new lease had gone into effect on April 26, we would have until May 26, only six days, to draw up a new petition, get signatures, and have it filed. It was now obvious that even if we could have performed such a miracle, Standard Oil, UTC, and the port commission would merely draw up still another lease. A few weeks later we discovered that Judge Cohn was a personal friend of Barnet Adelman, president of UTC, and that their children attended the same Sunday school class. We now knew, however, that this relationship had little to do with his Alice-in-Wonderland decision. We had been forced to recognize that judges—like port authority commissions, city attorneys, police officers, FBI agents, newspapers, and armies—were there to do whatever corporations required of them.

The following day, Aaron Manganiello began a one-man fast and vigil across the road from the napalm plant. He had just been suspended from the College of San Mateo, the local public community college where he had been studying music, for distributing literature against the Vietnam War. Every hour of each night of his vigil and fast, men from UTC would hose him down. After six days, Aaron had pneumonia and had to give up the vigil. He also soon gave up his pacifism, later becoming minister of information of the Brown Berets, a militant Chicano organization, and head of the revolutionary California organization Venceremos.

On May 28, we officially launched the national campaign against napalm with a rally and a four-mile march through downtown Redwood City and out along the causeway to the gates of the napalm plant. The rally speakers included three antiwar congressional candidates, the publisher of *Ramparts* magazine, African-American publisher and California gubernatorial candidate Carleton Goodlett, Felix Greene, retired admiral Arnold True, and a truck driver running for the state assembly. Despite a virtual news blackout before the event, thirty-five hundred people, including many families with small children, showed up. The demonstrators were "mostly well-dressed and clean-shaven," noted the *Redwood City Tribune.*

The march ended with more speeches, delivered from a flatbed truck outside the front gates of the napalm plant. The principal speaker was Senator Wayne Morse, who rambled on for half an hour, telling a couple of anecdotes to show he was still good friends with Lyndon Johnson and never mentioning napalm. The rally concluded, and people began strolling to the buses we had chartered to take them back to their cars. Suddenly, dozens of squad cars appeared, as if from no place. They had been carefully concealed behind buildings surrounding the rally. We counted hundreds of police from five different agencies. Each of the squad cars displayed shotguns and carried six police in full riot gear, something most people there had seen only on TV. The Redwood City police and the San Mateo County sheriffs had prepared an elaborate ambush, and they were obviously disappointed they had not found a chance to "teach you some patriotism," as one yelled out a car window.

Only local newspapers reported that the march and rally had taken place, and they underestimated the size of the crowd, reporting that citizens of Redwood City were hostile to such activities. Bruce Brugmann, the *Redwood City Tribune* reporter who had been covering the napalm campaign, became so disgusted by the blatant censorship and rewriting of his stories that he left to found the radical weekly newspaper, the *Bay Guardian.* Even a mere twenty miles away, the press and radio in San Francisco imposed a total news blackout,which kept many people in ignorance of this particular issue but also educated tens of thousands about the role of the media. Almost everyone in the area knew an important event had taken place and could not help but wonder why it was not reported and how many events from other areas were not reported to us.

In fact, we had succeeded in breaking through the media isolation. Announced at the rally, the national boycott of Dow Chemical Corporation products had already begun. That very day, fifty picketers demonstrated outside the New York offices of Dow Chemical, and more than two hundred picketed Dow's big plant for production of polystyrene in Torrance, outside Los Angeles. None of us would have predicted, however, that in the next few years there would be hundreds of demonstrations, involving hundreds of thousands of people, against Dow Chemical, its campus recruiters, and its subcontractors. Through the campaign against napalm, millions of Americans and people around the world were to learn deep lessons about the nature and causes of America's war against Vietnam.

The Responsibility Of Intellectuals

NOAM CHOMSKY

TWENTY YEARS AGO, Dwight Macdonald published a series of articles in *Politics* on the responsibility of peoples and, specifically, the responsibility of intellectuals. I read them as an undergraduate in the years just after the war and had occasion to read them again a few months ago. They seem to me to have lost none of their power or persuasiveness. Macdonald is concerned with the question of war guilt. He asks the question: To what extent were the German or Japanese people responsible for the atrocities committed by their governments? And, quite properly, he turns the question back to us: To what extent are the British or American people responsible for the vicious terror bombings of civilians, perfected as a technique of warfare by the Western democracies and reaching their culmination in Hiroshima and Nagasaki, surely among the most unspeakable crimes in history? To an undergraduate in 1945–46—to anyone whose political and moral consciousness had been formed by the horrors of the 1930s, by the war in Ethiopia, the Russian purge, the "China Incident," the Spanish civil war, the Nazi atrocities, and by the Western reaction to these events and, in part, complicity in them—these questions had particular significance and poignancy.

With respect to the responsibility of intellectuals, there are still other, equally disturbing questions. Intellectuals are in a position to expose the lies of governments, to analyze actions according to their causes and motives and often hidden intentions. In the Western world, at least, they have the

 Originally published in *The New York Review of Books,* Feb. 23, 1967, 16–26.

power that comes from political liberty, from access to information and freedom of expression. For a privileged minority, Western democracy provides the leisure, the facilities, and the training to seek the truth lying hidden behind the veil of distortion and misrepresentation, ideology and class interest, through which the events of current history are presented to us. The responsibilities of intellectuals, then, are much deeper than what Macdonald calls the "responsibility of peoples," given the unique privileges that intellectuals enjoy.

The issues that Macdonald raised are as pertinent today as they were twenty years ago. We can hardly avoid asking ourselves to what extent the American people bear responsibility for the savage American assault on a largely helpless rural population in Vietnam, still another atrocity in what Asians see as the "Vasco da Gama era" of world history. As for those of us who stood by in silence and apathy as this catastrophe slowly took shape during the past dozen years, on what page of history do we find our proper place? Only the most insensible can escape these questions. I want to return to them later on, after a few scattered remarks about the responsibility of intellectuals and how, in practice, they go about meeting this responsibility in the mid-1960s.

It is the responsibility of intellectuals to speak the truth and to expose lies. This, at least, may seem enough of a truism to pass over without comment. Not so, however. For the modern intellectuals, it is not at all obvious. Thus, we have Martin Heidegger writing, in a pro-Hitler declaration of 1933, that "truth is the revelation of that which makes a people certain, clear, and strong in its action and knowledge"; it is only this kind of "truth" that one has a responsibility to speak. Americans tend to be more forthright. When Arthur Schlesinger was asked by the *New York Times* in November 1965 to explain the contradiction between his published account of the Bay of Pigs incident and the story he had given the press at the time of the attack, he simply remarked that he had lied; and a few days later, he went on to compliment the *Times* for also having suppressed information on the planned invasion in "the national interest," as this term was defined by the group of arrogant and deluded men of whom Schlesinger gives such a flattering portrait in his recent account of the Kennedy administration. It is of no particular interest that one man is quite happy to lie in behalf of a cause that he knows to be unjust, but it is significant that such events provoke so little response in the intellectual community—for example, no one has said that there is something strange in the offer of a major chair in the humanities to a historian who feels it to be his duty to persuade the world that an American-sponsored invasion of a nearby country is nothing of the sort. And what of the incredible sequence of lies on the part of our government and its spokesmen concerning such matters as negotiations in Vietnam? The facts are known to all who care to know. The press, foreign and domestic, has presented documentation to refute each falsehood as it appears. But the power of the government's propaganda apparatus is such that the citizen who does not undertake a research project on the subject can hardly hope to confront government pronouncements with fact.[1]

The deceit and distortion surrounding the American invasion of Vietnam is by now so familiar that it has lost its power to shock. It is therefore useful to recall that although new levels of cynicism are constantly being reached, their clear antecedents were accepted at home with quiet toleration. It is a useful exercise to compare government statements at the time of the invasion of Guatemala in 1954 with Eisenhower's admission—to be more accurate, his boast—a decade later that American planes were sent "to help the invaders" (*New York Times,* October 14, 1965). Nor is it only in moments of crisis that duplicity is considered perfectly in order. "New Frontiersmen," for example, have scarcely distinguished themselves by a passionate concern for historical accuracy, even when they are not being called upon to provide a "propaganda cover" for ongoing actions. For example, Arthur Schlesinger describes the bombing of North Vietnam and the massive escalation of military commitment in early 1965 as based on a "perfectly rational argument . . . so long as the Vietcong thought they were going to win the war, they obviously would not be interested in any kind of negotiated settlement" (*New York Times,* February 6, 1966).

The date is important. Had this statement been made six months earlier, one could attribute it to ignorance. But this statement appeared after the UN, North Vietnamese, and Soviet initiatives had been front-page news for months. It was already public knowledge that these initiatives had preceded the escalation of February 1965 and, in fact, continued for several weeks after the bombing began. Correspondents in Washington tried desperately to find some explanation for the startling deception that had been revealed. Chalmers Roberts, for example, wrote in the *Boston Globe* on November 19 with unconscious irony: "[late February, 1965] hardly seemed to Washington to be a propitious moment for negotiations [since] Mr. Johnson . . . had just ordered the first bombing of North Vietnam in an effort to bring Hanoi to a conference table where the bargaining chips on both sides would be more closely matched."

Coming at that moment, Schlesinger's statement is less an example of deceit than of contempt—contempt for an audience that can be expected to tolerate such behavior with silence, if not approval.[2]

To turn to someone closer to the actual formation and implementation of policy, consider some of the reflections of Walt Rostow, a man who, according to Schlesinger, brought a "spacious historical view" to the conduct of foreign affairs in the Kennedy administration.[3] According to Rostow's analysis, the guerrilla warfare in Indochina in 1946 was launched by Stalin,[4] and Hanoi initiated the guerrilla war against South Vietnam in 1958 (*The View from the Seventh Floor*, pp. 39 and 152). Similarly, the Communist planners probed the "free world spectrum of defense" in Northern Azerbaijan and Greece (where Stalin "supported substantial guerrilla warfare"—ibid., pp. 36 and 148), operating from plans carefully laid in 1945. And in Central Europe, the Soviet Union was not "prepared to accept a solution which would remove the dangerous tensions from Central Europe at the risk of even slowly staged corrosion of Communism in East Germany" (ibid., p. 156).

It is interesting to compare these observations with studies by scholars actually concerned with historical events. The remark about Stalin's initiating the first Vietnamese war in 1946 does not even merit refutation. As to Hanoi's purported initiative of 1958, the situation is more clouded. But even government sources[5] concede that in 1959 Hanoi received the first direct reports of what [Ngo Dinh] Diem referred to[6] as his own Algerian war and that only after this did they lay their plans to involve themselves in this struggle. In fact, in December 1958, Hanoi made another of its many attempts—rebuffed once again by Saigon and the United States—to establish diplomatic and commercial relations with the Saigon government on the basis of the status quo.[7] Rostow offers no evidence of Stalin's support for the Greek guerrillas; in fact, though the historical record is far from clear, it seems that Stalin was by no means pleased with the adventurism of the Greek guerrillas, who, from his point of view, were upsetting the satisfactory postwar imperialist settlement.[8]

Rostow's remarks about Germany are more interesting still. He does not see fit to mention, for example, the Russian notes of March–April 1952, which proposed unification of Germany under internationally supervised elections, with withdrawal of all troops within a year, *if* there was a guarantee that a reunified Germany would not be permitted to join a Western military alliance.[9] And he has also momentarily forgotten his own characterization of the strategy of the Truman and Eisenhower administrations:

"to avoid any serious negotiation with the Soviet Union until the West could confront Moscow with German rearmament within an organized European framework, as a *fait accompli*"[10]—to be sure, in defiance of the Potsdam agreements.

But most interesting of all is Rostow's reference to Iran. The facts are that there was a Russian attempt to impose by force a pro-Soviet government in Northern Azerbaijan that would grant the Soviet Union access to Iranian oil. This attempt was rebuffed by superior Anglo-American force in 1946, at which point the more powerful imperialism obtained full rights to Iranian oil for itself, with the installation of a pro-Western government. We recall what happened when, for a brief period in the early 1950s, the only Iranian government with something of a popular base experimented with the curious idea that Iranian oil should belong to the Iranians. What is interesting, however, is the description of Northern Azerbaijan as part of "the free world spectrum of defense." It is pointless, by now, to comment on the debasement of the phrase "free world." But by what law of nature does Iran, with its resources, fall within Western dominion? The bland assumption that it does is most revealing of deep-seated attitudes toward the conduct of foreign affairs.

In addition to this growing lack of concern for truth, we find in recent published statements a real or feigned naïveté about American actions that reaches startling proportions. For example, Arthur Schlesinger, according to the *Times,* February 6, 1966, characterized our Vietnamese policies of 1954 as "part of our general program of international goodwill." Unless intended as irony, this remark shows either a colossal cynicism or the inability, on a scale that defies measurement, to comprehend elementary phenomena of contemporary history. Similarly, what is one to make of the testimony of Thomas Schelling before the House Foreign Affairs Committee, January 27, 1965, in which he discusses two great dangers if all Asia "goes Communist"?[11] First, this would exclude "the United States and what we call Western civilization from a large part of the world that is poor and colored and potentially hostile." Second, "a country like the United States probably cannot maintain self-confidence if just about the greatest thing it ever attempted, namely to create the basis for decency and prosperity and democratic government in the under-developed world, had to be acknowledged as a failure or as an attempt that we wouldn't try again." It surpasses belief that a person with even a minimal acquaintance with the record of American foreign policy could produce such statements.

It surpasses belief, that is, unless we look at the matter from a more his-torical point of view and place such statements in the context of the hypo-critical moralism of the past—for example, of Woodrow Wilson, who was going to teach the Latin Americans the art of good government and who wrote (1902) that it is "our peculiar duty" to teach colonial peoples "order and self-control . . . [and] . . . the drill and habit of law and obedience." Or of the missionaries of the 1840s, who described the hideous and degrading opium wars as "the result of a great design of Providence to make the wickedness of men subserve his purposes of mercy toward China, in break-ing through her wall of exclusion, and bringing the empire into more immediate contact with western and Christian nations." Or, to approach the present, of A. A. Berle, who, in commenting on the Dominican inter-vention, has the impertinence to attribute the problems of the Caribbean countries to imperialism—*Russian* imperialism.[12]

As a final example of this failure of skepticism, consider the remarks of Henry Kissinger in his concluding remarks at the Harvard-Oxford television debate on America's Vietnam policies. He observed, rather sadly, that what disturbs him most is that others question not our judgment, but our motives, a remarkable comment by a man whose professional concern is political analysis—that is, analysis of the actions of governments in terms of motives that are unexpressed in official propaganda and perhaps only dimly perceived by those whose acts they govern. No one would be disturbed by an analysis of the political behavior of the Russians, French, or Tanzanians questioning their motives and interpreting their actions by the long-range interests concealed behind their official rhetoric. But it is an article of faith that American motives are pure and not subject to analysis (see note 1). Although it is nothing new in American intellectual history—or, for that matter, in the general history of imperialist apologia—this innocence becomes increas-ingly distasteful as the power it serves grows more dominant in world affairs and more capable, therefore, of the unconstrained viciousness that the mass media present to us each day. We are hardly the first power in history to combine material interests, great technological capacity, and utter disregard for the suffering and misery of the lower orders. The long tradition of naïveté and self-righteousness that disfigures our intellectual history, however, must serve as a warning to the Third World, if such warn-ing is needed, as to how our protestations of sincerity and benign intent are to be interpreted.

The basic assumptions of the "New Frontiersmen" should be pondered

carefully by those who look forward to the involvement of academic intellectuals in politics. For example, I have referred above to Arthur Schlesinger's
objections to the Bay of Pigs invasion, but the reference was imprecise.
True, he felt that it was a "terrible idea," but "not because the notion of
sponsoring an exile attempt to overthrow Castro seemed intolerable in
itself." Such a reaction would be the merest sentimentality, unthinkable
to a tough-minded realist. The difficulty, rather, was that it seemed unlikely
that the deception could succeed. The operation, in his view, was ill-conceived
but not otherwise objectionable.[13] In a similar vein, Schlesinger quotes
with approval Kennedy's "realistic" assessment of the situation resulting
from Trujillo's assassination: "There are three possibilities in descending
order of preference: a decent democratic regime, a continuation of the
Trujillo regime or a Castro regime. We ought to aim at the first, but we
really can't renounce the second until we are sure that we can avoid the
third" (p. 769).

The reason why the third possibility is so intolerable is explained a few
pages later (p. 774): "Communist success in Latin America would deal a
much harder blow to the power and influence of the United States." Of
course, we can never really be sure of avoiding the third possibility: therefore,
in practice, we will always settle for the second, as we are now doing in
Brazil and Argentina, for example.[14]

Or consider Walt Rostow's views on American policy in Asia.[15] The basis
on which we must build this policy is that "we are openly threatened and
we feel menaced by Communist China." To prove that we are menaced is
of course unnecessary, and the matter receives no attention; it is enough
that we *feel* menaced. Our policy must be based on our national heritage
and our national interests. Our national heritage is briefly outlined in the
following terms: "Throughout the nineteenth century, in good conscience
Americans could devote themselves to the extension of both their principles
and their power on this continent," making use of "the somewhat elastic
concept of the Monroe doctrine" and, of course, extending "the American
interest to Alaska and the mid-Pacific islands. . . . Both our insistence on
unconditional surrender and the idea of post-war occupation . . . represented
the formulation of American security interests in Europe and Asia." So
much for our heritage. As to our interests, the matter is equally simple.
Fundamental is our "profound interest that societies abroad develop and
strengthen those elements in their respective cultures that elevate and protect
the dignity of the individual against the state." At the same time, we must

counter the "ideological threat"—namely, "the possibility that the Chinese Communists can prove to Asians by progress in China that Communist methods are better and faster than democratic methods." Nothing is said about those people in Asian cultures to whom our "conception of the proper relation of the individual to the state" may not be the uniquely important value—people who might, for example, be concerned with preserving the "dignity of the individual" against concentrations of foreign or domestic capital, or against semifeudal structures (such as Trujillo-type dictatorships) introduced or kept in power by American arms. All of this is flavored with allusions to "our religious and ethical value systems" and to our "diffuse and complex concepts," which are to the Asian mind "so much more difficult to grasp" than Marxist dogma and are so "disturbing to some Asians" because of "their very lack of dogmatism."

Such intellectual contributions as these suggest the need for a correction to De Gaulle's remark, in his *Memoirs,* about the American "will to power, cloaking itself in idealism." By now, this will to power is not so much cloaked in idealism as it is drowned in fatuity. And academic intellectuals have made their unique contribution to this sorry picture.

Let us, however, return to the war in Vietnam and the response that it has aroused among American intellectuals. A striking feature of the recent debate on Southeast Asian policy has been the distinction that is commonly drawn between "responsible criticism," on the one hand, and "sentimental" or "emotional" or "hysterical" criticism, on the other. There is much to be learned from a careful study of the terms in which this distinction is drawn. The "hysterical critics" are to be identified, apparently, by their irrational refusal to accept one fundamental political axiom—namely that the United States has the right to extend its power and control without limit, insofar as is feasible. Responsible criticism does not challenge this assumption, but argues, rather, that we probably can't "get away with it" at this particular time and place.

A distinction of this sort seems to be what Irving Kristol, for example, has in mind in his analysis of the protest over Vietnam policy (*Encounter,* August 1965). He contrasts the responsible critics, such as Walter Lippmann, the *Times,* and Senator Fulbright, with the "teach-in movement." "Unlike the university protesters," he points out,

> Mr. Lippmann engages in no presumptuous suppositions as to "what the Vietnamese people really want"—he obviously doesn't much care—or

in legalistic exegesis as to whether, or to what extent, there is "aggression" or "revolution" in South Vietnam. His is a realpolitik point of view, and he will apparently even contemplate the possibility of a nuclear war against China in extreme circumstances.

This is commendable and contrasts favorably, for Kristol, with the talk of the "unreasonable, ideological types" in the teach-in movement, who often seem to be motivated by such absurdities as "simple, virtuous 'anti-imperialism,'" who deliver "harangues on 'the power structure,'" and who even sometimes stoop so low as to read "articles and reports from the foreign press on the American presence in Vietnam." Furthermore, these nasty types are often psychologists, mathematicians, chemists, or philosophers (just as, incidentally, those most vocal in protest in the Soviet Union are generally physicists, literary intellectuals, and others remote from the exercise of power), rather than people with Washington contacts, who of course realize that "had they a new, good idea about Vietnam, they would get a prompt and respectful hearing" in Washington.

I am not interested here in whether Kristol's characterization of protest and dissent is accurate, but rather in the assumptions on which it rests. Is the purity of American motives a matter that is beyond discussion or that is irrelevant to discussion? Should decisions be left to "experts" with Washington contacts—even if we assume that they command the necessary knowledge and principles to make the "best" decision, will they invariably do so? And, a logically prior question, is "expertise" applicable—that is, is there a body of theory and of relevant information, not in the public domain, that can applied to the analysis of foreign policy or that demonstrates the correctness of present actions in some way that psychologists, mathematicians, chemists, and philosophers are incapable of comprehending? Although Kristol does not examine these questions directly, his attitude presupposes answers, answers that are wrong in all cases. American aggressiveness, however it may be masked in pious rhetoric, is a dominant force in world affairs and must be analyzed in terms of its causes and motives. There is no body of theory or significant body of relevant information beyond the comprehension of the layman that makes policy immune from criticism. To the extent that "expert knowledge" is applied to world affairs, it is surely appropriate—for a person of any integrity, quite necessary—to question its quality and the goals it serves. These facts seem too obvious to require extended discussion.

A corrective to Kristol's curious belief in the administration's openness to new thinking about Vietnam is provided by McGeorge Bundy in a recent issue of *Foreign Affairs* (January 1967). As Bundy correctly observes, "on the main stage . . . the argument on Vietnam turns on tactics, not fundamentals," although, he adds, "there are wild men in the wings." On stage center are, of course, the president (who in his recent trip to Asia had just "magisterially reaffirmed" our interest "in the progress of the people across the Pacific")and his advisers, who deserve "the understanding support of those who want restraint." It is these men who deserve the credit for the fact that "the bombing of the North has been the most accurate and the most restrained in modern warfare"—a solicitude that will be appreciated by the inhabitants, or former inhabitants, of Nam Dinh and Phu Ly and Vinh. It is these men, too, who deserve the credit for what was reported by Malcolm Browne as long ago as May 1965: "In the South, huge sectors of the nation have been declared free bombing zones, in which anything that moves is a legitimate target. Tens of thousands of tons of bombs, rockets, napalm and cannon fire are poured into these vast areas each week. If only by the laws of chance, bloodshed is believed to be heavy in these raids."

Fortunately for the developing countries, Bundy assures us, "American democracy has no taste for imperialism," and "taken as a whole, the stock of American experience, understanding, sympathy and simple knowledge is now much the most impressive in the world." It is true that "four-fifths of all the foreign investing in the world is now done by Americans" and that "the most admired plans and policies . . . are no better than their demonstrable relation to the American interest"—just as it is true, so we read in the same issue of *Foreign Affairs,* that the plans for armed action against Cuba were put into motion a few weeks after Mikoyan visited Havana, "invading what had so long been an almost exclusively American sphere of influence." Unfortunately, such facts as these are often taken by unsophisticated Asian intellectuals as indicating a "taste for imperialism." For example, a number of Indians have expressed their "near exasperation" at the fact that "we have done everything we can to attract foreign capital for fertilizer plants, but the American and the other Western private companies know we are over a barrel, so they demand stringent terms which we just cannot meet" (*Christian Science Monitor,* November 26), while "Washington . . . doggedly insists that deals be made in the private sector with private enterprise" (ibid., December 5).[16] But this reaction, no doubt, simply reveals, once again, how the Asian mind fails to comprehend the "diffuse and complex concepts" of Western thought.

It may be useful to study carefully the "new, good ideas about Vietnam" that are receiving a "prompt and respectful hearing" in Washington these days. The U.S. Government Printing Office is an endless source of insight into the moral and intellectual level of this expert advice. In its publications, one can read, for example, the testimony of Professor David N. Rowe, director of Graduate Studies in International Relations at Yale University, before the House Committee on Foreign Affairs (see note 11). Professor Rowe proposes that the United States buy all surplus Canadian and Australian wheat so that there will be mass starvation in China. These are his words: "Mind you, I am not talking about this as a weapon against the Chinese people. It will be. But that is only incidental. The weapon will be a weapon against the Government because the internal stability of that country cannot be sustained by an unfriendly Government in the face of general starvation" (p. 266).

Professor Rowe will have none of the sentimental moralism that might lead one to compare this suggestion with, say, the *Ostpolitik* of Hitler's Germany.[17] Nor does he fear the impact of such policies on other Asian nations, for example, Japan. He assures us, from his "very long acquaintance with Japanese questions," that "the Japanese above all are people who respect power and determination." Hence, "they will not be so much alarmed by American policy in Vietnam that takes off from a position of power and intends to seek a solution based upon the imposition of our power upon local people that we are in opposition to." What would disturb the Japanese is "a policy of indecision, a policy of refusal to face up to the problems [in China and Vietnam] and to meet our responsibilities there in a positive way," such as the way just cited. A conviction that we were "unwilling to use the power that they know we have" might "alarm the Japanese people very intensely and shake the degree of their friendly relations with us." In fact, a full use of American power would be particularly reassuring to the Japanese because they have had a demonstration "of the tremendous power in action of the United States . . . because they have felt our power directly." This is surely a prime example of the healthy, "*realpolitik* point of view" that Irving Kristol so much admires.

But, one may ask, why restrict ourselves to such indirect means as mass starvation? Why not bombing? No doubt this message is implicit in the remarks, to the same committee, of the Reverend R. J. de Jaegher, regent of the Institute of Far Eastern Studies, Seton Hall University, who explains that like all people who have lived under communism, the North Vietnamese "would be perfectly happy to be bombed to be free" (p. 345).

Of course, there must be those who support the communists. But this is really a matter of small concern, as the Hon. Walter Robertson, assistant secretary of state for Far Eastern Affairs from 1953 to 1959, points out in his testimony before the same committee. He assures us that "The Peiping regime . . . represents something less than 3 per cent of the population" (p. 402).

Consider, then, how fortunate the Chinese communist leaders are compared to the leaders of the Viet Cong, who, according to Arthur Goldberg (*New York Times,* February 6, 1966), represent about "one-half of one percent of the population of South Vietnam"—that is, about one-half the number of new southern recruits for the Viet Cong during 1965, if we can credit Pentagon statistics.[18]

In the face of such experts as these, the scientists and philosophers of whom Kristol speaks would clearly do well to continue to draw their circles in the sand.

Having settled the issue of the political irrelevance of the protest movement, Kristol turns to the question of what motivates it—more generally, what has made students and junior faculty "go left," as he sees it, amid general prosperity and under liberal, welfare state administrations. This he notes, "is a riddle to which no sociologist has as yet come up with an answer." Because these young people are well-off, have good futures, etc., their protest must be irrational. It must be the result of boredom, of too much security, or something of this sort.

Other possibilities come to mind. It may be, for example, that as honest men, the students and junior faculty are attempting to find out the truth for themselves rather than ceding the responsibility to "experts" or to government; and it may be that they react with indignation to what they discover. These possibilities Kristol does not reject. They are simply unthinkable, unworthy of consideration. More accurately, these possibilities are inexpressible; the categories in which they are formulated (honesty, indignation) simply do not exist for the tough-minded social scientist.

In this implicit disparagement of traditional intellectual values, Kristol reflects attitudes that are fairly widespread in academic circles. I do not doubt that these attitudes are in part a consequence of the desperate attempt of the social and behavioral sciences to imitate the surface features of sciences that really have significant intellectual content. But they have other sources as well. Anyone can be a moral individual, concerned with human rights and problems, but only a college professor, a trained expert, can solve technical problems by "sophisticated" methods. Ergo, it is only problems of the latter sort that are important or real. Responsible, nonideological experts will give advice on tactical questions; irresponsible, "ideological types" will "harangue" about principle and trouble themselves over moral issues and human rights, or over the traditional problems of man and society, concerning which "social and behavioral science" has nothing to offer beyond trivialities. Obviously, these emotional, ideological types are irrational, since, being well-off and having power in their grasp, they shouldn't worry about such matters.

At times, this pseudoscientific posing reaches levels that are almost pathological. Consider the phenomenon of Herman Kahn, for example. Kahn has been both denounced as immoral and lauded for his courage. By people who should know better, his *On Thermonuclear War* has been described "without qualification" as "one of the great works of our time" (Stuart Hughes). The fact of the matter is that this is surely one of the emptiest works of our time, as can be seen by applying to it the intellectual standards of any existing discipline, by tracing some of its "well-documented conclusions" to the "objective studies" from which they derive, and by following the line of argument, where detectable. Kahn proposes no theories, no explanations, no factual assumptions that can be tested against their consequences, as do the sciences he is attempting to mimic. He simply suggests a terminology and provides a facade of rationality. When particular policy conclusions are drawn, they are supported only by ex cathedra remarks for which no support is even suggested (e.g., "The civil defense line probably should be drawn somewhere below $5 billion annually" to keep from provoking the Russians—why not $50 billion or $5.00?). What is more, Kahn is quite aware of this vacuity; in his more judicious moments he claims only that "there is no reason to believe that relatively sophisticated models are more likely to be misleading than the simpler models and analogies frequently used as an aid to judgment." For those whose humor tends toward the macabre, it is easy to play the game of "strategic thinking" à la Kahn and to prove what one wishes. For example, one of Kahn's basic assumptions is that "an all-out surprise attack in which all resources are devoted to counter-value targets would be so irrational that, barring an incredible lack of sophistication or actual insanity among Soviet decision makers, such an attack is highly unlikely."

A simple argument proves the opposite. *Premise 1:* American decision makers think along the lines outlined by Herman Kahn. *Premise 2:* Kahn thinks it would be better for everyone to be red than for everyone to be dead. *Premise*

3: If the Americans were to respond to an all-out countervalue attack, then everyone would be dead. *Conclusion:* The Americans will not respond to an all-out countervalue attack, and therefore it should be launched without delay. Of course, one can carry the argument a step further. *Fact:* the Russians have not carried out an all-out countervalue attack. It follows that they are not rational. If they are not rational, there is no point in "strategic thinking." Therefore, . . .

Of course, this is all nonsense, but nonsense that differs from Kahn's only in the respect that it is of slightly greater complexity than anything to be discovered in his work. What is remarkable is that serious people actually pay attention to these absurdities, no doubt because of the facade of tough-mindedness and pseudoscience.

It is a curious and depressing fact that the "antiwar movement" falls prey all too often to similar confusions. In the fall of 1965, for example, there was an International Conference on Alternative Perspectives on Vietnam, which circulated a pamphlet to potential participants stating its assumptions. The plan was to set up study groups in which three "types of intellectual tradition" would be represented: (1) area specialists; (2) "social theory, with special emphasis on theories of the international system, of social change and development, of conflict and conflict resolution, or of revolution"; (3) "the analysis of public policy in terms of basic human values, rooted in various theological, philosophical and humanist traditions." The second intellectual tradition would provide "general propositions, derived from social theory and tested against historical, comparative, or experimental data"; the third would "provide the framework out of which fundamental value questions can be raised and in terms of which the moral implications of societal actions can be analyzed." The hope was that "by approaching the questions [of Vietnam policy] from the moral perspectives of all great religions and philosophical systems, we may find solutions that are more consistent with fundamental human values than current American policy in Vietnam has turned out to be."

In short, the experts on values (i.e., spokesmen for the great religions and philosophical systems) will provide fundamental insights on moral perspectives, and the experts on social theory will provide general empirically validated propositions and "general models of conflict." From this interplay, new policies will emerge, presumably from application of the canons of scientific method. The only debatable issue, it seems to me, is whether it is more ridiculous to turn to experts in social theory for general well-confirmed propositions or to the specialists in the great religions and philosophical systems for insights into fundamental human values.

There is much more that can be said about this topic, but, without continuing, I would simply like to emphasize that, as is no doubt obvious, the cult of the experts is both self-serving, for those who propound it, and fraudulent. Obviously, one must learn from social and behavioral science whatever one can; obviously, these fields should be pursued as seriously as possible. But it will be quite unfortunate, and highly dangerous, if they are not accepted and judged on their merits and according to their actual, not pretended, accomplishments. In particular, if there is a body of theory, well tested and verified, that applies to the conduct of foreign affairs or the resolution of domestic or international conflict, its existence has been kept a well-guarded secret. In the case of Vietnam, if those who feel themselves to be experts have access to principles or information that would justify what the American government is doing in that unfortunate country, they have been singularly ineffective in making this fact known. To anyone who has any familiarity with the social and behavioral sciences (or the "policy sciences"), the claim that there are certain considerations and principles too deep for the outsider to comprehend is simply an absurdity, unworthy of comment.

When we consider the responsibility of intellectuals, our basic concern must be their role in the creation and analysis of ideology. And, in fact, Kristol's contrast between the unreasonable ideological types and the responsible experts is formulated in terms that immediately bring to mind Daniel Bell's interesting and influential essay "The End of Ideology," which is as important for what it leaves unsaid as for its actual content.[19] Bell presents and discusses the Marxist analysis of ideology as a mask for class interest, quoting Marx's well-known description of the belief of the bourgeoisie "that the *special* conditions of its emancipation are the *general* conditions through which alone modern society can be saved and the class struggle avoided." He then argues that the age of ideology is ended, supplanted, at least in the West, by a general agreement that each issue must be settled in its own terms, within the framework of a welfare state in which, presumably, experts in the conduct of public affairs will have a prominent role. Bell is quite careful, however, to characterize the precise sense of "ideology" in which "ideologies are exhausted." He is referring to ideology only as "the conversion of ideas into social levers," to ideology as "a set of beliefs, infused with passion, . . . [which] . . . seeks to transform the whole of a way of life."

The crucial words are "transform" and "convert into social levers." Intellectuals in the West, he argues, have lost interest in converting ideas into social levers for the radical transformation of society. Now that we have achieved the pluralistic society of the welfare state, they see no further need for a radical transformation of society; we may tinker with our way of life here and there, but it would be wrong to try to modify it in any significant way. With this consensus of intellectuals, ideology is dead.

There are several striking facts about Bell's essay. First, he does not point out the extent to which this consensus of the intellectuals is self-serving. He does not relate his observation that, by and large, intellectuals have lost interest in "transforming the whole of a way of life" to the fact that they play an increasingly prominent role in running the welfare state; he does not relate their general satisfaction with the welfare state to the fact that, as he observes elsewhere, "America has become an affluent society, offering place . . . and prestige . . . to the onetime radicals." Secondly, he offers no serious argument to show that intellectuals are somehow "right" or "objectively justified" in reaching the consensus to which he alludes, with its rejection of the notion that society should be transformed. Indeed, although Bell is fairly sharp about the empty rhetoric of the "new left," he seems to have a quite utopian faith that technical experts will be able to cope with the few problems that still remain—for example, the fact that labor is treated as a commodity and the problems of "alienation."

It seems fairly obvious that the classical problems are very much with us; one might plausibly argue that they have even been enhanced in severity and scale. For example, the classical paradox of poverty in the midst of plenty is now an ever-increasing problem on an international scale. Whereas one might conceive, at least in principle, of a solution within national boundaries, a sensible idea of transforming international society to cope with vast and perhaps increasing human misery is hardly likely to develop within the framework of the intellectual consensus that Bell describes.

Thus, it would seem natural to describe the consensus of Bell's intellectuals in somewhat different terms from his. Using the terminology of the first part of his essay, we might say that the welfare state technician finds justification for his special and prominent social status in his "science"—specifically, in the claim that social science can support a technology of social tinkering on a domestic or international scale. He then takes a further step, ascribing in a familiar way a universal validity to what is in fact a class interest: he argues that the special conditions on which his claim to power and authority are based are, in fact, the only general conditions by which modern society can be saved and that social tinkering within a welfare state framework must replace the commitment to the "total ideologies" of the past, ideologies that were concerned with a transformation of society. Having found his position of power, having achieved security and affluence, he has no further need for ideologies that look to radical change. The scholar-expert replaces the "free-floating intellectual" who "felt that the wrong values were being honored, and rejected the society," and who has now lost his political role (now, that is, that the right values are being honored).

Conceivably, it is correct that the technical experts who will (or hope to) manage the "industrial society" will be able to cope with the classical problems without a radical transformation of society. It is conceivably true that the bourgeoisie was right in regarding the special conditions of its emancipation as the only general conditions by which modern society would be saved. In either case, an argument is in order, and skepticism is justified when none appears.

Within the same framework of general utopianism, Bell goes on to pose the issue between welfare state scholar-experts and Third World ideologists in a rather curious way. He points out, quite correctly, that there is no issue of communism, the content of that doctrine having been "long forgotten by friends and foes alike." Rather, he says, "the question is an older one: whether new societies can grow by building democratic institutions and allowing people to make choices—and sacrifices—voluntarily, or whether the new elites, heady with power, will impose totalitarian means to transform their societies."

The question is an interesting one. It is odd, however, to see it referred to as "an older one." Surely he cannot be suggesting that the West chose the democratic way—for example, that in England during the industrial revolution, the farmers voluntarily made the choice of leaving the land—giving up cottage industry, becoming an industrial proletariat—and voluntarily decided, within the framework of the existing democratic institutions, to make the sacrifices that are graphically described in the classic literature on nineteenth-century industrial society. One may debate the question whether authoritarian control is necessary to permit capital accumulation in the underdeveloped world, but the Western model of development is hardly one that we can point to with any pride. It is perhaps not surprising to find Walt Rostow referring to "the more humane processes [of industrialization] that Western values would suggest" *(An American Policy in Asia).*

Those who have a serious concern for the problems that face backward countries and for the role that advanced industrial societies might, in principle, play in development and modernization must use somewhat more care in interpreting the significance of the Western experience.

Returning to the quite appropriate question, whether "new societies can grow by building democratic institutions" or only by totalitarian means, I think that honesty requires us to recognize that this question must be directed more to American intellectuals than to Third World ideologists. The backward countries have incredible, perhaps insurmountable problems and few available options; the United States has a wide range of options and has the economic and technological resources, though evidently neither the intellectual nor moral resources to confront at least some of these problems. It is easy for an American intellectual to deliver homilies on the virtues of freedom and liberty, but if he is really concerned about, say, Chinese totalitarianism or the burdens imposed on the Chinese peasantry in forced industrialization, then he should face a task that is infinitely more important and challenging—the task of creating in the United States the intellectual and moral climate, as well as the social and economic conditions, that would permit this country to participate in modernization and development in a way commensurate with its material wealth and technical capacity. Large capital gifts to Cuba and China might not succeed in alleviating the authoritarianism and terror that tend to accompany early stages of capital accumulation, but they are far more likely to have this effect than lectures on democratic values. It is possible that even without "capitalist encirclement" in its various manifestations, the truly democratic elements in revolutionary movements—in some instances, soviets and collectives— might be undermined by an "elite" of bureaucrats and technical intelligentsia. But it is almost certain that capitalist encirclement itself, which all revolutionary movements now have to face, will guarantee this result. The lesson, for those who are concerned to strengthen the democratic, spontaneous, and popular elements in developing societies, is quite clear. Lectures on the two-party system, or even on the really substantial democratic values that have been in part realized in Western society, are a monstrous irrelevance, given the effort required to raise the level of culture in Western society to the point where it can provide a "social lever" for both economic development and the development of true democratic institutions in the Third World—and, for that matter, at home.

A good case can be made for the conclusion that there is indeed something of a consensus among intellectuals who have already achieved power and affluence or who sense that they can achieve them by "accepting society" as it is and promoting the values that are "being honored" in this society. It is also true that this consensus is most noticeable among the scholar-experts who are replacing the free-floating intellectuals of the past. In the university, these scholar-experts construct a "value-free technology" for the solution of technical problems that arise in contemporary society,[20] taking a "responsible stance" toward these problems, in the sense noted earlier. This consensus among the responsible scholar-experts is the domestic analogue to that proposed internationally by those who justify the application of American power in Asia, whatever the human cost, on the grounds that it is necessary to contain the "expansion of China" (an "expansion" which is, to be sure, hypothetical for the time being)[21]—that is, to translate from State Department Newspeak, on the grounds that it is essential to reverse the Asian nationalist revolutions or, at least, to prevent them from spreading. The analysis becomes clear when we look carefully at the ways in which this proposal is formulated. With his usual lucidity, Churchill outlined the general position in a remark to his colleague of the moment, Joseph Stalin, at Teheran in 1943:

> The government of the world must be entrusted to satisfied nations, who wished nothing more for themselves than what they had. If the world-government were in the hands of hungry nations there would always be danger. But none of us had any reason to seek for anything more. . . . Our power placed us above the rest. We were like the rich men dwelling at peace within their habitations.

For a translation of Churchill's biblical rhetoric into the jargon of contemporary social science, one may turn to the testimony of Charles Wolf, senior economist of the Rand Corporation, at the congressional committee hearings cited earlier:

> I am dubious that China's fears of encirclement are going to be abated, eased, relaxed in the long-term future. But I would hope that what we do in Southeast Asia would help to develop within the Chinese body politic more of a realism and willingness to live with this fear than to indulge it by support for liberation movements, which admittedly depend on a great deal more than external support. . . . [T]he operational question

for American foreign policy is not whether that fear can be eliminated or substantially alleviated, but whether China can be faced with a structure of incentives, of penalties and rewards, of inducements that will make it willing to live with this fear.

The point is further clarified by Thomas Schelling: "There is growing experience, which the Chinese can profit from, that although the United States may be interested in encircling them, may be interested in defending nearby areas from them, it is, nevertheless, prepared to behave peaceably if they are."

In short, we are prepared to live peaceably in our—to be sure, rather extensive—habitations. And, quite naturally, we are offended by the undignified noises from the servants' quarters. If, let us say, a peasant-based revolutionary movement tries to achieve independence from foreign powers and the domestic structures they support, or if the Chinese irrationally refuse to respond properly to the schedule of reinforcement that we have prepared for them—if they object to being encircled by the benign and peace-loving "rich men" who control the territories on their borders as a natural right— then, evidently, we must respond to this belligerence with appropriate force.

It is this mentality that explains the frankness with which the U.S. government and its academic apologists defend the American refusal to permit a political settlement in Vietnam at a local level, a settlement based on the actual distribution of political forces. Even government experts freely admit that the National Liberation Front (NLF) is the only "truly mass-based political party in South Vietnam";[22] that the NLF had "made a conscious and massive effort to extend political participation, even if it was manipulated, on the local level so as to involve the people in a self-contained, self-supporting revolution" (p. 374); and that this effort had been so successful that no political groups, "with the possible exception of the Buddhists, thought themselves equal in size and power to risk entering into a coalition, fearing that if they did the whale would swallow the minnow" (p. 362). Moreover, they concede that until the introduction of overwhelming American force, the NLF had insisted that the struggle "should be fought out at the political level and that the use of massed military might was in itself illegitimate. . . . The battleground was to be the minds and loyalties of the rural Vietnamese, the weapons were to be ideas" (pp. 91–92; cf. also pp. 93, 99–108, 155ff.); and, correspondingly, that until mid-1964, aid from Hanoi "was largely confined to two areas—doctrinal know-how and leadership personnel" (p. 321). Captured NLF documents contrast the enemy's "military superiority" with their own "political superiority" (p. 106), thus fully confirming the analysis of American military spokesmen who define our problem as how, "with considerable armed force but little political power, [to] contain an adversary who has enormous political force but only modest military power."[23]

Similarly, the most striking outcome of both the Honolulu conference in February and the Manila conference in October was the frank admission by high officials of the Saigon government that "they could not survive a 'peaceful settlement' that left the Vietcong *political* structure in place even if the Vietcong guerrilla units were disbanded," that "they are not able to compete *politically* with the Vietnamese Communists" (Charles Mohr, *New York Times,* February 11, 1966, italics mine). Thus, Mohr continues, the Vietnamese demand a "pacification program" that will have as "its core . . . the destruction of the clandestine Vietcong political structure and the creation of an iron-like system of government political control over the population." And from Manila, the same correspondent, on October 23, quotes a high South Vietnamese official as saying that "Frankly, we are not strong enough now to compete with the Communists on a purely political basis. They are organized and disciplined. The non-Communist nationalists are not—we do not have any large, well-organized political parties and we do not yet have unity. We cannot leave the Vietcong in existence."

 Officials in Washington understand the situation very well. Thus, Secretary Rusk has pointed out that "if the Vietcong come to the conference table as full partners they will, in a sense, have been victorious in the very aims that South Vietnam and the United States are pledged to prevent" (January 28, 1966). Max Frankel reported from Washington in the *Times* on February 18, 1966, that

> Compromise has had no appeal here because the Administration concluded long ago that the non-Communist forces of South Vietnam could not long survive in a Saigon coalition with Communists. It is for that reason—and not because of an excessively rigid sense of protocol—that Washington has steadfastly refused to deal with the Vietcong or recognize them as an independent political force.

In short, we will—magnanimously—permit Viet Cong representatives to attend negotiations only if they will agree to identify themselves as agents of a foreign power and thus forfeit the right to participate in a coalition government, a right that they have now been demanding for a half-dozen years. We well know that in any representative coalition, our chosen delegates could not last a day without the support of American arms. Therefore, we must increase American force and resist meaningful negotiations until the day when a client government can exert both military and political control over its own population—a day that may never dawn, for as William Bundy has pointed out, we could never be sure of the security of a Southeast Asia "from which the Western presence was effectively withdrawn." Thus, if we were to "negotiate in the direction of solutions that are put under the label of neutralization," this would amount to capitulation to the communists.[24] According to this reasoning, then, South Vietnam must remain, permanently, an American military base.

All of this is, of course, reasonable, so long as we accept the fundamental political axiom that the United States, with its traditional concern for the rights of the weak and downtrodden, and with its unique insight into the proper mode of development for backward countries, must have the courage and the persistence to impose its will by force until such time as other nations are prepared to accept these truths—or simply, to abandon hope.

If it is the responsibility of the intellectual to insist upon the truth, it is also his duty to see events in their historical perspective. Thus, one must applaud the insistence of the secretary of state on the importance of historical analogies—the Munich analogy, for example. As Munich showed, a powerful and aggressive nation with a fanatic belief in its manifest destiny will regard each victory, each extension of its power and authority, as a prelude to the next step. The matter was very well put by Adlai Stevenson when he spoke of "the old, old route whereby expansive powers push at more and more doors, believing they will open until, at the ultimate door, resistance is unavoidable and major war breaks out." Herein lies the danger of appeasement, as the Chinese tirelessly point out to the Soviet Union—which, they claim, is playing Chamberlain to our Hitler in Vietnam. Of course, the aggressiveness of liberal imperialism is not that of Nazi Germany, though the distinction may seem academic to a Vietnamese peasant who is being gassed or incinerated. We do not want to occupy Asia; we merely wish, to return to Mr. Wolf, "to help the Asian countries progress toward economic modernization, as relatively 'open' and stable societies, to which our access, as a country and as individual citizens, is free and comfortable." The formulation is appropriate. Recent history shows that it makes little difference to us what form of government a country has so long as it remains an "open society," in our peculiar sense of this term—that is, a society that remains open to American economic penetration or political control. If it is necessary to approach genocide in Vietnam to achieve this objective, then this is the price we must pay in defense of freedom and the rights of man.

In pursuing the aim of helping other countries to progress toward open societies, with no thought of territorial aggrandizement, we are breaking no new ground. In the congressional hearings that I cited earlier, Hans Morgenthau aptly describes our traditional policy toward China as one that favors "what you might call freedom of competition with regard to the exploitation of China" (p. 128). In fact, few imperialist powers have had explicit territorial ambitions. Thus, in 1784, the British Parliament announced: "To pursue schemes of conquest and extension of dominion in India are measures repugnant to the wish, honor, and policy of this nation." Shortly after this, the conquest of India was in full swing. A century later, Britain announced its intentions in Egypt under the slogan "intervention, reform, withdrawal." It is obvious which parts of this promise were fulfilled within the next half-century. In 1936, on the eve of hostilities in North China, the Japanese stated their Basic Principles of National Policy. These included the use of moderate and peaceful means to extend her strength, to promote social and economic development, to eradicate the menace of communism, to correct the aggressive policies of the great powers, and to secure her position as the stabilizing power in East Asia. Even in 1937, the Japanese government had "no territorial designs upon China." In short, we follow a well-trodden path.

It is useful to remember, incidentally, that the United States was apparently quite willing, as late as 1939, to negotiate a commercial treaty with Japan and arrive at a modus vivendi if Japan would "change her attitude and practice towards our rights and interests in China," as Secretary Hull put it. The bombing of Chungking and the rape of Nanking were unpleasant, it is true, but what was really important was our rights and interests in China, as the responsible, unhysterical men of the day saw quite clearly. It was the closing of the open door by Japan that led inevitably to the Pacific war, just as it is the closing of the open door by "communist" China itself that may very well lead to the next, and no doubt last, Pacific war.

Quite often, the statements of sincere and devoted technical experts give surprising insight into the intellectual attitudes that lie in the background of the latest savagery. Consider, for example, the following comment by the economist Richard Lindholm, in 1959, expressing his frustration over the failure of economic development in "free Vietnam":

> the use of American aid is determined by how the Vietnamese use their incomes and their savings. The fact that a large portion of the Vietnamese imports financed with American aid are either consumer goods or raw materials used rather directly to meet consumer demands is an indication that the Vietnamese people desire these goods, for they have shown their desire by their willingness to use their piasters to purchase them.[25]

In short, the Vietnamese *people* desire Buicks and air-conditioners, rather than sugar-refining equipment or road-building machinery, as they have shown by their behavior in a free market. And however much we may deplore their free choice, we must allow the people to have their way. Of course, there are also those two-legged beasts of burden that one stumbles on in the countryside, but as any graduate student of political science can explain, they are not part of a responsible modernizing elite and therefore have only a superficial biological resemblance to the human race.

In no small measure, it is attitudes like this that lie behind the butchery in Vietnam, and we had better face up to them with candor, or we will find our government leading us toward a "final solution" in Vietnam and in the many Vietnams that inevitably lie ahead.

Let me finally return to Dwight Macdonald and the responsibility of intellectuals. Macdonald quotes an interview with a death camp paymaster who burst into tears when told that the Russians would hang him. "Why should they? What have I done?" he asked. Macdonald concludes: "Only those who are willing to resist authority themselves when it conflicts too intolerably with their personal moral code, only they have the right to condemn the death camp paymaster." The question, "What have I done?" is one that we may well ask ourselves as we read each day of fresh atrocities in Vietnam—as we create or mouth or tolerate the deceptions that will be used to justify the next defense of freedom.

Declaration of Independence from the War in Vietnam (April 1967)

MARTIN LUTHER KING, JR.

OVER THE PAST two years, as I have moved to break the betrayal of my own silences and to speak from the burnings of my own heart, as I have called for radical departures from the destruction of Vietnam, many persons have questioned me about the wisdom of my path. At the heart of their concerns this query has often loomed large and loud: Why are *you* speaking about the war, Dr. King? Why are *you* joining the voices of dissent? Peace and civil rights don't mix, they say. Aren't you hurting the cause of your people, they ask. And when I hear them, though I often understand the source of their concern, I am nevertheless greatly saddened, for such questions mean that the inquirers have not really known me, my commitment or my calling. Indeed, their questions suggest that they do not know the world in which they live.

In the light of such tragic misunderstanding, I deem it of signal importance to try to state clearly why I believe that the path from Dexter Avenue Baptist Church—the church in Montgomery, Alabama, where I began my pastorage—leads clearly to this sanctuary tonight.

I come to this platform to make a passionate plea to my beloved nation.

Originally published in *Ramparts,* May 1967, 33–37

This speech in not addressed to Hanoi or to the National Liberation Front. It is not addressed to China or to Russia.

Nor is it an attempt to overlook the ambiguity of the total situation and the need for a collective solution to the tragedy of Vietnam. Neither is it an attempt to make North Vietnam or the National Liberation Front paragons of virtue, nor to overlook the role they can play in a successful resolution of the problem. While they both may have justifiable reasons to be suspicious of the good faith of the United States, life and history give eloquent testimony to the fact that conflicts are never resolved without trustful give and take on both sides.

Tonight, however, I wish not to speak with Hanoi and the NLF, but rather to my fellow Americans who, with me, bear the greatest responsibility in ending a conflict that has exacted a heavy price on both continents.

Since I am a preacher by trade, I suppose it is not surprising that I have seven major reasons for bringing Vietnam into the field of my moral vision. There is at the outset a very obvious and almost facile connection between the war in Vietnam and the struggle I, and others, have been waging in America. A few years ago there was a shining moment in that struggle. It seemed as if there was a real promise of hope for the poor—both black and white—through the Poverty Program. Then came the buildup in Vietnam, and I watched the program broken and eviscerated as if it were some idle political plaything of a society gone mad on war, and I knew that America would never invest the necessary funds or energies in rehabilitation of its poor so long as Vietnam continued to draw men and skills and money like some demonic, destructive suction tube. So I was increasingly compelled to see the war as an enemy of the poor and to attack it as such.

Perhaps the more tragic recognition of reality took place when it became clear to me that the war was doing far more than devastating the hopes of the poor at home. It was sending their sons and their brothers and their husbands to fight and to die in extraordinarily high proportions relative to the rest of the population. We were taking the young black men who had been crippled by our society and sending them eight thousand miles away to guarantee liberties in Southeast Asia which they had not found in Southwest Georgia and East Harlem. So we have been repeatedly faced with the cruel irony of watching Negro and white boys on TV screens as they kill and die together for a nation that has been unable to seat them together in the same schools. So we watch them in brutal solidarity burning the huts of a poor village, but we realize that they would never live on the same block in Detroit. I could not be silent in the face of such cruel manipulation of the poor.

My third reason grows out of my experience in the ghettos of the North over the last three years—especially the last three summers. As I have walked among the desperate, rejected and angry young men, I have told them that Molotov cocktails and rifles would not solve their problems. I have tried to offer them my deepest compassion while maintaining my conviction that social change comes most meaningfully through nonviolent action. But, they asked, what about Vietnam? They asked if our own nation wasn't using massive doses of violence to solve its problems, to bring about the changes it wanted. Their questions hit home, and I knew that I could never again raise my voice against the violence of the oppressed in the ghettos without having first spoken clearly to the greatest purveyor of violence in the world today—my own government.

For those who ask the question, "Aren't you a Civil Rights leader?" and thereby mean to exclude me from the movement for peace, I have this further answer. In 1957 when a group of us formed the Southern Christian Leadership Conference, we chose as our motto: "To save the soul of America." We were convinced that we could not limit our vision to certain rights for Black people, but instead affirmed the conviction that America would never be free or saved from itself unless the descendants of its slaves were loosed from the shackles they still wear.

Now, it should be incandescently clear that no one who has any concern for the integrity and life of America today can ignore the present war. If America's soul becomes totally poisoned, part of the autopsy must read "Vietnam." It can never be saved so long as it destroys the deepest hopes of men the world over.

As if the weight of such a commitment of the life and health of America were not enough, another burden of responsibility was placed upon me in 1964; and I cannot forget that the Nobel Prize for Peace was also a commission—a commission to work harder than I had ever worked before for the "brotherhood of man." This is a calling that takes me beyond national allegiances, but even if it were not present I would yet have have to live with the meaning of my commitment to the ministry of Jesus Christ. To me, the relationship of this ministry to the making of peace is so obvious that I sometimes marvel at those who ask me why I am speaking against the war. Could it be that they do not know that the good news was meant for all men—for communist and capitalist, for their children and ours, for black and white, for revolutionary and conservative? Have they forgotten that my ministry is in obedience to the One who loved His enemies so fully that He died for them? What then can I say to the Viet Cong or to Castro or to Mao as a faithful minister of this One? Can I threaten them with death, or must I not share with them my life?

And as I ponder the madness of Vietnam, my mind goes constantly to the people of that peninsula. I speak now not of the soldiers of each side, not of the junta in Saigon, but simply of the people who have been living under the curse of war for almost three continuous decades. I think of them, too, because it is clear to me that there will be no meaningful solution there until some attempt is made to know them and their broken cries.

They must see Americans as strange liberators. The Vietnamese proclaimed their own independence in 1945 after a combined French and Japanese occupation and before the communist revolution in China. Even though they quoted the American Declaration of Independence in their own document of freedom, we refused to recognize them. Instead, we decided to support France in its reconquest of her former colony.

Our government felt then that the Vietnamese people were not "ready" for independence, and we again fell victim to the deadly Western arrogance that has poisoned the international atmosphere for so long. With that tragic decision, we rejected a revolutionary government seeking self-determination and a government that had been established not by China (for whom the Vietnamese have no great love) but by clearly indigenous forces that included some communists. For the peasants, this new government meant real land reform, one of the most important needs in their lives.

For nine years following 1945 we denied the people of Vietnam the right of independence. For nine years we vigorously supported the French in their abortive effort to recolonize Vietnam.

Before the end of the war we were meeting 80 percent of the French war costs. Even before the French were defeated at Dien Bien Phu, they began to despair of their reckless action, but we did not. We encouraged them with our huge financial and military supplies to continue the war even after they had lost the will to do so.

After the French were defeated it looked as if independence and land reform would come again through the Geneva Agreements. But instead there came the United States, determined that Ho should not unify the temporarily divided nation, and the peasants watched again as we supported one of the most vicious modern dictators—our chosen man, Premier Diem.

The peasants watched and cringed as Diem ruthlessly routed out all opposition, supported their extortionist landlords and refused even to discuss reunification with the North. The peasants watched as all this was presided over by U.S. influence and then by increasing numbers of U.S. troops who came to help quell the insurgency that Diem's methods had aroused. When Diem was overthrown they may have been happy, but the long line of military dictatorships seemed to offer no real change—especially in terms of their need for land and peace.

The only change came from America as we increased our troop commitments in support of governments which were singularly corrupt, inept, and without popular support. All the while, the people read our leaflets and received regular promises of peace and democracy—and land reform. Now they languish under our bombs and consider us—not their fellow Vietnamese—the real enemy. They move sadly and apathetically as we herd them off the land of their fathers into concentration camps where minimal social needs are rarely met. They know they must move or be destroyed by our bombs. So they go.

They watch as we poison their water, as we kill a million acres of their crops. They must weep as the bulldozers destroy their precious trees. They wander into the hospitals, with at least twenty casualties from American firepower for each Viet Cong–inflicted injury. So far we may have killed a million of them—mostly children.

What do the peasants think as we ally ourselves with the landlords and as we refuse to put any action into our many words concerning land reform? What do they think as we test out our latest weapons on them, just as the Germans tested out new medicine and new tortures in the concentration camps of Europe? Where are the roots of the independent Vietnam we claim to be building?

Now there is little left to build on—save bitterness. Soon the only solid physical foundations remaining will be found at our military bases and in the concrete of the concentration camps we call "fortified hamlets." The peasants may well wonder if we plan to build our new Vietnam on such grounds as these. Could we blame them for such thoughts? We must speak for them and raise the questions they cannot raise. These too are our brothers.

Perhaps the most difficult but no less necessary task is to speak for those who have been designated as our enemies. What of the NLF—that strangely anonymous group we call VC or communists? What must they think of us in America when they realize that we permitted the repression and cruelty of Diem which helped to bring them into being as a resistance group in the South? How can they believe in our integrity when now we speak of "aggression from the North" as if there were nothing more essential to the war? How can they trust us when now we charge *them* with violence after the murderous reign of Diem, and charge *them* with violence while we pour new weapons of death into their land?

How do they judge us when our officials know that their membership is less than 25 percent communist and yet insist on giving them the blanket name? What must they be thinking when they know that we are aware of their control of major sections of Vietnam and yet we appear ready to allow national elections in which this highly organized political parallel government will have no part? They ask how we can speak of free elections when the Saigon press is censored and controlled by the military junta. And they are surely right to wonder what kind of new government we plan to help form without them—the only party in real touch with the peasants. They question our political goals and they deny the reality of a peace settlement from which they will be excluded. Their questions are frighteningly relevant.

Here is the true meaning and value of compassion and non-violence—when it helps us to see the enemy's point of view, to hear his questions, to know of his assessment of ourselves. For from his view we may indeed see the basic weaknesses of our own condition, and if we are mature, we may learn and grow and profit from the wisdom of the brothers who are called the opposition.

So, too, with Hanoi. In the North, where our bombs now pummel the land, and our mines endanger the waterways, we are met by a deep but understandable mistrust. In Hanoi are the men who led the nation to independence against the Japanese and the French, the men who sought membership in the French commonwealth and were betrayed by the weakness of Paris and the willfulness of the colonial armies. It was they who led a second struggle against French domination at tremendous costs, and then were persuaded at Geneva to give up, as a temporary measure, the land they controlled between the thirteenth and seventeenth parallels. After 1954 they watched us conspire with Diem to prevent elections that would have surely brought Ho Chi Minh to power over a united Vietnam, and they realized they had been betrayed again.

When we ask why they do not leap to negotiate, these things must be remembered. Also, it must be clear that the leaders of Hanoi considered the presence of American troops in support of the Diem regime to have been the initial military breach of the Geneva Agreements concerning foreign troops, and they remind us that they did not begin to send in any large number of supplies or men until American forces had moved into the tens of thousands.

Hanoi remembers how our leaders refused to tell us the truth about the earlier North Vietnamese overtures for peace, how the president claimed that none existed when they had clearly been made. Ho Chi Minh has watched as America has spoken of peace and built up its forces, and now he has surely heard the increasing international rumors of American plans for an invasion of the North. Perhaps only his sense of humor and irony can save him when he hears the most powerful nation of the world speaking of aggression as it drops thousands of bombs on a poor, weak nation more than eight thousand miles from its shores.

At this point, I should make it clear that although I have tried here to give a voice to the voiceless of Vietnam and to understand the arguments of those who are called enemy, I am as deeply concerned about our own troops there as anything else. For it occurs to me that what we are submitting them to in Vietnam is not simply the brutalizing process that goes on in any war where armies face each other and seek to destroy. We are adding cynicism to the process of death, for our troops must know after a short period there that none of the things we claim to be fighting for are really involved. Before long they must know that their government has sent them into a struggle among Vietnamese, and the more sophisticated surely realize that we are on the side of the wealthy and the secure while we create a hell for the poor.

Somehow this madness must cease. I speak as a child of God and brother to the suffering poor of Vietnam and the poor of America who are paying the double price of smashed hopes at home and death and corruption in Vietnam. I speak as a citizen of the world, for the world as it stands aghast at the path we have taken. I speak as an American to the leaders of my own nation. The great initiative in this war is ours. The initiative to stop must be ours.

This is the message of the great Buddhist leaders of Vietnam. Recently, one of them wrote these words: "Each day the war goes on the hatred increases in the hearts of the Vietnamese and in the hearts of those of humanitarian instinct. The Americans are forcing even their friends into becoming their enemies. It is curious that the Americans, who calculate so carefully on the possibilities of military victory, do not realize that in the process they are incurring deep psychological and political defeat. The image of America will never again be the image of revolution, freedom and democracy, but the image of violence and militarism."

If we continue, there will be no doubt in my mind and in the mind of the world that we have no honorable intentions in Vietnam. It will become clear that our minimal expectation is to occupy it as an American colony, and men will not refrain from thinking that our maximum hope is to goad China into a war so that we may bomb her nuclear installations.

The world now demands a maturity of America that we may not be able to achieve. It demands that we admit that we have been wrong from the beginning of our adventure in Vietnam, that we have been detrimental to the life of her people.

In order to atone for our sins and errors in Vietnam, we should take the initiative in bringing the war to a halt. I would like to suggest five concrete things that our government should do immediately to begin the long and difficult process of extricating ourselves from this nightmare:

1. End all bombing in North and South Vietnam.
2. Declare a unilateral cease-fire in the hope that such action will create the atmosphere for negotiation.
3. Take immediate steps to prevent other battlegrounds in Southeast Asia by curtailing our military buildup in Thailand and our interference in Laos.
4. Realistically accept the fact that the National Liberation Front has substantial support in South Vietnam and must thereby play a role in any meaningful negotiations and in any future Vietnam government.
5. Set a date on which we will remove all foreign troops from Vietnam in accordance with the 1954 Geneva Agreements.

Part of our ongoing commitment might well express itself in an offer to grant asylum to any Vietnamese who fears for his life under a new regime that included the NLF. Then we must make what reparations we can for the damage we have done. We must provide the medical aid that is badly needed, in this country if necessary.

Meanwhile, we in the churches and synagogues have a continuing task while we urge our government to disengage itself from a disgraceful commitment. We must be prepared to match actions with words by seeking out every creative means of protest possible.

As we counsel young men concerning military service we must clarify for them our nation's role in Vietnam and challenge them with the alternative of conscientious objection. I am pleased to say that this is the path now being chosen by more than seventy students at my own Alma Mater, Morehouse College, and I recommend it to all who find the American course in Vietnam a dishonorable and unjust one. Moreover, I would encourage all ministers of draft age to give up their ministerial exemptions and seek status as conscientious objectors. Every man of humane convictions must decide on the protest that best suits his convictions, but we must *all* protest.

There is something seductively tempting about stopping there and sending us all off on what in some circles has become a popular crusade against the war in Vietnam. I say we must enter that struggle, but I wish to go on now to say something even more disturbing. The war in Vietnam is but a symptom of a far deeper malady within the American spirit, and if we ignore this sobering reality we will find ourselves organizing clergy- and laymen-concerned committees for the next generation. We will be marching and attending rallies without end unless there is a significant and profound change in American life and policy.

In 1957 a sensitive American official overseas said that it seemed to him that our nation was on the wrong side of a world revolution. During the past ten years we have seen emerge a pattern of suppression that now has justified the presence of U.S. military "advisors" in Venezuela. The need to maintain social stability for our investments accounts for the counterrevolutionary action of American forces in Guatemala. It tells why American helicopters are being used against guerrillas in Colombia and why American napalm and Green Beret forces have already been active against rebels in Peru. With such activity in mind, the words of John F. Kennedy come back to haunt us. Five years ago he said, "Those who make peaceful revolution impossible will make violent revolution inevitable."

Increasingly, by choice or by accident, this is the role our nation has taken—by refusing to give up the privileges and the pleasures that come from the immense profits of overseas investment.

I am convinced that if we are to get on the right side of the world revolution, we as a nation must undergo a radical revolution of values. When machines and computers, profit and property rights are considered more important than people, the giant triplets of racism, materialism, and militarism are incapable of being conquered.

A true revolution of values will soon cause us to question the fairness and justice of many of our past and present policies. True compassion is more than flinging a coin to a beggar; it is not haphazard and superficial. It comes to see that an edifice that produces beggars needs restructuring. A true revolution of values will soon look uneasily on the glaring contrast of poverty and wealth. With righteous indignation, it will look across the seas and see individual capitalists of the West investing huge sums of money in Asia, Africa and South America, only to take the profits out with no concern for the social betterment of the countries, and say: "This is not just." It will look at our alliance with the landed gentry of Latin America and say: "This is not just." The Western arrogance of feeling that it has everything to teach others and nothing to learn from them is not just. A true revolution of values will lay hands on the world order and say of war: "This way of settling differences is not just." This business of burning human beings with napalm, of filling our nation's homes with orphans and widows, of injecting poisonous drugs of hate into the veins of peoples normally humane, of sending men home from dark and bloody battlefields physically handicapped and psychologically deranged, cannot be reconciled with wisdom, justice, and love. A nation that continues year after year to spend more money on military defense than on programs of social uplift is approaching spiritual death.

America, the richest and most powerful nation in the world, can well lead the way in this revolution of values. There is nothing, except a tragic death wish, to prevent us from re-ordering our priorities, so that the pursuit of peace will take precedence over the pursuit of war. There is nothing to keep us from molding a recalcitrant status quo until we have fashioned it into a brotherhood.

This kind of positive revolution of values is our best defense against communism. War is not the answer. Communism will never be defeated by the use of atomic bombs or nuclear weapons. Let us not join those who shout war and through their misguided passions urge the United States to relinquish its participation in the United Nations. These are the days that demand wise restraint and calm reasonableness. We must not call everyone a communist or an appeaser who advocates the seating of Red China in the United Nations and who recognizes that hate and hysteria are not the final answers to the problem of these turbulent days. We must not engage in a negative anti-communism, but rather in a positive thrust for democracy, realizing that our greatest defense against communism is to take offensive action in behalf of justice. We must with positive action seek to remove those conditions of poverty, insecurity, and injustice that are the fertile soil in which the seed of communism grows and develops.

These are revolutionary times. All over the globe men are revolting against old systems of exploitation and oppression, and out of the wombs of a frail world, new systems of justice and equality are being born. The shirtless and barefoot people of the land are rising up as never before. "The people who sat in darkness have seen a great light." We in the West must support these revolutions. It is a sad fact that because of comfort, complacency, a morbid fear of communism, and our proneness to adjust to injustice, the Western nations that initiated so much of the revolutionary spirit of the modern world have now become the arch anti-revolutionaries. This has driven many to feel that only Marxism has the revolutionary spirit. Therefore, communism is a judgment against our failure to make democracy real and follow through on the revolutions that we initiated. Our only hope today lies in our ability to recapture the revolutionary spirit and to go out into a sometimes hostile world declaring eternal hostility to poverty, racism, and militarism.

We must move past indecision to action. We must find new ways to speak for peace in Vietnam and justice throughout the developing world—a world that borders on our doors. If we do not act, we shall surely be dragged down the long, dark and shameful corridors of time reserved for those who possess power without compassion, might without morality, and strength without sight.

Now let us begin. Now let us rededicate ourselves to the long, the bitter—but beautiful—struggle for a new world. This is the calling of the sons of God, and our brothers wait eagerly for our response. Shall we say the odds are too great? Shall we tell them the struggle is too hard? Will our message be that the forces of American life militate against their arrival as full men, and we send our deepest regrets? Or will there be another message, of longing, of hope, of solidarity with their yearnings, of commitment to their cause, whatever the cost? The choice is ours, and though we might prefer it otherwise we *must* choose in this crucial moment of human history.

8

Why I Joined the Resistance

MICHAEL FERBER

I DON'T FEEL very historical yet, but to college students taking a course in the history of the Vietnam war, where I make regular guest appearances, I am already a living document or source, an expanded oral version of the thirty-year-old text they were assigned to read, "A Time to Say No." I am received with dutiful respect but also with some skepticism or boredom, so my challenge each time is to put across a lively picture of "what it was like" in the war-resistance movement. Of course, I never succeed entirely. Some students (I learn much later) are impressed by it, others duly note it and wonder if it will show up on the exam.

Usually I find in the class an older man or woman, often a combat veteran, who comes up to me afterward to talk; we quickly feel a friendly bond that bespeaks our sense that "our generation" underwent something together that transcends the divisions among us during the war, something that we cannot easily convey to young people today. Our memories of those days remain so vivid that what passes before us now, the world of those young faces in the classroom, seems pale, transitional, already itself historical, lacking in the intense, mythic clarity of our time. And some students feel this themselves: they feel they were born too late and can only sigh for the Age of Miracles.

I try to tell them the right things: that all times are "now" and equally important, that the end of the Cold War brings interesting possibilities for social change, that many students are doing good political work across the country, and so on. And I admit that there is something illusory about my own feelings about the war years, for at some deep level we all live off our experiences at about twenty-one, and I happened to turn twenty-one in 1965, the year the war began with a vengeance. Yet it is not just an illusion, after all, to believe that America as a whole went through a crisis in the late 1960s and has not yet gotten over it. That is a journalistic commonplace; it is also true. The Myth of the Sixties is not just a myth.

For most of what follows, then, I will not try to correct my youthful memories with what I have learned from books and conversations since. If I am mistaken or biased, I will at least try to be a useful document or source; there are good scholars of the period who will know what to do with me.

✳ ☮ ✳

By the beginning of 1965, having pondered the Tonkin Bay Incident and read a few books about Southeast Asia, I decided U.S. policy there was fundamentally wrong, and I joined the Students for a Democratic Society (SDS) march in Washington that April. So did twenty thousand others, most of them about my age, and I felt a surge of pleasure in seeing that a common spirit or mood of protest was spreading faster than anyone had guessed. I went on every major march for the next five years, and they grew larger and larger. Students today who know something about American politics ask me why we marched, and demonstrated, and sat in, and did things with our draft cards, rather than lobby Congress, which had the power to declare a war and end it. What they do not appreciate is that the war was conducted by a Democratic president who had a tight grip on a Democratic Congress, and the liberals who ought to have been lobbyable were afraid to oppose Lyndon Johnson, whose Great Society programs they were grateful for. Johnson had just been elected by a large majority over Barry Goldwater. It seemed hopeless to write letters and send petitions to congresspeople.

In the summer of 1965, I gave a sermon in the church I had grown up in, the Unitarian Church of Buffalo, New York, in which I presented all the reasons I could think of that America should get out of Vietnam, and I sent it with a letter to my congressman, a liberal Democrat named Max McCarthy. I remember sitting on our next-door neighbor's front porch that summer arguing with McCarthy about the war. I sensed he had some sympathy for my position, but he was reluctant to concede anything; he had faith, I think, that LBJ would take care of things before they got out of hand. Our neighbor was Joe Crangle, Democratic Party chairman for Erie County; he sat with us but said little until the end, when he wrapped things up with a jocular command: "As your party chairman, Max, I order you to support your president in his Vietnam policy." It was a chilly little moment. After that, at least until 1968, there seemed little point in spending a lot of time lobbying in Washington. We had to find another way.

I had been interested in nonviolence since I learned about Gandhi in Unitarian summer camp, and then, having plunged into the civil rights movement when I was a student at Swarthmore College, I was deeply impressed by Martin Luther King, Jr., and by the Student Nonviolent Coordinating Committee (SNCC). The Quaker ambience of Swarthmore was also a factor, but probably the strongest influence came from David Dellinger, whom I met with his family when they came to visit his eldest son, Patch, who roomed across the hall from me during our freshman year. Dellinger represented a world I had not known much about: men and women who had come of age in the thirties, lived through all the ins and outs of left-wing politics, but held to an ideal of nonviolence and radical egalitarianism, and often of anarchism, with great courage and flair. *Liberation* magazine, which Dave edited, for a while became my most important read-ing, and I came to cherish A. J. Muste, Paul Goodman, Barbara Deming, Bayard Rustin, and Staughton Lynd.

Many Swarthmore students had begun to work closely with the local civil rights leadership, and I joined them, learning something about the White power structure of Chester, Pennsylvania, about how to organize, about how to sing in church (Unitarians are terrible at hymns) and clap on the offbeats, and about how not to worry about getting arrested. It was a cru-cial experience for me because of both the lore it taught me and the taste or sense of a different and difficult reality it gave me, a counter to the world of libraries and classrooms where I had thus far spent much of my life.

I graduated in 1966, and by then Vietnam loomed larger than civil rights, in my view, as the most urgent national issue. The prospect of the draft, too, wonderfully concentrated my mind. By early spring of 1967, while I was a graduate student at Harvard and finding its classes rather dull after the intense seminars of Swarthmore and too otherworldly beside the ferocities of the daily news, I decided to declare to my local draft board that I was a conscientious objector (CO). I was still entitled to a student deferment, as I carefully pointed out, but I wanted it on record that I could not in good conscience serve in any army. Had my draft board done nothing (as it turns out they were legally obliged to do), or had it granted my CO request right away, it is likely that I would not have gone much further in my resistance, but by return mail it denied my request, took away my deferment, and reclassified me 1-A (draftable).

And so began what came to be called the Conscientious Objector's Gavotte, where one danced to the categories and schedules of an ignorant draft board. Did I believe in a Supreme Being? Did I oppose all wars (except "theocratic" ones)? Would I use force against a Nazi trying to rape my grandmother? I filled out forms, I rounded up testimony from Unitarian ministers, I appealed, I appealed again. Being a Unitarian was not much help, as it was not a traditional "peace church" and therefore, in the eyes of the gentlemen on my draft board, could not give religious sanction to my pacifism. (A year later, as I was preparing for my conspiracy trial, my lawyer and I went to see Rev. George Hunston Williams of Harvard Divinity School, a great scholar of the Reformation, to see if he could inject a little pacifism into the Unitarian tradition. He told me about the Socinians, who had been antitrinitarian and pacifist, and offered me books about them in Polish and Hungarian. But I had known little about them when I had my encounters with Local Board 87, and I rather doubt they would have done the trick for me.) By the end of the summer, I was sick of the dance and began to feel guilty for even trying to be a CO instead of just turning my back on the whole thing.

The news from Vietnam relentlessly drove home the urgency to do more. And a new understanding of the draft itself began to take hold of me when a Selective Service System document called "Manpower Channeling" was published in *Ramparts* magazine and elsewhere. There it was made clear that providing men for the army was only a minor function of the draft. Its real purpose was to control the entire national male workforce between eighteen and forty-five, which it accomplished by devising a system of deferments and exemptions for jobs it deemed in the national interest and by wielding the "club of induction" to drive young men into them. This was the American or indirect way of doing what foreign countries do by edict; it was "pressurized guidance" into the channels of essential jobs.

This was a revelation. It was fascism with a human face. And it occurred to me that conscientious objector status was itself a little sluice in the system, like the escape atop a pressure cooker, to allow intractable Christians a way out lest they cause trouble. Even Canada was a channel: the U.S. government seemed content to see thousands of young men emigrate rather than cope with them here. A strategy then presented itself: refuse to be channeled or, rather, choose the narrowest channel, the one most cloggable, and clog it. That was obviously the federal court system and the federal prisons.

During that summer of 1967, a small group of students from the Bay Area, including David Harris of Stanford and Lennie Heller of Berkeley, began organizing something to which they gave the mighty name The Resistance, consciously echoing not only the resistance to the Nazi occupation of Europe but the recent Jeune Resistance against the French war in Algeria. They announced that on October 16 groups of draftable men would return their draft cards to the government—not burn them—pledge to refuse induction, stay in this country, stand trial, and go to prison. Lennie Heller came east, spoke in a few places, and though he found himself baffled by the low-key "Harvard style" that prevailed among antidraft activists in Boston, he planted the idea.

The idea, he tried to make clear, was very different from draft-dodging; it was just the opposite, in fact, for most of the new resisters had deferments already and would in effect disavow them by returning their cards. Later, as I became a spokesperson for The Resistance, I constantly harped on the difference between evaders (not that I blamed them) and resisters: the resisters, not the evaders, were the ones who might have an impact on the Selective Service System and the war, for the government could not lock up thousands of forthright nonviolent young men who were defying the law out of conscience. Nonetheless, much of the public and much of the press couldn't or wouldn't see the difference. Even James Fallows—in his 1975 memoir, "What Did You Do in the Class War, Daddy?"—got draft resistance muddled with draft counseling and even attributed to me the view that "as committed opponents of the war, we had a responsibility to save ourselves from the war machine." That may have been the view of the Marxist-Leninist vanguard types, but it was not mine: I felt our place was up against the war machine, and in prison.

By the end of the summer, two or three graduate students picked up the Resistance idea and began working on it; I joined them. One, Alex Jack at Boston University Divinity School, had the brilliant idea of holding a ceremony in a church, where ministers and priests of all denominations would receive draft cards from young men, declare themselves moral accomplices, and then convey the cards to the government. Right, I thought, all we need is a church that will allow multiple federal felonies to take place in its sanctuary (refusing to carry a draft card was a crime punishable by five years in prison), but Alex found one, the Arlington Street Unitarian Universalist Church. I had not attended church for several years, though I had kept up friendships among Unitarian ministers, but this news brought me home. The Arlington Street congregation went back to William Ellery Channing, I learned, who had armed his parishioners and sent them to the Boston jailhouse to liberate recaptured fugitive slaves. Compared with that, what were a few draft cards? That was how Jack Mendelsohn felt, the current minister, and he enthusiastically welcomed us.

The little group of organizers divided tasks, and I was assigned to do most of the public speaking, mainly at campuses and churches, to invite supporters to come. We had no idea how many men would return their cards with us. Perhaps fifty? On October 16 about five thousand people showed up for a rally in Boston Common, where, among others, Howard Zinn and Noam Chomsky spoke—the largest turnout so far to a Boston antiwar rally. After a march to the church, William Sloane Coffin, chaplain at Yale, and several other clergymen spoke; I gave a short sermon called "A Time to Say No." When George Williams gave the call, about two hundred young men walked solemnly down the aisle and handed their cards to about a hundred clergymen; about sixty men also burned cards (we had to carry two cards!) at Channing's candlestick. At the end, someone thoughtfully gathered up the ashes and put them in a large envelope while I collected the unburnt cards.

By this time, a group of older men and women, many of them very prominent writers and scholars, had offered to lend their support by meeting with resisters in Washington, collecting draft cards from across the nation, and carrying them into the Justice Department building. They had published a statement, "A Call to Resist Illegitimate Authority," in a couple of journals, and it had drawn a lot of attention. At the end of the week, I flew to Washington with my two bags and gave them to Coffin, Dr. Spock, Mitchell Goodman, Marcus Raskin, and several others, who carried them to a deputy of Attorney General Ramsey Clark. The next day I joined the thousands who sat down in front of the Pentagon, watched the federal marshals club people, and inhaled my first whiff of tear gas.

Back home in Boston, I helped our Resistance group get organized, took part in another draft card turn-in (this time in a Methodist church), and rather distractedly returned to my studies at Harvard. The FBI was all over the place, calling everyone who returned his card; we learned later that FBI agents had been sitting in the room next to the deputy assistant attorney general's, who had been afraid even to touch the large bag of draft cards. I was reclassified 1-A Delinquent by my draft board. While I was riding back on the bus from Christmas holidays, I remember thinking that with probably just a few months to go before I stood trial and perhaps went to prison, I had better settle down and read some more English literature.

With that resolution in mind, I entered my apartment to find the phone ringing. It was United Press International. "Mr. Ferber, do you have any comments?" "About what?" I puffed, putting down my bags. "Oh, you haven't heard?" the reporter chuckled. "You've been indicted for conspiracy with Dr. Spock." "No shit!" I thoughtfully commented. "Is that your comment, Mr. Ferber?" "No, wait a minute, . . ." and I came up with something properly defiant and quotable. The phone rang constantly for the next several hours. Even TASS, the Soviet news agency, called: I denounced U.S. foreign policy to TASS, too, and then added that Dr. Spock and I and the other three (Coffin, Raskin, Goodman) wished to declare our solidarity with Sinyavsky and Daniel, the current dissidents jailed in the USSR. "Thank you very much. Good-bye." Click.

I finally got through to a lawyer, Bill Homans, who had generously offered to help any draft resister in trouble. "I rather thought I would hear from you," he said. He became my lawyer, and his generosity was very great because my family and I could not afford to pay his normal fees. So was his skill in court, and I much appreciated the thoughtful way he let his legal work yield to my political purposes during the trial; avoiding prison, after all, was not the goal. It was not until after the weekend that I finally got my official notice of the indictment, a letter from Boston Federal Court saying "Greeting" (in the stingy singular) and listing the counts and "overt acts." It occupied my mailbox with one other letter, this one from Local Board 87, which also began "Greeting": I was drafted and ordered to show up at an induction center in Buffalo. I had to laugh. Indeed, it turned out I could not be drafted because I had a federal felony case pending. I got to write a very enjoyable letter back to my draft board.

When the five of us co-conspirators finally got together at Leonard Boudin's house in Manhattan (he was representing Spock), Coffin had to introduce us because he was the only one who had actually met each of us. The lawyers were grim, and so was Marc Raskin, who had recently worked in the National Security Council under Kennedy and had inside lore about administration plans. We were facing "the decimation of the intelligentsia," Raskin thought: soon the government would round up Noam Chomsky,

Herbert Marcuse, Susan Sontag, even Norman Mailer. This was in early January 1968, before the Tet Offensive, before Eugene McCarthy's near upset of LBJ in the New Hampshire primary, before a section of the governing elite made its move to end the war, so we were in no position to question Raskin's gloom. But I felt cheerful. Indict more intellectuals? Great! That would only strengthen the Resistance strategy. And I felt a little flattered too, to be included, at age twenty-three, among the intelligentsia.

Coffin made the proposal that we raise the basic issues—the unconstitutionality of this undeclared war, the unconstitutionality of the draft deferment and exemption system, the violations of international law, and so on; then, if the judge dismissed all these questions (as he eventually did), we would stand mute and go to prison. I liked that idea, but the gloom and the clucking of lawyers prevailed, and we agreed to a lawyerly defense. The one good argument for such a defense was that the conspiracy law itself is a bad law and should not be applied to an open, nonviolent campaign like ours, so we owed it to the peace movement to try to defeat it. The result, however, was a trial in which the legal points made by a battery of defense lawyers sometimes drowned out the simple moral and political points the defendants tried to make when they took the stand. Some of the Chicago conspiracy defendants have criticized us on this ground. I believe, however, that we reached more people who were on the fence in their opinions about the war or about taking action against it than were reached by the Chicago group for their continual shenanigans in response to the judge's behavior also distracted attention from their main points. In any case, by taking the stand in our own defense, we convicted ourselves and at the same time got our arguments out to the press.

The story of the trial has been well told by Jessica Mitford in *The Trial of Dr. Spock*. Four of us, all but Raskin, whom the jury thought the government had mixed up with someone else, were convicted, fined, and sentenced to two years in prison. A year later, the conviction was reversed on technical grounds (the gloomy lawyers smiled knowingly), although the appellate court left the way open for a new indictment. By then, Nixon was in the White House and Republican prosecutors had no interest in cleaning up a Democratic embarrassment; the case was dropped. By then, too, public opinion had grown increasingly hostile to U.S. policy in Vietnam, and draft calls were beginning to decline.

The downside of my acquittal is that I was now draftable again. After many months, my draft board awoke to that fact and summoned me once more. I was by then vacationing in Ireland, and from the shores of Lake Killarney I wrote another enjoyable letter. I was not about to rush back just so I could refuse induction, I told the gentlemen of my board, but when I returned, I would cheerfully do so. I had in mind that I would take sanctuary in my church in Buffalo, which had already offered it to Bruce Beyer, a friend of mine from Sunday school, and had withstood a melee as the police broke in to arrest him. A few months later, for reasons I never fathomed, my draft order was canceled, along with the orders for a few hundred others around the country who fell under a certain age category.

So it ended with a whimper. Some of my friends spent a year or two in prison, and a few of them paid an emotional price. Most of the Resistance men, whether they went to prison or not, came through that time with a greater moral stamina, I think, than, say, the typical SDS activist or even the Chicago group. At a reunion twenty years later, we learned about several hundred of us: none of us was rich or even seriously trying to be; lots of us were teachers; if we were lawyers, we were public defenders; and quite a few were working for small wages with public interest groups. One or two had committed suicide; one went mad and shot and killed his mentor, Allard Lowenstein. There was no way to total it up, and we were only in midlife anyway, but I felt proud to have been among these brothers at a time, in the Reagan years, when many others of my generation seemed to give up, sell out, or sink into despair.

In 1993, the five Spock trial defendants had a reunion in Boston, courtesy of the Massachusetts Civil Liberties Union, the first time we had all been in the same room since the trial. Besides the pleasure of seeing everyone again, the high point of the reunion was the appearance of John Wall, the prosecutor in our case. He had done a good job, I thought, and had been a tough guy. He had been a paratrooper in the Korean War, and he did not seem to like us much, particularly not the traitorous Bill Coffin, who had been in the army during World War II and in the CIA in the 1950s. But now Wall had changed, and he diffidently asked us if he could say a few words. It was our case, he said, and those of the draft resisters he prosecuted, that brought him to oppose the war, join the ACLU, and become a defense attorney. "Gentlemen, you were right, and I was wrong. You converted your prosecutor." We shook his hand.

9

A Time to Say No

MICHAEL FERBER

WE ARE GATHERED in this church today in order to do something very simple: to say No. We have come from many different places and backgrounds, and we have many different ideas about ourselves and the world, but we have come here to show that we are united to do one thing: to say No. Each of our acts of returning our draft cards is our personal No; when we put them in a single container or set fire to them from a single candle, we express the simple basis of our unity.

But what I wish to speak about now is what goes beyond our saying No, for no matter how loudly we all say it, no matter what ceremony we perform around our saying it, we will not become a community among ourselves or effective agents for changing our country if a negative is all we share. Albert Camus said that the rebel, who says No, is also one who says Yes, and that when he draws a line beyond which he will refuse to cooperate, he is affirming the values on the other side of that line. For us who come here today, what is it that we affirm, what is it to which we can say Yes?

To be honest, we have to admit that we in the Resistance still disagree about a great many things, whether we speak out about them or not. For example, here we all are in a church, and yet for some of us, it is the first time we've been inside one for years. Here, we are receiving the help of many clergymen, and yet some of us feel nothing but contempt for the organized religions that they represent. Some of us, therefore, feel a certain hypocrisy in being part of this service.

Originally published in *Liberal Context,* Fall 1967.

But it would not surprise me if many of the clergymen who are here today feel some of the same contempt for organized religion that our unreligious or antireligious brothers feel. They know better than we do the long and bloody history of evils committed in the name of religion, the long history of compromise and Erastian subservience to political power, the long history of theological hair-splitting and the burning of heretics, and they feel more deeply than we do the hypocrisy of Sunday (or Saturday) morning. Perhaps the things that made some of us leave the church are the very things that made some of them become ministers, priests, and rabbis, the very things that bring them here today. Many of them will anger their superiors or their congregations by being here, but they are here anyway.

There is a great tradition within the church and synagogue that has always struggled against the conservative and worldly forces that have always been in control. It is a radical tradition, a tradition of urgent impulse to go to the root of the religious dimension of human life. This tradition in modern times has tried to recall us to the best ways of living our lives: the way of love and compassion, the way of justice and respect, the way of facing other people as human beings and not as abstract representatives of something alien and evil. It tries to recall us to the reality behind religious ceremony and symbolism, and it will change the ceremony and symbolism when the reality changes.

As a part of this service we will break bread together. We do this, however, not because some churches happen to take communion; we do this for one of the root reasons for communion itself: that men around the world and for all time have found it good to eat together when they are sharing in something important.

The radical tradition is still alive; it is present here in this church. Those of us who disregard organized religion, I think, are making a mistake if they also disregard this tradition and its presence today. This tradition is something to which we cay say Yes.

There is another disagreement among us, or if not a disagreement, then a difference in attitude toward what we are doing today. It is a difference that cuts through the other differences, perhaps because it is a little inside each of us, and it leads to a mistake that we are liable to make no matter how else we agree or differ. In religious terms, it is to dwell too much on the possibility of the apocalypse; in political terms, it is to dwell too much on the possibility of a utopian society. We must not confuse the ceremony and symbolism of today's service with the reality that we are only a few hundred people with very little power. And we must not confuse the change inside each of us, important though that may be, with the change that we have yet to bring about in this country and the world. Neither the revelation nor the revolution is at hand, and to base our hopes and plans on them would be a tragic blunder.

Maybe all of us—leftists or liberals, reformers or revolutionaries, radical religionists or hippies—maybe all of us are apocalyptarians; I don't know. Surely something else besides a cold rational calculation of sociological options has brought us here to this church. And surely we eat in this church partly to celebrate the occasion of our noncooperation (and many of us will celebrate in a somewhat different way at parties with friends tonight). But let us not be deceived. The sun will rise tomorrow as it does every day, and when we get out of bed, the world will be in pretty much the same mess it is in today. American bombers will continue to drop incendiary bombs on the Vietnamese people, and American soldiers will continue to "pacify" their villages. The ghettos will continue to be rotten places to live in. Black and Mexican farm workers will continue to get miserable wages. America's schools will continue to cripple the minds and hearts of its pupils. And the American Selective Service System will continue to send young men out to the slaughter.

Today is not the End. Today is the Beginning.

This is the Beginning because, very simply, we have to dig in for the long haul. It is not going to be easy to change this country. To change it is going to mean struggles and anguish day in and day out for years. It will mean incredible efforts at great human cost to gain a few inches of ground. It will mean people dedicating their lives and possibly losing them for a cause we can only partly define and whose outcome we can only guess at. We must say Yes to the long struggle ahead, or this service will be a mockery.

We are brought to a third difference among us. Earlier today, Nick Egleson spoke out against the kind of resistance whose primary motivation is moralistic and personal rather than political. He is saying that we must make ourselves relevant to the social and political condition of the world and must not just take a moral posture for our own sake, even though that too is a risk.

To some extent, this argument depends on terminology rather than fact. Today we have heard our situation described in religious terms, moral terms, political terms, legal terms, and psychological terms. Very few of us are at home in all these different modes of speech, and each of us habitually uses only one of them to talk and think in. But what is happening today should make it clear that these different modes of speech all overlap one another, and they often all say the same essential things. Albert Camus, who struggled in a more serious resistance than ours, believed that politics is an extension of morality, that the truly moral man is engaged in politics as a natural outcome of his beliefs.

To return to Nick's concern, the real difference is not between the moral man and the political man, but between the man whose moral thinking leads him to political action and the man whose moral thinking leads him no farther than to his own "sinlessness." It is the difference between the man who is willing to go dirty himself in the outside world and the man who wishes to stay "clean" and "pure."

Now this kind of "sinlessness" and "purity" is arrogant pride, and I think we must say No to it. The martyr who offers himself meekly as a lamb to the altar is a fool unless he has fully taken into account the consequences of his sacrifice not only to himself but to the rest of the world. We cannot honor him for his stigmata or his purple hearts unless he has helped the rest of us while he got them.

So then what are we to do? We must look at ourselves once more. We all have an impulse to purification and martyrdom, and we should not be ashamed of it. But let us be certain that we have thought through the consequences of our action in the outside world and that these consequences are what we want to bring about. Let us make sure we are ready to work hard and long with each other in the months to come—working to make it difficult and politically dangerous for the government to prosecute us, working to help anyone and everyone to find ways of avoiding the draft, to help disrupt the workings of the draft and the armed forces until the war is over. Let us make sure we can form a community. Let us make sure we can let others depend on us.

If we can say Yes to these things and to the religious tradition that stands with us today and to the fact that today marks not the End but a Beginning and to the long hard dirty job ahead of us—if we can say Yes to all this, then let us come forward together to say No to the United States government.

Then let our Yes be the loudest No our government ever heard.

Poems

DANIEL BERRIGAN, S.J.

Night Flight to Hanoi

In a bar in Ventiane
they said to us
like Job's mockers;
thanks to your own everloving bombers
you may never see
the northern lights, Hanoi.

Then, by bat radar
we crawled that corridor
blind as bats,
a wing and a prayer.

Came in!
the big glare of a kleig eye
held us, hooked, death's open season.
We held breath, fish
baited, not landed.
Ended: the pale faces of flowers

Poems originally published in Daniel Berrigan, S.J., *Night Flight to Hanoi* (New York: Macmillan, 1968).

said suddenly, out of season
something than death other, unuttered.

Exiles we went in
safe kept, cherished by strangers.

Song

The maids sing at their scrubbing
the cooks at the stove—
shame women; such lightness of mind
ill becomes; think rather on
Death   Judgment   Heaven   Hell

the names of the bombers
that bear in their skull
your names, memorized in fire.

Children in the Shelter

Imagine; three of them.

As though survival
were a rat's word,
and a rat's end
waited there at the end

and I must have
in the century's boneyard
heft of flesh and bone in my arms

I picked up the littlest
a boy, his face
breaded with rice (his sister calmly feeding him
as we climbed down)

In my arms fathered
in a moment's grace, the messiah
of all my tears. I bore, reborn

a Hiroshima child from hell.

Alert

The sirens are loosed on Hanoi
a Stalingrad
ringed round, rained upon, fired—

the air force calls
like a whistle of game cocks at dawn
like a song of songs
like the embassy eagle
on whom the sun never sets
the celibate, the almost
    (for self will
    for lack of an equal
    killer or climber)

extinct of its kind.

Bombardment

Like those who go aground
willfully, knowing that man's
absurd estate can but be bettered
in the battering hands of the gods—
yet mourning traitorously the sun and moon
and one other face, and heat of hearth—

went under
like a blown match. The gases flare on the world's
combustible
                        flesh.

Chicago 1968:
Street-Fightin' Man

CARL OGLESBY

At St. Patrick's

AFTER MIDNIGHT TWO days later, RFK's coffin arrived in New York to lie in state at St. Patrick's. Among the small group to meet the body and sit all night in silent vigil were SDS's Tom Hayden and Chicago's Mayor Richard J. Daley. In two more months, Hayden and Daley would become the opposing field generals of the great week-long battle of Grant Park, the confrontation that was in a strong and complex sense the Tet Offensive—the political showdown—of the antiwar movement. And just as hard to read.

But this night in early June, in this huge cathedral in the Bronx, Hayden and Daley were united in mourning for the one man who might have united them in politics. Imagine Hayden walking down the aisle to find Daley on his knees, then joining him.

The word on the SDS grapevine the morning after the RFK shooting was that when Hayden heard the news of Bobby Kennedy's assassination at two or three that morning, "he immediately freaked out," first phoning all his friends and comrades to call them to arms, summoning us all at last to real

From *Ravens on the Wing: A Memoir of the Movement Against the Vietnam War,* by Carl Oglesby. Copyright © 1995 by Carl Oglesby. Published by permission of the author.

rebellion, real resistance, in real streets. There were windows to be smashed, cars to be rolled, barricades to be built and burned. Was this the spirit of '76, or what? Image: masses of impassioned antiwar citizens and equally impassioned police units rushing up and down the Village's quaint, narrow, twisting streets, each side sometimes chasing and sometimes being chased.

And the same scene was reenacted with variations in D.C., Akron, San Francisco, Ames, Milwaukee, Detroit, Baltimore, Tucson, Roanoke, and on and on, more than a hundred demonstrations varying in scale and militancy but in message always the same: get out of Vietnam, and deal with racism and poverty, or else this street shit will get worse and worse.

"Look what Black people did when King was killed," Hayden yelled at me later. "They tore the place up! Now what will we White people do when the victim is another Kennedy?"

But Hayden did not get the response he hoped for, neither from me nor any of the other dozen people he tried to wake for hitting the streets at three or four A.M. In the first place, there was the matter of getting out of bed. In the second place, Hayden's implication here was that RFK was to Whites what MLK was to Blacks. But besides me, nobody I knew in the movement believed this.

For my part, I felt closer to the Catholic in Hayden at this point. As I saw it, Hayden defined the RFK of June 1968 as a savior in an almost religious sense—a very small-scale savior, naturally, and all too human (see the Marilyn Monroe story, for example)—and perhaps less for any spiritual reason than because RFK seemed uniquely positioned to offer a political way out of the gathering national impasse, seemed to be the one person in national political life who stood a chance of bringing the troops home, reconciling dissenters and loyalists, and restoring that ineffable sense of legitimacy that American government appeared to have lost with the assassination of his brother. And note: all without alienating the right wing. But now this was all lost.

Frustrated, outraged, wild with grief, Hayden ran bellowing out into the Village night, calling people to the nearly empty streets, looking for and failing to find a riot to join.

Another Messiah crucified!

How long would the people sit still for this?

The public position of the Chicago organizing group did not change after the L.A. murder. The promise of nonviolence in Chicago was not taken back. And because movement radicals had always been so dismissive of RFK, they seemed to have no reason now to ask if his assassination had really changed anything more than one member of the cast.

This was pure posturing. Movement people did finally notice that, in fact, the RFK assassination had changed the whole strategic equation, had changed the lay of American politics deeply, perhaps irreversibly, and, from the movement's standpoint, vastly for the worse.

In the context of this unvoiced but common realization, an equally unvoiced but common new attitude began to take shape. This new attitude welcomed the prospect of violence in Chicago—not because silly people had begun to think of street fighting as something they might at long last learn to enjoy, but because, now that the messiah had once again been crucified, violence was no longer avoidable. Perhaps it was also necessary. That was a different question. Necessary or not, it could no longer be avoided. If the movement went to Chicago, it would be to fight in the streets.

But what is necessary must also be in some sense good. Right? Did Plato not teach us that? Yes, so war, being sometimes necessary, is sometimes good. Questions?

My reaction to this was to get scared. If the movement wanted to get physical, then so did the cops. If there could be a new and deeper revolution, then there could also be a new and deeper terror.

Evacuate Chicago

Sometime in July, it became clear to me that the Chicago convention demonstration planning group was not only expecting violence but was in some sense prepared to welcome it, not in any desire for it per se, but rather in a belief that the American people (or perhaps one should say, "the American viewing audience" because this was from top to bottom and on all sides supremely a media event) would viscerally turn against whichever party seemed to throw the first low blow.

SDS planners assumed there would be a clash in the streets between the people involved in any serious antiwar demonstration and the Chicago police. Mayor Daley's honor was on the line. Could he not guarantee the security of his own streets? Moreover and more important, could Daley and Chicago and Illinois and the industrial Midwest not guarantee a hospitable, old-time welcome to Hubert Humphrey? If not, then what was his basically criminal administration worth? Could the larger Chicago powers not replace him with someone who could at least pacify Chicago itself?

So a conflict was just something that was going to happen, like winter. Just as inevitably, the police would represent to the (viewing) public the prowar side of the Vietnam debate, and, to begin with, the (viewing) public would sympathize with that official and pro-war side.

But if we were correct in our analysis, the relationship between the police and the demonstration would come to parallel the relationship between the American forces in Vietnam and the Vietnamese population. In one elaboration of this thought, some antiwar activists began calling themselves "the Americong." Certainly, within the prelude to Chicago there was much conspicuous "training" in what might be called aggressive nonviolence techniques.

SDS continued to claim publicly that the Chicago demonstration would be nonviolent, while more quietly a leadership consensus developed around the propositions that violence in Chicago might be (1) unavoidable no matter what we did or did not do, and (2) good for the movement in any case. Unavoidable because the cops wanted it, Daley wanted it, the FBI wanted it, and the president of the United States wanted it.

And so did a certain part of the movement. The thought was that a little police violence against us might be just about all right. It would show the Panthers that we were for real and willing to bleed. It would win us sympathy through the media images that were bound to be transmitted to the world.

Later in July, I began to argue on pure instinct against any Chicago demonstration at all and became embroiled in a running (and quite fraternal) dispute with the Chicago organizing group around Hayden, Davis, and Dellinger—the Loop Offensive's strategic high command. I heard myself saying that the movement should be anywhere but Chicago during the Democratic Party's convention week, that Chicago in August was a trap we were setting for ourselves. "Evacuate Chicago in convention week," I heard myself suggesting when someone said, "Well, what would you do?" I would stay the hell out of Chicago. I would sit down with a room full of smart people with good hearts who had been seriously looking at the problems—racism, poverty, urban blight, a growing tendency to militarism—that our country simply had to find a way to grapple with.

My alternative, which I had begun to make explicit in the misadventure with Business International, was for SDS to be active during the convention period in many small-scale, local-level conventions—scores of them, a hundred—in an attempt to generate a more powerful national agenda than the two-party system seemed capable of. Our little conventions would show how Blacks and Whites could work together. They would show what the issues were and how they ranked and interrelated. They would define an authentic popular agenda. They would show how the big parties might manage their conventions if they really were republican and democratic, and if they really did want, instead of only pretending to want, to involve all the people seriously in the political life of our culture. They would bear out the movement's basic faith in the wisdom of the people as a whole. They would show the world a solid, first-draft concept of a new American polis. They would show how larger numbers and all kinds of people could involve themselves in political life, even in a megastate, to the enrichment of all. They would show how well ordinary people could manage the city and reinvent the nation. The implied comparison between us and the Republicans and Democrats would flatter us and thus help us build our base.

But this was not going to happen. Movement people were committed to the idea of going to Chicago in August. Chicago and the Democrats at convention time possessed a magnetism that had become irresistible to the movement.

What the Chicago organizers brought out finally was an anti-Republican protest turned against the Democrats, so we got the worst of both worlds. The Hayden-Davis-Dellinger week might conceivably have seemed appropriate and been effective if it had been staged at the Republican instead of the Democratic convention. But there was no serious discussion in SDS of the political significance of staging demonstrations against both presidential parties rather than against one or the other or none. The decision to point the movement toward Chicago in August simply appeared full-blown sometime early in 1968: we were all going to Chicago in August. That was what was going to happen. It was going to happen because Tom and Rennie were doing it. Yes, the same Tom and Rennie who, until this point, had being saying that the Vietnam War was a distraction for the movement and that our key organizing issues would always be domestic ones.

If hindsight clarifies, what the antiwar Democrats needed in the Chicago of August 1968 was a week of nonviolent, legal, mass demonstrations aimed at an informal coalition between the movement and the growing numbers of civil rights Democrats who were starting to worry about Vietnam.

Of course, even for a movement heavy like Hayden, the open espousal of such a coalition would have been political suicide within the movement, which constantly fretted about co-optation by liberals. Therefore, this purpose, no matter how important it might be, still had to be concealed. And clearly the best way to conceal a sympathy for such a coalition was to denounce it.

As I saw it, the tough talk of the Chicago Seven's first period was to hide the fact that the underlying (subliminal?) aim of the Chicago action was to begin a reconciliation between "progressive youth" and the Democratic Party, the main vehicle and cause of this reconciliation to be RFK's presidential campaign.

The Chicago Seven realized that the murder of RFK in June overthrew the whole premise of such a reconciliation. There was no longer anyone to speak for the Democrats and say, "I'm sorry about racism, I'm sorry about poverty, I'm sorry about Vietnam, and I want to be president in order to help solve these problems." Such a simple speech. But after the Ambassador Hotel, there was no one to speak it.

The result was that in June New Left tough talk suddenly lost its undercurrent of irony and its mantle of innocence. The RFK assassination arrested the new left at a rhetorical stage it badly needed to outgrow, and the first signs of the dangers of this fact appeared in the action of Chicago.

If the Chicago Seven had staged their week of protest at the Republican convention, it might have seemed appropriate and even affecting. Staged as it was, it could only shatter both sides' illusions, the Democrats' illusion that a dialog with the antiwar movement was possible and the movement's illusion that it could end the war without a fight.

But when the question put to me that summer was where would I personally be during Democratic convention week, I finally started answering that I myself planned to be in Chicago, not to run riot, certainly not to be clubbed by a zealous cop or bayoneted by a frightened soldier. I would be there to see what happened. I would be a member of a small, loose group—an affinity group, a foco, maybe five or six of us, maybe loosely bonding with a few other such groups—all of us to keep an eye out for each other, able to get news and spread it, able to float around the edges of violence and to know which alley to run up.

And the question to me then became: why go at all when you have always opposed this action and have been consistently advising others not to go?

Well, it was not exactly as if I had been advising people not to go. I was only trying to discuss what seemed an open-secret consensus that violence was more than likely. Since the demo was being billed as nonviolent, should this not be discussed? Maybe the likelihood of violence was a reason to stay away. Maybe it was only a reason to be prepared. Where, in any case, was the discussion?

Question: No, you said stay away. You said, "Evacuate Chicago, make it a ghost town." Quote, unquote.

Answer: Well, yes, but then I lost that debate, didn't I? And now the Chicago action had become inevitable, and there was nowhere else to go to make a statement about the war and the political process, a statement badly in need of being made.

So I went to Chicago backward, in a sense, and hunched over, bitching and cursing, internally opposing my every step, but nevertheless putting one foot in front of the other.

At the Bandshell

It was mid-afternoon of the third day of the convention, and the cops had begun openly jeering us. Tension was high.

A rally was in progress at the bandshell, a few minutes' walk from the main campground of the protesters, Grant Park in front of the Hilton Hotel. I was in Grant Park with my affinity group when a guy came by and said that Dave Dellinger was paging me and I should go to the stagedoor at the bandshell.

So some friends and I went over to see what was up. Because I had been critical of all this, I had not been involved in any part of the program. But now Dellinger, looking frazzled, told me they needed speakers to fill some time before some other speakers showed up, so would I please do a turn. Well, okay, fine. Two speakers later, I stepped up to the mike.

The scene before me was a battleground before the battle. The crowd was crawling with anxious energy. Almost everyone was standing. I could see that people were dividing their attention restlessly between me in front of them and the line of police encircling them behind.

I had just started my talk when I saw maybe a hundred cops leave the larger circle and collect behind the crowd off to my right. I saw a lot of SDS people looking over their shoulders, a lot of drawn faces. I kept trying to make a speech about what the war was doing to America, but when you were right face-to-face with a clear and present instance of what it was doing, it was hard to find a tone that seemed appropriate short of just yelling my head off. But the energy of the crowd was too weird and I couldn't find the right words.

Then, apparently at some command—or was it something I said?—the hundred cops formed into a spearhead-shaped phalanx formation and marched straight into the crowd, their line of march bristling on both sides with riot sticks. People screamed and tried to pull back, but their chairs and benches got in the way, and they stumbled horribly over each other. Many in the line of the attack were trapped. I saw a young couple from Columbus fall right at the feet of two cops, both of whom took serious cracks at the woman's ribs and head as her husband struggled to protect her and pull her back from them.

Standing helplessly at the mike, I could only scream in impotent rage, "Look at this! Look at this!" What can you say? What can you ask the crowd to do?

But trust the people. This crowd knew how and when to put up a powerful, full-throated chant, and this chant became the slogan under which this entire protest might have been organized: "The whole world is watching!" And the crowd began to chant this even though at this particular place and time, the world was not watching at all, not any of it, because there were no electronic media at the bandshell then. For whatever reason, none.

I turned to Dellinger and said, "We've got to help these people get out of here." He agreed and got on the system and beautifully organized a crowd retreat to Grant Park. My affinity group and I left the bandshell area to find that the bridge we had come over on was now barricaded by National Guard barbed wire. But the third bridge north was still open, and the crowd coming over from the bandshell soon found it.

The police were at that point still trying to block Michigan Avenue in front of the Hilton, but fate intervened with the unscheduled arrival of a big farm wagon pulled by mules, part of a civil rights demonstration organized in the South and approved by the city long before this date. The police opened the barricade for the mule team and then could not close it again as the crowd spontaneously poured through behind the wagon.

That night, the electonic media and thus the whole world were watching again as the angriest physical confrontations between protesters and police took place in front of the Hilton and in the streets around it, lit intermittently by the eerie blue light of the TV crews and with a lot of tear gas clouding the air.

The Media Balance

Our feeling that the police assault on us must have played well for us in Peoria was all the stronger because the Soviet tanks had just rolled into Prague. We began calling Daley's city "Chiprago" to make the point.

But that reading did not altogether work out. What really happened was more complex.

First, there was a strong radicalizing of the media workers who were on the scene. Too many times did they find themselves seemingly targeted by the police. They could not help being affected by it. They were much clearer as to their own innocence than they had ever been as to ours, so they finally began to ask why the cops were doing these things to them. In the great sixties term, many media people were in this way "radicalized" at Chicago and began to see American politics in a new and more critical light. So far so good.

But second, this radicalizing process turned out not to work nearly so well over TV as in the street. Or perhaps it was just (1) that the event's actual power lay in its dramatic presence, a function of its scale, and (2) that such an event can lose its radicalizing power when it is mediated, i.e., when its power is reduced to the scale of the medium that contains it. In other words, maybe you had to be there.

Thus, what motivated so many media people in Chicago to question their basic assumptions about power in America was what they experienced in Chicago, not necessarily what they reported or what got shown. And what they did report, i.e., the story of "the police riot," struck much of Middle America as the story of fathers finally getting down to business with some very bratty kids. Should have been done it a long time ago.

So, yes, the whole world was watching, but as usual it was only seeing what it expected to see.

At Maggie's Farm

I moved in thickening confusion through the days after the August battle of Chicago.

First, at a place we called Maggie's Farm, a house in the country in Indiana not too far from Chicago, the SDS National Interim Committee (NIC) held a special meeting to consider the question of movement strategy in view of the recent events.

The strategy as of June 1 had been implicitly premised on the coming ascendancy of antiwar liberals behind Bobby Kennedy, but now this was not to be. Humphrey seemed committed to the war. Nixon was worse than Johnson. How to deal with this?

So a group of fifty or sixty antiwar activists had met at Maggie's Farm to try to deal with the situation.

The troubled mood quickened tempers. I came out of a reverie to hear a bristling, confrontative Mike Klonsky, one of the three SDS national secretaries, barking out, "What is Oglesby trying to prove with this company called Business International? A company with a name like that has got to be a CIA front. And even if it's not, it's still a voice for the big bourgeoisie. I thought Oglesby was against these guys. I thought he was with us in the fight against imperialism. Now here he comes wanting us to have programs with something called Business International and a guy named Eldridge Haynes. What about it, Carl? Who is this guy Haynes? What's going on here?"

I fumbled for an answer. I liked Klonsky but found him oddly threatening. He was a spare, broad-shouldered, rugged man of twenty-five or so with an angular face and a great hooked nose, close-shaven, brownish-blond hair cut workingman short. I knew from our games of touch football that he was an athlete. He came from a family of American Communist Party labor organizers involved in the West Coast dock unions.

Hayden, for his own reasons, said to me, "Klonsky is going around saying that you are the most dangerous man in the movement." Dangerous, as it developed, because of my extreme moderation and the fact that I could persuade unformed minds that my bad ideas were okay.

What could I say to this man? Especially about the Business International connection?

The phone rang and a guy at the side of the room, Rick Dodge, a grad student at Dartmouth, picked it up. We all waited a moment. Then Rick said, "Just a sec," and held the phone out to me. "Who is it?" I said, a little worried it might be some family thing. "Who's calling, please?" Rick asked, then looked back to me and said, "Eldridge."

My first thought was that Rick had to be jiving me. I could not believe such a coincidence—to be arguing in this group about Haynes, and then at that very moment he calls. A little titter fluttered around the room. I had the impression that a few people somewhat enjoyed my sudden predicament. And so chummy! "Eldridge," yet!

I crawled unenthusiastically over people's legs to get to the phone at the side of the room. Everybody was going to listen, so I didn't even try to talk in a low voice.

"Hello?" I said. "Hello, Eldridge?"

"Hey, Brother Carl, my main man, how you doin'?"

The voice was deep, a little husky, the words spoken with a ghetto lilt. This was not Eldridge Haynes, not at all. This was Eldridge Cleaver, the leader of the Black Panther Party. Instead of the Whitest man in the world, it was the Blackest!

Cleaver was calling to say that he was running a write-in presidential campaign in several states as the candidate of the Peace and Freedom Party. "I need somebody to do the vice president thing, you dig?" he said. "And it ought to be a White boy." He could think of a thousand reasons why this White boy should be me, but the main one was that everybody else on his list had turned him down.

I was naturally startled and begged an hour in which to discuss this new thing with my cohorts. "Well," Cleaver said, "if you've got to fuck off about it, go ahead. But listen, I need this."

My inclination was to say yes right away. I liked Cleaver, and he was in trouble and so were the Panthers. It would be a good gesture for SDS to make. By Black consensus, the Panthers and Cleaver had emerged as the successor to the Student Nonviolent Coordinating Committee (SNCC) and Stokely Charmichael, who himself became a Panther. But I had been elected to SDS national office on a group-discipline program, so now I had to be disciplined by the SDS executive group, the National Interim Committee. The NIC would have to decide this.

Now a really odd debate got going. I say odd because it bore at the same time, and through the sheer coincidence of this shared name of "Eldridge" (rather an odd name, too), on my relationships both to Haynes and Cleaver, both to Business International and the Black Panthers. In the debate of the two Eldridges, the Maggie's Farm group tried to figure out what each of these relationships meant in itself, what they meant occurring together, and how SDS must act in a world where such things go on.

I did not win this debate in terms of either Eldridge. With respect to Business International, I didn't even try to. An SDS link-up with Business

International could only have begun to make political sense in the context of an RFK presidential campaign. And as to Eldridge Cleaver's request, the SDS leadership was at that point more than normally disdainful of "movement personalities" and critical of the whole political mindset underlying the Cleaver campaign.

So I was not to do it. Klonsky was the one who stated the main arguments against it and prevailed in the debate. My only little consolation was that Klonsky was also the one who had to explain this all to Cleaver.

Cleaver's entrance made it easier for me to defend my relationship with Haynes. But I knew at the end of this two-day nonstop session that most people at the NIC level were listening to Klonsky about me and Business International. I could see that I was going to get away less and less as somebody who stood above movement politics and just spoke truth to power. I would more and more have to involve myself in the difficult game of internal politics—at least, if I wanted to keep up my relationship with SDS. I was being challenged. The basic complaint was that I was too moderate, that I should learn to moderate my moderation.

East Lansing

A few weeks after Maggie's Farm, I was in East Lansing a few blocks from the Michigan State campus. I was there to help the local SDS chapter deal with the appearance on campus of several pro-war politicians at a big awards ceremony. Certain fraternities and the football team had organized a peace-keeping committee to keep the radicals beyond a certain line, outside the line of sight of the great men. There was a lot of surging back and forth in the course of the evening, often as physical as a football scrimmage and with a lot of vigorous chanting.

Then somewhere around ten P.M. Billy Ayers, the campus traveler for this area in Michigan and northern Ohio, found me at the side of the main crowd of seven or eight hundred demonstrators. He pointed out a certain TV camera team taking pictures of the crowd, one guy with a video camera on his shoulder and another with a battery pack and a set of lights. Other news stations had come and gone, but these two had kept busy all night. They liked to work us from the inside, getting right up into people's faces.

Billy Ayers was at this point a close family friend from Ann Arbor. He would be a Weatherman within a year, but now he was still full-of-fun, warm-hearted, handsome Billy who gave my kids piggyback rides.

"The thing about these two guys," said Billy, "is that they routinely turn their tapes over to the Red Squad. We happen to know this through a contact in local TV. They are media people, but they are also doubling for the pig."

So I asked him what was to be done. He asked me what did I think. I thought of what I had heard about my lack of a taste for struggle. It was true. I hated to see politics get physical. I said to Billy, "I guess we have to take their toys away." I could see right away that he agreed.

So Billy and Diana and Terry and I assembled a very simple little plan. The three others would distract the spy-cameraman and his assistant, then I would step in and give the camera a push so that it would fall to the pavement and get smashed up.

This all pretty much happened, went pretty much the way we had wanted. One little detail, unforeseen in the scripting and rehearsal, emerged in the act. When I grabbed the camera, the guy yelled, "What!" and turned toward me, staring straight into my eyes. I had anticipated this to the extent of wrapping Diana's red bandanna around my face as a mask. But I had not foreseen the fear in this guy's eyes, or his courage, strength and quickness. He almost got back under his camera, but it was too heavy and my leverage was too good. It fell with a great crunching smash, bits of it flying everywhere.

The bystanders absorbed all this in a split second and without the least hesitation instantly opened up a passageway out for me, Billy, Diana, and Terry, then closed behind us to block any attempt at pursuit. We were swallowed up in the great sea of the people.

But where did this leave me? At best, I might have shown to someone who should not have asked that I could be a street-fightin' man, sort of, if I really wanted to, maybe. That I could be less immoderately moderate, maybe. That I could dare to struggle and dare to win, maybe.

And I had to wonder: was this really what everything was coming down to at last? Being tough and nasty enough to fight in the streets?

12

From the Suburbs to Saigon

JEFF JONES

I MET KIM PHUC on a steamy Saigon summer afternoon in 1986. It was during my second trip to Southeast Asia and my first to Vietnam. Both times, I had gone as part of a delegation of peace activists. In a quiet voice, she told us about her life.

Everyone over the age of thirty—and many younger—know the photo of Kim Phuc, taken when she was a young child, running naked, sobbing, down a Vietnamese road, her clothes and skin burned from a napalm attack. The picture won a Pulitzer Prize and became an icon of Vietnam War photo journalism. When we met Kim Phuc in 1986, she was in her twenties. Except for her beautiful, sad face, her body had been badly burned. "I want to be a scientist," she told us. But her skin cracks when the weather changes, and her pain is constant. She couldn't concentrate on her studies.

Once she had hope. The Axel Springer publishing company had brought her to West Germany for skin grafts. But the project—publicity stunt, really—was canceled after the Hitler diary fiasco. Springer had published what was purported to be the Nazi leader's writings, only to have it exposed as a forgery. Suddenly worried about money, Springer sent Kim Phuc home in mid-treatment. I looked into her eyes as we talked that afternoon and saw the scars on the hands and arms of an innocent child whose torment hadn't ended with the war.

I had opposed that war and had evolved from a peaceful demonstrator to an antigovernment radical. Some of my protests were effective, some not. Some were controversial, some were illegal. As a result of crossing state lines to incite a riot—so the indictment said—I had faced imprisonment.

Rather than submit to a costly and time-consuming trial when there was anti-war work to be done, I went underground in 1970 and remained a fugitive for eleven years.

As I sat there with Kim Phuc in Ho Chi Minh City Hall, the thought crossed my mind: I regret nothing I ever did to oppose the war. My only regret was that I hadn't done more.

The corner of California's San Fernando Valley where I lived in 1964 was still on the margins of suburbia. Sylmar, originally a desert, then a vast olive orchard, had been discovered by developers whose inexorable march across the Los Angeles Basin was busily turning the small town into another stereotypical suburb. My family moved to Sylmar from Van Nuys to be near The Farm, an intentional community of Quakers created by four couples after World War II. Their jointly owned acreage had been our Sunday destination for years. As kids, we played in the Farm's fields and gullies and found a community committed to tolerance and nonviolence.

The Farm men had been conscientious objectors, opposed to killing and to war, so during World War II they had either served jail time or were assigned to Civilian Public Service (CPS) camps. Their unwillingness to take human life was shared by my father, who had made his own difficult decision of conscience to become an objector. He was sent to a CPS camp on the eastern flanks of California's Sierra Nevada.

The larger Quaker community of Los Angeles, especially through the programs for teens created by the American Friends Service Committee (AFSC) had become the center of my intellectual life. At AFSC meetings we heard firsthand reports of the 1963 civil rights march on Washington, discussed U.S. foreign policy and wrote letters to our congressional representatives. We talked of our dislike for one particular California Quaker, Richard Nixon, who failed to live up to the values we were learning, although the committed elders among us continued to search for "that spark of good in every one," which Quaker belief emphasizes.

The Farm Meeting and the AFSC were also my political and moral center. They offered a reservoir of confidence as I set out on a teenage journey of discovery. I needed it, with the beginning of direct U.S. military involvement in Vietnam, the upheaval of the southern civil rights struggle, the lingering shadow of John F. Kennedy's assassination, and the Watts riots stalking my own upcoming decision: would I also register for the draft as a conscientious objector?

I did, in fact, seek and receive CO status when I turned eighteen in 1965.

But I gave it up later as my view of the war and U.S. policy—and nonviolence—radicalized, and I decided to support the Vietnamese's right to defend themselves. Despite being classified 1-A, however, I was never drafted because I had been arrested numerous times in antiwar demonstrations: it turned out that a person under the jurisdiction of a court could not be inducted. During the years of the Vietnam lottery, I was underground. The war was long over and the draft abolished by the time I was arrested in 1981.

I began thinking seriously about the war one fall day in 1964 when I went to hear Henry Cabot Lodge, Jr. At the time, he was the U.S. ambassador to South Vietnam. Lodge was the first Vietnam War propagandist I had heard. Lacking ideological beliefs to filter his comments, I seriously considered his talk of the need to stop communist infiltration and how the strategic hamlet program would save the peasants of Vietnam. The rhetorical "light at the end of the tunnel" shone brightly in those early days of the war. Lodge, President Lyndon B. Johnson, and others in the administration spoke so glibly of this important but inconsequential war. Indeed, LBJ ran in 1964 as a peace candidate. With my father, I carried his petitions. Johnson's postelection escalation was the betrayal that marks the moment I learned never to trust a politician—before I had ever cast a vote.

Still, I considered Lodge's arguments for a time. But my views soon changed. I arrived at Antioch College in September 1965. The town of Yellow Springs, Ohio, was more southern than northern. Students there had been active in the civil rights movement. The previous year, a student sit-in had closed the main state highway to protest a local barber who refused to cut Black students' hair.

On October 15, 1965, I went to an antiwar protest in Cincinnati, part of the First International Days of Protest Against the Vietnam War. Participating in that demonstration in front of the federal building changed my life. Our numbers were small—no more than forty—and the counterdemonstration was threatening. But taking a stand against a war I had grown to oppose was liberating. From that moment until April 30, 1975, the day the war officially ended, fighting the government became my main concern.

Although I didn't drop out of college for another year and a half, that first demonstration led to the end of my undergraduate career. Antioch became a place to organize. In April 1967, I left to become New York City regional coordinator for Students for a Democratic Society (SDS). This was SDS's largest region, with twenty-three chapters.

Johnson was escalating the war, buying General William Westmoreland's contention that victory could be achieved with one hundred thousand more troops. Our opposition was escalating, too. In those days in New York City, our peace demonstrations were joined by a militant group that carried the flag of the National Liberation Front (NLF) of South Vietnam. By utilizing genocide—like carpet bombing, napalm, antipersonnel weapons and massive defoliation, Johnson, Westmoreland, and Secretary of Defense Robert McNamara had led us to this: looking for answers to their lies, we realized not only that the United States was wrong in Vietnam, but that the Vietnamese were right and deserved to win. Our government wasn't in Vietnam on humanitarian grounds—as Lodge had maintained three years earlier at UCLA—but to protect economic interests half a world away.

In October 1967, I helped organize the SDS contingent at the Pentagon demonstration, the most important antiwar protest in which I participated. SDS was evolving an anti-imperialist outlook on U.S. foreign policy. As the excuses for U.S. participation in the war continued to lose credibility, we came to see it as part of a larger global conflict. We believed the United States was wrong—not only to have intervened in Vietnam's civil war, but to have created the conditions for that war by preventing the implementation of the 1954 Geneva Peace Accords and forcing the division of the country after Ho Chi Minh was elected president.

With liberation movements sweeping the Third World, and student and worker protests spreading in industrial countries, SDS was beginning to see itself as part of the world's new revolutionary movement. As the Pentagon demonstration drew near, we debated competing proposals. A militant New York City faction wanted us to break away from the main march and, emulating Japanese student protests, move into the streets of downtown Washington. We decided, however, to remain as an anti-imperialist contingent in the larger march. And so we found ourselves with tens of thousands of others face-to-face with troops of the Eighty-second Airborne, surrounding the U.S. military's world headquarters.

The standoff lasted for more than twenty-four hours. The Youth International Party attempted to levitate the building, while, as the long night wore on, soldiers and police arrested demonstrators at the confrontation line. In a day of dramatic moments, one moment that stands out for me was the sight of a group of men standing on top of the building, looking out at the protest. I was sure I recognized Secretary of Defense Robert McNamara. Years later, it was reported that McNamara did indeed survey the protest. "We've lost," he is reported to have commented. Imagine the lives that would have been saved if that insight, which turned out to be true, had been translated into policy.

The next month, November 1967, I joined an SDS delegation invited by the North Vietnamese Student Union to visit Hanoi. It had been twenty-three months since the first delegation of U.S. peace activists—Tom Hayden, Herbert Apthecker, and Staughton Lynd—went to the enemy capital for a firsthand look. Since that time, only a few such trips had been made.

Four of us left New York, flying via Paris to Phnom Penh. In the Cambodian capital, we learned that our trip to Hanoi had been canceled. A U.S. bombing escalation made it impossible to guarantee our safety. Instead, we spent a week in Cambodia, meeting with representatives of the North Vietnamese and the NLF, and traveling to visit the incredible jungle temples of Angkor Wat. Coming home, I landed at Los Angeles International Airport to read in the *Los Angeles Times* that we had been turned back as a propaganda stunt to bolster North Vietnamese propaganda about U.S. bombing of civilian targets. At the time, Johnson and McNamara denied that Hanoi was being attacked. Later, the secret bombings of North Vietnam—Operation Rolling Thunder—were confirmed in the *Pentagon Papers*.

In Cambodia, the North Vietnamese representatives were affable, regretting that we had come such a long way only to be turned back. The NLF representative was more stern. He was a professor whose wife had been tortured to death by the French during the First Indochina War. He let us read some letters written by young American troops who had recently been killed at the battle remembered as Hamburger Hill. He told us that the night before our visit, more than thirty-four regional and district capitals had been attacked by NLF troops in a coordinated military campaign.

Twelve weeks later, any thought that the United States could militarily defeat the Vietnamese liberation army ended with the Tet Offensive. Those November attacks were part of Vietnamese General Giap's plan to spread U.S. and South Vietnamese troops thin across the country. Compounding the problem for the United States, Johnson and Westmoreland had blundered into a standoff at Khe Sanh, a Marine base of limited strategic but critical symbolic importance near the Demilitarized Zone. "We don't want no Din Bin Foos," Johnson said. The general assured the president he would avoid the French mistake at Dien Bien Phu, the remote northern Vietnamese valley where they were forced to surrender after weeks of a debilitating siege. Instead of repeating that scenario, however, the Vietnamese military seduced Westmoreland into a political trap. While he concentrated his resources and prestige, the NLF launched its offensive, attacking targets across Vietnam that included the U.S. embassy in Saigon and the Citadel in Hue, the country's historic capital.

Some military historians still argue that the Tet Offensive was a defeat for the NLF. Despite the Front's military losses, however, the real significance of Tet was the political impact it had on American public opinion. After all the GI deaths, all the ordnance fired and bombs dropped, and all the money that had been spent, the promised U.S. victory was more elusive than ever.

And yet the war continued for another seven years.

Throughout the next decade, I remained part of the antiwar movement. Most of that time, it seemed that no matter what we did, no matter how many people we mobilized, LBJ and then Nixon only escalated and intensified the war. I worked with the Dayton Area Coordinating Committee to End the War and joined Students for a Democratic Society. I protested in Cincinnati, Columbus, and Indianapolis. I marched in Washington, D.C. and New York City. I became a radical and then a revolutionary. Our inability to affect a policy change through legal, peaceful means eventually forced me outside the system. After participating in scores of teach-ins, marches, sit-ins, and picket lines, after attending hundreds of meetings and issuing thousands of leaflets, I joined with like-minded activists driven to break the law in order to end an illegal war.

In the fall of 1969, the Weatherman faction of SDS (the name came from a line in Bob Dylan's song "Subterranean Homesick Blues") planned a Bring the War Home demonstration in Chicago. It was timed to coincide with the beginning of the Chicago Conspiracy Trial, the court case against the organizers of the antiwar demonstrations during the Democratic National Convention the previous summer. There I had avoided arrest, outrunning one cop in a deserted downtown parking lot and escaping down a Lincoln Park ally as another policeman jumped from his squad car firing his gun. Fourteen months later, we were back, about eight hundred of us, many wearing motorcycle and football helmets. On October 8, the first anniversary of the death of Argentine revolutionary Che Guevara in Bolivia, and the first night of the four-day protest that became known as the "Days of Rage," I announced in Lincoln Park that our goal was to march to the home of Judge Julius Hoffman, who was presiding in the conspiracy trial. We never made it. As we took to the streets, glass began breaking all around. The police raced to stop us. Attempting to run by them, I was grabbed, maced, and hauled off to jail. Before the confrontation was over, more than six hundred of us had been arrested. Some demonstrators were badly beaten, and several were wounded by police gunshots.

To the extent that we believed thousands of other alienated young people would join an antigovernment revolt, we were wrong. But as a marker of how alienated we had become, the Days of Rage were noticed. Later, I was part of an organization—the Weather Underground—that targeted the symbols and the property of those who were bombing Vietnam. Angry and appalled by a government that had betrayed its alleged values, we made mistakes. But militantly opposing the war wasn't one of them.

Vietnam Comes to Lexington: Memorial Day 1971

EUGENIA KALEDIN

BIRTHPLACE OF AMERICAN LIBERTY proclaims a neat circle of golden letters under the flag waving perpetually over the Battle Green of Lexington, Massachusetts. This small triangle of grass committed to helping visitors think about the American Revolution may come as close to being sacred as any piece of ground in America. The statue of the minuteman at one end—so clearly an ordinary citizen, a farmer, not a professional soldier—suggests the responsibility of all of us for what our government does; the white steepled clapboard church at the other reminds people that morality and religion defined New England from the beginning.

If historians remain unsure about who shot the first round on the Green in 1775, few question the fierce sense of injustice that propelled colonists to rebel against the Crown. If in the 1770s, as in the 1970s, most people wanted to respect law and order as part of a new country's obligation to civic tranquillity, moral outrage nevertheless propelled many good citizens into breaking their king's laws. When Bostonians dumped 342 chests of tea into Boston Harbor in 1776, when local abolitionists hid fugitive slaves in the 1850s, New Englanders were proud to be breaking man's laws for what they saw as higher law. And when in 1971, in a gesture of solidarity with the Vietnam Veterans Against the War (VVAW), many local citizens chose to break a town ordinance forbidding anyone to sleep on the sacred Green, the arrest that followed became the largest arrest in Massachusetts' history.

At the time the *Boston Globe* reported that when the riot police moved onto the historic spot at three A.M., 500 people were loaded onto buses headed for the snowplow barn. The official police record later published the number as 410 (juveniles were protected). Sharp-eyed citizens who counted names printed in the local paper got 458. When the court docket was finally brought out for a 1993 interview with the presiding judge, the official number counted, including those who paid bail, was 402. Yet it was still the largest mass arrest recorded in this feisty commonwealth of dissenters!

In terms of the history of protest in the Bay State the future should note the significance of the Lexington arrest alongside the Boston Tea Party and Shay's Rebellion, especially because it was a community gesture of civil disobedience, not of violence. If the police had arrested the crowd at ten P.M., the moment the ordinance became effective, twice as many people would have gone to jail. But no place in town could have held so many dissenters. The protest was entirely peaceable. No shots were fired; no menacing gestures were necessary. The police treated their law-breaking neighbors with respect. Indeed, the largest local repercussion was political; at the next election, the people of Lexington voted in great numbers to turn out of office the powerful selectman most responsible for the arrest.

Yet such arrests in the 1970s were never just local. The people put in jail believed that such massive protests taking place all over America would help to end the war. By bringing their dissent to Lexington, the Vietnam Veterans Against the War reminded us of the town's strong heritage of protest. The veterans had all agreed that if they were arrested, they would give their birth date as April 19, 1775.

Ostensibly, the arrests were made because no one, not even the Girl Scouts, had ever been allowed to sleep on the Green. The selectmen had voted three to two that the VVAW could not be given special permission to spend the night on the Battle Green as part of their protest march from one historic site to another, dramatizing their turn against the Vietnam War. Earlier, a telephone campaign had alerted politically active citizens to what might happen, and local radio stations announced an impending confrontation. All sorts of people, not just antiwar activists, came from all over the Boston area to show support for the veterans and disapproval of the inhospitality of the selectmen. In an interview in the 1990s, the police chief said there were probably more than one thousand people on the Green at the height of the evening. Although the arrest turned out to be the largest in Massachusetts history, the power of the moment has been ignored in town records. Even in the 1990s, a few people still prefer not to talk about what happened. The need to reinforce the myth of a harmonious community seems greater than the need to look honestly at the tensions that so often characterize our past. If a group of local citizens had not begun to make an oral history of survivors the entire historical moment might have disappeared. Was this also happening in other parts of America? Is our social fabric so weak that it will tear if we look squarely at recent controversies? What can we do as a civilization to preserve a vaunted tradition of dissent if people do not want to examine the most painful moments? What records shall we keep in an era of excess information? What questions do we want our children to ask of us? How shall they judge future moments when good citizens might again feel compelled to break the law?

On April 19 every year in Lexington, men dressed in authentic minutemen costumes reenact the battle that took place on the Green in 1775. Local citizens are justly proud of that glorious morning when a few dissidents in homespun organized against the militia that had come three thousand miles to quell their demand for self-determination. Most of the townspeople in the 1970s understood well why the VVAW had chosen special historic sites to protest their government's failure to represent them. It was easy to identify these Vietnam veterans' hard-wrought patriotism with the original minutemen's; they too felt betrayed by their political spokesmen. That most of the people in that vast crowd in 1971 were there to support the veterans' freedom of speech and assembly, to honor their right to bear witness against the government for which they had put their lives on the line, seemed clear. Only the twentieth-century town fathers failed to recognize this commitment to constitutional rights. Instead, they made the sacredness of the Green the main issue; they would not allow themselves to look beyond the park ordinance to the connection with the conflict that had been shattering the whole country for so many years. Although the town archives would produce photographs of haying on the Green and picnics and baseball games on the same spot, the idea of its sacredness dominated the thinking of the selectmen: "Hallowed ground," they said. The town report for 1971 notes under "Year in Headlines": "Veterans and Supporters Defy Bivouac Injunction: 410 Arrested." Lexington's proud heritage, the report goes on to suggest, was "blurred by those who forgot that the Battle Green is not only a historic shrine but it is also the cemetery of the honored dead of April 19, 1775." Thousands of visitors walk all over this Green every year; few realize that the Revolutionary volunteers are actually buried under the grass. A stone commemorating the lost lives of the brave men willing to defend their rights at a minute's notice stands apart from the Green. Most people in 1971 had no idea that the hallowed ground they were trespassing on did *not* belong to all the American people or that the selectmen had the power to restrict its use to "a quiet and orderly behavior in keeping with a respectful regard and reverence for the memory of the patriotic service there so nobly rendered." Ironically, the behavior of the vast crowd on the Green was entirely orderly and respectful. When the charges were drawn up for their arrest, the charge of "disorderly conduct" had to be dropped. By dredging up a town ordinance to deny this living group of patriots the right to sleep on the Green, the selectmen called forth two hundred years of revolutionary ghosts to be arrested at their side. We all should have given our birth date as April 19, 1775.

Many people, perhaps most of those who came from nearby towns, went home before midnight because the threatened confrontation seemed so unlikely. People could not believe that the selectmen would actually arrest veterans in wheelchairs or uniformed soldiers with obvious disabilities. Indeed, the police did not want to arrest them. They seemed embarrassed by what was happening. One man in a wheelchair had to argue with them to take him to the jail in the snowplow barn. Perhaps it is this terrible embarrasssment that endures. No formal apology was ever offered the vets. Not only did the town of Lexington not welcome young men who had offered their lives in Vietnam for their country's ideals, it also treated them like criminals, asking them to walk in single file through the town and finally arresting them: putting the sanctity of property, the hallowed Green, before the sanctity of the moral need to bear witness against what they saw as an unjust war.

After the arrest, letters poured into the *Lexington Minuteman* for three weeks. The majority by far were against the selectmen's decision, and many were by people who had never before written a public letter—people who were not involved in politics, but good citizens who were outraged by the failure of democratic manners in their hometown. Perhaps a sense of fairness must always be the strongest motivation in a working democracy. Those individuals arrested understood that men who had sacrificed so much for their country deserved attention. To shift allegiance in the middle of a war took great courage; to throw away their medals, as many of these vets had, required amazing valor. No actions ordinary people could offer on the veterans' behalf seemed adequate to compensate for their sacrifices. Did similar demonstrations take place on a local level in other American cities and towns? After they watched nightly television newsreels about Vietnam, how were other Americans finding ways to express their sense of national betrayal? What records remain of the less dramatic protests? As more and more people came to realize that our own young men were being damaged by what they were required to do in Vietnam, Americans lost their sense of patriotism.

Although the editor of the local newspaper did not support the veterans' petition to sleep on the Green that night, she took her responsibility to report the event seriously, and the paper's publisher supported her. Not only did they publish a complete list of all the people arrested, thereby furnishing researchers with a public record that might otherwise be gone, but in the weeks that followed, the paper also printed every single letter about the arrest. There were so many the first week that a supplement had to be added to contain all the opinions. The publisher's sense of democratic responsibility, however, was greater than his concern for advertising profits. Although it is fashionable to malign the media, we need to be aware of how important the press remains in providing records that may be deleted in official documents. If the town had reason to be ashamed of its selectmen, it had reason to be proud of its newspaper.

"When people believe in something as strongly as the people of Lexington," the editor of the *Minuteman* wrote, "their belief must be appraised. But when these beliefs extend beyond the law then they must be reexamined." One conciliatory spirit wrote: "Who knows what you or I would have done?" But most of the letters were irate. An eloquent retired U.S. Air Force colonel protested: "The grass on the Lexington Green can be replaced; the lives of those who must now die cannot be replaced." One town mother summarized her life: "I have lived here seven years, teach Sunday school, am a Brownie leader, have only one previous traffic violation in thirty-five years. . . . I don't think the Selectmen are trying to teach me not to sit on the Green at night," she concluded, "I think they want to inhibit my right to express dissenting views."

"When the Lexington Commons ceases to serve as a meeting ground for peaceful political protest, the liberties of all citizens are at stake," one man asserted. A family writing together articulated what many people were thinking: "Has our town become a showplace for tourists only . . . blindly echoing the words of fallen patriots only to ignore the needs and purposes of their contemporary counterparts?" A few letters congratulated the selectmen on their stand for law and order. A "native and life long resident" resented the extra cost for police and buses. Of the people born in Lexington, it might be said that they felt especially proprietary about the town Green. They did not appreciate the exhilarating sense the outsiders had that the Green belonged to them too, that for one night, "the Battle Green had come alive again." Simply by being challenged, the "Birthplace of American Liberty" had reinforced all its symbolic power.

Changes in the town since the 1950s had made the older natives uncomfortable. Post–World War II building developments turned Lexington from a farm community to a commuter suburb. Near Harvard and MIT and the Route 128 technology industries, the town started to house individuals who cared as much about the world as they cared about the birthplace of American liberty. The town meeting government now had to address issues such as integrating the schools and setting aside money for conservation. Although we have no occupational breakdown of the people arrested on Memorial Day 1971, it would be safe to conclude that almost all of them were "new" people who arrived after the Second World War, changing Lexington from a small town where everyone knew everyone else to a community that would probably house more Nobel Prize winners than any other place in America. In the 1990s, the town could also boast that the secretary of the U.S. Air Force and the head of the CIA. had both lived there. Scholars of world reknown—Noam Chomsky, Henry Lewis Gates, and John Rawls—continue to live in Lexington. But the two dry goods shops, the three hardware stores, the Woolworth's, and the Rexall store that defined the town center until the 1970s are gone. In some peculiar way, the Vietnam veterans' appearance in Lexington exacerbated all the new social conflicts as well as the political differences. Perhaps such conflicts lurk beneath the surface in many places in America, where so many different traditions and attitudes are forced to live side by side. A few people were honestly afraid that holiday weekend. If we look at newsreels of the rest of America during this period, reminding ourselves of the Chicago Democratic Party Convention, the march on the Pentagon, and the murders at Kent and Jackson State, such fears might well have been justified. Yet the Lexington police were as restrained and polite as the crowd was. The great arrest seemed to bring into the open a vast sympathy for the veterans. Although the atmosphere on the Green was often jolly, the people involved were far from indifferent to the deeper meaning of law and order.

For almost twenty-four hours the people arrested experienced a rare and satisfying sense of being part of a moral community of concern. Even the ongoing squabble between Lexington and Concord about where the Revolution actually began was shelved. The people of Concord, no longer rivals, came to the jail with coffee and doughnuts for the Lexington prisoners, and they handed out five-dollar bills to the vets to help pay their fines. Proud of their own town's record of hospitality the previous night in allowing the VVAW to camp out on the nationally owned Old North Bridge, they also helped drive all the criminals home after the massive trial.

Among the later letters in the local paper was one signed by a group of distinguished professionals requesting money to publish a page of apology in the *Boston Globe.* They wanted especially to praise the veterans: "These men, having risked their lives in a far-off war, now return to raise grave moral issues. It is both ironic and tragic that they should find themselves arrested on the very spot where American liberty was born." Perhaps more important were the many letters urging everyday readers to remember that "the prejudiced persons" who caused the arrest could be voted out of office when the town went to the polls the following spring. Almost immediately, an active group of local newcomers enlisted an MIT professor with impeccable credentials to run for selectman against the incumbent. The professor won easily.

Several weeks later, a movement arose to try to get all the criminal records expunged, although many of those arrested did not want pardons. They were as proud of their one night in jail as Henry David Thoreau had been when he refused to pay taxes to extend slavery through the Mexican War. The Lexington library owns an elegant edition of Thoreau's essay on civil disobedience published in 1969, at the height of the resistance to the Vietnam War. This edition concludes the famous lecture on resistance to civil government with a clarifying note: "In a small sense, Thoreau tried to explain to his neighbors why on a July night 1846 he had chosen to go to jail rather than pay a trifling poll tax." The numbered edition goes on to define Thoreau's broader aims: "In a larger and deeper sense, he was probing a far more delicate and critical problem, as relevant in his day as our own, the relation of the individual to the state." Although the extreme individualism Thoreau's life represents is deeply rooted in the nineteenth century, his influence as a writer of ideas belongs to every century and to every country. The people who still pay homage to him at Walden Pond wear many costumes and speak many languages. Although today people seem to want to separate his ecological vision from his political concerns, all his ideas are intertwined. Lives of quiet desperation still abound. The transcendental exhilaration Thoreau tried to communicate has never been easy to understand because life offers most of us few chances to define ourselves outside of daily routines. That Memorial Day 1971 provided such a moment.

Even if Thoreau's dramatization of the power of nonviolent dissent was not known to the great number of people who were arrested that night, such ideas are so powerful—especially in Massachusetts—that they do not need to be studied to be understood. To most of the people involved in the largest arrest in the state's history, their night locked in the snowplow barn was not anymore local in its implications than was Thoreau's experience in the Concord jail. There is also real evidence that Thoreau remained a culture hero for many students and vets throughout the entire period of Vietnam dissent, another important local ghost on the scene.

In the end, the pardon petition seemed to get lost in bureaucratic red tape, and the criminal records for more than four hundred people on file were not readily available until summoned by the judge for his interview. As time went on, more and more people began to see the costly folly of the Vietnam War—just as many of Thoreau's contemporaries came to see the Mexican War as he did—as a situation in which comparatively few individuals were "using the standing government as their tool." By 1990, many more local citizens viewed the great arrest with sympathy.

As the twentieth anniversary of the event approached in 1991, realizing that the town yearbook gave no sense of the size and the exhilaration of that experience of dissent, a local citizen wanted to create some sort of collective commemoration and wrote a letter to the *Minuteman* that brought out several groups of survivors eager to talk about their experiences at the time. The local cable TV station also called to urge the production, for the entire community, of a videotape based on an oral history of the survivors. Although a few local citizens thought such moments should be forgotten, many more wanted to put their recollections on record, and several wanted to be involved in the project. By 1995, eight members of the community who formed a tax free group, the Lexington Oral History Projects, had collected sixty-five videotapes. They first created a short tape to urge greater public participation in the video planning, and they finally offered the town a panel discussion on the event with a seventeen-minute film of some of the most moving tapes. The town hall presentation room was mobbed. Among those interviews now recorded are: a number of involved veterans, two selectmen, women who made spaghetti sauce for the vets, policeofficers, ministers, newspaper editor, judge, probate officer, experienced radicals, newcomers, and several conservatives who disapproved strongly of what the VVAW were doing on the Green. Since then, a number of interested citizens have given the oral history group money to prepare the tapes for presentation to both the Cary Memorial Library in Lexington and the Joiner Center for the Study of War and Social Consequences at the University of Massachusetts in Boston. From this collection of oral history tapes, future students of dissent in America will be able to learn much about how history shapes itself. With the help of a humanities grant and the skills of a major filmmaker, the group is also hoping to produce a longer video to make this moment of protest less easy to forget.

Questions vital to the nature of democracy emerge at such moments. All those law-abiding citizens would like to believe that their action helped shorten the war in Vietnam. We still need to look at the role of family background and education in determining the behavior of the moment. Almost every church and both temples in Lexington were split down the middle regarding the war. Did some fiery young ministers influence young people as they had at earlier times in America? When the actual arrest began, a few teenagers locked themselves into the belfry of the First Parish Church at the edge of the Green and kept on ringing the bells. Perhaps the sense of solidarity of the moment also grew because in churches and schools so many of those present had counseled many other young men to avoid that war. As they sat with the brave, less fortunate returned soldiers who had gone to war instead of the students they knew, their sense of guilt had to be real. The videotapes are full of soul-searching patriotism as well as happy memories of working for a cause. The twentieth anniversary of the "Great Arrest" has come and gone. Another editor of the *Lexington Minuteman* telephoned Senator John Kerry to ask about his personal recollections of being arrested that night as a leader of the Vietnam Veterans Against the War. Like most of the townspeople, he remained proud of the experience. Later, he would address a high school history class that had prepared questions in advance for him.

The Cary Library had offered an exhibition case outside the Henry David Thoreau Room to display a small collection of artifacts related to the Memorial Day 1971 arrest. Many citizens had collected posters and brochures at the time; some wrote poems and cartoons; others saved their speeches and the cards they enclosed with telephone bills refusing to pay war taxes. But when the Gulf War came along, the exhibit was canceled: "The committee in charge of the display case has decided to feature a recent donation

from the Japanese Association of Greater Boston. Due to the recent developments in the Gulf, it would be inappropriate to allow your exhibition to
take place." Thoreau would have smiled. When it is needed most, the idea
of dissent may never be appropriate.

As the veterans marched from Concord to Lexington that Memorial
Day, many ordinary people gave them flowers and held high their posters
of welcome. One local citizen, in a deliberate reversal of the Revolutionary
slogan inscribed on the Battle Green, proclaimed: *If they mean to have peace,
let it begin here.* Perhaps we can fantasize a twenty-first century when the
tour guides in tricorn hats also wear bell bottom trousers and tell visitors
from all over the world that along with the killing of eight men that began
the American Revolution, another event occurred on the same spot in 1971
when more than four hundred people were peacefully arrested in an act
of civil disobedience in protest against the war in Vietnam.

14

"Where Are You Now, My Son?"

JOAN BAEZ

IT RAINED WHEN I was in Hanoi. It rained into the bomb craters and made brown swimming pools. The people were carrying their bicycles over the ruins, packing up with nowhere to go.

After the first few nights of bombing, most of the city was evacuated. During the seventh and eighth days of bombing, the city began to fill up again. The B-52s were hitting the countryside at the edges of the city, and I suppose people felt they'd rather die at home. I didn't want to die anywhere.

This is the story of my thirteen-day stay in Hanoi, eleven of them the days of the Christmas bombing, the result of the "most difficult decision" President Nixon had to make during his term in office. That Christmas bombing was, as it turned out, the heaviest bombing in the history of the world.

In December of 1972, I was on the road in the eastern United States when I received a telephone call from Cora Weiss. The group the Liaison Committee, which Cora headed, had been sending a steady flow of American visitors to North Vietnam to try to keep up some kind of friendly relations with the Vietnamese people even as our country continued to bomb the hell out of them, burn their villages, and napalm their children. Before Watergate, anyone who talked or wrote about the atrocities the U.S. military was performing in Vietnam was looked upon skeptically or with great annoyance and anger by a high percentage of the American population.

Originally published in Joan Baez, *And a Voice to Sing With: A Memoir* (New York: Simon and Schuster, 1987), 193–225.

I would be the guest of a North Vietnamese group called the Committee for Solidarity with the American People. No serious fighting had taken place in the north for many months, and four Americans were being invited, among other things, to deliver Christmas mail to the POWs in Hanoi. Gabriel would be with his dad at the time. I could return home by Christmas Day.

I sat alone in a motel room in Erie, Pennsylvania, chewing on my cuticles and wondering if I could haul myself and my truckload of neuroses halfway around the world to see things I was afraid of seeing, eat food I was afraid of eating, take night flights, which are anathema to me, and travel with three other people I'd never met. I was practically paralyzed with fear and disgusted with myself. At the same time, the prospect of the trip became more and more irresistible. Little did I know—while sitting in that crummy motel room with the snow falling outside, my three-year-old child off at a coffee shop in the arms of his loving grandma—that I would come within eight blocks of never returning home.

I made a couple of hundred calls from a New York hotel room, telling everyone I knew that I was going to visit Hanoi.

I would be traveling with a conservative lawyer, former brigadier general Telford Taylor; a liberal Episcopalian minister, Michael Allen; and Maoist Vietnam veteran against the war Barry Romo. We met for the first time a couple of hours before departure, in the SAS lounge at Kennedy airport. Displaying the big sack of mail that we would be delivering to the POWs, we bluffed our way through a press conference. We were carrying cameras, tape machines, batteries, film, and a minimal amount of clothing. Tucked in our bags were personal messages to members of the solidarity committee from people who'd gone before us and lists of what people wanted brought back, chess sets being the big priority.

We flew at night, Mike Allen and Telford downing a few and chatting noisily in the row behind me, and Barry dozing off across the aisle. As I think back, the preacher and the general, as we came to call them, were a little anxious, and Barry, who had been in Vietnam in battle and under fire, was (in my opinion) terrified of what he would feel coming back as a friend to a place where he had once been, frankly, a paid killer. I was feeling pretty good because of a smooth flight and plenty of Valium.

I vaguely remember a hotel in Denmark where we floated in and out of the restaurant, nodding at each other and looking jet-lagged. On another flight, I remember leaning over toward Telford as we watched the sun making its hazy way up through the clouds. Telford said, "On the road to

Mandalay, where the flying fishes play, . . ." and I finished, "And the dawn comes up like thunder over China, 'cross the bay," then felt like a terrible hypocrite because I was afraid Telford would think I knew something about poetry or that I read books. I simply have a good memory, and my mother and father used to say that poem whenever we were driving to the beach.

In Bangkok, Barry started to get sick with what I figured to be his internal conflict about returning to Vietnam, and I began pumping him full of tetracycline and trying to talk to him. I got cramps in the Bangkok airport and a uniformed woman from Thai Airlines managed to find me a Tampax, the last of that luxury I was to see during nature's long and eerily early visit to me that month.

Somehow, we were in Vientiane, Laos. We had dinner with a terribly sweet *New York Times* correspondent who was bitterly disgusted that nothing he sent in ever got printed without being massacred first. Jet lag hit with all its force at dinner, and I excused myself and went to bed. The next day we obtained visas from the Provisional Revolutionary Government to enter North Vietnam the week before Christmas.

We boarded our final aircraft, along with a gathering of dour-looking Russians and some Japanese. The flight was short and hot, and the Russians remained dour throughout.

I remember landing on the short runway, piling out of the plane, and being met by a group of the loveliest people one could imagine. Our hosts were all men, and they gave us flowers and invited us to sit down while our things went through customs. Quat was the leader of the group, lively and intelligent and full of jokes. During the time we were there, Quat's wife would give birth to a baby during a bomb raid; one member of the committee would lose his wife and eight children; another would lose track of his wife's whereabouts and spend all of the time he wasn't with us trying to track her down, not knowing whether she was alive or dead; but they looked after us as though they were our personally assigned guardian angels and had nothing else in the world to do.

I rode with Telford to the Hoa Binh Hotel, past thousands of people along the route and miles-long traffic jams. I was looking at the children, of course, and what I had heard about them was true so far: they were delicate and reserved, yet full of laughter, and they thought we were hilarious. While our car sat pinned in traffic, the children began to gather. One of them gave me a flower, and all the rest laughed with amusement. Later, I tried to give the same flower to a shy little girl who looked on from the edge of the group, but the others would not allow it. They said (and it was translated to me) that the flower had been given to me, and I must keep it.

Telford was much more interested in the automobiles that were passing us going in the other direction. "That one's Czechoslovakian, I believe, isn't it?" he'd say to the driver. I was amused by the way we were seeing things. "Look at those beautiful kids," I said to him, and he replied with a very genuine, "Where?"

I saw Barry get out of his car and walk off. Of course, I thought, how stupid to sit here. I got out and was immediately surrounded by ten or fifteen children who were grabbing at my hand and apparently trying to lead me somewhere. I laughed and let them tug me along, and it wasn't until they took me off the regular dirt bicycle path to an even smaller footpath that I began to understand what was happening. We were approaching a combination lean-to, chicken house, and outhouse. It had two "walls" of rusty corrugated steel backed up against a frail fence. The facilities themselves were even sportier, a couple of broken bowls, properly being put to use instead of thrown out. I had no choice. I made a little bow to the children and left them standing about fifteen feet from the structure, went steadfastly forth and squatted with as much dignity as I could muster, hoisting my tweed skirt and causing much mirth among my small audience. Unfortunately, due not only to the peanut gallery, but also to the Russian convoy inching past about seventy-five yards away, I wasn't able to produce anything, but I pretended to be very relieved and pleased as I stood up and smoothed my skirt and bowed a thanks to the children.

Traffic thinned out as we came into the city. The streets were lined with trees, and the sidewalks were lined with people. The beauty of the women was stunning. Dressed in white blouses and black pajama pants, they held a baby or a bundle resting on one hip, their heads cocked in placid curiosity under a pointed straw hat. Wisps of hair blew loosely around their faces, the bulk of it gathered into a magnificent braid. The women aged quickly and mercilessly. The faces of the old showed hundreds of lines, and their teeth flashed empty gaps and silver. The young men had skin that would be coveted by Western women.

We had all seen the Vietnamese men in the marketplaces, sauntering about the streets, and staring into the intrusive cameras. We'd seen their eyes in a thousand daily papers. And we'd seen them—these soft men of steel—with bullet holes in their flesh, lying dead in their own rice paddies. On the streets of Saigon, they seemed Westernized in the worst possible sense of the word. Here on the streets of North Vietnam, their eyes were not suspicious, but amused. We were intruders, but we must be friends or we would not have been allowed to visit, so most people smiled immediately upon making eye contact.

We arrived in Hoa Binh at midafternoon. Our hosts suggested that we wash up and rest, and then gather for dinner. My room, like all the others, was spacious old French architecture, with a ten-foot-high ceiling, wooden floor, and a modest balcony looking out over a tiny street. Across the street were tiny houses of the poor with mud courtyards and tropical-looking trees hung with laundry.

My room was furnished with a single bed, with a mosquito net drawn back for daytime. Next to it was a small table with an ashtray, matches, a white candle, and a bottle of drinking water. Near the balcony two chairs were placed on either side of another table holding a thermos of hot water, a small container of tea, and two cups.

The bathroom was a huge tiled affair, with a big lion-footed tub, stained at the bottom from the yellow and brown water that usually preceded the flow of clear water. Hanoi had been bombed before, and it was difficult to keep running water operating at all. The toilet was a pull-chain and worked in its own good time. There was another bottle of water above the sink, a piece of soap, and a couple of worn but clean towels.

I lay down on the creaky bed and listened to the sounds of a busy city almost devoid of cars. Some Vietnamese music was coming from a loud-speaker across the alley, and I fell into a heavy sleep.

I was awakened an hour or so later for my official chat with a member of the committee. Each of us had separate talks at that point; mine was at my coffee table with Quat, who told me of the plan they hoped to follow for us: trips to local places of interest, visits to war memorials, and talks with North Vietnamese who would, I assumed, try to impress upon us the horrors of America's invasion of their country. On the third day they hoped to pile us into jeeps and head out into the country for Haiphong. The ride was supposed to be beautiful. . . . Haiphong had once been beautiful.

I watched Quat's face as he spoke. It was a gentle and considerate face. It was patient. We talked a little about pacifism. He seemed to respect me for my beliefs and, like people I meet everywhere in the world, reasoned that pacifism had no place in his own country. I asked him if he knew that the National Liberation Front had once used nonviolent tactics against the French with some success. He laughed politely and said that things were different now. I told him that I had not come there to proselytize, but to meet people and make friends. Later on in the bomb shelter, it would be for Quat and a man named Chuyen that I would weep because I couldn't bear the thought of them coming to any harm. Chuyen was one of the very few people I would see cry during my entire visit. And Quat and Chuyen were the ones who consistently halted the traditional toasting of a fallen B-52 if I happened to be in the room when the news came. I think Chuyen was a pacifist at heart.

At dinner there were fifteen to twenty people. I remember the yellow vodka, which I refused to drink, and dish after dish of delicious food. The only dish I couldn't cope with was a whole bird with its head flopped over the side of the bowl, beak open. Aside from that, I had my neuroses under control and began to enjoy watching everyone loosen up. Quat drank like a fish, and Telford and Mike joined him. Barry hadn't been challenged yet, but his turn was to come.

The level of gaiety rose to new heights with the telling of jokes: first a Vietnamese joke, which would need a dozen explanations to cover the culture gaps, and then an American one that got the same treatment. When the joke was finally understood, there was triumphant and uproarious laughter, not so much at the joke as at the feat of having figured it out. Quat dashed over to my place with two little glasses of vodka. I couldn't refuse his offer, nor could I guzzle it down with a "bottoms up." Eventually, Quat thought of a way to let me off the hook by saying that vodka was injurious to my throat, and no one must make me drink anymore. Barry was challenged and rose to the occasion like a trouper, drinking two, three, four, I'm not sure how many little glasses of that awful yellow stuff, his shyness diminishing and his cheeks reddening with each glass.

At the height of the noise and laughter Quat raised his arms in the air and said, "Now, music!" Two Vietnamese singers rose to their feet. Their voices were trained, crystal clear and powerful. The men sang like Irish tenors and the women like nightingales. I got my guitar and asked them what they would like to hear. They liked Pete Seeger songs and anything recognizable as an antiwar song. Quat liked traditional music, and in the end the song that was his favorite was "Hush little baby, don't say a word, daddy's gonna buy you a mockingbird."

In the midst of our rumpus, I suddenly noticed that Barry seemed extremely tense, as if the guilt he had been burying had slowly unearthed itself and now, with the help of the vodka, was suddenly unbearable. I dedicated a song to all the Vietnamese and Americans who had died in the war, and then to all the men who had refused to fight it from the beginning, and finally to those who had quit fighting when they had become disillusioned (or, illuminated). I said it was necessary that we forgive them what they could not forgive themselves. I sang "Sam Stone," the story of a Vietnam veteran. Barry put his head down and wept through the song. I supposed he was seeing private reruns of the horrors he'd lived through, that the rest of us had sat home and paid for. I sang my heart out to him. When the song was over, Quat offered him another vodka, and Barry blew his nose and laughed and cried at the same time. Then the Vietnamese did a strange thing. They took him to the head of the table and sat him down as though to protect him from any harm, hovering about him, chatting and joking casually for a few minutes until he dried up. And in this way, Barry Romo, former marine, was forgiven, no questions asked, for his part in what had taken place in these people's jungles.

We joked and sang for a little while longer, until it was time for bed. We would be up at seven for breakfast and then taken to see a war memorial. They asked us if we would like to eat American, French, or Vietnamese food during our stay; we all said Vietnamese. I went to bed exhausted under my mosquito net and floated off to the sound of the loudspeaker still playing the haunting melodies that had played all afternoon.

The next morning we saw the war memorial. It was boring. I hated the pictures of babies with bullet holes in their heads and women with their intestines falling out into the mud. I hated the horror stories. I'd heard and seen them for years. It was my business to know them. I also hated the maps and long descriptions of what was bombed and when. Chuyen could feel my restlessness, and he gave me a sympathetic glance. I shrugged and smiled.

Most of the details were directed at Telford, who was there as a lawyer to determine whether or not war crimes had been committed. Legally, I was of no use, especially because of my deep-seated opinion that war itself is a crime—that the killing of one child, the burning of one village, the dropping of one bomb sinks us into such depths of depravity that there's no use bickering over the particulars. But Telford was a terribly conscientious man and was carrying out his duties to the last detail with endless questions about logistics, dates, and so forth. I tried to be patient, reasoning that Telford was probably the most important member of our group as far as credibility at home was concerned. I also liked him very much and was, in spite of my boredom with maps and details, fascinated at the way his mind worked.

We were given tea and tangerines and eventually let out of the little building. Later, in between propaganda sessions, there were lovely walks and a visit to a restaurant on the lake where the waitresses sang to me in exchange for my song to them. Chuyen took me to a music school, where the students and I exchanged songs for more than an hour and where we ended up having a political discussion about American involvement in Vietnam. By then I was taping everything.

Always there was Quat, smiling and laughing and animatedly telling stories and jokes, but listening attentively to any questions we might have and trying to explain things to us. It was during one of these talks that Quat innocently said the things that would haunt me in the shelter later on. We were sitting in the lobby of the hotel, where we gathered before and after meals to drink and talk, when I asked Quat what he would do if the insanity ever stopped and he had some free time.

"Oh!" he said. His face lit up, and he looked past his glasses and past me to what he was imagining. "There are islands north of Haiphong that I have never been to. I would take a little boat and go around to all of them, taking my time and stopping at each one. They are supposed to be so beautiful. All of Vietnam was beautiful once. But these islands are supposed to be special." It was as if he knew the islands, and they were his Shangri-la. It was also clear that there had been no time for Shangri-las in his lifetime. He finished talking and with a smile said, "Yes, that's what I would do." His smile was not sad; it wasn't a forced stiff-upper-lip smile. It was a truly optimistic and cheerful smile. So that's what this lovely man would do. Take a small boat to some islands. Not very much to ask, it seemed to me. Not very extravagant. I said I hoped he would someday have his dream. "I don't know," he said and laughed.

The second night in the hotel dining room we were shown patriotic films about the people of Vietnam. There was one about the Viet Cong in training, sliding down poles and swinging from ropes and shooting at targets, looking an average age of fourteen, though I know they were older. A pleasant-looking officer gave a demonstration in Vietnamese to his juniors about antiaircraft, and he used two little plywood planes to show how one shoots down the other most efficiently. Heroic music played between narrations. I excused myself and went to my room. When I came down later, one of the committee said, "Were you tired? You must have needed a nap."

"I wasn't tired," I said to him. "I just didn't like the film." He smiled.

And so the first two days went, more visits to places with reminders and explanations of the war. We ate three good meals a day and drank jasmine tea. (I can no longer smell jasmine tea and not think of Hanoi.) I was looking forward to the trip to Haiphong, as our days were too organized. I was longing to walk the streets of Hanoi alone, without a group and without a schedule. Until now, what I had liked best was sitting alone on my balcony and listening to that strange music, or talking with Quat or Chuyen alone without the propaganda.

On the third night, I cleaned up and went down to dinner. From that point on, my mind contains only strong flashbacks of what took place. I remember that we were again shown films, but these interested me because they were about children and what the different kinds of poison chemicals used by the U.S. military had done to unborn infants. I remember a sequence of a cat in a cage dying from a kind of gas and a monkey dying from the same thing. I remember an American soldier shooting fire from a hose at a small hut and planes spraying miles of jungle with poisonous white clouds. There was a picture of a baby born abnormal because of chemicals. She was lying on her stomach and appeared to have no muscles. A nurse and doctor were standing next to her; they lifted her arm, and when they let it go, it dropped to her side like a piece of butterfish.

Nervous and afraid that I would feel faint if I watched any more, I was about to retreat, make myself small and apart from the things and people around me, set up the armor that would keep me from seeing, when right in the middle of that whole familiar series of regressive emotions, the pattern was jolted.

The electricity in the building failed, leaving us sitting in the dark. Everyone stiffened, the Americans uneasy, the Vietnamese speaking rapidly to each other in quiet tones. Then, as though I'd been whirled back in time, like Dorothy in *The Wizard of Oz,* I heard a siren coming from a distance, starting at zero bass and rising evenly to a solid, steady high note where it stayed for a second or two and then slid back down through all the notes like a glider. All I could think of was the civil defense drills we'd had in grammar school. I sat still, aware that my heart had doubled in pace, and waited for instructions from the Vietnamese. By the time the siren began its second wail, one of our hosts had lit a candle and broken out of Vietnamese to say to us, calmly and with a smile, "Please excuse me. Alert."

How ironic. Please excuse whom? But I didn't think of the irony yet. I thought of standing up carefully and not banging into anything in the dark. I also thought that we were having a drill, a routine drill, being led at a careful but rapid pace out the door and down the hall. At the end of the hall there was a turn, a small room filled with bicycles. We were bumping into each other and making wisecracks about I don't remember what.

The flickering from the candle half helped and half hindered, blinding the eyes when it came too close, but giving us our only light. The tiles were uneven, and we walked by feel. The rest of the hotel guests were appearing from other halls and floors, forming a bottleneck at the rear door of the hotel. The candles were put out, and we poured and stumbled into a court-yard bright with moonlight.

There were Mike and Telford. Now I saw Indians, Latins, and others whom I later learned were Poles and French. "What's going on?" I asked a Latin man. He was Cuban.

"They don't know anything. Maybe planes. I don't hear them. We'll just wait. Hasn't been any bombing for a long time."

Bombing? I heard the word, and I had surely suspected that's what the sirens were all about, but hearing this man say it as he looked so matter-of-factly at the sky was something different. I realized that we were standing just outside of a bomb shelter. The Indians began making jokes, and everyone laughed. I thought I was the only one who was nervous. Telford had been in war zones before. Barry was not around. Mike may have been as nervous as I was, but he was chatting away and seemed fine. I relaxed a little.

A tall Indian held up his forefinger and said, "Shhh." In the distance, I heard them . . . the planes. Everyone went on standing there in the moon-light, but now we were not talking. The sound faded into the distance, and the voices came back, only much softer. People let out sighs. My heart was slamming again. I felt alone with my panic. There were a few more jokes, the voices almost back to normal.

And then it hit.

The planes were coming fast, and they were loud. The group jumped as a unit, heading for the door of the shelter down the narrow stairs. A big boom happened somewhere, and it shook the shelter walls and sent a wave of adrenaline through all of us. People hurried down the steps. The Cuban sat me down at the end of a long narrow bench that faced another long narrow bench. I had to go to the bathroom. There was another blast.

"That was close," was all the Cuban said. He and the other veterans were trying to assess the seriousness of the situation.

I didn't know what was happening. My ears were fluttering and popping as if I were on a plane gaining altitude quickly. The Cuban was telling me to lean away from the wall, to keep swallowing and pop my ears. I grabbed his arm with both hands. For awhile, all I could think of was my straining sphincter muscles. The bombs were coming down continuously. The Cuban was shouting in my ear. "It will be all right. They are not as close as they sound. Don't worry."

But I could see that I was not the only one who was worried. The big Indian sat forward with his head down. He was very dignified. People would look up at each other and shake their heads. When there was a lull, they would look at the ceiling. When the bombing started up each time, it did so with such force that we were almost knocked out of our seats with the plain shock. Every muscle in my body was tight and ready to move. I must have cut off the blood to the Cuban's hand. With every fresh concussion I bent over his lap, feeling that I would be protected next to his chest. I was desperately afraid. I said to him, "I am scared."

"I know," he said. "That's okay. After awhile, you get used to it. You'll be a veteran after a few more raids."

A few more raids! I'd be dead by a few more raids! More concussion, more fluttering, more deafening roar. Down went my head. I didn't like losing control like that; I decided to try to keep my head up.

There was a lull. We heard the sound of the planes getting softer. I loosened my grip. Murmuring started up among the group.

"Maybe they are leaving."

"Yes, perhaps. But they could be circling."

"Had you heard any rumors of this?"

"Nothing."

"An early Christmas package from Nixon, perhaps." And we all laughed.

I looked around the shelter. We'd come down a concrete stairwell, wide enough for one person to pass at a time. There was a narrow eight-foot hall that turned left at the end. A few steps later, there was a small door on the right leading to the cement room where most of us sat. The room was about twelve feet long and so narrow that when you sat on one of the two long benches that were placed lengthwise against the walls, your knees almost touched the knees of the person sitting opposite you. There was a bare bulb dimly lit in the middle of the ceiling. At the far end of the room was a door leading to an annex, the shelter for the Vietnamese who worked at the hotel. They had a separate entrance. It was only many raids later that Barry and I rebelled and took blankets in to sit with the Vietnamese.

There were about five Indians who were with the International Control Commission and had been in Hanoi for sixteen months. The Cubans were off of a ship that had been hit by our bombs in Haiphong harbor. There were three Pathet Lao (the Laotian Communist Liberation Movement), and the wife of one held a three-day-old baby in her arms. Most of the French didn't come down to the shelter. They were with Agence France Press, and they remained on the third floor of the hotel, watching out the balcony window or wandering the streets trying to guess what was going on so that they could report it.

I introduced myself to the Cuban. His name was Monti. I told him that I was trying to stop shaking and thanked him for the loan of his arm. We Americans exchanged glances, shaking our heads in amazement. The Vietnamese in their annex sat patiently, the children now beginning to play. I was coming out of shock. I'd forgotten how badly I'd needed a bathroom.

CRACK-BOOM! This time the bomb exploded before any of us heard the planes. I took a deep breath and felt like vomiting. I took Monti's hand again, breathed deeply and waited. This time I made a conscious effort to keep my head up. I was only partially successful. Monti explained that we were hearing carpet bombing. It was like thunder, the kind of thunder that rolls and rolls when you see purple lightning like strobe-lit twigs hurled into the air at the edge of a desert horizon. The intermittent cracking of antiaircraft seemed to be coming from the hotel patio. I didn't understand that it was ground to air, and its volume added to my panic.

We rode out the minutes. Carpet bombing is relentless. I realized with shame and horror that to pray for the planes to go away was to pray that they would drop their bombs somewhere else. I was kneading Monti's hand and sweating all over, my body shaking again as badly as before. But I was beginning to get a grip on myself. As soon as the noise became less than deafening, I felt like making a joke.

"I wonder if Macy's is open till nine this evening."

"What is Macy's?" asked the big Indian.

"It's a department store in the States. There's some last-minute Christmas shopping I have to do." They began to laugh. The bombing was in the distance now.

"Oh yes, Christmas. Your country has an amusing way of celebrating." It was not said bitterly.

"I think it's stopped," Monti said, and again I let go of his hand. My body began to unclench, a long process of relaxing muscle knots like untying an old-fashioned buttonhole shoe. Then I was limp. The fear was gone, and all that remained was a light anxiety.

The Vietnamese stirred from their squatting positions in the annex. The siren started its low rumble and soared to the all-clear note, staying there for about fifteen seconds. Everyone stood up, talking, joking, speculating, and we walked back up the stairs into the moonlight.

I followed Mike back through the hotel, past the room where we'd been watching the film before the lights went out. I peeked in. The Vietnamese were setting up to roll the movie again. They acted as though nothing had happened.

"Christ," I muttered to Mike. "No thanks, I'm going to bed."

I passed the lobby where all the people from the shelter were gathering to drink yellow vodka and beer, and trudged on up to my room. Barry's door was closed. He'd slept through the entire raid.

The music from the scratchy little speaker sounded like Russian marching music. I laughed. It wasn't completely Russian, but the influence was obvious. I leaned over the balcony, feeling strangely calm. People were moving about as usual. The only difference was the sound of sirens in the distance and the fact that the sky was eerily bright.

I remember taking a bath and getting into a long woolen nightgown. What innocence! I didn't even lay my clothes out so they would be easy to find, but dumped them over a chair on the other side of the room. I lit the candle and climbed under the mosquito netting. I must have been asleep in three minutes.

A strident voice was squawking at me in a language I didn't understand. From somewhere inside the hotel, through the window, enveloping every-thing, encasing my head, came the siren. It was so matter-of-fact. There were footsteps in the hall. I was out from under the mosquito net reaching for the candle. There was a knock at the door, and Mike Allen came in.

"Want some help? Want me to take you down?"

"Yeah, okay. Thanks. Just let me get some clothes on."

Mike stood near the door holding his candle. "Okay," he said, "but hurry."

I was feeling around for my clothes, finding only a pea coat, leaning over the chair groping for my long johns, when the sky lit up, and there was a RATTA-TAT-TAT that seemed to come from the balcony. I jumped back from the window, grabbed the pea coat, and Mike came hulking over to grab my arm.

"Screw the clothes! Let's get moving!" My heart was bouncing around the back of my throat and head. My candle was out. We bumped down the hall in the dark. The sky was bright: when we passed a window, we could see. Something happened, and I was alone on the stairs. I think Mike went to find Barry and Telford. I saw the black-and-white tile floor of the lobby like a checkerboard with men dashing across it. Very suddenly I became disgusted and angry and sat down on the bottom step. I'm not going this time, I thought; it's stupid. A group of Cuban sailors passed. One of them said: "Come. You mustn't stay there. It's dangerous."

"It's all dangerous. It disgusts me."

"Please come. The bombs could start any minute. Come, I'll take you." I got up and walked with him.

My bravery dwindled to nothing at the sound of the planes. We began to run. The Cuban had me by the elbow. The planes were overhead, and we were scrambling like rabbits across the courtyard. The sky lit up just as we made it to the stairs. This time the shelter was full, the entrance and hallway jammed. Mike and Telford hurried in. The concussions started. The sound was deafening. I remember distinctly that my nightgown was fluttering. Again I was shaking uncontrollably. I wanted to bend over and curl up on the ground. Fortunately, there was no room, so I went on standing. My nightgown continued its mysterious fluttering. (I learned later that the fluttering was caused by drafts made by the concussions.) There was a lull. Mike Allen was right next to me; I was pretty sure he was praying.

The planes were back. Down went my head, this time onto Mike's chest. He put his arms around me, but there was not a thing to say. If anything, this was the worst the bombing had been so far. It seemed to last forever. Even some of the French had joined us. Finally, the racket stopped, and there was only the sound of the planes droning away from the city. There weren't any jokes this time. The Vietnamese appeared at the shelter door just as the all clear sounded. We left solemnly. The Vietnamese asked where Barry Romo was, and Mike said he had wanted to stay in bed. They smiled.

I said goodnight to Mike and the people in the hallways, went to my room, and got dressed in long johns, a turtleneck, blue jeans, boots, and my pea coat. I made myself some tea, lit the candle, turned out the lights, and sat in a chair trying to think. But the music was like hypnosis. Just before I climbed into bed, I put my little cassette machine on the night table.

I couldn't have been asleep for more than half an hour when I heard the voice on the loudspeaker again. I sat up and waited. The voice came again—that singsong, clipped, woman's voice delivering its elaborate message. I climbed out from under the mosquito net and put my cassette under my arm. The hall lights went out at the same time that the siren started. I blew out the candle and felt my way toward the door. The sky lit up, and I heard a plane approaching tremendously fast. It didn't sound like the other planes. I began to run, trying to turn the tape recorder on as I ran. I was alone in the hall. Either the others weren't up yet, or they'd all gone downstairs. I passed a window and there came a white flash accompanied by a RATTA-TAT-TAT, and I hit the floor on one knee, the tape recorder dropping onto the tiles. What am I doing down here? I thought. I didn't know what was happening. I huddled low to get past the window and wondered if anyone had seen me. Then I stood up and realized with great lucidity that I did not want to die running. I could die scared, but not running. I tested the recorder and found it was working; it had picked up the siren, the running footsteps, the RATTA-TAT-TAT, and the clunk as it dropped to the floor. My unheroic flight had all been recorded. Good. I'd keep it to remind myself that it's embarrassing to run like a puppy. In the eleven days of bombing that followed, I ran only once, and it was at the instructions of and along-side members of the Swedish embassy, who had to cross two streets to get to their shelter.

There were ten raids that first night. Monti was right: by dawn, I was a veteran. I had even started singing to everyone during the less intense raids. When we stumbled out into the air after the last raid of the night, the sun was up, and there was a rooster strutting around the yard, crowing. Women were hanging out wash, and children were puttering in the yard.

To my amazement, I was told that the trip to Haiphong was still on. We brought all our things downstairs and stood around the lobby. Quat's men handed us each a helmet. I immediately left mine behind a door because I knew I could never wear it.

And then, looking tired and distressed and apologetic, as though they were parents who had just ruined a weekend for the kids, the Vietnamese informed us that the roads to Haiphong were dangerous, both in their condition and in their location, and we would have to stay in Hanoi. I was relieved and dis-appointed at the same time. I was already addicted to the bomb shelter. Being under fire on the open road did not appeal to me, but a sense of adventure lingered on, pushing me to get out into the country, out of Hanoi.

We went to the outskirts of the city, Telford and I in the same car, passing through what had been a village the evening before. Now small huts were left standing between huge craters filled with muddy water, and people were busy hunting for the remains of their things in the ruins. The Vietnamese always gave us the impression that few people were hurt. I know now that they did not want us to know the death toll.

Telford asked a series of questions of the guide while I stood silently at the edge of a bomb crater, looking down into it and then up at the people. They paid us no mind. We got back into the car. As we were bumping slowly back over the bricks and mud that had once been a country road, a girl passed by the car, carrying her bicycle. She looked in the window and said something to the driver. I had to pump a translation out of him. I heard her say, "Nixon."

"What did she say about Nixon?" I asked.

"She say, 'Do they come to take a look at Nixon's peace?'"

We returned to the hotel, having been spared seeing anything but a sampling of what fresh bomb craters look like. There was a raid during lunch. We all said, "Shit," and grabbed some food and headed for the shelter. The Air Force was setting a pattern for the days to come: raids all night, one at noon, one in midafternoon. We rested as much as possible in between. Those funny Viet-Russian marches played over the speaker all day long now. After the noon raid, I slept.

The second night of bombing was similar to the first, only not quite as severe. I asked Barry if he would help me out. I have never found a way to thank him. He was a fanatic Maoist who disliked the pacifist rhetoric that armed-struggle advocates referred to as "sunshine talk" as much as I hated his endless jabber about the fascist, racist, imperialist pigs. Each time the siren rumbled to a start and all the lights in the city went out, Barry would come to the door and say, "Are you ready?" would take my hand and walk me to the shelter. I told him to make me keep my head up during the heavy bombing. When there was a loud concussion, it would often be followed by a "tsk, tsk, tsk," which was Barry reminding me to get my chin up. One night, we stayed in the shelter to continue a discussion we'd begun on violence versus nonviolence. We were frustrated that we could get nowhere with each other's dogmas. We'd both heard it all before, and each believed vehemently that the other was wrong. It ended in a state of near tears, and at that point we made a pact never to talk about it again. I don't know if I was of much help to Barry, but he was the person in the group who was most able to help me with my terror. I spoke no more about Gandhi, and he never again referred to bullets of love. And we laughed a lot. I was especially grateful to him for spending so many long hours in the shelter because I found out later that if he had any fears at all, they were of being caught and sealed into a shelter to die of suffocation.

For me, the mercury that measured fear and anxiety soared up and down totally out of my control. Eventually, even with the bombs crumping nearby, I would find myself joking and singing, adding ridiculous verses to lighten things up. One night as we waited in the shelter, someone asked me to sing "Kumbaya." As the verse progressed, we heard the planes in the distance, heading toward the city. I'd been squatting and singing near the tape recorder. The planes droned onward, getting louder. The next verse was "Save the children, Lord." In the middle of the second line, the bombs began raining so close to our bunker that the tape recorder fell over with the concussion. I rose to my feet, grabbed on to Barry, who was standing, and went on singing. When the bombing finally stopped, someone said that was the last time they'd ask me to sing when the night was quiet.

On the third day, the Bach Mai Hospital was bombed. I saw a dead woman laid out by the roadside. There were corpses around her carefully covered with mats. She had not yet been covered up. She was old. I wanted to go and lie next to her and put my arms around her and kiss her. I would have done it if there had been no people around, but I was afraid that I would offend someone or that the press would take a picture, and I would be accused of being theatrical. We walked around what had been the largest hospital in North Vietnam. The head of the hospital was speaking rapidly, pointing to the wreckage of three-sided rooms on second stories where beds hung partially over the floor's edge, bits of sheet dangling in the breeze.

"This was X-ray," he said, waving toward the remnants of a wall, as we labored over slippery debris. Telford had his notepad out and was asking those awful questions again.

A woman hurried by carrying a bandaged boy on her back, her face set, but the tears undried on her cheeks. Telford was asking the dates of when certain craters had been made. Was this one fresh, or was it from the June bombing? The Vietnamese spoke quickly, explaining everything. Quat was there. He asked me to sit down and not go any further while the others went ahead. Barry stayed with me. From around the corner came the smell of burnt flesh. Near the entrance of the grounds, we could see a crane and some small equipment struggling to lift concrete and bricks from the mouth of the shelter in which a number of people were still alive. The last I heard, the attempt was not successful, and eighteen people died there.

It was at the hospital that I saw Chuyen cry. He simply walked away from our group, where he had been translating. Someone called him, and when he kept his back turned, another member of the committee took up where Chuyen had left off. When he joined us again, his eyes were red and full. I put my arm around him for a moment. He just shook his head. It wasn't until the night after we'd seen the Bach Mai disaster that I finally began to feel what I had absorbed.

I had gone down to the shelter. Barry spread my blanket in the Vietnamese quarters. I was catching a cold, and my body was uncomfortable and restless. Sleep seemed impossible. One of the Indians had brought his blanket down and was lying in the guest section of the shelter. Barry fell asleep. The little bunker was so damp and cold, so unhealthy. Our guardians were upstairs now, taking turns resting three on a bed near the rear entrance to the hotel. They were the most patient people I'd ever known . . . and the bravest. Chuyen's tearful face passed before my eyes. And then Quat's face, animated and cheerful: "There are islands north of Haiphong . . . I would take a little boat and go around to all of them." Very suddenly I was sobbing. Barry was awake, sitting up and encouraging me to cry.

"Get it out. You've been holding it in there too long. Go ahead and cry."

My racket woke the Indian, and he began telling me not to cry, that I was upsetting myself. "No! You must not. Here. Here's a tangerine. Eat something. You will feel better."

"I don't want any fucking tangerine," I mumbled, and Barry began to laugh. He was encouraging me to cry, and the Indian wouldn't hear of it: a cultural difference, I assumed, and took the tangerine.

"Here, I'll peel it for you," the Indian said, grabbing it back. It occurs to me that he just wanted desperately to help out.

"Thank you." I sighed.

Well, I had scratched the surface. I wondered what was really going on inside of me. I wondered about the children who spent their lives ducking bombs. The ones I'd met seemed very stable. Perhaps it was better to have something real to deal with than to conjure up, as I had, symptoms and phobias all of your childhood. Here was the difference I'd thought about so often, between victims of ourselves and victims of circumstance. Me and my years of therapy. Me and my friends who went in and out of psychiatric hospitals, trying to decide whether to live or die. And here, where the children had always known war, perhaps here life was a little more precious, just the opposite of the nasty cliché I'd heard all my life about Asians—"life is cheap over there." Perhaps there was no time for phobias here on the battlefield.

And so it went. Eleven days and nights of bombing, and then going out to see it in the mornings. I came to know the French press people, Jean Thoroval and his wife, who lived on the top floor of the Hoa Binh Hotel. They seemed fearless. Mike Allen suggested I spend some time out of the shelter, so I began going up to the Thorovals'. The French were fun and distracting. They gave me great courage. I took my guitar up, and we sat around—Mike, Jean and Marie Thoroval, Telford, two other members of the French press, and Barry—and I sang. Thoroval's favorite song was "Até Amanha," a Brazilian carnival song. His face would light up, and he would do a little dance. When the voice came over the microphone, Jean would go to his desk and mark down the number of the raid. When the bombing started, I would put down the guitar and pick up a cigarette. I don't smoke.

One night, we were up in the Thorovals' room chatting, drinking beer, and waiting. I was nervous. There had already been several raids that night, which I had sweated out in the shelter. When the next raid began, Mike called me over to the window.

I went unhappily to the balcony and looked out over a city already burning from the preceding raids. The planes were on their way. Mike stood there, boldly cheering me on. We could hear the droning of the B-52s getting steadily louder, bringing the war closer. I wilted and took his arm. "I don't want to see," I said and went over to Marie, who was perched on an armchair, smoking casually. I could see her by the light from outside that was bouncing around the room. I took her hand.

"J'ai peur," I said.

"Moi aussi," she said. She patted my hand. "There is nothing to do but wait."

A fresh wave of carpet bombing rolled persistently. Marie uttered a "mon Dieu." Then came a crash that set the windows flapping and objects dropping from desks. I was on my feet.

"Ah. Bon. Descendons à l'abri." It was Jean, the stoic, saying, "Let's go to the shelter," as he walked at an even pace to his bedroom and came out with a carton of Gauloises. We went slowly down the three flights of stairs. Marie was telling him to hurry, but he would not. He had never been to the shelter. It was again filled to capacity, and we crowded in under a display of fireworks.

The Indians were in the hallway looking somber. They did not make light jokes or ask me to sing. Jean kept rushing out into the courtyard to see if any planes were being shot down, and Marie kept calling desperately for him to get back inside. I was breathing deeply again. I remembered an expression I'd heard from old Doner, ten years before. I turned to Mike.

"You speak French, don't you?" I yelled in his ear.

"Oui, un peu."

"You'll like this one. Je n'ai pas peur—Je tremble avec courage!" ("I am not afraid—I tremble with courage!") He loved it. It began doing the rounds of the shelter, translated into various languages. Meanwhile, Barry was out running around the streets counting B-52s as they exploded in the sky.

There was much publicity over the first six pilots shot down. What a tiny victory, I thought, as we began to see their faces on posters all over town. We were invited and taken to the press conference to see them.

Heavy security surrounded the building where the pilots were to be shown to the international press. There were city officials, military personnel, and tons of cameras and tape machines. I did not want to sit in the front row where places had been saved for us; all four of us sat a couple of rows back. Barry was on one side of me and was not in good shape. Perhaps he was afraid he would see himself when the pilots came out. He called people in the U.S. military "pigs." Perhaps he was wondering if he had made a total transition himself. Telford was taking notes, and Mike and I were getting our tape recorders ready for whatever was about to happen.

What did happen was unspectacular. The prisoners were driven into a courtyard adjoining the press room. One at a time, they were led around in a circle in the patio while people took pictures of them. They were bandaged and in shock. I was astounded that they hadn't been torn to shreds by the Vietnamese. They looked young, and I felt sorry for them. One by one, they stepped up to the microphone and gave their name, rank, and serial number. If they had a message to give the press, they could. One of them said he hoped "this terrible war would come to an end real soon." Another sent his love to his wife, Sally, and wished his family a Merry Christmas. My God, they were oblivious. These guys were guilty of genocide, and I don't think it had ever occurred to them. In spite of the fact that I hated the press conference, I thought it was carried out with great restraint by the North Vietnamese. And I, too, hoped the war would end soon, and that Sally and the family would be joined by their daddy, and that he would get a nice civilian job—like a fireman or forester—and burn his uniform and send all his medals back to the White House.

Our visit to the POW camp was even more bizarre than the press conference. It began with the same red tape I'd been through at prisons everywhere, except that I was never before given tea in the warden's office. The sun was going down, which meant that the evening raids could start at any minute. I had my guitar, Mike had his Bible, Telford had his notepad, and Barry had a stomachache. It didn't really matter what we had with us or what we planned to say or do. In this prison, as in all others I've ever seen, the main issue was boredom and loneliness for home and for one's friends and family. We were closely supervised as the pilots showed us around their barracks. Flying shrapnel had severely damaged their bunkhouse the night before, and they were irate about not having any shelters provided for them. So was Telford. They were scared. They didn't understand what was happening. One of them held up a large piece of shrapnel.

"This thing came right through the ceiling. We was hiding under the beds. We've kinda made our own shelters, but they don't amount to much. I don't understand."

"What don't you understand?" I asked.

"This," he said, holding up the deadly looking piece of steel again. "I mean, I don't understand what's happening." He was absolutely serious.

"Well," I ventured. "There are these planes flying over here every night carrying bombs."

"I know that. But I don't understand what's happening," he repeated for the third time.

"Well, it's really very simple," I explained. "These people drop the bombs out of the planes, and the bombs fall to the earth where they explode and cause tremendous damage to people and things. Apparently, one or several of these bombs landed close enough to your compound to send that piece of metal flying through your roof."

"But what I mean is," he persisted, "Kissinger said peace was at hand, isn't that what he said?" The sarcasm drained out of me like milk pouring from the tipped cup of a child. I wanted to cry.

"That's what he said," I told the expectant pilot. "Maybe he didn't mean it. They lie a lot."

Mike kneeled and said a prayer. They kneeled with him. I sang the Lord's Prayer, thinking I should keep things Christmas-like. Then I asked them what they'd like to hear. The consensus was unanimous: "The Night They Drove Old Dixie Down."

I laughed out loud and sang it. Then we all sang "Kumbaya." Fighter pilots, lost in a strange land, standing with an American brigadier general, a preacher, a Maoist, and a pacifist, all under supervision of the "enemy," joining hands and singing with tears in their eyes, "No more bombing, Lord, Kumbaya . . ." I embraced them one by one, and we left. The last thing I heard one of them say was, "Get us out of here . . . if you can."

On the ride home, Telford announced to me that the POWs' having no shelters was the most disgusting thing he'd seen since he'd been in Vietnam. The prison officials had assured us a number of times that shelters were being built; in fact, the prisoners were digging them themselves.

At dinner, Barry and Telford exploded at each other, and Barry finally moved to another table. I felt he needed support and took my plate over to where he was sitting. It was not the first rent within our group, nor the last. Mike refereed, and Barry and Telford seemed to make a silent agreement similar to the one shared by Barry and me. Mike held things together through his good nature and a bit of preaching and storytelling. Barry hated the church, but he, too, seemed relieved at Mike's boisterous good spirits.

Toward the end of the week, we learned that the airport had been bombed, causing considerable damage to the runway as well as to the airport building. There would be a slight delay in our departure.

As Christmas drew nearer, there was no letup in the bombing. Occasionally, a Chinese plane would land and take off. We did not have visas to go through China, and it became clear we were going to celebrate my favorite holiday in the Hoa Binh Hotel.

The Vietnamese put a two-foot-high replica of a tree on a table in the middle of the hotel lobby, and hung bits of decoration on it. It sat fifteen feet from the bar as our only visual reminder that the Prince of Peace had come into the world to redeem all of our sins in the hopes that the people of the world would be a little kinder to each other. Mike and I planned a small service to take place in the lobby for the hotel guests and for our hosts, who I thought would at least be amused. There had been a lull in the raids, and I was hoping that a twenty-four-hour cease-fire had begun.

All the stories about Christmas have been written. They are of abounding love, sacrifice, rebirth, and forgiveness. They are about children in their time, their joy, their magic. Every year, they are told again and again, and they are fresh and warming to the souls of the weary and the old. They become true even if they are only wondrous fantasies. Because it is the one time in the year that those of us who celebrate it have an unwritten alibi to be nicer to each other. An extra inch or two of love. Christmas, to me, is exquisite.

I don't know what Christmas was to the U.S. president and secretary of state in 1972, but some of the true spirit escaped them. Surely there is a time zone chart somewhere in Washington, D.C. They must have known that it was Christmas Eve in Hanoi even if it wasn't yet Christmas Eve in the "real world."

Mike led a prayer in English and gave a short improvisational sermon to suit our situation. There were no more than twenty-five people in the lobby. I was ready with my guitar to share in whatever the Christmas spirit dictated on that strangest of all Christmas Eves of my life. I sang "The Cherry Tree Carol," and after Mike did a reading in French, I sang a calypso version of the Lord's Prayer.

My head was stuffed up with a cold, but the voice was coming out fine. Our Father who art in heaven, hallowed be Thy name. What a strange and pitiful Christmas. Give us this day our daily bread. Hallowed be Thy name. Perhaps Quat would eventually get to his islands. That will be my prayer for him. Forgive us all our trespasses. Hallowed be Thy name. God, bless and keep Gabriel. Give him a good Christmas. And keep his daddy well. As we forgive those who trespass against us. Hallowed be Thy name. I wonder if my family got the last telegram we sent out. It told them we were all right and wished them a Merry Christmas. Best not to think of home. And lead us not to the devil to be tempted. Hallowed be—a bomb exploded somewhere in the city. I went on singing—Thy name. But deliver us from all that is evil. The lights went out. I stopped my song. The French were telling me to keep going, and the Vietnamese were asking us to go to the shelter. The siren commenced. Mike was swearing. People lit candles, and I tried to go on singing. My voice came out so weak that I thought it was someone else's. I realized later that I was trying to keep quiet so that the bombs wouldn't know where we were. I strummed on the guitar, waiting for the hotel to be blown to bits or my voice to return. Either would have been a relief. I cut a verse, and amidst the shuffling of feet, encouragement from the French, and the closing notes of the siren, I finished the Lord's Prayer. Amen, Amen, Amen, Amen. Hallowed be Thy name.

"Those bastards," I said to Mike as we hurried to the shelter. "If there's one thing I can't stand, it's being interrupted in the middle of a performance." Mike had been swearing steadily under his breath ever since the bombing started.

Later that evening, we went to a midnight mass. I was in a near panic. The church was full, the streets outside lined with soldiers and police, obviously an emergency unit to lead people to shelters in the event of a raid. The service was awful. The priest gave the sermon in Vietnamese, French, and German. Each time he ran through his lines, he appeared more pompous and colder than the time before. This was one time I was some help to Barry: I think if I hadn't kept him joking with rude remarks under my breath, he might have run up to the rostrum and throttled the priest. When the collection plate came around, he was delighted to see Quat ignore it. Mike was so excited to be inside a house of God that he managed to work himself into a state of religious fervor; I think he even took communion. Telford looked serious and reminded me of my father in Quaker meeting. There were roving news cameras with bright lights, which also kept me from being a public outrage. The choir sang familiar Christmas carols in French, and I taped them on my cassette recorder. When the service was over, I didn't feel one bit holier than I had when it began, but only wanted to go home and go to bed and not hear any sirens, planes, or explosions for a full day.

I got my wish and slept for sixteen hours straight. I think we all did. Even our hosts took a break. A twenty-four-hour truce is an amazing feeling.

There is something I feel I must say here. During this "truce," a great psychological and probably physical change took place in me. The exhaustion, the sleep, the calm were, by the end of the twenty-four hours, almost boring. It was like the letdown that follows a long prepared for performance in a play or an exciting tour of concerts. Odd as it seemed, and frightened as I had been for so many days, something in me actually missed living on the edge of the knife. I would be ashamed of saying this, but I have heard others express the same feelings about their experiences in the Second World War. At least I knew I was alive during those raids because I was treasuring my life as I had never done before. Why be ashamed to admit that I missed the excitement? Because to wish it back was insanity, was wishing back death for hundreds more people and possibly myself. And, sure enough, as soon as the raids began again, I wanted to be out of Hanoi, and my thoughts returned more and more to my home and to Gabe. And once again, I became afraid.

One morning after a particularly bad night, we were taken to a business district called Kan Thiem that had been devastated by carpet bombing. It shook us all more severely than anything else had so far. Even our hosts seemed shocked. Maybe it was because the raid had occurred near dawn, and there hadn't been time to clean things up. People were dashing about or just standing and facing the ruined area, talking rapidly and shaking their heads. Within a few yards of the road, we were walking on mud, brick, and debris, staring into the small rooms that lined what had so recently been a street. There was a woman quietly picking up a few scraps of her life. There was a man weeping to himself and a surviving family moving about their small area like zombies. Everywhere were headbands of white cloth, the symbol of mourning for a relative.

After the long row of what had been buildings the night before, we struggled over an area of even more jagged and slippery terrain leading out into the open. Hundreds of people struggled past us, carrying their bicycles. Some looked at the ruins; others simply kept walking. I glanced up and saw, amidst the flow of people stumbling toward me, an old, old man. He had a long white beard and a kind face and was bent forward with his hands low to the ground so that when he slipped he could catch himself before he fell. Just as his footing became unstable again, I reached out auto-matically to take his hand. He allowed me to help him and then looked up. He peered deep into my eyes, straining for a second, and then smiled cheer-fully and nodded his head. He said, "Dankeschön! Dankeschön!" and clasped my hand in both of his. I bowed to him as he bowed to me, and off he went.

I saw a woman sitting on a small heap of rubble, pounding her fists on her thighs and crying with a despair that was ferocious. She would go from a wail to a moan to almost a growl, then sob wretchedly from her island of misery. Her husband was tugging her gently by the hand, looking some-what embarrassed, scolding her softly to get up and come with him. She would attempt to rise to her feet, and then she would give in to the anguish that had taken away all her strength and pride and sensibilities. Cry, I wanted to say. Cry, for God's sake. Keep crying until there is nothing left in the well, until the next turn of the hourglass. All my common sense told me to stay away from her, but I could not. I squatted next to her, putting my arm around her. Some people looked on, as they looked on at the many other scenes taking place all around. For one desperate moment, she wailed and put all her weight against me. Then she looked up and saw that I was not only a stranger but a foreigner as well, and she became visibly uneasy, though her sobbing didn't change. I got up immediately, found my way back to Barry, and took his hand.

We came to what looked like a large expensive movie set of a piece of the moon. Men were standing atop craters banked with mud and trash, shout-ing out the number of the dead. Today, they wanted us to know. The num-ber was mounting into the hundreds. The white headbands were a part of the moon people's costume. Some of the younger children were laughing excit-edly and scrambling from crater to crater like extras. Many people walked in slow motion. Barry guided me around the edges of a crater. We were walk-ing on top of what had been people's homes. Here was a shoe, here a half-buried little sweater, a piece of broken dish jammed into the earth, a book lying open, its damp pages stuck together. The press were there with their cameras. Barry and I were walking just behind Jean Thoroval and his inter-preter. On the other side of a thirty-foot abyss I saw a woman bending low to the ground singing a strange little song as she hobbled back and forth over an area of ten or twelve feet of ground. At first I thought she was singing a song of joy, that she was all right, and her family had been spared. But as we got closer, her song grew strange to my ears. She was alone. Thoroval asked his interpreter what she was singing. The interpreter listened closely for a few seconds and said to him, "Elle dit, 'Mon fils, mon fils, ou êtes vous maintenant, mon fils?'—My son, my son. Where are you now, my son?"

Oh, heaven and earth. Such depths of sadness cannot exist. I crumpled to the ground and covered my face and sobbed. That woman's boy lay somewhere under her feet, packed into an instantaneous grave of mud, and she, like a wounded old cat, could only tread back and forth over the place she'd last seen him, moaning her futile song. Where are you now, my son?

Barry raised me to my feet and said, "Let's go now." I couldn't walk very well, and he supported me. I was sick of mud, sick of craters, sick of death. Not for me, but for these people who had been living here for so many years. We passed a younger member of the French group. He was furious. "Ah, bon. Now what do you say, eh? You still think like a pacifist? After all this you would still say to put down your arms?" I waved my hand to indicate the moon set. "This is supposed to change my mind?" I said in a quiet fury. "You are a fool." But he was beckoning to Barry. I was not supposed to notice, but what he pointed out was a child's hand lying a few feet from us in a pile of debris. It was like a doll's hand that pops out at the wrist, and the rest of the doll was nowhere to be found. Barry took me back to the car.

After our visit to Kan Thiem, an air of desperation spread over all of us. Thoroval became ill. His wife said he could not eat. He called it indigestion, but it was more like a case of revulsion. He'd been in Hanoi for two years. The Vietnamese children looked drained and colorless. I had begun to dress like the Vietnamese, wearing black pajama bottoms and sandals with my shirts and pea coat. I was afraid to think of home. Telford read books patiently during the raids by the light of a candle. The Frenchmen looked tired. The Pathet Lao couple with their tiny child couldn't make it up and down the stairs anymore. The mother was too sore. I bought five chess sets and jewelry from a woman who had lost her brother the night before. She let me hold her a minute. Our Vietnamese hosts went out and bought a jumper for Gabriel, as though to reassure me that I would see my child soon. We'd already made two unsuccessful trips to the airport, being turned back at a checkpoint. No planes. And the ghastly unspoken fantasy slowly formulating in the minds of all of us finally began to be voiced.

I think it was first spoken, in broken English, up in the Thorovals' quarters over beer and cigarettes. It made perfect sense. By now, it was clear that the American administration's strategy was to bomb the North Vietnamese back to the bargaining table. The strategy was not working. There was the insult of the new Russian missiles that were shooting B-52s out of the sky like fat crows. By now, Nixon was so insulated from the American people that there was no way for him to sense that he was losing their confidence and that he had completely overstepped the boundaries of everyone's sensibility, except the extreme right wing and idiots. On Christmas day, a tree had been delivered to the White House, its branches broken and all the ornaments smashed. The message was clear.

Why was the administration sticking to a strategy of losing B-52s and Phantoms by the score when Hanoi could be wiped off the map forever with one nuclear bomb? Certainly China or Russia would not retaliate over such a small item as Vietnam. No, dear Barry, China would not have done a thing. We were, as the expression goes, sitting ducks.

At this point, Quat began a campaign to restore our good spirits and hope. He planned a series of farewell dinners as though we were actually going to leave Hanoi alive. I distinctly remember two of these parties at which we again drank, laughed, made music, and said good-bye to many people we'd met during our stay. At one of the parties, a woman sang to us in Vietnamese, and then told us in a tearful voice that her son was at the front and that she would sing her favorite song in English for us and for her son. She clasped her hands together and stood rocking back and forth next to me, choking back the tears and singing an old Stephen Foster song, verse by verse. She knew the words phonetically, and it was only because we all knew the song from high school music class that it was at all comprehensible, but it was unbearably beautiful and moving. Mike began a seizure of throat clearing, and even Telford's eyes could not stay dry. I tried to sing with her, but could not hold the notes. She soared to the high notes and broke on the lower ones, and with each break, tears rushed from her eyes. She ended on a wavering note and then reached her arms out to me, saying, "Sank you, sank you," to which I could respond nothing. I sang, too, all of their favorites, and Quat passed around the vodka.

At the other farewell dinner there were raids, and we went singing into the shelter. Beneath the bombs, two women sang steadfastly and clear-eyed, in two voices that sounded like one, in perfect harmony, accompanied by an accordion drowning out the sound of the planes. I think during the few minutes that they sang, I would have been able to face death with some dignity. That night after the party was over, I stood out on the Thorovals' balcony, at Barry's prompting, and breathed in the night air while waiting for the planes to return. He had persuaded me that I would feel better if I faced up to the fear and watched the sky.

"If you really want to have courage," Barry said softly, "you will sing."

I began to sing "Oh, Freedom," quietly at first and then more and more boldly. "And before I'll be a slave, I'll be buried in my grave . . ." The notes were coming out loud and sure. I sang a few verses, and when it was over, there was the sound of clapping from the little street shelters below us. I smiled at Barry.

"You see?" he said. "You made them feel good."

I sang some more. I sang through the entire blackout, feeling many things as I went along. How I would miss my son if I died; but then no, I would be dead: he would miss me. I still didn't want to die. I was not brave like the people walking below. I was hanging on desperately to my life. But I was singing.

"Ain't gonna let nobody turn me around, turn me around, turn me around, walkin' up to freedomland . . ."

No bombs came down during that raid. Perhaps it would have been very different if they had, but as it was, I came in from the balcony feeling triumphant.

It was decided that we would try to leave Hanoi through China since the Chinese planes were still the only ones attempting the Hanoi airstrip. This would mean a trip to the Chinese embassy to obtain transit visas.

Telford, Mike, Barry, and I arrived fifteen minutes early in the afternoon. We were ushered into a dark and gloomy old French building, down a hallway hung with pictures of Ho Chi Minh and Mao, and were seated in the receiving room, which was also hung with pictures of Ho Chi Minh and Mao. There were two interpreters—one to get us from Chinese to Vietnamese, and the other to get us from Vietnamese to English. Barry was sitting across from me trying to hide his delight at being in the embassy of his beloved Mao. We were served Chinese beer, offered cigarettes, and at long last the ambassador arrived. We stood up to greet him, and all he said was, "Hmmmmm." He was wearing little round glasses and a Mao jacket. He seated himself and said, "Hmmmmm," again. He spoke to the interpreter, who in turn spoke to the other interpreter, who then spoke to us.

"The ambassador says he hasn't been sleeping too well lately."

We shifted around in our chairs trying to think of appropriate responses to his statement, but he spoke again.

"He says perhaps it is because of the bombing that goes on all night."

"No doubt, no doubt," said Telford.

"Tell him we haven't been sleeping so well either, and apologize about the bombing," I ventured. It was interpreted and the ambassador said, "Hmmmmm."

"The ambassador wants to know why you have come here to see him today." He knows damn well why we're here, I thought.

"Well." It was Telford's turn now as spokesman of the group. "The ambassador is surely aware of the fact that it is very difficult to find a way out of Hanoi, and we understand that the Chinese planes are the only ones that seem to be functioning with any regularity at all." More interpreting.

"The ambassador wants to know, is this the only reason you came to visit the Chinese embassy?"

"Oh!" said Telford hurriedly. "No, of course not. But we did think it would be a wonderful experience for us to see even a small portion of your great country on our journey home."

Telford, you hypocrite, I was thinking. And who do you think you're fooling? At this point, Mike Allen commented on the beer. Marvelous beer, the Chinese beer. Made in Peking? Marvelous! Barry was squirming in his chair and probably plotting how he could get a Peking beer bottle for a souvenir. The ambassador was looking almost comically inscrutable and was no doubt enjoying nailing us all into a corner.

"I don't wish to be rude," I blurted, "but please tell the ambassador that speaking for myself, I'm scared stiff and would like to get the hell out of this city as soon as possible, and that's why I came to see him today." The ambassador smiled faintly with his next "Hmmmmm." Mike and Barry laughed, and I don't remember if Telford responded.

After more small talk, the ambassador had our passports collected for what he had probably intended to do all along, which was to give us visas for the next day. We tried to muffle our excitement and relief. I wanted to rush up and hug him, but that seemed definitely out of order. We all stood up and made gratuitous gestures and speeches and shook hands and bowed. Barry had been silent the whole while. His moment had now arrived. Just as we were filing toward the exit, he plunged his hand into his pocket and gathered a fistful of Vietnam Veterans Against the War buttons. Walking stiffly up to the ambassador, he placed the buttons on the tea table, saying, "I am with you in your fight to stamp out the fascist, imperialist aggressor." The ambassador looked baffled, peering at the pile of tiny buttons with their incomprehensible logo, which had been delivered with the equally incomprehensible short speech. "Oh, for Christ's sake, Barry," I mumbled to him. "He doesn't know what the hell you're doing."

"He'll understand," said Barry.

Back in my room at the hotel, I packed for the third time. It was beginning to look as though we would actually leave Hanoi, and I wanted to listen to the music from my balcony window and think about the people and enjoy feeling hopeful about returning home. There would be raids all night, but there was a general air of optimism about the arrival of the Chinese plane.

In the morning, we ate breakfast and met for the final time in the lobby, dragging our bags, tape recorders, cameras, gifts. Once again, I tried to leave my helmet behind, but when I got in the car, I found it had been placed by my feet. For the third time, we headed off in three cars for the airport. Again we passed the skeleton of a train depot, the wrecked huts, the craters. We came to a pontoon bridge. I popped two Valium. The pontoon bridge was the only way left to cross the river. The traffic went one direction for a half hour and then the other direction for the next half hour. I shrank down in my seat and waited for the sound of sirens. Getting caught on that bridge during a raid was my idea of hell. It would mean getting out and climbing under the car. There would be a fight about the helmet. But worst of all was the great expanse of open sky above the bridge. I felt sure we were a perfect target. The ride across the bridge took about an hour.

At the airport, the chairs were lined up the way they had been when we'd arrived two weeks before, but the room had only half a roof and part of its walls. Debris had been pushed into corners, and the room swept and wet-mopped, but there was a dull finish everywhere, an endless amount of dust. The bar was standing. I asked for the ladies' room and was directed to a cubicle just intact enough to ensure partial privacy. The plumbing was out. From the broken window I could see some Russians, some Vietnamese, and a group of wounded Polish soldiers arriving outside for the same flight.

We wandered outside, looking at the damage. While I was strolling around peering at the rubble, I saw partially buried in the thick mud, halfway down the inside of a crater, a piece of metal that had a startling shape to it. I climbed in and pulled it out of the dirt. A piece of an airplane, no doubt, had melted into the shape of a bird sitting on a branch. I slipped it into my purse. The lobby was filling up, and I knew there would be a raid. A phone rang, and everyone sauntered across the pockmarked area in front of the terminal toward the airport shelter.

There were eleven Polish soldiers, counting two who were in coffins. Like Monti's, their ship had been hit in Haiphong harbor. When we reached the area just outside the shelter, people struck up conversations. Some of the Poles asked me for autographs, and I obliged and shook hands with them; others were very much in pain and just looked on.

We were ushered down into the shelter. It was pitch-black until someone lit a candle. There was a fat lady who was embarrassed about trying to make it down the stairs. The shelter was like a catacomb, each new room black until a candle bearer caught up with us. Ten or twelve of us reached a small cubbyhole and sat down to wait. A Pole stood in the doorway. I was next to Barry and Mike. Near me sat a wounded Pole with his head sunk into his knees. All the Poles looked exhausted and shell-shocked. We heard the planes in the distance. Every soldier in the bunker stiffened. One began to cry. I reached out my hand and stroked the head of the one nearest me. He looked up wearily and put his head back down. I began to sing, "Hush, little baby, don't say a word, Papa's gonna buy you a mockingbird." I kept stroking his head. "If that mockingbird don't sing, Papa's gonna buy you a diamond ring." Get those goddamned planes out of the sky, and let these guys get out of here. "If that diamond ring is glass, . . ." I finished the song and the planes were gone. No one spoke as we got up and headed slowly for the open air.

The Chinese plane was landing. The soldiers were too tired to smile. We walked back to the runway and lined up. The coffins were loaded first, then the Poles, and next the Americans. We turned around at every other step to wave good-bye again and again to Quat, Chuyen, and the others. The plane was small and hot. Directions were given in Chinese, and Chinese music played over the speakers. The engines started up. As we taxied down the wreck of a runway, I looked out the window and saw our little band, still waving. Suddenly, en masse, they all turned their heads around and sky-ward, and I knew that the B-52s must be coming back. And then, as though nothing had happened, they turned back and continued to wave to us until we were airborne, and they were specks on the pockmarked land below.

We arrived home safely on New Year's Day. My son stepped out of the crowd at the San Francisco International Airport and handed me a bouquet of acacia that was as big as he was, and he said, "Hi, Mom." I picked him up in my arms and said, "Hi, sweetheart," and gave him a fire truck I'd bought at the Tokyo airport.

The first two weeks I was back, I stayed at David's house, where I slept most of the time and spent the remainder giving interviews to newspapers and magazines. Every time I fell asleep on the couch, I could hear Gabriel hollering around the house, and the only thing that woke me up was when he'd drop a Tonka truck on my head or the cat on my stomach or himself on my chest. Then I would grab him and hug him and tell him I'd play in a few days when I was back on my feet. At night, I left a candle lit so that when a plane went over and I found myself sitting up in bed reaching for my pea coat, I could orient in a hurry to the fact that I was home. But part of my psyche was still in Hanoi.

When I had fully recovered my physical strength, I went to my own house and listened to the fifteen hours of cassettes I had taped in Vietnam, including the sirens, the bombs, Phantoms, B-52s, antiaircraft, the children laughing, Monti talking, the Vietnamese singing, myself singing in the shelter. I did a rough edit and took the results to the record company to record as best I could the story of my Christmas in Hanoi. It is one long poem partially sung and begins with a run to the Swedish bomb shelter during a raid, some bombing, and then the old woman at Kan Thiem chanting, "Oh, my son, where are you?" The last verse of the title song goes:

> Oh, people of the shelters
> > what a gift you've given me
> To smile at me and quietly let me share your agony
> And I can only bow in utter humbleness and ask
> Forgiveness and forgiveness for the things
> > we've brought to pass.
>
> The black pajama'd culture that we tried to kill
> > with pellet holes
> And the rows of tiny coffins we have paid for
> > with our souls
> Have built a spirit seldom seen in women and in men
> And the White Flower of Bach Mai will surely
> > blossom once again.
> I've heard that the war is done
> Then where are you now, my son?

The album is called *Where Are You Now, My Son?* and it is my gift to the Vietnamese people and my prayer of thanks for being alive.

PART THREE

Soldiers Against the War

What Did You Do in the Class War, Daddy?

JAMES FALLOWS

MANY PEOPLE THINK that the worst scars of the war years have healed. I don't. Vietnam has left us with a heritage rich in possibilities for class warfare, and I would like to start telling about it with this story.

In the fall of 1969, I was beginning my final year in college. As the months went by, the rock on which I had unthinkably anchored my hopes—the certainty that the war in Vietnam would be over before I could possibly fight—began to crumble. It shattered altogether on Thanksgiving weekend when, while riding back to Boston from a visit with my relatives, I heard that the draft lottery had been held, and my birth date had come up number forty-five. I recognized for the first time that, inflexibly, I must either be drafted or consciously find a way to prevent it.

In the atmosphere of that time, each possible choice came equipped with barbs. To answer the call was unthinkable—not only because in my heart I was desperately afraid of being killed, but also because, among my friends, it was axiomatic that one should not be "complicit" in the immoral war effort. Draft resistance, the course chosen by a few noble heroes of the movement, meant going to prison or leaving the country. With much the same intensity with which I wanted to stay alive, I did not want those things either. What I wanted was to go to graduate school, to get married, and to enjoy those bright prospects I had been taught that life owed me.

Originally published in *The Washington Monthly,* Oct. 1975, 5–19.

I learned quickly enough that there was only one way to get what I wanted. A physical deferment would restore things to the happy state I had known during four undergraduate years. The barbed alternatives would be put off. By the impartial dictates of public policy, I would be free to pursue the better side of life.

Like many of my friends whose numbers had come up wrong in the lottery, I set about securing my salvation. When I was not participating in antiwar rallies, I was poring over the army's code of physical regulation. During the winter and early spring, seminars were held in the college common rooms. There, sympathetic medical students helped us search for disqualifying conditions that we, in our many years of good health, might have overlooked. Although, on the doctor's advice, I made a half-hearted try at fainting spells, my only real possibility was beating the height and weight regulations. My normal weight was close to the cut-off point for an "underweight" disqualification, and, in a diligence born of panic, I made sure I would have a margin. I was six feet and one inch tall at the time. On the morning of the draft physical, I weighed 120 pounds.

Before sunrise that morning, I rode the subway to the Cambridge city hall, where we had been told to gather for shipment to the examination at the Boston Navy Yard. The examinations were administered on a rotating basis, one or two days each month for each of the draft boards in the area. Virtually everyone who showed up on Cambridge day at the Navy Yard was a student from Harvard or MIT.

There was no mistaking the political temperament of our group. Many of the friends wore red armbands and "stop the war" buttons. Most chanted the familiar words, "Ho, Ho, Ho Chi Minh / NLF is Gonna Win." One of the things we had learned from the draft counselors was that disruptive behavior at the examination was a worthwhile political goal, not only because it obstructed the smooth operation of the criminal war machine, but also because it might impress the examiners with our undesirable character traits. As we climbed into the buses, and as they rolled toward the Navy Yard, about half of the young men brought the chants to a crescendo. The rest of us sat rigid and silent, clutching x-rays and letters from our doctors at home.

Inside the Navy Yard, we were first confronted by a young sergeant from Long Beach, a former surfer boy no older than the rest of us and seemingly unaware that he had an unusual situation on his hands. He started reading out instructions for the intelligence tests when he was hooted down. He went out to collect his lieutenant, who clearly had been through a Cambridge day before. "We've got all the time in the world," he said and let the chanting go on for two or three minutes. "When we're finished with you, you can go, and not a minute before."

From that point on, the disruption became more purposeful and individual, largely confined to those whose deferment strategies were based on antiauthoritarian psychiatric traits. Twice, I saw students walk up to young orderlies whose hands were extended to receive the required cup of urine and throw the vial in the orderlies' faces. The orderlies looked up, initially more astonished than angry, and went back to towel themselves off. Most of the rest of us trod quietly through the paces, waiting for the moment of the confrontation when the final examiner would give his verdict. I had stepped on the scales at the very beginning of the examination. Desperate at seeing the orderly write down 122 pounds, I hopped back on and made sure that he lowered it to 120. I walked in a trance through the rest of the examination, until the final meeting with the fatherly physician who ruled on marginal cases such as mine. I stood there in socks and underwear, arms wrapped around me in the chilly building. I knew as I looked at the doctor's face that he understood exactly what I was doing.

"Have you ever contemplated suicide?" he asked after he finished looking over my chart. My eyes darted up to his. "Oh, suicide—yes, I've been feeling very unstable and unreliable recently." He looked at me, staring until I returned my eyes to the ground. He wrote "unqualified" on my folder, turned on his heel and left. I was overcome by a wave of relief, which for the first time revealed to me how great my terror had been, and by the beginning of the sense of shame that remains with me to this day.

It was, initially, a generalized shame at having gotten away with my deception, but it came into sharper focus later in the day. Even as the last of the Cambridge contingent was throwing its urine and deliberately failing its color blindness tests, buses from the next board began to arrive. These bore boys from Chelsea—thick, dark-haired young men, the White proles of Boston. Most of them were younger than we were because they had just left high school, and it had clearly never occurred to them that there might be a way around the draft. They walked through the examination lines like so many cattle off to slaughter. I tried to avoid noticing, but the results were inescapable. Whereas perhaps four out of five of my friends from Harvard were being deferred, just the opposite was happening to the Chelsea boys.

We returned to Cambridge that afternoon, not in government buses but as free individuals, liberated and victorious. The talk was high-spirited, but there was something close to the surface that none of us wanted to mention. We knew now who would be killed.

The Thinking Man's Route

As other memories of the war years have faded, it is that day in the Navy Yard that will not leave my mind. The answers to the other grand questions about the war have become familiar as any catechism. *Q:* What were America's sins? *A:* The Arrogance of Power, the Isolation of the Presidency, the Burden of Colonialism, and the Failure of Technological Warfare. In the abstract, at least, we have learned those lessons. For better or worse, it will be years before we again cheer a president who talks about paying any price and bearing any burden to prop up some spurious overseas version of democracy.

We have not, however, learned the lessons of the day at the Navy Yard, or the thousands of similar scenes all across the country through all the years of the war. Five years later, two questions have yet to be faced, let alone answered. The first is why, when so many of the bright young college men opposed the war, so few were willing to resist the draft, rather than simply evade it. The second is why all the well-educated, presumably humane young men, whether they opposed the war or were thinking fondly of A-bombs on Hanoi, so willingly took advantage of this most brutal form of class discrimination—what it signifies that we let the boys from Chelsea be sent off to die.

The "we" that I refer to are the mainly White, mainly well-educated children of mainly comfortable parents—who are now mainly embarked on promising careers in law, medicine, business, academics. What makes them a class is that they all avoided the draft by taking one of the thinking man's routes to escape. These routes include the physical deferment, by far the smartest and least painful of all; the long technical appeals through the legal jungles of the Selective Service System; the more disingenuous resorts to conscientious objector (CO) status; and, one degree further down the scale of personal inconvenience, joining the reserves or the National Guard. I am not talking about those who, on the one hand, submitted to the draft and took their chances in the trenches, or, on the other hand, those who paid the price of formal draft resistance or exile.

That there is such a class, identifiable as "we," was brought home to me by comparing the very different fates of the different sorts of people I had known in high school and college. Hundreds from my high school were drafted, and nearly two dozen killed. When I look at the memorial roll of names, I find that I recognize very few, for they were mainly the anonymous Mexican Americans (as they were called at the time) and poor Whites I barely knew in high school and forgot altogether when I left. Several people from my high school left the country; one that I know of went to jail. By comparison, of two or three hundred acquaintances from college and afterward, I can think of only three who actually fought in Vietnam. Another dozen or so served in safer precincts of the military, and perhaps five went through the ordeal of formal resistance. The rest of us escaped, in one way or another.

The fifth anniversary report of my class at Harvard gives a more precise idea of who did what. There were about twelve hundred people in the class, and slightly fewer than half wrote in to report on what had happened to them since 1970. Of that number, twelve said that they had been in the army, two specifying that they had served in Vietnam. One had been in the marine reserves. Another thirty-two people, most of whom had held ROTC scholarships in college, had put in time with the navy. Two were in the Coast Guard, two in the National Guard, and seven more in unspecified branches of the military. That was the bite the military took from half my class at Harvard during a bloody year of the war—fifty-six people, most of them far from the fighting. Besides them, seven of my classmates performed alternate service as conscientious objectors; and, though no one reported going to prison, one wrote from England that he was a "draft resister; beat the rap on a legal technicality," and another that he had "several years of legal entanglement with the draft and the Justice Department."

A few of the personal reports are worth quoting for what they tell about the way the burden of the war fell on the men of Harvard. Here are two reports from people who felt the pinch:

> Number four in the draft lottery sparked my idealism, and I entered the Peace Corps following graduation. After eighteen or so peaceful and mostly enjoyable months in and around a peasant village in Senegal, West Africa, I returned home and ended up in the jungles of Harvard Law School."

> I got a lucky draft, number 13. That was good for six months in the Reserves. There I got in-depth training on how to be a "Petroleum Supply

Storage Specialist," i.e., a service station attendant. But the six months was put to good use by the Nixon Administration; that is how long it took to get me a security clearance for a job in the Executive Office. Six months after my arrival there, the Wage Price Control Program was hatched, and the next three years were spent diverting public attention from other matters that were attracting that attention. With a briefcase of anecdotes, I decided to divert my attention back to my studies in economics at Wisconsin.

Meanwhile, those men who did not go were preparing themselves, each by his own lights, for their contributions to the world:

My wife and I graduated from Harvard Law School in 1973, and we are both working for New York City firms. She is associated with Cravath, Swaine and Moore, and I am with Davis, Polk & Wardwell.

With four unpleasant medical school years behind me, I am enjoying Philadelphia and internship. I hope to deliver babies on Maui someday.

After the usual three-year stint (at Columbia) I find myself in the unusual position of practicing law in the entertainment field. Clients include Norman Lear, Burt Reynolds, Ryan O'Neil, Valerie Perrine, et al., as well as a number of "struggling young artists"—the latter pro bono, of course.

Am practicing corporate law (mostly tax), working fairly hard, enjoying my schizophrenic law firm—Berkeley happy life very much.

At a minimum, the record of my class should help Midge Decter over her fears that the people of my generation have somehow strayed from the straight and narrow path. More than that, it does sum up the home front's story of the war; we happy few were sped along to Maui or the entertainment law firm, or at worst temporarily waylaid in the reserves, while from each of our high schools the less gifted and industrious students were being shipped off as cannon fodder. There are those who contend that the world has always worked this way, and perhaps that is true. The question is why, especially in the atmosphere of the late sixties, people with any presumptions to character could have let it go on.

Learning from Lyndon

First, we should consider the conduct of the people who opposed the war. Not everyone at Harvard felt that way, nor, I suspect, did even a majority of the people throughout the country who found painless ways to escape the draft. But I did, and most of the people I knew did, and so did the hordes we always ran into at the antiwar rallies. Yet most of us managed without difficulty to stay out of jail. The tonier sorts of antiwar literature contained grace-note references to Gandhi and Thoreau—no CO application would have been complete without them—but the practical model for our wartime conduct was our enemy LBJ, who weaseled away from the front lines during World War II.

It may be worth emphasizing why our failure to resist induction is such an important issue. Five years after Cambodia and Kent State, it is clear how the war could have lasted so long. Johnson and Nixon both knew that the fighting could continue only so long as the vague, hypothetical benefits of holding off Asian communism outweighed the immediate, palpable domestic pain. They knew that when the screaming grew too loud and too many sons had been killed, the game would be all over. That is why Vietnamization was such a godsend for Nixon, and it is also why our reluctance to say No helped prolong the war. The more we guaranteed that we would end up neither in uniform nor behind bars, the more we made sure that *our* class of people would be spared the real cost of the war. (Not that we didn't suffer. There was, of course, the *angst,* the terrible moral malaise we liked to write about so much in the student newspapers and undergraduate novels.)

The children of the bright, good parents were spared the more immediate sort of suffering that our inferiors were undergoing. And because of that, when our parents were opposed to the war, they were opposed in a bloodless, theoretical fashion, as they might be opposed to political corruption or racism in South Africa. As long as the little gold stars kept going to homes in Chelsea and the backwoods of West Virginia, the mothers of Beverly Hills and Chevy Chase and Great Neck and Belmont were not on the telephone to their congressmen screaming, *"You killed my boy";* they were not writing to the president that his crazy, wrong, evil war had put their boys in prison and ruined their careers. It is clear by now that if the men of Harvard had wanted to do the very most they could to help shorten the war, they should have been drafted or imprisoned en masse.

This insight was not such a difficult one, even at the time. Lyndon Johnson clearly understood it, which was the main reason why the *graduate school* deferment, that grotesque of class discrimination, lasted through the big mobilizations of the war, until the springtime of 1968. Even when the deferment was done, Johnson's administrators came up with the intelligence-test plan for draft deferments, an even bolder attempt to keep those voluble upper classes off the president's back. What is interesting is how little of this whole phenomenon we at Harvard pretended to understand. On the day after the graduate school deferments were snatched away from us, a day Johnson must have dreaded because it added another set of nasty enemies to his list, the Harvard *Crimson* responded with a magnificently representative editorial entitled "The Axe Falls." A few quotes convey its gist:

> The axiom that this nation's tangled Selective Service System is bound to be unfair to somebody fell with a crash on the Harvard community yesterday. The National Security Council's draft directive puts almost all college seniors and most graduate students at the head of the line for next year's draft calls. Three-fourths of the second-year law class will go off to war. . . . Yesterday's directive is a bit of careless expediency, clearly unfair to the students who would have filled the nation's graduate schools next fall.

That was it, the almost incredible level of understanding and compassion we displayed at the time—the idea that the real victims of General Hershey's villainous schemes were *"the students who would have filled the nation's graduate schools next fall."* Occasionally, in the *Crimson* and elsewhere, there were bows to the discriminatory nature of the whole 2-S deferment system and the virtues of the random lottery that Edward Kennedy, to his eternal credit, was supporting almost singlehandedly at the time. But there was no mistaking which emotions came from the heart, which principles really seemed worth fighting for.

X-Ray Vision

It would be unfair to suggest that absolutely no thought was given to the long-run implications of our actions. For one thing, there were undercurrents of the sentiment that another *Crimson* writer, James Glassman, expressed in an article early in 1968. "Two years ago, Harvard students complained that the system was highly discriminatory, favoring the well off," Glassman wrote. "They called the 2-S an unfair advantage for those who could go to college." But as the war wore on, "the altruism was forgotten. What was most important now was saving your own skin—preventing yourself from being in a position where you would have to kill a man you had no right to kill."

Moreover, a whole theoretical framework was developed to justify draft evasion. During many of the same meetings where I heard about the techniques of weight reduction, I also learned that we should think of ourselves as sand in the gears of the great war machine. During one of those counseling sessions I sat through a speech by Michael Ferber, then something of a celebrity as a codefendant in the trial of Dr. Spock. He excited us by revealing how close we were to victory. Did we realize that the draft machine was tottering toward its ultimate breakdown? That it was hardly in better condition that old General Hershey himself? That each body we withheld from its ravenous appetite brought it that much nearer the end? Our duty, therefore, was clear: as committed opponents of the war, we had a responsibility to save ourselves from the war machine.

This argument was most reassuring, for it meant that the course of action that kept us alive and out of jail was also the politically correct decision. The boys of Chelsea were not often mentioned during these sessions; when they were, regret was expressed that they had not yet understood the correct approach to the draft. We resolved to launch political-education programs, some under the auspices of the Worker-Student Alliance, to help straighten them out. In the meantime, there was the physical to prepare for.

It does not require enormous powers of analysis to see the basic fraudulence of this argument. General Hershey was never in danger of running out of bodies, and the only thing we were denying him was the chance to put *us* in uniform. With the same x-ray vision that enabled us to see in every Pentagon subclerk, in every Honeywell accountant, an embryonic war criminal, we could certainly have seen that by keeping ourselves away from both frying pan and fire, we were prolonging the war and consigning the Chelsea boys to danger and death. But somehow the x-rays were deflected.

There was, I believe, one genuine concern that provided the x-ray shield and made theories like Ferber's go down more easily. It was a monstrous war, not only in its horror, but in the sense that it was beyond control, and to try to fight it as individuals was folly. Even as we knew that a thousand or ten thousand college boys going to prison might make a difference, we knew with equal certainty that the imprisonment and ruination of any one of us would mean nothing at all. The irrational war machine would grind on as if we had never existed, and our own lives would be pointlessly spoiled. From a certain perspective, it could even seem like grandstanding, an exercise in excessive piety, to go to the trouble of resisting the draft. The one moral issue that was within our control was whether we would actually participate—whether, as Glassman put it, we would be forced to kill—and we could solve that issue as easily by getting a deferment as by passing the time in jail.

Not Worth the Gesture

We were not the first to face the dilemma. In his new book, *World War II*, James Jones describes how the same considerations affected men in combat. As an infantryman in the Pacific, Jones had survived months of deadly action only to come up with a twisted ankle, an aggravation of an old injury. He heard from the company's medical officer that the injury might be enough to get him a medical discharge and return to the States:

> He had presented me with a serious moral problem. I talked it over with a few of my buddies. . . . All of them urged me to go up to division medical with it. They would certainly go up with it if they had it, if they were me, and maybe it would get them out of there. . . . I would be crazy not to try. "But what about the company," I asked the mess sergeant, and the supply sergeant, and a couple of the field sergeants—"Would you leave the company?"
>
> "Are you kidding?" the supply sergeant said. "I'd be out of here like a shot."
>
> I was smart enough to understand that if I did go, and did get sent out, it was not going to affect anything in any appreciable way. Some poor-ass, bad-luck replacement would replace me, and one of the guys would get my corporal's ratings. I understood that numbers were what counted in this war, vast numbers of men and machines. I was intelligent enough to see that.

Jones decided that it was not worth the gesture, that it would not be intelligent to run any more risks, and so did we. The difference is that Jones had already been through half of the worst campaigns of the war, and we had not been through much of anything at all. We told ourselves that the rallies and sit-ins were the real thing, but they never involved a substantial risk, nothing more serious than the threat of a night in jail. That was one reason why Kent State was so deeply appalling to many students; it changed the rules, it added an element of risk.

Expiation

Lord Jim spent the rest of his days trying to expiate his moment of cowardice aboard the *Patna*. The contemporaries of Oliver Wendell Holmes felt permanent discomfort that Holmes, virtually alone among his peers, had volunteered to fight in the Civil War. I have neither of those feelings about Vietnam, so they are not the reason I feel it important to dredge up these hulks. Rather, the exercise can serve two purposes—to tell us about the past and to tell us about the present.

The lesson of the past concerns the complexities of human motivation. Doubtless because the enemy we were fighting was so horrible in its effects, there was very little room for complexity or ambiguity in the antiwar campaigns. On the black-and-white spectrum by which we judged personal conduct, bureaucrats were criminals if they stayed inside the government, and politicians were cowards if they failed to vote for resolutions to end the war; the businessmen of Dow and Honeywell were craven merchants of death; and we, meanwhile, were nothing less than the insistent voice of morality, striving tirelessly to bring the country to its senses. The easiest way to see those feelings revived is to attend a showing of the movie *Hearts and Minds* in the company of the young. When the lone heralds of morality, the antiwar protestors, finally appear, the audience breaks into cheers. *We were right.*

Of course, we were right to try to stop the war. But I recall no suggestion during the sixties that it was graceless, *wrong* of us to ask the Foreign Service officers to resign when we were not sticking our necks out at the induction center. Granted, there is a difference between those two risks; imprisonment for a felony is a serious matter, and it was perhaps one degree more perilous to refuse induction as a twenty-one year old than to throw aside a career as a forty-five-year-old father of three. But our calculations rarely even reached that point. The normal benchmark of morality was this: if we were showing our stuff by taking to the picket lines (meanwhile continuing our cruise through college), then our elders were shameful, middle-aged cowards if they did not do their part, too. If nothing else, a glance back at our own record might give us an extra grain of sympathy for the difficulties of bringing men to honor, let alone glory.

The implications for the present are less comforting and go back to the question asked several pages ago. The behavior of the upper classes in so deftly avoiding the war's pains is both a symptom and a partial cause of the class hatred now so busily brewing in the country.

Tom Joad v. Edmund Wilson

The starting point for understanding this class hatred is the belief, resting just one layer beneath the pro forma comments about the unfortunate discrimination of the 2-S system, that there was an ultimate justice to our fates. You could not live through those years without knowing what was going on with the draft, and you could not retain your sanity with that knowledge unless you believed, at some dark layer of the moral substructure, that we were somehow getting what we deserved. A friend of mine, a former Rhodes scholar now embarked on a wonderful career in corporate law, put the point more bluntly than most when he said, "There are certain people who can do more good in a lifetime in politics or academics or medicine than by getting killed in a trench"; in one form or another, it was that belief that kept us all going. What is so significant about this statement is not the recognition of the difference in human abilities—for that, after all, has been one of the grand constants of the race—but the utter disdain for the abilities, hopes, complexities of those who have not scrambled onto the high road. The one-dimensional meritocracy of Aldous Huxley's *Brave New World* is not so many steps away from the fashion in which we were content to distribute the burden of the war.

This claim about class hostility is a relative one—that the seeds of class warfare now fall on more fertile ground than they have for many years. The war in Vietnam was not the sole cause, but it did contribute, in a way that may become more clear through a comparison of that war and the years leading up to World War II.

At the beginning of the forties, the United States was leaving behind an era of class division nearly as poisonous as what the seventies seem to be producing. The rich feared the poor, the poor envied the rich, and only the perseverance of an old American myth kept the envy from shading over into more violent emotions. In the movies, the downtrodden of the thirties saw that miracles could still happen—the chorus girl could marry the millionaire, rags could turn into riches. On the sports fields, a few athletes could hit it big; pretty girls had a chance in Hollywood. As long as there were enough of these brass rings, perhaps one for every ten thousand people reaching out to grab, one kind of class hostility was neatly blunted. The poor were encouraged to think of *joining* the rich, rather than overthrowing them.

The more trenchant political theorists of the era did not fall into this trap, but they did display another symptom of class stratification: That was the romanticized, simplistic notion of egalitarianism that the upper-class intellectuals seemed eager to spout. The socialists and communists of New York and Boston might never have seen an Okie in their lives, but they often seemed to imagine themselves as citified versions of Steinbeck's Tom Joad, making a common cause against the bankers and the privileged classes. Workers of all social classes were united in one great effort: if you looked deep enough into the coal mines or the cotton fields, you would find replicas of Granville Hicks, John Dos Passos, and the other luminaries of the left—a little grimy, perhaps, and with quaint regionalisms in their speech, but nonetheless possessed of the same fine qualities of mind and spirit. There were, of course, similarities between the political ideals of both groups, but the unity between worker and intellectual could be romanticized out of all proportion to reality, as it was in this manifesto issued by Edmund Wilson and signed by several dozen other "brain workers" in 1932:

> Very well, we strike hands with our true comrades. We claim our own, and we reject the disorder, the lunacy spawned by grabbers, advertisers, traders, speculators, salesmen, the much-adulated, immensely stupid and irresponsible "business men." We claim the right to live and function. It is our business to think and we shall not permit business men to teach us our business. It is also, in the end, our business to act.
>
> We have acted. As responsible intellectual workers we have aligned ourselves with the frankly revolutionary Communist Party, the party of the workers. In this letter we speak to you of our own class—to the writers, artists, scientists, teachers, engineers, to all honest professional workers— telling you as best we can why we have made this decision and why we think that you too should support the Communist Party in the political campaign now under way.

If this manifesto recalls anything, it is the equally pie-eyed rhetoric of the

Worker-Student Alliance during the late sixties. All we lacked was our own Clifford Odets to sing the revolutionary consciousness of the factory worker.

The coming of World War II changed this attitude, and many others, for one predominant reason: this broad national effort required some mixing between the classes. Unlike my college class, which lost not a single member in Vietnam, thirty-five men from the Harvard class of 1941 had died by the time the war was over, and hundreds more had fought. Across class lines, young men were all expected to serve. The mixing, if incomplete, still provided a degree of cross-exposure not known before or since. And the mutual sacrifice created a basis for mutual respect.

The benefits of this exposure should not themselves be romanticized, for at war's end the Vanderbilts and the poor white trash were hardly ready to consider themselves brothers under the skin. But, even as members of each class remained sharply aware of their respective positions, even as the postwar era brought in the vigorous upward striving of the status seekers, two vastly important things had happened because of the wartime cross-exposure.

The first was the purging of the oversimplified romanticism of the intellectuals of the thirties. Plays such as *Waiting for Lefty* had imputed to the working classes a purity of motive and a clarity of vision that would have done credit to St. Francis. It cannot have taken too many months of living and eating and fighting together for the college-educated elite to see that a more complicated mixture of motives was propelling the representatives of the proletariat. When some son of the backwoods South charged off bravely into battle, it was not under the banner of the populist alliance against the barons of Wall Street, but because of an ideology of a different sort—part a sense of duty, part the crazy Southern mystique about gallantry and masculine heroism, part a sense of fatalism and inescapability. The true voice of this united national war effort was not Edmund Wilson's manifesto or the duty-honor-country propaganda films turned out by Hollywood or even Ernie Pyle, with his occasional spells of romanticizing the fighting man. It was Bill Mauldin, absolutely free of pretense and absolutely on key about the mixture of cynicism and backhanded honor that kept the troops going. Anyone who participated in that effort, or even read the cartoons, could no longer believe that *Waiting for Lefty* was an accurate portrait of American life.

The second effect was the reduction of the opposite sort of oversimplification: the tendency to ridicule, condemn, even hate people from the classes different from your own. The war taught the country not that Tom

Joad and Edmund Wilson were identically gifted, but that there were qualities to be honored in each, abilities in one that the other might count on for survival. The literature of the war is full of examples. To take *The Caine Mutiny,* one of the high-class characters, the novelist Tom Keefer, turns out to be a coward when the others are relying on him, whereas his brother dies saving his own ship, and the mama's boy from Princeton, Willie Keith, becomes a kind of hero. The enlisted men they work with have the same range of qualities—some posses the coolheadedness that saves their shipmates during the typhoon, others are lower-class versions of Tom Keefer. The importance of these portrayals and of the more widespread ethic they represented was that, without relying on the old fiction that all men are identical, they allowed some room for mutual respect and mutual dependence. People who had spent months in a hut with strangers would, in the future, probably be one step slower to oversimplify and hate than they would have been in the past. This is why the military's racial segregation during World War II was such a tragedy; it kept any of the ameliorating balm from being spread between the races. The effect was limited to the different classes of White America, but even that was something of value.

The American society that grew out of the war certainly was no utopia. Still, the United States of Truman and Eisenhower at least could say for itself that it was not colored by the kind of entrenched class hostility that now seems to be on the rise. The difference between the two eras is symbolized by the difference between the great national effort of the forties—the war—and the two broad-based struggles of the last fifteen years, the crusade for civil rights and the effort to end our participation in Vietnam.

Contempt for the Proles

In that happy time before racism was discovered in the North, the civil rights crusade took the convenient form of a virtuous nation lecturing to its sinning minority—in this case, that favorite reprobate, the South. Early in the sixties, a new twist was added when the bright, young college student went trooping down from the Ivy League, ready to protect the downtrodden but virtuous Black people from the tyranny of the immoral Whites. This may be caricature, but not by much; I joined the crusade long after its heyday had passed, and even then the essential elements were intact. Like the characters in *Waiting for Lefty* or *Awake and Sing,* the Blacks of our dreams were well motivated, nature's noblemen types, and when their real-life counterparts fell short, we found ways of ignoring it. The Southern Whites, of course, were brutal, stupid rednecks whom, when we were feeling both compassionate and condescending, we could forgive by explaining that it was status anxiety about the Blacks that made them so nasty. We walked as through a fantasy world, seeing imaginary figures rather than real people; rarely were there bursts of understanding, or even realism, that could have helped explain how the South actually worked.

The "movement" of the sixties extended from the civil rights struggle through the campaign to end the war, and there was continuity as well in its view of the lower class. By the end of the sixties, when the antiwar campaign was going full steam, it exhibited contempt for the White proles in three clear ways. One was paying so little attention to the rate at which the Chelsea boys were dying—we mentioned the casualty rates, but not the fact that it wasn't our type of people being killed. The second was the bullying, supercilious tone that said that to support the war was not so much incorrect as *stupid*. (Recall how quickly arguments about the war reached the pedant's level with the question: "Have you read . . . ? If you haven't read . . . how can you presume to say anything?") And the third, rivaling even with the first in ugliness, was the quick resort to the phrase "pig" for the blue-collar, lower-class people who were doing the job they thought they were supposed to do. They had been "pigs" holding down the Black people in Mississippi; the children of "pigs" were being sent off to die in Vietnam; and now "pigs" were clubbing our chosen people, the demonstrators in Chicago. We hated the pigs, and let them know it, and it was no great wonder that they hated us in return.

Now that the war is over, there is a fourth demonstration of our contempt for the proles. Among any highbrow audience, it is scarcely possible to attract a minute's attention on the subject of Vietnam veterans. Ralph Nader sponsored a study of their predicament, written by Paul Starr, but apart from that, the intelligentsia has virtually willed them out of existence. The indignities they suffer rival those of any other oppressed group, but the only magazine to give sustained attention to this fact is *Penthouse*. On television, the veterans are painted with extremely unflattering strokes—as wartime junkies or pathological killers who keep reenacting the massacres they took part in—but no protests are heard about this crude stereotyping. The most frequently offered explanation for the neglect of the veteran is the *kind* of war we fought and our eagerness to forget it. No doubt that explanation is partly true. But our behavior is also shaped by *who* the veterans are. They are the boys from Chelsea, and if we were embarrassed to see them at the navy yard, when their suffering was only prospective, how much more must we shun them now?

The Decline of Public Schools

From its struggles in World War II, this country created a cushion of class toleration; our heritage from Vietnam is rich with potential for class hatred. World War II forced different classes of people to live together; Vietnam kept them rigidly apart, a process in which people like me were only too glad to cooperate. On either side of the class divide, the war has left feelings that can easily shade over into mistrust and hostility. Among those who went to war, there is a residual resentment, the natural result of a cool look at who ended up paying what price. On the part of those who were spared, there is a residual guilt, often so deeply buried that it surfaces only in unnaturally vehement denials that there is anything to feel guilty about. In a land of supposed opportunity, the comfortable hate to see the poor. Beneath all the explanations about self-help and just deserts, there remains the vein of empathy and guilt. Among the bright people of my generation, those who have made a cult of their high-mindedness, the sight of legless veterans and the memories of the Navy Yard must also touch that vein. They remind us that there was little character in the choices we made.

If the war were the only source of this mistrust, it would be bad enough, but it has worked its influence on a society already facing class division from three other sources. The first, and in the long run the most significant, is the decline of the public school system and the stratification by class, as well as by race, of the urban schools. Whatever their faults, the public schools of this country could usually be relied on to serve one end. They were the melting pot; they brought together children whose parents lived on different sides of the tracks and who themselves clearly were headed for different stations in life. If you were one of the people going on to college, in high school you got to know people who weren't. This contact did not guarantee that you would come to mutual affection, or even understanding, but it could dampen the chances for hatred in the same way the military did in World War II.

In some smaller communities, where one's high school serves the entire town and where the education remains good enough to meet the standards of ambitious parents, this end still is served. But in more and more of the urban schools, it has been abandoned altogether. As the Whites have fled to the suburbs, as the declining quality of urban education has made sure they will never come back, as the integration plans have stopped at the city limits rather than embracing the full racial mix of the metropolitan areas, the urban classroom has come to resemble the army in Vietnam, mainly lower-class Whites coexisting with lower-class Blacks (the middle-class Blacks having followed their White counterparts' example and headed for the suburbs or the private schools). In the past few years, the most obvious cost of this arrangement has been the desperate reaction of the Whites one rung up from the bottom—the Whites of Pontiac and Southie—when they fear they will be dragged back to the level of the lower-class Blacks. In the years to come, the more important cost may be the distorting effects of class segregation on people from both top and bottom.

The second development is the rise of a new professional class, closely corresponding to the educational elite. In the years since World War II, the number of people working for government has risen dramatically. The expansion hit the federal government first, in the forties and fifties, and is now most intense for local governments and the states. Within the last ten years, the type of people filling these jobs has also begun to change. The transformation, from patronage to professionalism, has been most obvious at the local level, where it means that the city clerk or the second-echelon health administrator for the state is less likely to be a local good ole boy and more likely to be a handsomely pedigreed young professional. (The young professional, in turn, is likely to be the good ole boy's son, full of disdain for the class he has risen above.) During the sixties, many of the same well-educated people were also filling new positions opening up in the foundation world and other public affairs sectors of the economy.

The effect of these developments has been to place the educationally privileged in jobs whose essence is telling other people what to do. No government can get along without such jobs, but the way they are developing now clearly aggravates class hostility. Among people on the top, it creates an impression that the "public" is a retrograde mass, which must be either fooled or "educated" into overcoming its brutish instincts. Congressional staffers, public education directors for foundations, producers for public TV constantly fret about how to make the public overcome White backlash, support the UN, and conserve energy by obeying the fifty-five-mile-per-hour speed limit. Any of these goals might be laudable, but as with the civil rights crusaders, little consideration is given to the reasons more complicated than bigotry, greed, and stupidity that shape people's behavior. When Lord Reith of the BBC set out unashamedly to bring the masses better material than what their own taste would guide them toward, he fit comfortably within the British tradition of dominant and inferior classes. As the professional elite of the United States acquire an arrogance that none of the governed can fail to notice, George Wallace gets his biggest cheers for his denunciation of the pointy heads—and that can hardly come as a surprise.

The third development is the right of the meritocracy of taste and the consequent shortage of charity and toleration among those on top. As family pedigrees have lost much of their import and as the ranks of the upper levels have been opened to the self-made, the American cultural race has become, as Suzannah Lessard has pointed out ("Taste, Class and Mary Tyler Moore," the *Washington Monthly,* March 1975), a subtle matter of multiple labels adding up to a person's taste—education, associates, profession, passions, dislikes. Even as this has made for a somewhat fairer society than the world of the 400, it has added a note of desperation to the quest for social standing. Because there is no permanent standard like the old standard of family pedigree, no one can feel completely secure. Those who hope to remain "in" must be constantly aware of which artifacts are right and which are wrong. (A recent ad for the *Village Voice* demonstrated this point nicely. A takeoff on the old ninety-seven-pound weakling pitch, it showed a couple on the beach being approached by Rodney Trendy. His weapon was not muscles but being able to put down hapless Stan for out-of-date taste: "Still waiting on line for 'Last Tango,' Stan? How's your Nehru jacket supply? Bet you think Arica's a high-school honor society. Haw, Haw, Haw.")

The insecurity of this kind of class structure is its most destructive feature and accounts for two unpleasant results. One is the remarkable phenomenon of people—who, by every outside standard, should be secure against criticism—flaring up in indignant and disproportionate defense against any imagined slight. The tangled history of literary politicking in New York is one long case study. The intellectuals understand that Nixon went to unreasonable lengths to defend himself against a few pitiful demonstrators, but let one bad review be written of a friend's book, and they roll out the heavy artillery. Leonard Bernstein held his party for the Black Panthers when they were still chic; anyone who held a party for them came out high on the taste charts. Soon afterward, Bernstein was turned into an object of ridicule by Tom Wolfe, who said (in *Radical Chic*) that the parties weren't chic at all; in fact, they were ludicrous. Then, for sharp observers, the way to go to win the taste game was to laugh at Bernstein. But no one associated with Bernstein and his kind of taste could sit still for that, and so abusive reviews were written of Wolfe's book in an attempt to put *him* down. For those of us whose fates are not played out in such public arenas, the put-down game has its more modest applications. The cultural gamesman who comes across a nasty review of *Ragtime* has a potent weapon to use the next time he hears someone praising the book.

The second result of this cultural insecurity is an intolerance toward mass culture. There is no such thing as a simple highbrow/lowbrow cultural distinction anymore; indeed, one of the important tricks in winning the taste stakes is to know when to pick up certain parts of popular culture—Harry Truman, roller derbies, country music—and when to drop them cold. It is the necessity of dropping, the importance of putting down the things not currently "in," that makes for the destruction because it leaves little room for toleration of the other classes. Oldsmobiles are not currently one of the chic items in mass culture, so Larry McMurtry, writing in the *Atlantic's* issue on Texas, defined the difference between himself and the mass of Texans this way:

> What I *really* felt, on my visit home, was that for three weeks I was surrounded by Oldsmobiles; probably I had been surrounded by them for the 32 years that I lived in Texas, but had simply accepted them without really noticing it, as one accepts chicken-fried steak without really tasting it.
>
> Exile is supposed to give one perspective, and mine has. I work in Georgetown, where I am surrounded by Mercedes and Volvos.

A disdain for Oldsmobiles, the segregation of school children, even the bitter residue of the war—perhaps none of these things will bring us to class warfare. But we have created a world in which they can.

War Memorial: Staying Close to a Buddy Twenty-five Years after His Death

GEORGE SWIERS

DURING THE MIDDLE watch, in the eerie midnight hour, every sound in the Vietnamese jungle seemed horribly intensified. Every shadow gave the appearance of death coming to call. If you were lucky, very lucky, it was merely your fatigue and anxiety and nothing more. But luck, in March's last week in 1969, was the lover that had fled the ninth Marines, leaving us with that collective foreboding familiar to the infantry in every war. The awful wisdom that something terrible was about to happen. Soon.

So I was grateful for the company that night when Paul, who was unable or unwilling to sleep, came and sat beside me on my watch. No company, in good times or bad, was better company than Paul Baker. That night, a night suffocating with apprehension, he actually sang. Sang in this ridiculous tone-deaf whisper—not Hendrix, the Doors, the Temptations, or any other secular grunt anthems—but this wonderfully corny song called "High Hopes." Sang this inspirational melody about ants moving rubber tree plants until we laughed so hard he had to clamp a hand over my mouth.

Of all the mysteries of the mind, the greatest is how it faithfully protects us. A quarter of a century later, whenever I hear "High Hopes" I burst into spontaneous laughter, and that night long ago, courtesy of my friend Paul,

Originally published in *The Daily Gazette,* Schenectady, N.Y., May 29, 1994.

I forgot that I was a hostage to tomorrow. "Stay close tomorrow," whispered Paul, after a long, mournful silence, "It'll be OK."

My son, Paul, is three now. Innocent enough to see life as a daily, delightful adventure. Bold enough so that the adventure is boundless. Among his favorite adventures are the once in awhile visits to the comfortable North Troy neighborhood where John and Marion Baker raised their four children. Marion Baker, he knows, will tirelessly produce toys, books, and juice to indulge him, will laugh lovingly at his silly attempts at conversation, will tenderly take his hand when he wishes to explore her home.

As I watch this warm, dignified woman enjoying my son, I wonder if she thinks about her own Paul. Perhaps proudly recalling the class president, gifted athlete, valedictorian at Troy's Catholic Central. Perhaps painfully recollecting the helplessness she surely felt that evening when he called to say that he'd quit college, joined the marines, and had volunteered for Vietnam because, he insisted, so many less fortunate were required to serve. And I wonder, too, about the bond, forged by chance, that we share. She had been with him when he came into this world, and I was with him when he left it.

I was beside Paul that afternoon, staying close, part of a long horizontal line moving up the wooded hillside—moving up in the relentless heat, against an objective we knew could never be taken. Then, just in front of Paul and me, the khaki blur of a North Vietnamese soldier and the distinct pops of an AK-47 rifle. That quickly. Leaving me to forever wonder why he chose my friend, not me, leaving me with the most profound, instant loneliness I ever knew.

Then the khaki blurs were everywhere, and the rest of the horizontal line began to die. Died all that afternoon. Mostly teenagers. Sometimes in twos or threes. White, Black, Red, and Brown. At nightfall, isolated and devastated, we formed a circle around our dead and dying friends and hoped for morning. That night I lay beside Doc Tom, our hospital corpsman, and told him about the song Paul had sung the night before. Tom wept unashamedly for the friend he loved and missed, then said something extraordinary. He said he was thankful that Paul had been the first to die, that seeing what had happened would have broken his heart.

Some people go to war and lose their lives. Others go to war and find that life has given them a second chance.

Each night when I look in on my son, usually in the midnight hour, I adjust the lighting in the hall just so, and let a soothing circle of light drip through his open doorway. Each night he looks the same. Smiling the sleep that only children can know. His blankie, worn more thin and ragged by the day's adventure, is balled in a tiny pillow.

In frequent moments of moral outrage, I promise myself that he will never go to war. In calmer moments, I know that if he always acts on principle and follows his conscience, as I hope he will, the path will sometimes lead there anyway. The fact is, I have not yet learned myself whether the greater madness lies in war or in the casual indifference to it.

"Stay close tomorrow." I whisper to him each night. "It'll be OK."

American War Crimes and Vietnam Veterans

TOD ENSIGN

ALMOST EVERY AMERICAN over thirty-five knows about the My Lai massacre and its impact on public opinion about the Vietnam War. Less well known is the organizing among Vietnam combat veterans that followed the disclosure of this gruesome atrocity. They testified in grassroots citizens commissions across the country about policies conceived at the highest levels of command that led, inevitably, to the commission of war crimes in Vietnam.

Some of us in the antiwar movement recognized that the Nixon administration's cynical scapegoating of a few low-ranking GIs for the My Lai massacre provided a unique opportunity to organize veterans to speak out against the war in general and against their victimization in particular.

In the wake of the My Lai disclosures, antiwar groups were not alone in asking whether international law had been violated. Thirty-four law professors and eminent attorneys, led by former Supreme Court justice Arthur Goldberg, signed a letter asking President Nixon to appoint a special presidential commission to investigate whether the war "is being conducted in a manner inconsistent with . . . international law."

Unfortunately for Nixon and Secretary of State Henry Kissinger, My Lai came to light at a particularly delicate stage of negotiations with the Vietnamese. Historians tell us that both men feared that any in-depth probe of our military policies in Vietnam would further undermine support for continuing the war—if they decided that such a continuation was necessary.

In *Kissinger: The Price of Power* (1983), Seymour Hersh reports that behind closed doors, Nixon blamed the entire My Lai controversy on "those dirty rotten Jews from New York."

Actually, Nixon gave the *New York Times* and the other national media far too much credit for journalistic zeal in unearthing the truth about the atrocity. For more than eight months, Ron Ridenhour, a freelance journalist, repeatedly sent out a detailed report about the massacre to public officials and the media, but he never generated any interest—except for a secret army investigation of his charges. Ridenhour was serving as a combat soldier in Vietnam when he learned about the atrocity from other GIs who had witnessed it.

America's allegedly antiwar media was so passive about exposing My Lai that the charge against Lt. William Calley for multiple murder counts of "Oriental human beings" had been public for more than two months before any national story appeared. That article, which earned Seymour Hersh a Pulitzer Prize, was broken by an independent news service—not by the "big guys" in New York or at the *Washington Post.*

In 1992, two British journalists took a fresh look at the My Lai massacre by producing an award-winning TV documentary and a book, both entitled *Four Hours in My Lai.* By relying on many previously unavailable military documents, they confirmed what we in the antiwar movement had said in 1969: that the U.S. military had organized a systematic coverup of the atrocity just hours after it occurred. They also unearthed army reports of another massacre of ninety civilians carried out by another company of the same brigade in Co Luy hamlet, one and one-half miles from My Lai, on the same morning. The army was able to deflect any concern about this second massacre by falsely blaming it on the South Vietnamese military.

Within a week after the My Lai storm hit, Jeremy Rifkin and I, both antiwar activists, met with staff members of the Bertrand Russell Peace Foundation to discuss their public call for the creation of citizens commissions to collect testimony from Vietnam veterans. Two years earlier in Sweden and Denmark, Lord Russell had initiated tribunals on war crimes in Vietnam. At the second tribunal in Roskilde, Denmark, three American veterans—Peter Martinsen, David Tuck, and Don Duncan—provided eyewitness accounts of wanton killing and torture to the tribunal, which was composed of such distinguished members as Jean-Paul Sartre, James Baldwin, and Simone de Beauvoir.

Although the Russell hearings received extensive coverage in Europe, reports about them were virtually blacked out in the United States. The

New York Times did, however, find space for an editorial that lambasted the Russell panel as a kangaroo court that lacked any moral or legal authority.

And although the Russell proceedings were well-known within the American antiwar movement, two more years would pass before Vietnam veterans would have a forum from which they could expose and denounce policies that they'd been forced to implement and that led to the commission of war crimes.

From the first disclosures about My Lai, the Pentagon adopted a game plan for handling allegations about war crimes that served it well in the next few years. It chose to treat Vietnam atrocities as a strictly criminal matter. Therefore, military police agencies were given complete control over all investigations. When eyewitnesses to various atrocities refused to be interviewed or couldn't be found, these cases were simply closed for "insufficient evidence." Also, by treating each atrocity as an isolated act, unconnected to larger policies, the investigators could focus all their attention on a few low-ranking GIs rather than trace the source of war crimes up the chain of command to policymakers in Saigon or Washington.

I learned for the first time, while reading the book *Four Hours at My Lai,* which Michael Bilton and Kevin Sim published in 1992, that the army had created a Vietnam War Crimes Working Group in 1970. The creation of this panel of high-ranking officers signaled the Pentagon's deep concern about the impact My Lai would have on its continued prosecution of the Vietnam War. They likely feared that the exposure of additional war crimes might further erode public confidence.

Unfortunately, the activities of the working group were kept secret, at least from the public and press. In retrospect, we could have predicted that the military would probably create a mechanism of this type to control negative publicity and, to use today's lingo, to put the Pentagon's "spin" on the issue of war crimes in Vietnam. If we'd been less confrontational and more adept at finding allies within the press and Congress, we probably could have smoked out the working group's existence, which would have allowed us to challenge it aggressively at every turn and demand that it broaden the scope of its investigations to include strategy and tactics passed down from Washington.

Even in 1969, we understood that the disclosure of American war crimes was politically explosive. We also knew that many combat vets felt personally threatened by Nixon and the Pentagon's insistence that war crimes were isolated events for which sadistic or deranged soldiers should be held accountable.

We believed that by creating public forums at which veterans could condemn both the command's policies, which led inevitably to the commission of war crimes, and its scapegoating of individual GIs, we would be able to undermine whatever public support still existed for U.S. intervention in Vietnam. We hoped that members of Nixon's "silent majority" would be willing to listen to the testimony of their own sons, who were returning from the war.

Unfortunately for Jeremy and me, all the Bertrand Russell folks were offering us was the concept of the citizens commissions and their moral support. Beyond that, we were on our own. It may be difficult to understand in the cynical nineties, but Jeremy and I were eager to forge ahead. It's easy to believe that money and support will come your way when you feel yourself to be part of a large, progressive movement.

Trained as a lawyer, I was given the assignment of researching what legal risks, if any, existed for veterans who publicly admitted to participating in or witnessing war crimes while serving in Vietnam. The Supreme Court had ruled after the Korean War that a discharged veteran could not be ordered back to active duty solely for the purpose of trying him or her at court-martial. It later occurred to me that the Pentagon was also happy with this precedent. It meant that if their investigators were called to probe allegations of war crimes that had occurred years earlier, few of the lower-ranking GIs would still be on active duty. Because it was not their practice to prosecute high-ranking career officers (only one colonel was ever court-martialed for war crimes), the military was spared embarrassing court-martials in most cases.

Next, Jeremy and I had to consider ways of involving veterans' organizations in our investigations. The "big three" veterans groups—the American Legion, the Disabled American Veterans, and the Veterans of Foreign Wars—with a combined membership of more than six million, were still rabidly pro-war. Their conventions were one of the few venues left where presidents could still hope to find a warm reception for their plans to continue the war. Clearly, their leaders were not going to cooperate with our efforts to demolish one of America's best-guarded myths—that our intervention in Vietnam was prompted by high moral purpose.

At that time, only two national vet groups were against the war: the Chicago-based Vets for Peace and Vietnam Veterans Against the War (VVAW), which was then headquartered in New York City. Both groups were quite small, a few hundred members at most, and neither group had full-time staff. The midwest group had actively demonstrated against the war, but most of its members were World War II or Korean War vets. We sought the support of both groups and, in the case of VVAW, were able to obtain membership lists, which we used for leads to potential witnesses.

I vividly recall our first in-depth interview with Vietnam combat veterans. Jeremy and I had traveled to Toronto in December 1969, reasoning that deserters from the Vietnam War might be more willing than other veterans to publicly disclose war crimes they'd witnessed. We spent an unforgettable afternoon in the Toronto suburbs listening as two baby-faced GIs described, in horrific detail, what it was like to fight with the 173d Airborne Brigade. Their description stripped away the facade created by antiseptic phrases such as *free fire zones* and *harassment and interdiction fire,* forcing us to confront the gruesome reality that lay behind them.

That night, I slept fitfully, tortured by graphic nightmares in which I was a combat soldier in Vietnam. In one vision, I helped to scalp a corpse in the same manner described to us earlier. After that night, however, my psyche made some sort of adjustment because never again did I have a strong emotional reaction to the gruesome testimony I was helping to gather and publicize.

When I look back at what we did, I realize we were insensitive to the psychological turmoil that could be stimulated when a veteran began to disclose long-buried memories of truly horrible events. At least some of the veterans we worked with at the various citizens commissions were suffering from post-traumatic stress disorder. It's difficult to say, however, whether the act of publicly disclosing their participation in war crimes would have exacerbated a previously existing mental condition. What I do know, however, is that as New Leftists, we regarded as paramount our political goal of undermining and discrediting U.S. military intervention in Vietnam. When we encountered what appeared to be an emotionally shaky veteran who had strong and credible evidence about atrocities, we encouraged him to testify. We shared a belief that getting a veteran to shift responsibility for war crimes to his military and civilian leadership would help ease his own personal guilt and torment.

Word about our efforts to organize citizens commissions spread rapidly throughout the antiwar movement. We conducted our first hearing in Annapolis, Maryland, in February 1970, with the Maryland Veterans for Peace as cosponsor. With Canadian antiwar groups in Toronto, we also organized a simultaneous hearing at which several American deserters detailed their Vietnam experiences to the press.

Déjà Vu All Over Again

After finally learning of the military's War Crimes Working Group, I traveled to the National Archives in College Park, Maryland, in April 1997 to sift through its records and files. It was fascinating to read, almost three decades later, what the "other side" did in response to our activities.

The working group was established in 1970 in an effort to coordinate the military's response to new allegations of atrocities, which began to surface after the My Lai massacre became an international scandal in November 1969. Although some allegations trickled in from individual veterans, the group was primarily concerned with allegations being made at various commissions that we sponsored. By February 1971, the working group was busy enough to justify a weekly "Talking Paper" memo, which was edited by the unit's commander, an army colonel. This memo provided status reports on the various probes being conducted by its military investigators, along with summaries of news reports about new allegations of atrocities. In 1972, this report became a monthly publication. It was discontinued in June 1973.

The first citizens commission to receive national attention with a story in the *New York Times* was one I had organized in April 1970 in Springfield, Massachusetts. There, a former helicopter pilot, David Bressem, described witnessing the aftermath of what he called a "turkey shoot" in which U.S. helicopters mowed down at least thirty-three unarmed Vietnamese civilians, including several children. Bressem inspected the death scene, where he saw no weapons. He vividly recalled that a small boy was still clutching the halter of his water buffalo.

Unknown to us, the War Crimes Working Group launched one of its first investigations by probing into Bressem's allegations. Following what was to become their standard practice, they placed strict limits on the scope of the inquiry. They contacted Bressem and several others whom he had named. Bressem refused to provide a detailed statement, in part because he agreed with us that individuals shouldn't become scapegoats in the investigation of such policies as "body counting" which encouraged indiscriminate killing as a means of winning promotion and favorable ratings.

I also recall Bressem telling me that his former commander later telephoned, pleading with him not to cooperate with an investigation that would destroy his military career. Torn between his respect for the man as a military leader and his outrage that such killings could be swept under the rug as "body counting," Bressem decided not to cooperate with the army's investigators. According to the working group's files, the Bressem investigation was closed on November 25, 1970, with the notation, "insufficient evidence to prove or disprove."

In retrospect, I feel that we could have been more creative in our response to the Pentagon's search for scapegoats. One tactic would have been to encourage witnesses to cooperate if the military provided them with immunity from criminal prosecution. It's unlikely that military officials would have accepted this condition, given their prosecution of Lt. Calley, but it would have made it more difficult for them to blame their inaction on uncooperative witnesses. Our ultimate goal was to force the command to scrutinize strategic policies that inevitably resulted in the commission of atrocities. As long as they focused solely on the individual conduct of GIs, however, they could continue to avoid such an investigation.

An In-Depth Probe That Wasn't

As the waves of public disgust over My Lai continued to roil the political waters, the Pentagon felt it necessary to appoint a special investigative panel, composed of high-ranking officers and led by a respected two-star general, William Peers.

The Peers Commission labored mightily for months, interviewing hundreds of witnesses to reconstruct the massacre in all its horrific detail. Eventually, it published a massive, four-volume report. Unfortunately, it provides only an exhaustive look at the events at My Lai that morning; none of the army strategic concepts or "rules of engagement" are given serious scrutiny—sort of like an accident report on the sinking of the *Titanic* never discussing icebergs or other weather conditions.

One recommendation tucked away in the Peers report was that, in the future, commanders should not allow their troops to bring personal cameras into war zones. Remember, without the color photos taken by Ron Haeberle, the unit photographer, with his personal camera, it would have been much easier for the army to distort or deny the entire incident.

The Truth Is Told

Throughout 1970, we conducted citizens commissions in Los Angeles, Boston, New York City, Buffalo, Minneapolis, Portland, and Richmond,

Virginia. Usually, the antiwar coalition in each city would play a role, helping us to identify veterans who were witnesses and cosponsoring the public event. I particularly recall the Buffalo commission, during which five local veterans kept an overflow crowd of three hundred transfixed with accounts of war crimes committed, as policy, by their military units. U.S. Senator Charles Goodell (R-N.Y.) sat through this cathartic experience and then walked out with a stunned look on his face. We never heard from him again.

Each commission helped spread the word among a growing number of antiwar vets that they had a unique role to play within the antiwar movement. For many of these vets, testifying was their first conscious political act. As we hoped, the commissions often served as a springboard for vets to form advocacy groups to fight for their needs. Many chose to join the Vietnam Veterans Against the War, and new chapters sprang up across the country.

In addition, I think that these hearings helped convince many antiwar activists, especially pacifists, that active duty soldiers and veterans were eager to hear and embrace our antiwar message.

Proceeding along a parallel track to our work were film stars Jane Fonda and Don Sutherland, who had independently decided that they wanted to conduct what would be called the Winter Soldier investigations of U.S. policies that led to war crimes in Vietnam. Initially, they contacted the VVAW leaders, who passed them along to us.

In retrospect, we were naïve to think that pampered (and politically inexperienced) celebrities such as Jane Fonda or her sidekick, Kennedy-assassination lawyer Mark Lane (who later narrowly escaped death in Jonestown, Guyana) would accept the collective will of our steering committee.

A few months into the coalition, Mark Lane published a poorly researched book of accounts of war crimes told by veterans; it was denounced by book reviewers and many veterans as fraudulent. Because we felt strongly about the issue of credibility in making such allegations, we demanded that Lane separate himself from further involvement in Winter Soldier. Showing the poor judgment that she later demonstrated by allowing herself to be photographed astride an antiaircraft gun in Hanoi, Fonda blindly supported Lane and pressured the VVAW leadership to override our concerns.

As often happened in that volatile period, a split occurred, and the two camps then set about organizing separate national hearings on war crimes. We at the citizens commission decided to hold a National Veterans Inquiry (NVI) in Washington, D.C. (or the "belly of the beast" as some called it in those days), in December 1970. Meanwhile the Fonda/VVAW group continued with the original plan to conduct a Winter Soldier investigation in Detroit in January 1971.

James S. Kunen summarized the two hearings in his book *Standard Operating Procedure:* "The goal of both events was the same—to show that American policies lead to war crimes and the substance was similar. Some veterans testified at both. Winter Soldier got less attention in the mass media (than NVI) and more in the underground press."

One outgrowth of the Washington hearings was contact with active duty members of the Concerned Officers Movement—an antiwar group. We assisted them with the filing of formal charges against several American generals under the Uniform Code of Military Justice for their complicity in war crimes in Vietnam.

We also established a working relationship with Ronald Dellums, who had just been elected as congressman from Oakland, California. He agreed to take the lead in trying to pressure Congress to finally confront the explosive issue of who should bear the responsibility for war crimes committed in Vietnam. To the consternation of some of his colleagues, Ron also allowed us to set up in his office a photographic exhibit about the victims of war crimes.

Even though public opinion polls documented that a majority of Americans now favored an immediate withdrawal from Vietnam, Congress as a whole was still very reluctant to criticize the military for its conduct of the war. In the face of such cowardice, Representative Dellums bravely agreed to chair ad hoc hearings on policies that led to war crimes, once it was clear that established congressional committees would have nothing to do with the issue.

So for four mornings in early April 1971, Vietnam veterans were heard on Capitol Hill as they testified about their participation in the commission of war crimes as policy. About twenty U.S. representatives and one senator attended at least part of the hearings.

A United States Army Criminal Investigative Detachment (CID) memo submitted to the working group on August 10, 1971, provides a candid view of how some career officers regarded the war crimes issue.

"Out of 133 war crimes investigations [to date] only six were initiated by the CID," complained Colonel Henry H. Tufts. "Investigations have been based [instead] . . . on Executive and legislative interest, media impact, and the reaction of the Chief of Staff," he continued. "We all have been a party to what might be [called] an over-reaction."

After urging that sole authority for launching probes on war crimes be returned to the CID, Tufts reassured his commanders that "Everyone in the CID program, at every level, is dedicated to getting out of the war crimes investigation business."

In November 1973, the working group published a summary of the results from 250-plus war crimes cases it investigated: unsubstantiated allegations, 113; dismissed before court-martial, 28; acquitted by court-martial, 30; not tried for various reasons, 31; cases disposed of by nonjudicial punishment, 20; convicted by court-martial, 31; found insane, 2; and cases still under investigation, 7. Despite the military's insistence on pursuing only individual GIs for criminal conduct, only slightly more than 12 percent of those accused were ever convicted of a crime.

In retrospect nearly thirty years later, the fact that hundreds of Vietnam veterans were willing to bare their souls to document U.S. war crimes and the policies that led to them indicates just how little legitimacy the war had by 1970, yet U.S. troops fought on for three more years.

The hearings helped veterans—most of whom had been raised on a spiritual diet of virulent anticommunism and blind patriotism—to fight back in their own interest. Their courageous testimonies helped to destroy one of the Pentagon's most treasured myths—that we had an honorable purpose in Vietnam.

Recently, the issue of responsibility for war crimes has been raised again—this time in the former Yugoslavia. I believe that the refusal of our political leaders, including Congress, to hold our military and civilian commanders accountable for what happened in Vietnam has fostered an unhealthy cynicism about the applicability of international law and Nuremberg, which will bear bitter fruit in the years ahead.

18

The War Against the War

DAVID CORTRIGHT

Awakenings

IN A SENSE, the army did me a favor. When they drafted me in the summer of 1968, I was forced to become socially aware. My attention quickly focused on the world around me, especially on the war raging in Southeast Asia. Up to this point, I had not been politically active. In college, I bounced from one major to another and spent most of my time playing music or working. My family background was conservative, Catholic, and working class. My dad was a plumber, my mom a waitress and homemaker. Nothing in my background had prepared me for political activism. When the army came knocking on my door that summer, however, the world began to turn upside down. Service in the army ironically turned me into a peace organizer.

The summer of 1968 was not a good time to be a draft-eligible male in the small Pennsylvania town where I lived. Nearly all my friends had already been scooped up by Uncle Sam, and my turn was not long in coming. Returning home three days after my college graduation, I received notice from the draft board. A month later, I was classified 1-A (draftable), and a few days later my official induction order arrived. Faced with the inevitable and hoping to avoid the infantry, I reluctantly volunteered for a three-year hitch in the army band. By August, I was in basic training, crawling through the sands of Fort Dix, New Jersey.

I immediately began to question the entire process. The mindless brutality and depersonalization of basic training shocked me. The system is designed to break down your personality and instill a sense of violence and aggression. I began to feel hatred—not for the enemy, but for the drill sergeants. Their cruelty toward the less able among us was appalling. One overweight recruit obviously could not cross the overhead bars, but was forced to try repeatedly until his hands bled. When the boy fell from the bars and collapsed on the ground sobbing, the drill sergeants laughed and made fun of him. Anger and resentment boiled within me.

Troubling images of the war also began to intrude. The drill sergeant, who was Black, kept referring derisively to gooks, slopes, and dinks. "You're going to get your White college asses shot off," he kept saying, seeming to relish the prospect. We were forced to watch the absurd propaganda film, *Why Vietnam?* It began with and kept returning to Lyndon Johnson droning on in his Texas twang. Both he and the amateurish images of the film offered us unconvincing justifications for why we had to fight the war. The murmurs and hissing among the recruits began quietly but soon grew to outright hoots and howls. "You men quiet down and listen," the sergeant shouted. "You might learn something." We doubted it.

When I arrived at my first base, Fort Hamilton, New York, the impressions of order and discipline the army had tried to instill were immediately shattered. As I walked up the stairs of the barracks, duffle bag slung over my shoulder, a long-haired, bleary-eyed Spec four sauntered over and asked, "Hey man, wanna buy some acid?" Speechless, I hurried on my way. The drill sergeants hadn't prepared me for that one in basic training. I soon learned that drugs were everywhere on the base. Everyone—the guys in the band, the military police (MPs), supply clerks, medical technicians, and others—smoked pot and dropped acid.

Fort Hamilton was a processing center for GIs being discharged back to New York, which meant there was a constant flow of troops returning from Vietnam. Our commanders ordered the new guys like me to stay away from the returning vets. Naturally, we were curious and sneaked over to the coffee shop during breaks to find out why the brass tried to keep us apart. The answer was quickly evident. These vets were the most embittered, burned-out people I had ever met. They were slovenly in their military attire, angry at the world, and disdainful of authority. More than one said mockingly, "Wait 'til you get there, sucker."

My mind was reeling. Doubts and questions were building rapidly. I started to read books and articles about Vietnam and listened more carefully to the news. Opposition to the war was prevalent at that time, especially in the New York area, which also affected me. It didn't take long to realize that the war was, as Robert McNamara belatedly admitted, "terribly wrong." I came to see the war as not just a mistake, but a crime. Hundreds of Americans and thousands of Vietnamese were dying senselessly every week. Doubts, confusion, and even guilt swept over me as I faced the prospect that I too might be sent to Vietnam and that even if I stayed in the States, I was contributing to the war. My world began to fall apart. I just could not continue with business as usual.

For weeks, I went through an excruciating crisis of conscience. The thought of deserting to Canada crossed my mind, but I worried that this act would have a devastating impact on my mother, who was then a cook for the priests in my local parish back in Pennsylvania. Conscientious objection seemed a possibility, but I was not religiously opposed to all war and thus didn't qualify. My quarrel was not with the use of the military per se, but with this particular war. Then I read an article about soldiers opposing the war. GIs at Fort Sill, Oklahoma, were forming a union and were calling for an end to the war. Here was the answer, I thought. If active duty soldiers were to organize and speak out, this could have a powerful impact. Political leaders might finally take notice if their own soldiers were to demand peace. I knew that speaking out would entail risks, but that didn't bother me. The only question was selecting the most effective and appropriate method of dealing with the dilemma in which I had been placed. Joining the GI movement was the choice for me, and I was prepared to sacrifice and pay a price for making this choice.

Finding other soldiers who opposed the war was not difficult because they were all around me. The challenge was choosing a proper course of action and convincing others to join me. During this time, I was taking graduate courses at New York University in the evening, and I began to look at the many antiwar posters that were around the city for indications of GI involvement. A notice in the student union announced a meeting of GIs opposed to the war, and I decided to check it out. I remember being very hesitant as I made my way to the announced location, fearful that the meeting might be some kind of setup, but the civilians there were very friendly and welcoming, and other soldiers were present as well. The atmosphere was supportive, and I soon felt at ease. The group was discussing an antiwar rally planned for April 1969 in New York. I agreed to work on a GI planning committee to create a special contingent of antiwar GIs to lead the march. My peace-organizing days had begun.

Convincing fellow soldiers at Fort Hamilton to attend the rally was not easy. I pointed out that we would not be violating regulations because the army's own guidelines held that a soldier was free to speak his or her mind while off duty, out of uniform, and not on base. All of us knew, however, that such legal distinctions meant little to military commanders and that we would likely face reprisals for speaking out. In the end, only about a dozen colleagues joined the April demonstration, although the total GI contingent from Fort Dix and other surrounding bases numbered about two hundred. For many of us, this demonstration was our very first political activity. We felt nervous and self-conscious, doubly so for being conspicuously in the front of the march and wearing silly paper caps that said "GI for Peace."

The experience of participating in that first action was exhilarating. The commitment to speak out, once I had finally made it, was very satisfying. I felt a tremendous release of energy. The internal tensions eased, and I felt a positive sense of direction. Suddenly, my life had meaning and purpose. A year before, as I was completing college, I had no idea what I would do with my future. Now I was a committed antiwar activist, spending every waking moment agitating and organizing against the war. I brought antiwar literature on base, spoke incessantly with my fellow soldiers, and attended meetings with troops from other bases to build the broader GI movement. I became a full-time peace activist, working from within the system to subvert the war.

Who We Were

The conventional wisdom assumes that GI protest came predominantly from disgruntled draftees. One of the arguments later offered for switching to an all-volunteer force was that it would eliminate the problem of opposition within the ranks. As I became involved in the GI movement, however, I found that most of my fellow protestors at Fort Hamilton and later at Fort Bliss, Texas, were, like me, volunteers. Many also came, as I did, from working-class or lower-middle-income families. Although middle-class draftees played some role in dissent, the bulk of the GI protest movement came from working-class volunteers. To be sure, many had volunteered reluctantly, and some had been to college, at least for a time. Those men without any college education had volunteered primarily to seek employment or training, which made them, in effect, economic conscripts. Whatever the reasons for enlistment, volunteers were the most likely to resist the war and military authority. An explanation for this phenomenon was given with typical directness by Spec 5 Jim Goodman, a GI activist in Germany: "Draftees expect shit, get shit, aren't even disappointed. Volunteers expect something better, get the same shit, and have at least one more year to get mad about it."

Informal surveys during the Vietnam era confirm the predominance of volunteers among GI movement activists. In March 1970, the National Council to Repeal the Draft examined the backgrounds of twenty-five members of GIs United Against the War at Fort Bragg, North Carolina. Seventeen of the twenty-five activists had volunteered, and sixteen came from lower-income families. In November 1971, fifty-five GIs and recent vets attended a United States Serviceman's Fund conference on soldier organizing. Nearly all of us there had volunteered, and most of us came from working-class families. In April 1971, during the encampment on the Washington mall of the Vietnam Veterans Against the War, a survey of 172 antiwar veterans found that two-thirds had enlisted.

As I approached GIs in different units at Fort Hamilton and other bases, I noticed a sharp distinction in how different soldiers expressed their opposition to the military. Those soldiers who had some college education, including most of the members of the band in which I was assigned, tended to sign petitions and attend demonstrations. The ones with little or no college experience were more likely to express themselves through more direct forms of defiance: go AWOL (absent without leave), confront a company commander, or sabotage equipment. In this latter category were the military policemen at Fort Hamilton and the artillery men I later met at Fort Bliss, Texas. In many cases, these GIs were more embittered and resentful than the college-educated GIs. The more intellectual and verbal approach came to be known as the *GI movement,* but, the more direct forms of defiance were called the *GI resistance.*

During the 1970s, the army conducted several sociological studies on the motivations of GI protestors. One of the most interesting was a two-volume report by the Research Analysis Corporation (RAC) entitled *Determination of the Potential for Dissidents in the U.S. Army and Future Impact of Dissident Elements within the Army.* The report classified GI protest under two separate headings, *dissidence* and *disobedience.* Under *dissidence,* they grouped participating in a demonstration, signing a petition, attending a coffeehouse, or publishing a GI newspaper. Under *disobedience,* they placed insubordination, refusal to follow orders, individual sabotage, and the like. The first category involved more verbal forms of protest, whereas the second implied a more physical and immediate response. Dissidence was aimed at higher authorities: colonels, generals, and even the commander in chief.

Disobedience struck out at a more immediate target: the first sergeant or company commander. The army's distinction between *dissidence* and *disobedience* conformed to what GIs understood, without the benefit of sociology degrees, as the GI movement and the GI resistance.

The Research Analysis Corporation study also examined the social origins of protestors. The study found that *dissidents* and *disobedients* had different social backgrounds, the former being more middle class than the latter. Analyzing personnel records of more than one thousand dissenters (gleaned from files of the army's Counterintelligence Analysis Detachment), the report portrayed the dissident group as follows:

1. more than half were volunteers;
2. they were more likely to have had some college education than most GIs;
3. they scored above average on army classification tests (although they had high scores on verbal reasoning, they were slightly below average in mechanics categories such as automotive information).

The dissident group tended to be better educated and from a slightly higher class background than the disobedients, who were more likely to engage in direct confrontations with commanders and to run afoul of the military justice system. Dissenters employed verbal forms of expression and engaged in political action. Both groups posed difficult challenges to military discipline and together worked to undermine the U.S. war effort.

Suing the Army

Within our dissident group at Fort Hamilton, opposition to the war steadily mounted. During the fall of 1969, as momentum built for the historic Vietnam Moratorium events in October and November, many of us signed a GI petition calling for an immediate end to the war. This petition was very special, for it was signed exclusively by active duty service members and was to be published in the *New York Times*. We who signed knew that we would be committing ourselves in a very public way and might face reprisals as a result. Despite this possibility, thirty-five soldiers out of the sixty in our unit agreed to sign the petition, which appeared as a full-page ad in the Sunday edition of the *New York Times*. The ad was signed by 1,366 active duty service members from nearly eighty bases and ships throughout the world. It appeared on November 9, 1969, just a few days before the huge Moratorium rally that would take place on the grounds around the Washington Monument in Washington, D.C. The ad had a dramatic impact and helped to build momentum for the November 15 mobilization, which attracted nearly half a million participants. A dozen of us from Fort Hamilton attended the rally as part of a GI peace contingent that numbered several hundred.

The Moratorium events gave the antiwar movement unprecedented scale and legitimacy. As we drove back to New York following the November 15 rally, it seemed that every car on the New Jersey turnpike was coming from Washington, D.C. The rest stops along the way were filled with peace activists. When we listened to the radio, however, our spirits sank. The news broadcast reported that President Nixon was unimpressed and unfazed by the huge rally. He claimed to be watching college football on television that Saturday afternoon and made pointed reference to the decent patriotic young Americans who were back on their college campuses. We were depressed at the thought that so large a demonstration could not move or influence him. Little did we know that the White House was in fact extremely concerned about the antiwar movement, despite claims to the contrary. We didn't know at the time that the Moratorium events were having a very direct effect on U.S. policy. Nixon later admitted in his memoirs that these particular protests conducted in the fall of 1969 prevented him from carrying out his ultimatum to escalate U.S. military action against North Vietnam. In fact, the growing antiwar movement acted as a significant constraint on U.S. military options in general in Indochina.

At Fort Hamilton, the Moratorium actions and the GI petition had an immediate impact. Base commanders suddenly realized they had a "dissent problem" and acted swiftly to suppress it. We were called to a "command information" assembly and read the riot act. The commanders tried to sound like good liberals ("of course we are all entitled to our opinions"), but threatened to punish any further acts of protest, whether they be in the form of a petition or a demonstration. The warnings were vague and unspecified, but the implication was clear: keep your opinions to yourself or suffer the consequences.

Our response was not long in coming. We learned of a second GI petition to be published in the newspapers, and many of us added our names, choosing to ignore the command's threats. As the petition floated through the barracks, however, an officer noticed it lying on a desk and immediately notified the base commander, Major General Walter Higgins. The general blew his stack and demanded that we withdraw our names. The threats were now intense and specific. If the petition went ahead, everyone in the unit, signers and nonsigners alike, would be punished. Divisions surfaced within our group, as many argued for withdrawing the appeal, and the debate became very heated. We held a special meeting on base, which the brass allowed, to decide whether to proceed. I argued strenuously in favor of the petition—emphasizing that, despite the risks, we needed to take a stand against the killing in Vietnam. Most of the men agreed with me about the war, but many were concerned about their families and their future. Some wept, others shouted, and all agonized over the decision before us. After a grueling two-hour deliberation, we called for a show of hands. The proposal to proceed with the petition and defy the brass was rejected by a narrow margin.

Our respite from command repression did not last long. A few weeks later, the ax finally fell. Ironically, the precipitating event was not an action we committed, but a demonstration by our wives and girlfriends. On July 4, 1970, as our band prepared to play in a parade on Staten Island, the women appeared with signs and banners reading "GI Wives for Peace" and "Declare Independence: Stop the War." Their arrival caused a near riot among the conservative crowd gathering for the parade, and irate bystanders began shouting and throwing objects at the women. After much confusion and a hasty negotiation, the parade organizers allowed the women to march near the band. The parade finally got underway, but the entire event was a fiasco. The next day, the military's embarrassment was compounded when newspapers gave prominent coverage to the incident.

The harassment began immediately. Blaming us for not controlling "our" women, the command imposed a series of restrictions and punitive work details. Musical activities ceased, and a few months later the unit was effectively disbanded. Transfers were also announced. Eight of us, considered ringleaders by the brass, were summarily transferred to the far corners of the world: Korea, Germany, and in my case, Fort Bliss, Texas. Interestingly, only one of our group was sent to Vietnam. In earlier days of the GI movement, in 1967–68, dissenters were sent to the war zone, but by 1970, this practice was no longer considered wise. The army in Vietnam was already in an advanced state of decay, overflowing with dissenters and resisters, and the last thing commanders there wanted was an influx of additional troublemakers.

The brass's attempts to silence us backfired. Thirty-six of us immediately signed an Article 138 complaint (a seldom used but sometimes effective grievance mechanism) and vowed to fight the army's harassment efforts, initially by filing a suit against the army. Encouraged and coached by an officer on base who was a judge advocate general, we approached a group of civilian lawyers in New York City for help. We argued that the army's transfers and punitive restrictions were an unconstitutional attempt to suppress our First Amendment rights. Led by attorney Fred Cohn, a team of civilian lawyers at the Law Collective in Manhattan agreed to take our case. On July 23, we filed a class action suit against the army in the Federal Court for the Eastern District of New York in Brooklyn. The case became known as *Cortright v. Resor.* Initially we had been nervous and uncertain about suing the army, but the experience turned out to be great theater. National and local reporters converged on the courtroom, and news reports of our action appeared throughout the country. Suddenly, we were celebrities. Although I was indeed transferred to Fort Bliss on July 24 (the judge refused our request for a restraining order), the federal court accepted jurisdiction in the case and agreed to hold hearings and to issue a ruling on the matter.

At this point, the GIs remaining at Fort Hamilton decided to organize and founded both a newspaper, *Xpress,* and a committee, GIs United Against the War. The group began an intensive legal support effort. We needed to prove that the command's transfers and other actions were not required by military necessity, but rather were designed to silence our antiwar activities. We knew our allegations were true, but we needed evidence. The company clerk was a member of GIs United, and he remembered typing a letter written by a general that would provide the incriminating evidence. He and others plucked spent typewriter ribbons from the trash, and in one long evening, several of the GIs and their wives painstakingly unwound and reviewed the tapes. At last they found the incriminating letter. The lawyers were impressed with our resourcefulness, but they noted that the spent tape would not hold up as evidence in court. We needed either the letter itself or an admission by the general that he had written it. The general's letter was recreated and typed on official stationary. Cohn then brought the facsimile into court and waved it in front of General Higgins on the witness stand. Quoting the incriminating passages about "getting rid of Cortright" and the other ringleaders, Cohn thundered "Did you not write this letter, General?" Flustered and unaccustomed to being cross-examined in court, Higgins foolishly said yes. The judge rolled his eyes in disbelief, and those of us sitting in the courtroom smiled and silently cheered. Cohn quickly thrust the ersatz letter back into his briefcase and announced "no more questions." We had proven our point. A few months later, in February 1971, Judge Jack Weinstein ruled in our favor, invalidating my transfer and branding the army's actions unconstitutional. The army quickly appealed the ruling, however, which meant that I had to remain at Fort Bliss, and the higher courts eventually overturned Weinstein's ruling.

Blissed Out

Fort Bliss had a reputation as a hotbed of antiwar sentiment, and I was eager to meet members of the local group, GIs for Peace. Army spies were watching my every move, though, so I proceeded cautiously in making contact. When I finally located the group and went to their weekly meeting, one of the soldiers asked, "Where have you been?" They had heard on the national news about my court case and transfer, and were eagerly awaiting my arrival. GIs for Peace had been active for more than a year and published a thriving underground newspaper, *Gigline*. In recent months, the group had sponsored two antiwar rallies, conducted a prayer vigil on base during the Moratorium, and organized an antiwar protest at traditional Veterans' Day ceremonies. When I arrived in July 1970, however, the group was suffering from the sudden departure of several leading organizers. (Because soldiers rarely stayed at one post for more than a year, GI peace groups faced constant turnover.) The remaining members were happy to have an energetic new recruit, and we made plans to revive GIs for Peace and launch a new program of antiwar activities.

Our first action was to open a GI coffeehouse in downtown El Paso. Up to this time, GIs for Peace had used a meeting house known as the Ex-Pfc Wintergreen Center, named for the marvelous character from Joseph Heller's novel, *Catch-22*. When the lease ran out on this center, the group decided to open a more convenient organizing office and coffeehouse in downtown El Paso. We rented a large second-floor suite of offices above a storefront in the city's central square and installed a printing press. A new issue of *Gigline* was produced and distributed, and soon a steady stream of GIs flowed through the office every afternoon, evening, and weekend. Weekly peace meetings attracted an average attendance of twenty-five, most of them active duty GIs, along with a few wives and girlfriends and recent vets. The coffeehouse also featured speakers and films. Mostly, GIs came just to hang out, listen to music, and, at least for a few hours, escape the military.

Our strategy for funding GIs for Peace was delightfully simple and successful. We timed the publication of *Gigline* to coincide with payday. We then positioned ourselves on the bridges leading from El Paso to Juarez well in advance of the Friday afternoon buses that would disgorge crowds of recently paid GIs eager for an evening of entertainment and diversion. As the GIs approached the bridges, we hawked copies of our paper and asked for donations. Most of the guys were supportive, gladly taking a copy and giving contributions. In the space of a few hours, we would distribute nearly all of our press run of three thousand copies and collect several hundred dollars—enough to print the paper, pay our rent, and cover other expenses. After depositing our money and celebrating our success, we usually followed the trek across the Rio Grande and joined the Friday night festivities.

GIs for Peace sponsored several major peace actions during my tenure. In October 1970, as part of a coordinated program of local demonstrations across the country, we sponsored a rally on the campus of the University of Texas at El Paso. More than one thousand people attended, half of them active duty GIs. Our featured speaker was Rennie Davis of the Chicago Eight. Davis used his appearance to promote the May Day plan for massive civil disobedience in Washington, D.C. In December, at the traditional Christmas tree-lighting ceremony in downtown El Paso, approximately seventy-five members of GIs for Peace gathered at the front of the crowd with banners calling for peace on earth and immediate withdrawal from Vietnam. The commanding general at Fort Bliss was the featured guest at the ceremony, and as he prepared to throw the switch to light the tree, we gave a peace salute by raising our hands in the familiar two-finger V sign. The general was so angry he could hardly control himself. In his remarks, he made reference to the "decent" soldiers at Fort Bliss who were back in the barracks on the base.

Perhaps our largest and most successful action came in May 1971 on Armed Forces Day. For several years in the early 1970s, because GI movement groups observed the traditional militarist ceremonies of that day with peace actions, it became known as "Armed Farces Day." At Fort Bliss, we held a peace festival at a canyon near the base. Nearly one thousand active duty servicemen and women joined a crowd of more than fifteen hundred people. The day featured rock bands, organic food, information booths on a variety of causes, and a program of speeches. During my remarks, I read the decree that had been issued recently by the Provisional Revolutionary Government in South Vietnam, pledging not to fire upon American GIs carrying or displaying antiwar materials. In effect, our so-called Viet Cong "enemy" had declared a truce with rank-and-file GIs who were against the war. As I described the document, many of the soldiers in the crowd cheered. We concluded the program by reading from the People's Peace Treaty, which was then circulating widely within the antiwar movement. We declared ourselves at peace with the people of Vietnam and pledged to work for a speedy end to the war.

The issue of U.S. war crimes also became a major focus for GIs for Peace. When Lt. William Calley was convicted in 1971 for the massacres at My Lai, but every other officer involved in that incident, especially the ones higher up in rank, went free, many GIs and recent vets became angry. At Fort Bliss, a number of combat vets came forward to say that such mass murders had been common, if not always on so large a scale. One recently discharged vet, Bill Patterson, went to the El Paso sheriff's department and declared that he had committed acts similar to those of Calley and that he too should be arrested. A door gunner on a chopper, he had killed dozens of civilians walking along roads or working in rice paddies. Confused and uncertain, the local police told Patterson to go home. Soon he made contact with GIs for Peace. With Patterson's support and the involvement of other local GIs and vets, we decided to organize a war crimes tribunal. Our event was modeled on the Winter Soldier hearings held in Detroit by Vietnam Veterans Against the War. We invited Noam Chomsky to be the featured speaker of the panel. Half a dozen local GIs and vets took the podium to tell their painful stories of mass murder, and Chomsky offered a scathing, brilliantly argued indictment of the illegal and criminal nature of U.S. policy in Indochina. Our war crimes tribunal received extensive media coverage, and Chomsky was featured on several local television and radio interview programs.

GIs for Peace also played an important but little-known role in challenging the POW/MIA hoax that began in the early 1970s. As H. Bruce Franklin and others have documented, the POW issue was consciously used by the Nixon administration, with help from millionaire H. Ross Perot, to stir up public animosity against the Hanoi government and prolong the war by adding a new complication to the peace negotiations. In 1971, right-wing groups began to emphasize the POW issue in their own demonstrations around the country, and they scheduled a national "POW/MIA Day" for El Paso. They chose El Paso because of the large number of military retirees living in the area and because they assumed that an enthusiastic crowd could be mobilized. At GIs for Peace, we decided to become involved and spoil the

POW/MIA Day committee's party. We argued that the surest and quickest way to free the POWs would be to end the war. We took that message to the press, and we presented it at the planning committee meetings for the POW/MIA Day. We wrote and distributed fliers that called for turning the event into an antiwar rally. Thanks to our efforts, the heralded national POW/MIA Day was a flop. Only a few hundred people attended, and nearly half of them were member of GIs for Peace distributing antiwar literature. At least in El Paso, the attempt to use the POW issue to sustain Nixon's war policy failed.

Other, less political forms of resistance were also prevalent at Fort Bliss. When I first arrived in July 1970, my assignment was a Special Troops Detachment. We were the "troublemakers" who had not necessarily committed any major crimes, but were considered unfit to serve with regular units. The stockade and the Special Processing Detachment on base were already filled to overflowing, so command had no other place to put us. Many of the troops in our barracks exhibited open defiance of military regulations. The Black GIs were especially bold in flouting army dress regulations. Carrying "power sticks" (African walking sticks with a carved fist at the top), a group of ten or more of them, adorned with beads or African jewelry, would strut conspicuously across the quad between the barracks. Wearing their army caps perched atop oversize Afros, sneakers rather than combat boots, and shirts untucked and unbuttoned, they affronted the military dress code. But they received no reprimand. The company sergeants and commanders, who already had more than enough trouble dealing with the existing level of dissent, had no intention of stirring up more trouble by challenging them. The "heads" in the barracks were equally aloof, if less openly defiant, and spent most of their free time smoking pot and listening to music that blared loudly from sound systems. Many of the sergeants and lifers were on drugs, too, usually downers and alcohol. Morale and discipline were at rock-bottom levels.

Resistance sometimes had a countercultural flavor, especially among the troops at Fort Bliss's Defense Language Institute (DLI), where the army tried to teach Vietnamese to mostly college-educated GIs who knew only too well where their training would take them. Many of the DLI students were members and supporters of GIs for Peace, and they were determined to avoid going to Vietnam by whatever means they could. The use of marijuana and other drugs was pervasive, and a number of soldiers intentionally took overdoses to get medical discharges. The most inventive of the DLI resisters were Paul Fuhs and Dennis Oney, who were also key organizers for GIs for

Peace. Known as the fabulous furry freak brothers, after the R. Crumb comic book characters, Fuhs and Oney exhorted fellow classmates to drop acid and refuse orders to Vietnam. The army had foolishly named Fuhs section leader of his Vietnamese language class, and he used his authority to convince fellow students to resist the war. When twelve of the twenty-one members of his class either deserted, obtained early discharge, or filed for conscientious objector (CO) status, the army finally realized that something was wrong. Fuhs himself filed for a conscientious objector discharge and, after a federal court battle, won an early discharge. When Oney's CO discharge was rejected, he went crazy, quite literally. After an episode of heavy drug taking and ranting at army doctors and counselors, he finally received a mental disability discharge. His official medical release papers recount the wild tale of his "illness."

> *Chief complaint:* Someone injected LSD in my brain.
> *History of present illness:* . . . [H]e became increasingly convinced that war was evil, the army was run by psychotics and that he would be unable to live with his conscience if he stayed in the army. . . . [H]is friend advised him to take LSD and then the army wouldn't matter. On the following day patient was told that LSD would be injected into his brain. . . . patient since has felt he has been on a continual trip. . . . [P]atient describes specifically that whenever he sees something that is evil he can close his eyes and he will hear such things as voices sounding like the multitude of the heavenly hosts. He can also see and hear such things as nursery rhymes.

Resistance Everywhere

Opposition to the war and resistance to the military were pervasive not just at Fort Bliss, but throughout the U.S. military. As I recount in my book *Soldiers in Revolt,* the armed forces were racked by widespread antiwar protest and resistance, which began in 1968 and built to a peak in 1971–72. During these years, more than 250 antiwar soldier committees and underground newspapers existed. The rate of unauthorized absences soared to record levels, reaching seventeen AWOLs and seven desertions for every one hundred soldiers in the army in 1971. Harsher forms of rebellion also occurred—including drug abuse, violent uprisings, mutinies, and attacks against superiors. The result of this resistance was a breakdown in military discipline and the virtual collapse of the armed forces.

The pervasiveness of GI opposition is confirmed in the Research Analysis Corporation studies that I mentioned earlier in this essay. The RAC researchers surveyed 844 soldiers at five major army bases in the continental United States to determine the extent of dissidence and disobedience. Conducted in 1970 and 1971, the study found that one out of every four enlisted men had participated in dissident activities such as attending a protest action or receiving an underground GI newspaper. An equal number, one of four, had engaged in acts of disobedience such as insubordination or equipment sabotage. The combined results showed a startling 47 percent of lower-ranking enlisted soldiers involved in some form of dissidence or disobedience, with 32 percent involved in such acts more than once. If frequent drug use is added as another form of resistance, the combined percentage of soldiers involved in disobedience, dissidence, or drug use came to 55 percent. The army's own investigation thus showed that half of its troops were involved in some form of resistance activity—a truly remarkable and unprecedented level of disaffection.

The effects of this widespread opposition within the ranks were felt most dramatically in Vietnam itself. Although there were few formal GI movement committees or underground newspapers among troops in the field (where the civilian support and off-base resources necessary for such ventures were lacking), opposition to the war and resistance to command authority were widespread. The headline of an October 1970 *Life* magazine article captured the culture of defiance that had spread among combat units: "You Just Can't Hand Out Orders." Company commanders often had to negotiate with their troops—"working it out" was the phrase used—before sending them out on an assignment. This defiance was more than the usual grumbling of soldiers in war. It often became outright revolt and mutiny.

The specter of combat refusals in Vietnam struck home in a banner headline August 26, 1969, in the *New York Daily News:* "Sir, My Men Refuse to Go." The accompanying article told the story of A Company of the Third Battalion, 196th Infantry, in the Songchang Valley south of Da Nang. After five days of grueling combat and heavy casualties, the men of A Company refused orders to proceed. The captain in charge, Eugene Shurtz, was relieved of command, and new officer and noncommissioned leadership was brought in. After hours of cajoling and threatening, this new leadership persuaded most of the men of A company to continue their advance, albeit grudgingly. Mutiny in time of war is a cardinal offense, punishable by death, yet none of the men who balked on that August day in the Songchang Valley received even so much as a reprimand.

In April 1970, a mutiny incident was broadcast on CBS television news. Newsman John Lawrence was with C Company of the Second Battalion, Seventh Cavalry, when the company commander, Captain Al Rice, ordered his men down a jungle trail in the midst of a guerilla stronghold. The troops objected that a direct advance would almost certainly draw fire and produce casualties. The men refused the captain's order to advance and proposed an alternative route that would avoid contact with the enemy. The entire discussion was played out before CBS cameras as television viewers were treated to a real-life performance of "working it out."

Many other combat refusals took place among U.S. troops in Vietnam. The exact number of these incidents is not known and is unlikely ever to be revealed. In my research for *Soldiers in Revolt,* I uncovered ten major incidents of combat refusal. Military lawyers and fellow GIs at the time I was doing my research in the mid-1970s insisted that many other mutinies had occurred. I suspected they were right, but lacked solid documentation. A decade later, the publication of Shelby Stanton's *The Rise and Fall of an American Army* provided a glimmer of evidence confirming the prevalence of combat disobedience. In his 1985 book, Stanton thoroughly documents the breakdown of U.S. combat forces. Drawing on unit archives, Stanton reports that in the elite First Cavalry Division, thirty-five instances of combat refusal occurred during 1970, several involving entire units. Stanton's research does not focus on combat refusal, so it provides no evidence from other divisions and years. His revelation regarding the First Cavalry based on its own archives suggests, however, that probably hundreds of incidents of significant mutiny took place among army units in Vietnam, which undoubtedly had a significant impact in undermining U.S. combat capability and hastening the withdrawal of American forces.

The most shocking evidence of the rebellion within the ranks came in the frequency of "fragging"—attacks against sergeants and officers. As Senator Charles Matthias (R-N.D.) said on the floor of the U.S. Congress in April 1970: "In all the lexicon of war there is not a more tragic word than 'fragging' with all that it implies of total failure of discipline and depression of morale, the complete sense of frustration and confusion and the loss of goals and hope itself." In 1969, the army began keeping records of assaults with explosive devices. By the middle of 1972, as the last American troops were preparing to leave Vietnam, the total number of recorded incidents had reached 551, with 86 soldiers dead and more than 700 injured. Approximately 80 percent of the victims of these attacks were officers and noncommissioned officers, according to army statistics. These shocking figures reveal an army at war with itself. Gung ho young officers, eager to push their men into battle, often became the victims of assault by their own men. Stanton confirms a story widely rumored at the time: after the bloody and senseless ten-day battle on Hamburger Hill in May 1969, embittered troops placed a notice in their underground newspaper offering a reward of ten thousand dollars for the fragging of the officers in charge.

On some occasions, the breakdown in discipline became so severe that troops fought against each other. The best-known incident took place at the Long Binh jail in August 1968. Overcrowding and oppressive conditions among the mostly Black prisoners at LBJ, as it was known, produced a violent insurrection that killed one soldier and injured dozens. One group of resisters barricaded themselves in a section of the stockade and held out against riot-equipped military police for nearly a month. Another incident occurred at Whiskey Mountain in September 1971, when soldiers of the Thirty-fifth Engineer Group barricaded themselves in a bunker and battled MPs with automatic weapons and machine-gun fire. Military police were called in again at Praline Mountain near Dalat in late 1971 to quiet tensions in a company where fragging attacks against the company commander had occurred two nights in a row. Many other such incidents took place among U.S. forces in Vietnam, some racially motivated, others the result of general rebellion, as U.S. military capability in Vietnam steadily disintegrated.

The rebellion that racked the army and Marine Corps also spread to the navy and air force. As the Nixon administration intensified the air war against Indochina, the level of GI activity in the anitwar movement and the number of incidents of resistance multiplied in these services as well. In the navy, the most dramatic manifestation of revolt was the increasing prevalence of sabotage. In a 1972 report on navy disciplinary problems, the House Armed Services Committee disclosed "an alarming frequency of successful acts of sabotage and apparent sabotage on a wide variety of ships and stations"; it also reported "literally hundreds of incidents of damaged naval property wherein sabotage is suspected." The most significant of these incidents occurred in July 1972, when sabotage put two of the navy's aircraft carriers out of commission in a period of just three weeks. On July 10, 1972, a massive fire broke out aboard the *U.S.S. Forrestal* in Norfolk, causing seven million dollars in damage. This blaze, the largest single act of sabotage in U.S. naval history, was responsible for a two-month delay in the carrier's deployment. Three weeks later, another act of sabotage crippled the *U.S.S. Ranger* as it was about to depart Alameda, on the West Coast, for Indochina. A paint scraper and two twelve-inch bolts were inserted into the ship's reduction gears, causing nearly one million dollars in damage and forcing a three-and-one-half-month delay for extensive repairs.

Legal forms of political opposition also spread in the navy and air force. Dozens of protest committees and underground newspapers appeared at air force bases and on ships. In San Diego, sailors aboard the *U.S.S. Constellation* organized an informal vote, asking area citizens to approve or disapprove the carrier's scheduled sailing for the South China Sea. More than fifty-four thousand San Diegans voted in the October balloting, including sixty-nine hundred men and women on active duty. Eighty-two percent of the civilians and 73 percent of the people in service voted for the *Constellation* to stay home. The ship sailed nonetheless, but not before nine sailors held a press conference at a local church and publicly refused to go.

Within the air force, more than thirty organizing committees and underground newspapers operated at bases all over the world. Internal resistance and declining morale became especially acute among air force enlisted men and officers at combat bases in Thailand and Guam. In December 1972, during the Nixon administration's Christmas bombing against Hanoi and Haiphong, two pilots stationed in Thailand, Captains Dwight Evans and Michael Heck, refused to fly combat missions. In the spring of 1973, four B-52 crewmen stationed on Guam joined in a federal lawsuit filed by Congresswoman Elizabeth Holtzman (D-N.Y.) challenging the constitutionality of continued bombing. Within the air force and the navy, as in the army and Marine Corps, internal opposition to the war became widespread and undermined military capability.

My experience as a GI dissident at Fort Hamilton and Fort Bliss was a small part of an internal revolt that swept through every element of the U.S. military. For many of us, the experience of fighting against the war was a life-changing event, radicalizing our political consciousness and setting us on a path of enduring commitment to justice. By forcing us to serve during the Vietnam War, the army opened our eyes to the brutal realities of U.S. military interventionism and galvanized us into making difficult but essential moral choices. We joined the GI revolt and became veterans of a great crusade for peace.

Although little known or acknowledged in official history, the GI rebellion had an enormous impact on government policy and on the armed forces themselves. The decisions to pull out American troops and then accelerate the rate of withdrawal, the commitment to end the draft and create an all-volunteer force, and the Nixon administration's inability to fulfill its threats of escalating military pressure against the Vietnamese—all were significantly influenced by the rebellion within the ranks. In the final years of American involvement, the U.S. military became more a liability than an asset. No longer capable of sustaining effective combat action and rapidly deteriorating from within, the armed forces had to be withdrawn for their own survival. The United States could not continue the war against Vietnam because GIs would no longer fight. In the end, we won the war against the war.

PART FOUR

Consequences

Consequences of the Vietnam War and Government Policies of the Seventies

EUGENE J. McCARTHY

THE VIETNAM WAR had a disordering, disrupting, and even corrupting effect in major areas of government and politics. It corrupted the military establishment. Officers and spokesmen for the military not only made major misjudgments about the war but also misrepresented, even falsified, reports of what was happening in the war.

The military were further corrupted by the use of methods of warfare contrary to American tradition and the code of military conduct: firing on undefended villagers, making little or no distinction between combatants and noncombatants, using napalm and defoliants, resorting to executions. My Lai was the prime example.

Officers allowed themselves to be used to sustain the political case for the war. General William Westmoreland, a notable example, returned to defend the war before the Congress.

The war corrupted the administration, the presidency, the CIA, the Senate, the House of Representatives, and other institutions of government. It corrupted the press, the media, and the language, going well beyond Orwellian language until finally progress or lack of progress was reported in numbers, such as body counts and kill ratios.

Originally published in Eugene McCarthy, *Required Reading: A Decade of Political Wit and Wisdom* (New York: Harcourt, Brace, Jovanovich, 1977), 151–54.

It corrupted the Democratic Party, its procedures, and its substantive stand on the war in Vietnam.

It prepared the way for the fiscal disorder to follow, a disorder that was manifest in the inflation of the Carter administration and is reflected in the massive debt (federal) largely accumulated during the Reagan administration.

While too little attention was given to substantive disorders, too much attention was directed to procedural change as the answer to most long-recognized and troubling problems of government and society.

Evidently encouraged by a budget surplus of $3.2 billion in 1969 and a deficit of only $2.8 billion in 1971, Congress and the Nixon administration approved revenue sharing, something the states accepted quickly. Let the federal government (which some economists, projecting a growing economy and the end of the war, said would be hard-pressed to spend all of its collected taxes) distribute money to the states. The slogan for states operating on monies received from the federal government could well have been "Representation without Taxation." (Two governors exhibited fiscal responsibility in using those distributed federal funds: Carter and Reagan.) The federal government began to run short of money; the war did not end in 1970, and the growth of the economy slowed.

When the federal debt continued to grow, Congress did not choose to cut appropriations or raise more money as a solution, but passed a resolution on budget control. The budget process, it was held, would bring the budget under control. Obviously, it did not. Budget deficits have been greater since the passage of the 1974 budget resolution than they were at any time in the earlier history of the country.

With the budget out of control and inflation rates growing, Congress took another step toward automatic government. It indexed government salaries, including those of members of Congress, and indexed federal pensions and Social Security payments, without providing an adequately indexed base to support the inflation-moved increases.

Then, in the latter half of the decade, having come close to losing control of the economy through budget and fiscal reforms, Congress and the reformers turned to politics and to governmental procedure as the way to salvation.

In 1975–76, the new provisions of the Federal Election Campaign Law were passed. The theory was that if the government paid for political actions, corruption would be reduced, if not eliminated, and better persons would be elected to national offices. The financing, currently in effect, applies only to presidential races. Two presidents have been elected since passage of the law, Jimmy Carter and Ronald Reagan.

To improve its operation, Congress was reorganized. The principal target of reorganization was the seniority system, a system that, if it did nothing else, accomplished what Gilbert Chesterton said was accomplished by having the eldest son or daughter of a monarch follow his or her parent to the throne—"It saved a lot of trouble."

And then, from 1977 to 1979, with starts and stops, progress and retreat, the House and the Senate each adopted codes of ethics. Since the codes were adopted, but not necessarily because of their application or enforcement, public disclosure of moral failings on the part of members of Congress has demonstrated that the adoption of codes did not either ensure the election of "good men" or keep those in office on the straight and narrow.

In addition and of quasi-substantive significance was the War Powers Act, a kind of after-the-act defense by those who did not oppose the Vietnam War when it was in progress.

The decade of the eighties got off to a reasonably bad start. Taxes, the one immediate response to inflation and to its control, were indexed. There was pressure to extend federal funding of campaigns beyond presidential elections, where it has not worked well, to include congressional elections, where it is likely to work even less well, and support for constitutional amendments to balance the budget.

The whole reform record sustains Gilbert Chesterton's judgment cited earlier, that "the Puritans wind up killing St. George and keeping the dragon."

Passing It On: The Movement for Teaching the Vietnam War in the Schools

JEROLD M. STARR

THE U.S. WAR in Vietnam was the longest and second most costly in U.S. history. More than two million American youths were sent to fight. More than 58,000 were killed, more than 300,000 wounded, and almost 14,000 completely disabled. According to the U.S. Veteran's Administration, some 800,000 Vietnam veterans have been diagnosed as having "significant" to "severe" problems of readjustment. The war cost U.S. taxpayers hundreds of billions of dollars, and these costs will continue for generations in the form of veterans' benefits and interest on past loans.

In Vietnam today, more than two million dead are mourned. Four million were wounded and ten million displaced from their homes. More than five million acres of forest and croplands were laid waste by eighteen million gallons of poisonous chemical herbicides. The U.S. military exploded more than fifteen million tons of bombs and ground munitions in a country less than half the size of the state of Texas. This represented four times the total dropped by the United States in all theaters of war in World War II. Large areas of Vietnam are pockmarked by more than twenty million craters.

When the Tonkin Gulf Resolution was passed by Congress in August 1964, I was just about to be married and to begin graduate studies in sociology at Brandeis University. By April 1975, when North Vietnamese troops marched into Saigon, I was father to two sons and preparing to leave the faculty of the University of Pennsylvania. I never faced a draft notice forcing me to choose between military service, prison, or exile. I never led a demonstration and was never jailed for civil disobedience, yet it would be impossible for me to recall this eleven-year period without the war as a constant reference.

Throughout this period, I thought about the war every day. I attended rallies and marched in demonstrations, wrote letters to the editor, petitioned door-to-door, staffed telephone hot lines, sat in vigils for AWOL soldiers, worked in the campaigns of antiwar politicians. In short, I did whatever I thought would help bring the bloody madness to an end.

In the years after the war, I remained politically active as a democratic socialist working for peace and justice both in schools and in the public sphere. However, it took the reckless military adventurism of the Reagan administration in Central America to bring Vietnam back to the center of my activism. The hawks had learned their own lessons in Vietnam—use proxy troops and bombing to limit U.S. casualties, intimidate opposition in the Congress and in the streets, and keep a tight rein on press coverage. Still, it seemed to many that the conflicts in Nicaragua and El Salvador could become "another Vietnam," and now I had two sons verging on adolescence.

Although public opinion polls over the years consistently show that two of three Americans judge the Vietnam War to have been a "mistake," ignorance about the war is widespread. A 1985 poll, for example, found that 57 percent did not have "a clear idea" what the war was about. Polls in 1988 and 1989 found only a third could locate Vietnam on a world map; a third didn't even remember which side the United States supported. Of course, this ignorance is even more widespread among the generations who have come of age since the war ended. Such ignorance is a national liability if we see the Vietnam War as not just past but prologue.

When the Soviet Union collapsed near the end of the decade, spokespersons for the U.S. Army and U.S. Air Force rejected a post–Cold War peace in favor of "new missions" in which more Vietnams are possible. Such new missions are designed to combat "instability" in Third World "trouble spots" through "low-intensity conflict": guerrilla warfare, counterinsurgency, and pacification (e.g., Nicaragua, El Salvador); "rapid deployment forces" (e.g., Grenada, Panama, Iraq); and "surprise bombing raids" (e.g., Libya).

The United States moved on to more and more battlefields, but its war against the Vietnamese had never truly ended. The Vietnamese were frozen out of the Western world and forced to deal with massive problems of reconstruction with little more than Soviet military aid. Not only did the U.S. government refuse all requests for assistance, but it also actively obstructed assistance from private groups (such as churches and relief organizations), international agencies (such as the World Bank), and other countries.

In 1982, one of my college honors students proposed doing his term paper on the treatment of controversial issues in West Virginia public school books. I asked him to pay special attention to coverage of the Vietnam War. To my dismay, he reported an average of three paragraphs on the war per book.

Within a few weeks, I had confirmed that such neglect was typical. Numerous studies have documented that textbook coverage of the war ranges from a few paragraphs to a few pages and usually does not discuss Vietnamese geography, culture, or history; the personal experiences of combat soldiers and war protesters; or such moral issues as the My Lai massacre and chemical warfare.

I teach at the college level where the curriculum is more open to faculty input. In 1980, only two dozen colleges had courses about Vietnam, but by 1987, that number had increased to almost 350. Faculty reported that 58 percent of them had higher than normal enrollments, some in the hundreds. The most important catalyst in this development was production of the Public Broadcasting System's thirteen-part *Vietnam: A Television History,* licensed to more than two hundred colleges and universities by 1983. Stanley Karnow's companion volume, *Vietnam: A History,* sold 200,000 copies in hard cover and 150,000 in paperback from 1983 to 1985.

Although these changes were encouraging, I was personally focused on a curriculum that would be used at the secondary level as well as at the college level. I wanted to reach the potential cannon fodder who might never have the opportunity to take a college course. Moreover, I wanted them to be challenged to involve themselves actively in the issues and events of the war—analyzing, empathizing, and reflecting on the legacies and lessons for today.

Despite warnings that kids didn't care and that teachers were afraid of the controversy, I was hopeful that more would take on the subject if they knew good materials were available. I searched social studies clearinghouses for supplementary teaching materials, but was unable to find anything of professional quality or that was available nationally and still in print, let alone sufficient for a full-semester course. When I contacted established educational, peace, and veterans' organizations about this problem, they encouraged me to take on the challenge.

For about one and one-half years, I consulted with numerous global curriculum publishers who advised me on everything from pedagogy to economics. In 1984, I established the Center for Social Studies Education (CSSE) as a not-for-profit corporation. In my first grant application, I listed more than sixty outside consultants.

I sought to recruit people to the program by following every lead I ran across or was given. I put out a newsletter quoting responses, reporting progress, posing problems, and encouraging participation. I built consensus around the curriculum's basic approach—emphasizing student participation and critical thinking, presenting different points of view, and provoking the students to contrast and compare.

I advocated this approach as the only one that would appeal to the professionalism of administrators and teachers in the schools and undermine the predictable opposition of the militarists. I also supported it as the best pedagogical strategy to create effective democratic resistance to all forms of propaganda.

Because I have never believed in the abstraction of "objectivity" about something as huge and complex as a war involving millions of people, I encouraged writers to strive for a plurality of views by featuring in their teaching materials the personal statements of many different people involved in the war—not just political officials and the academics who criticized them, but also American soldiers, Vietnamese soldiers and peasants, and ordinary Americans for and against the war.

Very often, these "smaller truths" are presented in authentic voice. They take the form of interview responses, poetry, diary entries, court testimony, letters to the editor, songs, and so on. I hoped that the effect of using such materials in the classroom would be to humanize the issues and consequences of the war for the students in a way that traditional narrative accounts fail to do.

To better ensure fulfillment of these objectives, I sought a diversity of participants with complementary skills and differing political orientations. In particular, I recruited from among academic specialists, high school teachers, and Vietnam veterans. I hoped that the recognition of this diversity in our group would help people accept a nonpolemical, nonsectarian, critical-thinking approach.

Frequently, it was rough sailing. Several people became angry. Some quit. Others dropped out because they couldn't find the time to do the work. Still others were dropped because their contributions didn't fit or weren't good enough. Of the thirty people who in 1984 attended a two-day organizing meeting to launch the project, only two ultimately assumed responsibility for writing, editing, or developing activities for any unit in the curriculum. From June 1984 to June 1987, when all the pieces finally were in place, I talked or corresponded with more than three hundred people. The final "team" consisted of an editor and designer, thirteen writers, seven copy editors, twenty-one reviewers, seven curriculum developers, and eighty field testers. All the units in the curriculum were reviewed by a diverse panel of five or six authorities and field-tested by a network of about eighty participating teachers in about thirty states.

Our cause was given a boost near the end of 1986 when a viewer's guide for an NBC-TV drama on Agent Orange gave us a plug. We received requests with comments such as the following from more than five hundred teachers in forty-eight states: "I have tried for years to teach this topic, but available materials for high school students are scarce" (from Washington); "The book we use now has one page on the Vietnam War" (from Texas); "I am constantly in search of valuable information about the subject" (from Kansas).

The following year I edited a special issue on "Teaching the Vietnam War" for *Social Education,* the official journal of the National Council for the Social Studies. The issue went out to twenty-five thousand social studies teachers across the country and brought forth hundreds of prepublication orders.

Mindful of the time and money constraints faced by teachers, we designed the curriculum's format to minimize cost and maximize flexibility. Our "modular textbook" consists of a dozen thirty-two-page units that snap into a three-ring binder. Each unit covers a different topic, so teachers can select material to fit any course option. The individual modules can be purchased separately. A forty-eight-page teacher's manual includes projects and classroom activities, including role play simulations, with reproducible sheets.

I wanted Vietnam veterans to be included in the curriculum and the movement. I knew that many had been traumatized by the war and had difficulty talking about it. A vet from California confided to me he could not "read about Vietnam without the nightmares returning." Another from Texas shared, "My daughter asked me to speak to her high school class on the war. I couldn't do it for fear of losing my composure."

At the same time, after years of silence, many vets were feeling the need to talk about what they knew, and they wanted to talk to youths—people at the age they were when they went off to Vietnam. Many of them also were the parents or uncles of the students I wanted to reach. They were credible witnesses. However, they didn't have ready access to the schools and didn't fully understand teachers' needs and constraints. The challenge was to forge a collaboration that would provide a sound educational experience for everyone.

I invited Bobby Muller, founder of Vietnam Veterans of America (VVA), to serve on the center's advisory board, where he made several useful suggestions. By the end of 1988, after several meetings and negotiations, *Education Today* announced formation of a "Teacher/Veteran Partnership Program" between the Center for Social Studies Education, Vietnam Veterans of America (thirty-five thousand members in four hundred chapters) and Educators for Social Responsibility (fifteen thousand members in ninety chapters).

VVA sent copies of the curriculum to all four hundred chapters with advice on how to organize a speakers bureau for the schools in their communities. The VVA director of fundraising, Ken Berez, was chosen to lead this effort. He commented: "We realize that very few schools have courses dedicated to Vietnam, but teachers can adapt these materials to their needs. This will enable us to let the next generation coming of age to learn about the war."

In summer 1989, the partnership conducted a week long training program in Pittsburgh for 40 teachers, more than half of them veterans and including a Missouri social studies teacher of the year, a Kentucky history teacher of the year, Tennessee teacher of the year. We taped the entire sixty-some hours of demonstration lessons and edited it down to a seventy-two-minute videocassette, *Teaching the Vietnam War: Classroom Strategies*. Several hundred copies have been purchased. A twenty-five-minute version of the highlights is used by people who wish to present our program to prospective schools.

With coordination by the CSSE office, these master teachers developed a 132-page handbook on how to plan, market, and conduct workshops and conference sessions for other teachers. This resource, *Teacher Trainer Handbook: Professional Development Workshops,* has been used by the fifty-five teacher trainers now in our network and was made available recently as a new resource for teachers nationally.

In 1991, CSSE issued a paperback version of the curriculum to accommodate the many new courses it had helped to spawn. This book was revised again in 1994 and again in 1996; we then published *Resources for Teaching the Vietnam War: An Annotated Guide* to complete our package of support materials for teachers.

The teachers in the program have been extremely active in passing it on. For years, presentations on teaching about Vietnam have been given at scores of state, regional, and national social studies conferences, as well as in special workshops sponsored by many different organizations and schools. I myself have conducted workshops for teachers in California, Louisiana, Maine, Maryland, Michigan, New York, Pennsylvania, Texas, Virginia, and West Virginia. Along the way, we have been featured on dozens of TV and radio programs, including the CBS *Morning News* and CBS *News Nightwatch,* and in scores of magazines and newspapers including *Time, U.S. News and World Report, New York Times, Washington Post, Los Angeles Times,* and *USA Today.*

What are the results? About twenty thousand copies of the curriculum have been sold to about three thousand high schools, five hundred colleges, and scores of veterans and peace groups. Several colleges and universities have used *Lessons of the Vietnam War* as the basic text in a full-semester course on the war—including Butler, Central Michigan, Kent State, Illinois, North Carolina State, Syracuse, Temple, Virginia Tech, and Williams. It is a tribute to our critical-thinking approach that units are taught at the National Defense University and Army War College and that we were also awarded the 1989 Veterans for Peace Medal for Educational Achievement.

Our records indicate that about 175 full-semester high school courses are being offered now that use *Lessons* as the basic text. This number does not include numerous teaching initiatives in which selected materials from *Lessons* are utilized extensively, such as the six-week segment on Vietnam introduced in 1992 to all twenty-three secondary schools in the Montgomery County, Maryland, system. We have been sufficiently successful to provoke a lengthy vitriolic attack from some conservative veterans, principally organized by the right-wing censorship group Accuracy in Academia, yet nine years after publication, we still are very much "in business."

Our teachers have been marvelous. However, for personal reasons, I cherish most the contributions of the veterans—and these have been many. In Indiana, middle school teacher David Weckerly organized a two-week summer enrichment course for twenty-four students. The course featured presentations from six Vietnam era veterans, numerous videos, and a tour of Grissom Air Force Base. According to Weckerly, the speakers made "a great impact on the students about the realities of warfare," showing them that "statistics represent real people."

From New Mexico, Deryle Perryman has written, "so far this school year I've addressed over 2,000 students, teachers and parents in 13 schools throughout the state. It's been a bit of fun and a bit of pain, but I enjoy it. It helps the kids and their veteran parents and my healing from the war as well."

In Oklahoma, Bill McCloud wrote to scores of leaders and asked them all, "What Should We Tell Our Children about Vietnam?" The letters he collected were edited into a special issue of *American Heritage* magazine and then published by the University of Oklahoma Press. As one of the teachers in our program, Bill advised *USA Today,* "I tell my students that Rambo's not going to take care of it for us, he's not going to appear with a magic gun and destroy the enemy. Students need to be aware that war isn't easy—it's grim."

John Weigelt was a member of Students for a Democratic Society when he was drafted. He chose to go to Vietnam rather than to Canada or prison. He is one of our most active participants. Among his many accomplishments are a twelve-hour in-service program for secondary-level teachers in the Milwaukee Public Schools, sessions for the Wisconsin and Minnesota Education Associations, and a semester-long course for the University of Wisconsin–West Bend.

In Florida, Gene Cain, the social studies curriculum supervisor for Broward County, has been a regular contributor. Gene's special interest is in designing exercises to teach critical-thinking skills. In commenting on our work to interested reporters, Gene explained: "There are no right answers, but certainly questions worth bringing up, like the legality of the war, the conduct of soldiers in Vietnam."

In Pennsylvania, George Molnar and his VVA chapter wrote a $1,700 grant to supply twenty-seven teacher editions and twenty-three student editions of the curriculum to every high school and public community library in their area. They then followed up with each librarian and history department head, introducing them to their speakers bureau and asking them to consider expanding their teaching about the war.

In Ohio, Bob Clewell and his VVA chapter hosted an all-day workshop for almost fifty teachers and curriculum consultants, who were joined by about a dozen undergraduates and ten of the chapter's members. This workshop was followed by another on how to develop a full-semester course on the war, attended by twenty teachers. One of the teachers was most impressed with the curriculum, advising a newspaper reporter, "Critically, it's the best stuff in the field. And it's teacher friendly." In her class, students "learn that the world is no longer just black and white. They are now aware of gray areas. That's a big step to maturity and a big step to intellectual growth." After teaching the course, she said, "Of all my twenty-three years in teaching, this was my most rewarding."

Success with the teachers led to a two-day seminar on the war for 150 high school seniors. Thirty of these students subsequently signed up for a new course on the war at one local high school. Still another school announced a new course on the war for the next semester. Bob and his group then organized two more countywide workshops and a presentation to the Ohio Department of Social Studies.

In North Carolina, Bob Matthews lobbied his school tirelessly until he was allowed to teach his own course on the war. He even developed additional units to relate the issues to his North Carolina home (e.g., veterans, boat people, and refugees). He organized events and workshops and received lots of press. Eventually, he obtained a commitment from all the schools in the county to increase their teaching of the Vietnam War and its legacies. Moving on, Bob helped organize a veterans/educators tour of Vietnam, where he presented copies of the textbook to his hosts.

In New Jersey, Chris Wilkens, coauthor of our unit on My Lai, has lectured to audiences of up to three hundred students at Rutgers and elsewhere. At his own school, he introduced a semester-long senior elective called "The Vietnam Generation," which drew 119 students out of a class of 396. Word got out that the class was tough—emphasizing critical-thinking and problem-solving skills—but enrollment the next semester still held at 93 of 358.

In Massachusetts, Steve Sossaman founded the Veterans Education Project, which makes 150–200 school presentations per year. They also distribute a video, *Straight Talk: Vietnam-Era Veterans Speak Out;* a training manual, *Facts about Military Life: A Guide for Speaking in Schools;* and a pamphlet, *Alternative* [to the military] *Career and Job Training Opportunities.* When President Bush ordered his buildup of U.S. military forces in Saudi Arabia, Steve formed the Veterans Civic Action League, which included vets from World War II, Korea, and Vietnam. This group organized the first antiwar demonstration in the area, which was covered by the press. Steve then organized the first teach-ins in the area. His speeches at various rallies and colleges, as well as his informational flyers, brought attention to him, and he made appearances on CBS *News Nightwatch, World Monitor Television,* Bill Moyer's *Springfield Goes to War* town meeting, cable TV panels, local TV broadcasts, and radio call-in shows.

We are still a small boat floating in a sea of ignorance and conservatism, but we keep stirring the waters and dropping lifelines. By now, we have reached hundreds of thousands. In the process, we have learned as much about teachers and students out there as they have learned from us. There seems to be a spirit among the Vietnam generation that inspires them to do this work. According to Sandie Fauriol, the leading fundraiser for the Vietnam Veterans Memorial and first director of the Center for the Study of the Vietnam Generation, about two-thirds of the nation's 450 college teachers who teach about the war are themselves members of the Vietnam generation, as are the vast majority of participants in our movement.

Many teachers report that their students come into their class conservative, believing that the government tells the truth and that citizens should do what their government tells them to do. Moreover, they seem to have the fairly widespread view that war protesters were "unpatriotic" and to believe the urban myth that many protestors spat on veterans coming home from the war.

Then they hear from teachers such as Betty Simmons, who regrets not having been more active in opposing the war in her youth, and from Carol Transou, who feels she has "a duty to get some of it straight, at least to raise the questions that need to be raised." Although many students remain unchanged, they nevertheless learn to see specific aspects of the war years quite differently. For example, one of my own students told a reporter from the school paper, "After I took the class, I realized why people were so upset. A lot of people were disappointed in how America handled the conflict. It was never even declared a war. Families watched their sons go off to war, and they didn't know what their sons were fighting for." Such students will know to ask next time. Maybe that's all we can expect. Maybe that's enough.

Students do show great sympathy and respect for veterans. Many of them ask the usual questions: "What did it feel like to kill somebody?" "Would you go again?" And although the vets have differing political assessments of the war, when they get down to the nitty-gritty, they quickly dispel the students' Hollywood illusions. In Texas, former Green Beret Dan Giesel tells students, "There's nothing romantic about killing other people, and there's nothing adventurous about seeing friends killed or being shot at yourself." In Maryland, Ray Frappoli tells students Rambo is a "cartoon." In New York, Frank Campaigne tells students "what it was like to live in the jungle, to get into firefights, to get wounded." He advises, "At the least, I dispel their romantic notions about war."

For all of us, the war goes on. We work for the complete rehabilitation of

Vietnam and its people, U.S. veterans, peace activists, and any other casualties of the war. We work for a change in U.S. foreign and military policy—a turn away from being world policemen and toward becoming a development benefactor. And we work to help our youth to embrace peaceful values, question authority, and think for themselves. As Ken Berez, now involved in a worldwide campaign to outlaw land mines, says, "If we can help the next generation to understand what really happened in Vietnam, and we can encourage them to become active citizens, the war will not have been in vain." For all these reasons, we are committed to passing it on.

Visiting Vietnam

ARLENE ASH

The following is adapted from a talk I gave at a symposium entitled "Vietnam: The Choices We Made" offered at the twenty-fifth reunion of the Harvard Class of 1967 in June of 1992. My "special expertise" relates to my travels as a scientist to Vietnam in 1987 and 1990.

MY ANTIWAR ACTIVITIES had their roots in my family's history as once ardent and ultimately disillusioned communists. My father had traveled with his father in 1932 to the Soviet Union with a dream that they could establish a more just community in the 'Jewish Autonomous State' established by Lenin in Siberia (Birobidzhan). Winter was bitter, and there were enormous logistical problems. Although they returned to the United States because it seemed like a marginally better bet to survive the worldwide depression, my father still held to his political ideals: our family cheered the civil rights movement and believed that government should be used to support social justice. I was taught how to stand up for my outsider's perspective in our wealthy, conservative, Protestant community in southern Connecticut. When I went to school, my parents said, "If they're going to do a Christmas ceremony, ask the teacher if you can bring in a Menorah and explain what your tradition is about."

Philip Halle's book *Lest Innocent Blood Be Shed* has helped me understand how people learn to resist society's juggernauts; it tells how a Huguenot village in France came to shelter many people from the Nazis. But I read that book much later in my life. When I was growing up, I think my parents were honestly confused about what political advice to give. They were

259

being punished as communists in the McCarthy era witch hunts even as they came to terms with their own disillusionment over Soviet-style government. I lived through the McCarthy years without anybody talking about it. Like many teens, I was socially insecure, anxious to please, and politically ignorant. When I left for college in 1963 at the age of seventeen, my concept of "international travel" was a brief foray to Niagara Falls.

In my freshman year, South Vietnamese Madame Nhu spoke at my Radcliffe College dorm. She was a very sophisticated lady, and I was dazzled by her slinky Asian sexiness, by her French accent, and perhaps most of all by her long, bright red fingernails. She totally convinced me that our country should fight to preserve her brother-in-law's government.

The next year, a classmate whose "consciousness had been raised" during a summer in Europe recruited me to one of the first big marches against the war. My politics were pretty fuzzy, but the weather was great, and a walk with friends suited me just fine. To my total surprise, crowds lined the streets, and women were hissing at us, throwing eggs and stones. I didn't understand the class nature of the difference between us: these women's sons were already fighting this war, still so distant to me. All I knew were those maps I saw in the *New York Times*—not on the front page—of a funny-looking (scar-shaped) country. Usually I just turned the page.

One particular incident sticks in my mind from the summer before my senior year, 1966. I attended a speech by Hubert Humphrey at a National Student Association–sponsored "student leadership" conference. Always the "Happy Warrior," he urged us to rally behind our president in this fight for democracy. By this time I had serious doubts about the war, but I had a crush on the guy I was sitting next to, and when he jumped to his feet for the standing ovation that swept the room, I couldn't resist. I felt badly, but got up and applauded nonetheless.

I had older brothers who were avoiding military service with the small modifications in their career plans that still worked then—in other words, staying in the top half of their class, and studying science, not English literature. This war was something my family didn't believe in, didn't want, and was vastly relieved to be able to avoid.

Upon graduating in 1967, I spent two years in the Peace Corps teaching mathematics to scholarship students at Mindanao State University in the southern Philippines. Despite being nearer to the ever-escalating fighting, the war in Vietnam receded in my consciousness. My daily experiences challenged both my "left-wing political" and "patriotic" ideological stereotypes as I struggled to understand the profound effects—for good as well as for evil—of America's presence in the Philippines.

When I returned to the United States in 1969, I was drawn in by the quickening pace of the war and the momentum of the antiwar movement. I attended marches on Washington. I devoted hundreds of hours during the 1972 elections, knocked on more than five hundred doors in my Chicago precinct to say to my neighbors, "You're not really going to vote for Richard Nixon? How can I convince you not to do that?" I went to protest marches right up to 1975—although I hated them, although I felt that they were pointless, that nobody was watching. But I told myself, "If I don't go, 'they' will think we don't care anymore."

※　☮　※

About ten years later I saw an ad for a "scientific grant to teach in Vietnam" sponsored by the Kovalevskaia Fund, a small foundation put together by a couple who were very upset about the war in Vietnam. He's a mathematician, I'm a mathematician, and she is a historian. They have been using their money to encourage scientific exchange between the United States and Vietnam and Nicaragua.

I competed for the award and on December 31, 1986, found myself on a small plane from Bangkok to Hanoi. Going there seemed so exotic that I was astonished and somewhat deflated to find other passengers, such as an Italian tourist couple, for whom Vietnam was just another foreign country. Indeed, we landed in a beautiful city with vacation-perfect weather, and I spent my first night in Vietnam at a glorious New Year's Eve party at the International House in Hanoi. Would-be dance partners approached with wide-eyed curiosity; they had never met an American before. For my part, I had never before danced with so many good ballroom dancers. Well after midnight, I accepted an invitation from a local couple to return with them to their home. From my guest perch on the man's bicycle, I took in the sweet air and the sleepy streets of what looked to me like a charming French provincial town.

The next day I began my work, which was to give lectures in applied statistics at Vietnam's Advanced Institute for Mathematics. Later that month, I also participated in a Kovalevskaia Fund conference on "Women and Science in the Developing Countries."[1]

At the women's conference, I met people from "Iron Curtain" countries—

from parts of the world (Mongolia, Uzbekistan) that in a very real sense I barely knew existed. I was startled to hear Professor Vo Hong Anh, a Vietnamese woman and world-class theoretical physicist, speak of carrying out her graduate studies in 1972 when "the war of destruction by the U.S. Air Force in North Vietnam reached its high point of cruelty with twelve days—and nights—of B-52 bombardment of Hanoi."[2] As a graduate student, I had protested those bombings at a meeting of the American Association for the Advancement of Science in Washington D.C., but I had no sense of the people who were affected. How effortlessly my mind's eye had pictured a stereotype: people wearing peasant trousers and conical hats, cowering in huts under a hail of explosives. But here was an intellectual woman like me, struggling to complete her Ph.D. in the face of the various disasters and hardships of war. Here was empathy.

I returned to Vietnam in 1990, this time to Ho Chi Minh City (formerly, Saigon). I was traveling for a Boston-based Vietnam veterans group, the Joiner Foundation, which works to heal the personal and political wounds of the Vietnam War. The foundation is run by people whose lives were absorbed either by the antiwar movement or by wartime service or by both; many are veterans who came back with nightmares. The Joiner Foundation is a wonderful group. They can always use money and support, and they have helped many people make the connections they need. They put together groups that go back to Vietnam and initiate positive projects, such as building a hospital or getting people who fought each other to sit down and talk about what it's like to be a war veteran in either country.

I went to Vietnam the second time because I do quantitative studies in medicine. I was exploring the question, "Can we find an association between the poisons that the United States dumped on Vietnam during the war and the extraordinary incidence of molar pregnancies there?" A pregnancy is "molar" when a mass, rather than a fetus, develops in the womb. Such pregnancies occur once or twice per ten thousand births in Boston, whereas four out of one hundred pregnancies at the obstetric hospital in South Vietnam are molar.[3] Such data are terrible and tantalizing, but I came to believe that a solid scientific study was not feasible. For one thing, many years have passed and record keeping has been so poor that it is virtually impossible to measure levels of individual exposure to dioxin, the chief carcinogen in Agent Orange. For another, the war and subsequent economic hardship have disrupted referral patterns to the point that most "normal" pregnancies never come to the hospital; thus, problem rates among hospital cases cannot be readily compared with other rates either elsewhere in the world or even at the same hospital before the "American" war. Finally, the research infrastructure, despite some help from the French government, is too little developed. We in the United States have the resources and can still learn much from research in Vietnam about the health effects of exposure to war and poverty, but our political realities have, so far, prevented such collaboration.

Another significant event that happened during my second stay in Vietnam was that I met people I had never had any tolerance or respect for when I was in college—officers of the Army of the Republic of Vietnam (ARVN). We considered ARVN to be a joke because even with all the American help, they couldn't fight/win their own war. I had no doubt that they were wrong. And yet, one mild evening in 1990, I found myself on a Saigon River dinner cruise, dancing the night away with a former ARVN officer and his family. He had endured years of punitive "reeducation." One of their children was in a refugee camp in Cambodia. I don't know what this man did in the war—I don't want to know—but one thing's for sure, his life tragedy is no longer even remotely a "joke" to me.

✳ ☮ ✳

Going to Vietnam was wonderful for me. I came to feel a great affinity with the Vietnamese people and their intellectual, community-conscious culture. In Hanoi, I visited an ancient secular university, Van Mieu, which possessed tablets inscribed with the names of scholars (and the subjects of their dissertations) going back more than nine hundred years. The young men who pulled passengers in rickshaws often read while waiting for the next fare or worked to practice their English. City life, especially in Saigon during my second visit, was full of industrious bustle. In January, preparations for the great family reunion holiday, Tet, transformed society. Family is immensely important to the Vietnamese. On my first visit, I had spoken with Pham Van Dong, the prime minister, about women working in science and women having children. In an interview for TV in Hanoi, I was asked about the difficulties of being a scientist and a mother. My response—"I'm not a mother, which makes it easier to have the time to be a scientist"—was deleted from the nightly news broadcast because in Vietnam "everyone" wants children. I chided the prime minister that maybe my choice was OK, especially in a society where population growth was outpacing economic development. He just smiled graciously and reassured me: I didn't look so old. He wished that I "would still have the opportunity to have a family."

What I wish is that our nations will "still have the opportunity" to make peace. For middle-class Americans, it's actually quite feasible to get on a plane and go to Vietnam. But even without leaving home, you can still take that mental journey from stereotype to empathy. Real and fascinating people await you.

Chicago 1996: Despite Corporate Media Silence Many Powerful Protests

DAVE DELLINGER

IN CHICAGO DURING the Democratic Convention and the four days that preceded it, there were more demonstrations and protests on a variety of urgent issues than at any other event I have attended or know of in the past decade. An official spokesman for the Chicago Police Department said afterward that 10,300 demonstrators attended 104 protests. But the *Washington Post, New York Times,* and *Boston Globe*—three eastern papers that I checked—failed to report any account of these activities during the nine-day period in which they were taking place. And the major Chicago papers gave palpably dishonest reports on a few activities that they could not ignore because so many Chicagoans had to have seen them as we marched through the streets. Since my return to Vermont, I have received phone calls from a number of states wanting to know what happened in Chicago because they saw no information on it in either the print or TV media.

In fairness, I have to say that on at least six occasions, I either participated in live TV broadcasts or received calls from persons in New York City who had seen a broadcast there of a speech I had made at one of the rallies for Juvenile Justice. But, to my dismay, people who were not overpublicized in 1968 or at the Chicago Seven's five-month conspiracy trial in 1969–70 were mostly ignored by TV, even though they played a central role in some of the 1996 demonstrations and were more qualified than I to speak about them. Three of the times that I participated in a live broadcast were on CNN, including *Larry King Live,* along with Tom Hayden, Rennie Davis, Bobby

Seale, John Froines, Lennie Weinglass (our surviving trial lawyer), Eugene McCarthy, and Allen Ginsberg. McCarthy and I were the only ones who said that we would not vote for Clinton. The other two live broadcasts were on ABC and NBC. I also did countless other TV or video interviews that may or may not have been shown in some locations, as well as live interviews on several radio stations, including one for the Pacifica network and one on Public Radio.

Here are some of the activities in which I and my associates in the Not on the Guest List coalition and the Festival of Life participated. The main organizers of Not on the Guest List were middle-aged or older. The organizers of the festival were mostly two or three generations younger. On the Thursday and Friday before the convention, I spoke at demonstrations on the need for Juvenile Justice. One slogan was "Don't Plan for Our Children to Fail—Build Opportunities Not Jails." Another was "Locking up Nonviolent Juveniles Often Produces Hardened Criminals Not Better Citizens." On Saturday, I demonstrated in two rallies and a march to stop the drug war. On Sunday, there was a mostly centrist demonstration organized by Tom Hayden, a Democratic Party state senator in California, and by the *Nation* magazine. It was one of only two events I attended that charged a fee, probably to benefit the *Nation*. This was followed later the same day by a rally for Ecological Sanity and Closeness to Nature, organized by the Festival of Life under the leadership of Harvey Wasserman of Greenpeace. Another early demonstration was called "Protest the Anti-Immigrant and Anti-Poor Policies of the Democrats and Republicans." My contention is that the anti-human policies in California (and some other states) overlook the U.S. military invasion that seized land from Mexico and turned it into U.S. states. So Governor Wilson is an alien, if such terms would mean anything in a country that lived up to the inspiring words on the Statue of Liberty. Why don't we learn to be as welcoming and friendly as the inhabitants of Turtle Island were until Columbus, the early colonists, and the U.S. government instituted policies of slavery and genocide against them?

Beginning on Monday, there were several demonstrations to "stop the war on the people!" They called for "Jobs, Health, and Education, not Bombs, Prisons, and Exploitation!" One of these events that continued throughout the week was headed by Dr. Quentin Young of Cook County Hospital. A veteran of the sixties, he called for single payer health insurance for everyone and condemned Hilary and Bill Clinton's hypocritical alliance with the big insurance companies.

The other event that charged money (to benefit the countermedia) was on Monday evening. A number of us spoke to a packed auditorium on the widespread rise of local community organizing. I said, here and elsewhere, that the widespread emphasis on mutual interactions with sister cities in countries that the United States oppresses economically and militarily is an encouraging, grassroots expression of "Act Locally, Think Globally."

On Tuesday, there was an impressive rally and march through a poor, interracial neighborhood. We protested the racist and classist actions of the inJustice Department, demanded freedom for all political prisoners and an end to the death penalty and police brutality. Wednesday was Human Rights Day. Its major action was a rally and march organized by the African American Cash the Check coalition, with major assistance from the American Indian Movement (AIM). It emphasized current inequities imposed on people of color and the need for radical changes in the economy and culture to provide economic, political, and cultural equality for all races.

Next, a group went to the Justice Department to demand, once again, freedom for all political prisoners and an end to the death penalty. About twenty of us went inside and chanted the names of a series of political prisoners—including, among others, Leonard Peltier, Alejandra Torres, Mumia Abu-Jamal, Susan Rosenberg, Geronimo Praje, and Linda Evans. After each name, we chanted, "Free All Political Prisoners," or sometimes, "Free All Prisoners." We apologized to arriving and departing employees for the disruption and had good conversations with some of them. In the end, eleven of us were arrested, including my twenty-year-old grandson, Seth Dellinger, and my niece on my wife's side, Barbara Peterson. So now I am a member of the Chicago Eleven rather than the out-of-date Chicago Eight or Chicago Seven.

Several media followed us inside with cameras and video equipment, but the next day one Chicago paper said that we were calling for freedom for "unspecified political prisoners." Another Chicago paper said both in the headline and in the story that because the police wouldn't arrest us, we went to the feds in order to be arrested—as if we wanted to be martyrs rather than to free martyred political prisoners. But I had told the media of the planned action at the Justice Department when they interviewed me before I went to Chicago and in several interviews in Chicago itself. We were released after a few hours with orders to pay a citation charge of $50 or attend a trial at an unspecified future date. All eleven of us agreed not to pay the fine but to continue the protest before and during the trial. As the Chicago Seven did twenty-seven years ago, we will put the government on trial, this time for dishonest policies that crucify people who stand for justice and real democracy.

Given the situation in Chicago that week, we held two special demonstrations that had not been planned earlier. One was to protest the Chicago media's distortions and to tell those present why we went to the Justice Department and what we said and did there. The other was to protest the arrest of seven Chicago organizers on monstrously false charges. Andrew Hoffman, Abbie's oldest son, and I had been with the seven during the entire time that they were supposed to have committed violent crimes and knew that they were innocent. Yet five of the seven were charged with having committed three felonies, one for "mob action" and two for "aggravated battery of a police officer." The city's failure to charge Andrew and me with these crimes makes it clear that the authorities hoped to avoid widespread public attention to its outrageous charges and wanted to intimidate these five from continuing their preconvention work for justice and human rights in the local communities in which they live and work.

Finally, there was a rally for women's rights, but I couldn't attend. I had received a phone call from one of the arrestees, a much revered Baptist clergyman who said: "I have been arrested before for nonviolent actions I had done in good conscience. This time I am frightened by the arbitrary nature of the charges and the penalties that might accompany them." So I needed to visit him in the jail and be present at his arraignment. I wanted to assure him, the other four, and their lawyers that I would testify in their behalf at the trial. So I had to miss the women's event but was doubly glad that a few weeks before the convention I had flown specially to Chicago to attend a powerful event on women political prisoners and the sexual and other abuses that are inflicted on them and other women prisoners.

Here are a few words on two of the above demonstrations. At the Stop the Drug War rallies and march, former drug addicts spoke, as well as people who worked in drug-infested areas to provide hard-pressed youth with more positive forms of fulfillment than hard drugs. Others spoke in favor of decriminalizing all drugs so that addicts can be treated medically with understanding and love rather than be thrown into prison and treated as subhuman. Several spoke on the need to legalize marijuana. Unlike alcohol, marijuana is harmless and has never caused any deaths. Others spoke on the need to permit the growing of hemp as an alternative to the society's dependence on oil and other destructive but profit-making pollutants, and to stop the deforestation that flows from society's overdependance on paper, which could be eliminated by the use of industrial hemp. Dana Beal gave a convincing presentation on Ibogaine, a plant that provides a different form of temporary "high" than hard drugs. He said that after taking Ibogaine, one loses any desire for hard drugs, alcohol, and even tobacco, but suffers no withdrawal pains, not even from heroin. The CIA has known about the virtues of Ibogaine since the fifties but has kept them secret from the public. Recently, the Netherlands made Ibogaine legal and the results are positive, as testified by a few U.S. addicts who have traveled there to receive it and have been cured of their illness. Recently, Florida has passed a law permitting the University of Florida to conduct scientific experiments on Ibogaine.

Personally, I said that three-quarters of all federal prisoners are there for nonviolent offenses related to drugs. Under Clinton, the government allows local authorities to seize the property of people who are caught with drugs, whether they are found guilty or not. Those convicted of violent crimes in connection with drugs are often impoverished inner-city youths for whom the only way to get a few dollars for the necessities of life is to sell drugs supplied to them by hard-core criminals. Soon, some of the youths get a gun and, under pressure, shoot someone or get shot. I also said that some of the long-term prisoners I visit today are GI's to whom the CIA provided heroin in South Vietnam. The purpose was to keep them from protesting a war with which a growing number of them were becoming disillusioned. Besides discovering that even anticommunist Vietnamese opposed the U.S. invasion, they were finding it increasingly difficult to obey orders to mass murder and torture Vietnamese civilians and soldiers. Some of today's prisoners became addicts in Vietnam and, back home, held up a person, store, or bank in order to get drugs. Now, for example, my friend Frank Lovell gave up his addiction years ago, but so far has served twenty-three years for a crime that the CIA helped cause him to commit. Meanwhile, the FBI and CIA provide drugs to Harlem and other areas where people of color and other poor persons protest their oppressions.

Mentioning that I grew up during prohibition (I was nineteen when it was repealed), I discovered that the well-to-do had no trouble getting all the alcohol they wanted because profiteers like Joseph Kennedy made millions of dollars by working through the hard-core gangs that sold it. So I said, "John F. Kennedy wouldn't have become president except for the many millions that his father contributed to his campaigns, first for the

Senate and then for the presidency." Nowadays, the Cold War has ended, and there are pressures to reduce the role of the military. But rather than deal with the reasons that oppressed people turn to drugs, Clinton and Dole push the drug war to set up military installations in countries in which drugs are grown—even as the United States continues to get them distributed for its own sinister purposes.

The event sponsored by Tom Hayden and the *Nation* featured a number of well-known musicians and dancers, including Crosby, Stills, and Nash, who sang "Make the Children Happy." This song reflected Tom's desire to show some continuity between a few of those present at the 1968 convention, including five members of the Chicago Eight and their children or other descendants. He asked us to have a child or grandchild introduce us and then for us to say a few brief words. Later in the program, he said I would be one of the major speakers, but when I arrived at the theater he told me that the *Nation* had ruled that I would be limited to the three sentences that were to follow my introduction. The introduction was a brief, beautiful message sent by my son Danny and read by my friend Steve Sato. Unfortunately, someone, whether from the *Nation* or from Tom's staff, told Steve that he must omit the first two sentences, which I love. They were, "I know I'm supposed to be introducing my father, Dave Dellinger, but how could I do that without acknowledging his soul mate, my mother, Elizabeth Peterson? Together, they gave me the gift of a love divine—a sacred community of love beginning with our inner family and encompassing Mother Nature and the entire human family." Then my grandson Seth Dellinger made me proud by his brief but poignant introduction. When I followed with three or four sentences in which I said that both the Republicans and Democrats had been captured by the multinational corporations, rendering national elections and the national government obsolete, I was surprised to receive a tremendous ovation from the audience.

In conclusion, some intergenerational factors. Once again, I was thrilled to spend several days with Andrew Hoffman and to rediscover how sensitive and sensible his understanding of life is. His Soup Kitchen on Wheels is a typical effort to combine the personal and the political in his own way, but also in the spirit of his father, Abbie. He has learned so much from both the creativity and the mistakes of Abbie. Seth Dellinger and two young people from Boulder, Colorado, Josh Hershman and Gabe Deerman, age fourteen and seventeen respectively, stayed where I stayed, and along with our hosts, Steve Sato and Aimee Bass (in their thirties), were inspiring companions all week. Seth wrote a special song for the largest rally of the week, the one that was protesting the injustices of the Justice Department. He sang it while playing his guitar and received enthusiastic applause that lasted for a long, long time. Not at a rally, but on several occasions when thirty or forty organizers were evaluating events and making plans for future ones, I asked Josh to present his ideas on what had happened and to express any advice he could offer us. Having been impressed by some of Gabe's poems that he and his mother, Ellen Maslow, had mailed me, I asked him to recite a couple of them. These two youngsters proved then and all throughout the week, as did Seth, that adults need to learn at least as much from young people as young people need to learn from them. We all need each other, and we especially need the special insights of generations that were born at a different time than we were.

PART FIVE

Conclusions

What I Got Out of the War

JANE SASS COLLINS

GROWING UP IN the '50s, I was haunted by nightmares of World War III. I had some doozies, very specific and detailed: people stumbling around with their flesh falling off and their eyes melting down their faces, and so on. Holocaust stories in Hebrew school were a gold mine of basic imagery, as were the grainy black-and-white photos of Hiroshima I found in some book. In public school, during duck-and-cover air raid drills, I couldn't keep myself from imagining the blinding flash of white light and its aftermath. I was convinced it wouldn't be long before Armageddon. My worst dreams felt prophetic.

The more I learned of the world outside the small safe harbor of my family, the more certain I became that horror was coming, and there was no way to stop it. It seemed to me that institutionalized hatred, so nearly successful in wiping out the Jews, was about to destroy our whole species. The papers and the evening newscasts showed terrible things going on in the United States and in the world, every kind of injustice and cruelty in individual and organized forms, yet most people in my little world were content with the status quo. Passive acceptance was the order of the day. I couldn't understand why no one else seemed to be upset. Not even the Cuban missile crisis disturbed the calm surface of life for more than a fear-filled week or two. The only alternative to nuclear dare and double dare I remember hearing about was unilateral disarmament, but that meant we'd be letting the Nazis—I mean, communists—win, which was unthinkable.

It looked as if evil were ruling the world unchallenged. There wasn't much of a gleam on the horizon except for the civil rights movement, which seemed very distant from my junior high school in the Northeast. Then came Vietnam, and everything changed. Once again, horror was happening, and maybe there was no way to stop it, but people were going to try. That made all the difference in the world to me.

As a teenager with pressing personal issues to think about, I'd become resigned to the continual meaningless shedding of blood in distant places. If my actual and potential boyfriends hadn't been threatened with the draft, I might have gone on shunting world events as far back in my mind as possible, under the category of "Awful Things I Can't Change." But in college, early activists made sure the war stayed in front of our faces whether or not we read the papers or listened to the news. It took many arguments and months of leaflets and speeches to rouse me to conviction and action.

One of the first events I participated in was a college fast against the war, in '66 or '67. The organizers briefed us on the facts and gave us black armbands to wear. We did most of our talking in dormitory dining rooms. It was an amazing guilt trip, sitting at your table wearing a black armband and watching everyone eat, with all of them knowing why you weren't eating. As a way to bring the war home, this approach wasn't bad. Someone is eating; someone else is not. Someone is safe; someone somewhere else is in the line of fire.

It wasn't an intellectual argument or a question of strategy or history. Although we talked about how our government was lying to us, that point was a side issue. The main argument was emotional and spiritual. Our country wasn't forced to do this killing. Why, then, must we continue? Was this war an action befitting the brave and the free?

I heard that the American Friends Service Committee was organizing people to talk to the recruits themselves. It seemed like the next logical step, so I went to one of their training sessions.

Whoever called the vets "baby killers" when they came home, it wasn't the people who did draft counseling. The Friends and their trainees went door-to-door in pairs wherever a 1-A was living and tried to talk him out of going or at least to help him begin to think about what was going to happen. The 1-As would just break our hearts—peach fuzz on their faces, and they were going off to kill or be killed. All they knew was that the war had something to do with dominos and honor. You could see their moms and dads were proud. An eagle on the mailbox was a dead giveaway.

It was my impression from the training, though nobody said it exactly, that if you were a girl, and they sent you around with a guy, you weren't supposed to do much of the talking. The idea was that the guy could explain the issues to the 1-A, if anyone could; he stood the best chance of getting the 1-A to listen to him because they were in the same position; they both could get sent over, whereas the girls could not. We were safe. Just by her presence, however, a girl could get across to him that at least one woman wouldn't think he was less of a man for not going. Maybe he'd even be more of a man for running away. What a revolutionary concept. For the most part, they listened politely and just said that if their country called them, they would go.

I didn't go on many of those visits. I didn't think we were saving any lives. Maybe it happened, but not on my watch. I started feeling like the voice of doom. All that time, more images of horror appeared on the television, in the magazines, on posters around town—the faces, pictured up close, of people dying hard deaths because of decisions made by our elected representatives. Yes, we were protesting, but our government didn't seem to be paying any attention. I became discouraged and decided to leave the country. I didn't even know I had reached this decision until it popped out of my mouth during a casual conversation.

Without really thinking about my destination too much, I took a year off from school and went to Israel, like the good Jewish girl I was. This turned out to be a case of "out of the frying pan into the fire." At home, the killing wasn't being done where I could see it. I'd always lived in better neighborhoods. Even in Israel, I started out in the suburbs, in one of the old middle-class German kibbutzim, but soon I followed my new boyfriend out to the fringes, frontier country—the Golan Heights, taken from Syria only two years earlier.

In occupied Syria, the killing was closer. The closest I came to the real thing wasn't the time we were shelled and had to stay in the bunker for a few hours or the time the first bus on my route to a temp job in Kiryat Shmoneh hit a land mine. One morning there was some talk at breakfast about an incident the previous night: an army patrol found four Arabs on our side of the border trying to steal cattle and shot them all dead.

What affected me so much wasn't just the fact that these Arabs were unarmed. Our kibbutz had a ranch with several hundred head of cattle, scrawny little cows left behind by the Syrians when they fled to Damascus to escape the Israeli army. Now the Syrians were homeless, landless, penniless refugees. Why shouldn't they try to take back their own cattle? Was this some international game of finders keepers?

I hated most of all the light way my fellow kibbutzniks took the news. They would have been more upset if one of the horses had been shot. If anyone saw any injustice in what happened, he or she never let on. The Peace Now movement may have already been underway in the cities, but on the desolate plains of the Golan there was only indifference. Arabs were enemies. We were defending ourselves. End of story.

My Zionism evaporated. When people talking about the Holocaust said, "Never again," I had to wonder: never again for Jews, or never again for anybody? I thought I saw modern Jewry's answer on the Golan.

By the time I returned to the United States, I felt only despair for humanity.

But I was going to Harvard, and the campus had been energized during my absence. People had a sense of history swinging their way. The media were paying attention now. The status quo was being shaken. When I left in 1968, speaking out against the war was a fringe activity. When I returned in 1969, most people seemed to be doing it. It took a while for me to sort out the players because every male in Cambridge had grown a full beard while I was gone, and I had to mentally shave people to figure out who they were. But the rallies and marches and demonstrations kept growing bigger. You had to make detours to avoid them.

It was wonderful to see that so many people were outraged. Maybe humanity wasn't a lost cause. Maybe the United States was growing up. Maybe a new consciousness was rising that would shape a new era. Every time I saw a crowd gathered in protest, my heart would lift, even if I myself was just going to class.

Eventually, the campus movement grew so much that university life could not go on as usual. Classes were suspended, or professors deserted the syllabus to talk about Indochina instead of eighteenth-century drama. The more we talked, the more issues our protests covered. We couldn't indict the war without indicting the structures that led to it—not only the government of the United States, but the international business interests, the complacent and co-opted media, the dominant culture of violence and greed.

The evidence was everywhere once we started looking for it, that the culture that raised us in such privilege had done so and was continuing to do so at the expense of many millions of innocent people at home and around the globe. Because of our culture, not just Vietnam, but South Africa and Dorchester and the East Bronx were war zones.

I liked the politics of the Students for a Democratic Society (SDS), and they had great posters, so I went to a meeting. The only people who spoke at any length were the same alpha males who ruled every other meeting or class I'd ever attended. If you wanted to be heard, you had to be loud, sure of yourself, and dogmatic. More thoughtful or quieter voices didn't stand a chance. Women seemed to be too busy making coffee and taking notes to speak. The few who tried were bulldozed into silence. I didn't go to anymore SDS meetings.

I felt a bond not with the leadership, but with the other foot soldiers in this war against war. People wearing black armbands were my compadres. People milling around in the street demonstrations felt the same hope. We longed to see all human life equal and respected, without regard for status or nationality. When people dropped the elite styles of dress in favor of lower-class jeans and T-shirts, this philosophy was at work. It was no longer possible to tell Town from Gown. All of us were wearing the same clothes, listening to the same music, attending the same open air events. For the first time in my life, I felt I was living in a democracy instead of an aristocracy.

The antiwar movement was an act of grace for me. I had despaired, then I found God in the hearts of the People.

I can't remember how many times I went to D.C. I was never on the front lines, close enough to hear the speeches or face the National Guard. I was glad just to be there, though. We knew what was being said, and we knew our presence mattered, even if the media undercounted our living bodies just as they undercounted the bodies of the American dead. Much later, it occurred to me that all the chants we shouted were mantras of some kind—stop the war, stop the war . . . Hell no, we won't go. We said them as if we were saying a rosary, over and over. There was power in that.

It was a mind-bending experience to be part of a crowd gathered to high purpose. We felt the same exhilaration that must have sustained people in the civil rights movement. Sharing a common cause, we dropped barriers against one another, smiled at strangers, struck up conversations. We felt a great sense of possibility. If we could tear down the illusions built by our government, what else might we find that was sham?

We had ceased to be obedient citizens and good little boys and girls. Doors were opening whose existence we had never suspected: doors of perception, through drugs or meditation; doors of sensual experience, through sex that for one brief historical moment was, if not free, at least freer; doors of relationship, in which any random association of people might set up housekeeping together.

If there were truly a different way for nations to relate besides the old way of might making right, maybe there were different ways, better ways, to do many other things. The dream of peace brought with it related dreams of harmonious living with other species as well as with our own. If we could question the necessity of war, we could question the need to use pesticides on crops or to kill animals for their fur. A thousand social arenas regarding which we had previously accepted the status quo seemed ripe for reevaluation now that we could doubt the "experts" and listen to the counsel of our own hearts.

We gave ourselves permission to challenge any aspect of our culture. We were making a new culture based on the premise of mutual respect instead of a struggle for dominance. As part of this new culture, along with questioning conventional authorities, we began to question the very notion that people should leave it to any authority outside of themselves to save the world.

One thing the '60s generation learned early: heroes get shot. On some level, we must have figured there was more safety in numbers. Anyway, one of the most radical aspects of the antiwar movement was how many leaders we had. They popped up everywhere. People resisted the draft in such daring, such creative ways! People went to jail proudly or went voluntarily into exile. We had a million heroes. The media never heard of most of them, but we told their stories to one another and cherished them among ourselves.

The draft wasn't the only arena where dramatic choices were being made. Vietnam blew up the Ozzie and Harriet version of America. The two stories existed in different universes. In one story, young people's responsibilities were few and simple—homework, chores, obedience—and the consequences of any choice were transitory and mild. In the other story, young men could be faced with the starkest dilemmas—whether to obey God or country, conscience or authority—and consequences ranged from loss of freedom to their own deaths or the deaths of others. One of these stories could be true, not both.

Young people woke up from the sweet dreams of the '50s to realize that we had been raised on mass-produced illusions—designed, it seemed, to lull us into trusting in the beneficence of our culture. Besides the rationale for the Vietnam War, we had to wonder what other stories we had been told were actually deliberate lies. For one thing, it was obvious that the old culture was trying to sell us quantities of material goods that we didn't really need, while denying the necessities of life to billions.

So we stopped buying stuff. That was dangerous. We decorated our old clothes, became artisans, made do with what we had, tried to share things instead of hoard them. More dangerous. There was a new story afoot, and no one knew where it was going.

It seemed that the old world was brittle. Where we touched it with truth, it crumbled and was transformed. No wonder we thought victory was within our grasp. It was our time to advance. Unfortunately, as Paul Simon sang, nobody knew from time to time if the plans had changed.

The counterculture was born of belief in the power of loving, belief that humanitarianism could trump materialism. But in an America single-mindedly devoted to the accumulation of wealth, the gallant rags of the hippies were a call to battle.

One by one, as time went on, each person in the counterculture had to face a brutal reality: if you don't have any money, you can't survive. If you don't cut your hair, if you don't wear the right clothes, you can't make any money. Not many people can make a living off leatherwork, and you can't keep farming if your money runs out.

Because we had to survive, we began to dress for survival. We put our shoes back on (and, in some cases, our clothes). We cut our hair, and when we did this, we disappeared because the media had identified us as longhairs. Maybe nothing had changed at all in our hearts, but we had become invisible. Mainstream culture declared victory and got out.

That was the battle we lost twenty years ago. The story people seem to be buying these days is that in losing this battle, we lost the cultural war. The changes we sought were certainly easier to imagine than to manifest. A lot of people thought everything would change immediately because of all of us passionate teenagers, which was just silly. Slowly, however, many of the changes we hoped for have come to pass. The culture will never again be what it was in the '50s. We tolerate a much wider range of lifestyles, and we tend not to be so gung ho about America's role in the world. We're cynical about things our parents believed—that you can really serve both God and country, or that if you only conform and play by the rules, you have nothing to worry about. I think, though, that cynicism is beginning to get old in its turn and that people might soon be ready to give peace, love, and understanding another chance. Anyway, the story isn't over yet. Compared to other recent decades, the '60s look pretty good.

My own life has been totally different from what it would have been without the antiwar movement. I was on the kind of academic track that usually leads either to teaching English or to writing for magazines. If I'd gone to college in the '50s, I suppose I'd have married a Harvard man and spent the rest of my life among the upper middle classes. Instead, I married a carpenter and have spent what passes for my career in one part of the peace movement or another, always struggling and often broke. I've made much less money than I think I would have otherwise; on the other hand, I've had a great deal more fun.

After a few years of watching the government and media attempt to justify an unjust war, I began to feel, like many others, that conventional paths to success were somehow tainted. I was afraid that if I followed those paths, I'd go back to seeing through ruling-class eyes and lose my newfound connection to the rest of the world. I didn't want to fit into a society that kept being so wrong-headed. After graduation, I dropped out.

Some friends and I moved into an old house on a back road in New Hampshire. Getting back to basics seemed like one way to opt out of the dominant culture and evolve something different. We had no car, no telephone, no electricity, and no indoor plumbing. No problem. For the first time in my life, I learned how to do more than read and write. We grew and preserved food, taught ourselves to sew, hewed wood, and carried water. No one would have figured me for a country girl at the beginning of this adventure, but that's what I became.

This hippie idyll ended when my boyfriend's father was diagnosed with cancer. We got married and moved to Kentucky to be with his family. There, with my family's help, we bought a small farm in a "holler"—a narrow valley—between Mud Lick and Seed Tick Roads. For the next few years, my husband did construction, and I worked on the fringes of the local media, making documentaries of elders and craftspeople for public television.

When I became pregnant with our first child, I expected to go back to work a few months after the birth. But once again, the movement bias toward doing things yourself influenced a major decision: I found I couldn't accept the idea of other people raising my child. I ended up being a full-time mother for eleven years. I know how lucky I've been. Not only did I have a supportive husband, but my family was willing to step in when his income wasn't enough. Raising my own children has been the great luxury of my life.

Eventually, though, we ran into serious trouble. My husband had begun to build state-of-the-art, energy efficient housing for low-income families. We had just finished the first house when the oil crisis hit. All of a sudden, interest rates skyrocketed to higher than 20 percent. No ordinary family could afford a mortgage that high. We lost the business, the farm, and a lot of my family's money. For nine months, we were actually homeless: the five of us had to move in to my mother-in-law's four-room house.

That was the worst time we've had. We moved back up north, where the economy was better, and got back on our feet. The experience gave me a new focus. I went to work at a shelter for homeless adolescents and then did some organizing with homeless mothers, helping them become powerful advocates for their own families and others like them. For several years, I researched and wrote about human services issues for a liberal think tank. Along the way, I've also worked with environmental organizations and, in the '80s, with peace and justice groups trying to influence U.S. policies in Central America.

But I haven't been such a purist as it might seem. There have been times when our financial situation was so bad that I tried hard to sell out—but no one was buying. I haven't found a way to write my résumé so I look like good corporate material.

I don't have many regrets. I wish I hadn't caused my birth family so much worry, disappointment, and financial loss; I hate being the black sheep. But I'm happy with my husband and kids, and I have a wonderful and varied set of friends. I believe what Gandhi said, that we must be the change we want to see in the world. I want to see the world move from selfishness to compassion and from despair to hope, so that's the path I've been trying to follow ever since the antiwar movement gave me a place to begin. I'm still plenty selfish, and I still have seasons of despair—never quite living up to my principles—but I haven't found a way to live that makes more sense than the way of nonviolent resistance to evil.

Certainly, many idealists have fallen by the wayside in the past couple of mean decades. My friend Harry offers one explanation. His theory is that every kind of mental distortion has its opposite, just like mania and depression. It's been said, for example, that there's an opposite of paranoia called pronoia—the delusion that people like you more than they really do. Harry thinks that a lot of people in this society are suffering from the opposite of delusions of grandeur. He calls this state of mind "delusions of insignificance."

In this state, you think that nothing you do will make any difference. It's very convenient for the powers that be if a majority of people feel this way. Because of the way our schools and our electoral contests work, and the way big corporations can demand that employees conform to the corporate culture even in their personal lives, it's easy to convince people they have no power. And, of course, concern for our personal comfort has made many of us willing accomplices in this delusion.

Antiwar activists were stunned just as much as mainstream America by the strength we had when we made up our minds to take a moral stand. But what did our strength imply, if not that we had the power within ourselves to bring about peace on Earth? I think that power scared the shit out of us on a very basic level.

If we really confronted the implications of the '60s, we might have no excuse but to spend the rest of our lives trying to make this a better world. There is no denying the trouble our species is in—with nuclear proliferation, AIDS, the population explosion, environmental degradation, and (add your favorite looming disaster here). Humanity's survival still looks like a long shot. There are both moral and very practical reasons for having a sense of urgency. But then, what about our comfort, what about our personal ambitions, what about fun? Dedicating a teenage year or two was all very well, especially if we could get out of class, but a lifelong commitment? Too heavy, man.

If we convince ourselves that there is no real hope of solving these problems, we let ourselves off the hook. We might as well eat, drink, be merry, and drive a good car. It's easy to succumb to delusions of insignificance. The alternative is far too much like work.

American boomers might choose to forget what we are capable of, but we weren't the first people to discover soul power, and we won't be the last. When Filipinos saved the lives of soldiers in tanks by surrounding them with their unarmed bodies, they had soul power. The Berlin wall was hacked into souvenirs by soul power. A peaceful transition to majority rule in South Africa impossible to imagine a decade ago; species pulled back from near extinction, safaris transformed from hunts to photographic expeditions, negotiations in the Middle East—what else could be operating but the power of the spirit, or whatever you want to call it, some deep instinct, maybe a visceral impulse for species survival? As Auden said, we must love one another or die.

Change is coming, whether the United States is in the vanguard or at the rear. We simply can't afford to keep making war on one another. Short-term gains for the United States are coming at everyone else's expense. Sooner or later, this country is going to have to deal with the fact that we export more arms than the rest of the world put together. The military-industrial complex is still wreaking havoc in the lives of millions, and we still don't know how to stop it.

When we watched our country shooting people in the back and burying people alive in the desert sands, the Gulf War was over before we could get ourselves organized to protest. Maybe our children's generation will be quicker on the uptake. Kids raised with Bart Simpson as a role model are not likely to buy the rich old white man's version of reality.

Great television aside, life is tough for young people today. At least my generation had a glimpse of what society might be like if we loved one another, even if it sometimes seems like a hallucination now. All the present generation has seen is the rich getting richer and the poor getting poorer, and the rich saying, "The hell with them." It's so difficult to afford a college education these days and so difficult to find a good job even with a degree that kids don't have much room to experiment. There's a lot of despair among them and not much hope for decency in public life.

But I'm becoming more reconciled to the way life has changed. The vision we used to share is still around—in pieces. People who work on any part of the world, as we used to say, are working on the whole thing. Plenty of people are working on it, old and young—housing the homeless, feeding the hungry, saving the whales, and doing all the rest of it. It's just that we don't talk to one another anymore. We've specialized, and we've lost touch. We used to cruise around and notice how many people were trying to live in a new, more globally responsible, more loving way. Now most people seem to stay within their own small circles. It's easy to forget how many of us are out there—and how many friends we've made in the past twenty-five years.

The forces of evil receive a lot more media exposure, but one of these days I believe people of good will are going to rediscover one another. Though the '60s are history, the ripples from those days continue to spread. It's clear what we dropped out of. It's not yet clear what we dropped into. New technologies based on '60s environmental and social ideals have been developed and refined in the past twenty-five years—for example, in education, construction design, energy generation, and food production—but they remain present mostly as microcosms. Mainstream society has denied them the resources necessary for large-scale manifestation. They require a new paradigm; they fit into a world that doesn't yet exist.

It seems to me that the present situation is like a liquid in which fine particles—those microcosms of a new world—are suspended. More particles are being added to this liquid so that the solution is becoming supersaturated, but the particles are still invisible. What might happen is that perhaps something new will be dropped in, maybe something very small, and all of a sudden the suspended particles will precipitate out and make structures, crystals of complex form. One moment there would be no visible structure, and then in the twinkling of an eye, there it will be. In this way, unexpectedly, there might be a revolution, a deep and pervasive change, at the very time when it seems as if life will go on in the same way forever.

If this change ever happens, it might not even make the papers. The movements toward peace, economic justice, freedom, and a healed planet could come together again in a movement so big this time that we won't even be able to see it; we won't even give it a name. It'll just be the way things are.

24

Cherishing Vistas, Embracing Human Beings: Toward Peace and Freedom

WILLIAM AYERS

IN 1965—DURING the first "International Days of Protest" against the Vietnam War—I was arrested with thirty-eight others for disrupting the ordinary operation of the draft board in Ann Arbor, Michigan. Hundreds of us had rallied; we had marched; some of us, then, entered the office used by the draft board—the bureaucratic hub for selecting young men for war, a clean and efficient sorting machine for ranking people along all the predictable American dimensions of privilege and oppression—and blocked the doorways, the desks, the phones, and the cabinets, refusing to leave. As we were carried out by the police and placed in locked vans, we were jeered and assaulted by a hostile crowd.

We were trying, in our own way, to stand up for peace, to militantly display our opposition to war, to link our conduct to our developing consciousness. We wanted to irritate the war makers, of course, but mostly to energize and encourage the latent impulses toward peace—impulses we assumed to be there in all people. We spoke of "building a beloved community" and of "putting our bodies on the gears of the war machine"— metaphors that pointed, on the one hand, toward fragile vistas to be cherished, of human beings to be embraced, and, on the other, of the necessity of opening a space where forceful and effective action was doable, to sacrifice, perhaps, as prelude to coming together. We would sing when possible, but we were also prepared to scream when necessary.

Inside that draft board and later in the county jail where we were held, I glimpsed for the first time (and in a small way) what the French Resistance fighter Rene Char called an "apparition of freedom." Char spoke of people becoming "challengers" of found conditions, moving beyond passive acceptance of the world as somehow given and immutable, imagining a world that could be otherwise: "[the resistance fighters] had taken the initiative upon themselves and therefore, without knowing or even noticing it, had begun to create the public space between themselves where freedom could appear." Day after day—night after night—inside the county jail, we talked strategy and tactics, debated the proper role of the United States in the world, analyzed the role of racism in class oppression, linked the struggle for civil rights and racial justice with the movements for liberation exploding everywhere. In that jail at the moment, freedom had indeed appeared.

In those dark days, like a flash of lightning, I was shocked into new awarenesses, my imaginative space was dramatically expanded, and my life path was altered. I met a teacher affiliated with an alternative free school, an insurgent place built on principles of racial justice and social improvement, and I walked out of jail and into my first teaching job. From that moment, teaching was forever linked for me with organizing and activism around a basic message: you can change your life.

I was a teacher—or, more accurately, someone groping toward teaching, struggling to see my students as three-dimensional beings, each with hopes, dreams, skills, capacities, preferences, and unique experiences, struggling, as well, to create environments rich enough and deep enough to simultaneously nourish and challenge the wide range of people who actually appeared in my doorway. I was also a member of Students for a Democratic Society (SDS), the militant, eclectic, and insurgent youth group that challenged the cotton wool of consciousness afflicting the country, shaking some of us lucky ones from the scripted lives we were expected to lead, propelling us off in a wide range of unpredictable directions. SDS—and the broader movement that bore and sustained it—was part political, part cultural, part social, part intellectual, part emotional, part visceral. Attempts to sort it all out neatly today tend to murder it. How do you dissect a dream? Where is the incision that delineates hope? SDS was an outrageous and enormous act of imagination—as was the civil rights movement, as was the women's movement and the antiwar movement—and once released, imagination has a habit of exploding into exciting and dangerous places.

(I still struggle to teach, incidentally, and I am still a member of SDS.

My membership card still reads, "We are people of this generation . . . looking uneasily at the world we inherit"—and I still am.)

SDS was a strange soup, all mixed up: we were disaffected kids, hippies, freaks, street people, preppies, intellectuals, anarchists, cultural rebels, socialists, communists, red-diaper babies, children of the labor elite, sons and daughters of the power elite, beatniks, poets, free thinkers, artists, guttersnipes, rockers, diggers, wobblies, and a lot else. We smoked dope (OK, not all of us), grew our hair (some guys on their heads and faces more than others, some women on their legs and armpits, but not all), argued hard and hurt each other's feelings, and hugged and made up. We did all sorts of things: some of us organized in poor and working-class neighborhoods; some of us built counterinstitutions to provide a model of a new society inside the decaying husk of the old; some of us built mobilizations against the war; some of us stopped Marine and CIA recruiters on campus and exposed and opposed war-related research that was making our institutions wealthy; some of us fought for open admissions and student power; some of us, eventually, blasted away at the purveyors of war and death. I did all of that and more.

We were united by a vision of what could be, but was not yet: a democracy that is participatory, a society that is just, a planet at peace. None of that seemed possible when 6 percent of the world's people (the United States) consumed more than 50 percent of the wealth or for a country (ours) in which 1 percent of the population owns 48 percent of the wealth. No way. So we organized, fought, demonstrated, built the beloved community, and put our bodies on the gears of the machine.

I was a member of the Weather Underground Organization—initially a faction within SDS, later a group of political outlaws—and I lived underground for almost eleven years. Friends died and were mourned, babies were born, the wheel turned. That story has not been told.

How do young people today see the antiwar movement? I fear it is largely through the Hollywood myth-making machine. As I look at the enormously popular Vietnam War films today, I am reminded of my first lesson in cinematic text and subtext: when I discussed the anticapitalist classic *Bonnie and Clyde* ("What do you do?" "We rob banks.") with my very capitalist father, I found that he, too, loved the film, but for him it was a gangster classic. Even more jarring was my discovery that one of my favorite antiwar films of the seventies, *Patton,* was one of Richard Nixon's very favorite war films ever and that he showed it regularly to guests at the White House. To me *Patton* was the story of a megalomaniacal general bent on destruction and self-destruction, a clear parody of patriotism and a cautionary tale on the dangers of glorifying war. To Nixon, I discovered, it was the story of a true American patriot, a man of courage, wisdom, and erudition, and it was a story of men in battle, a tale of sacrifice and triumph. Slowly I realized that both were true, that it was all there, and that whatever sense the film made depended on the particular attitudes, experiences, and autobiographies that reached out and met it. In a sense, this multiplicity is the result of the Hollywood business ethic: make entertainment that means all things to all people and create, therefore, a huge paying audience. But more important for me was a rediscovery about the importance of interpretation and the ways in which reality has meaning for a person. This rediscovery made me less dogmatic, I think, less certain, less willing to insist that my viewing of a particular film or novel or event is necessarily the clearest or the truest. It opened me a bit to multiple interpretations and layered meanings.

War films can never be the same for me, not after the experiences and events of Vietnam. I realize that not much has changed for the filmmakers or the war makers. They are a bit more sophisticated, perhaps, subtle in new ways and with new technologies and gripping special effects, but the messages are frighteningly familiar, and the text and subtext are broad enough to drive a truck full of paying movie goers through.

In the Vietnam War films, we discover once again that war is hell. In Michael Cimino's Academy Award–winning film *The Deer Hunter,* the horrors of war are internal as well as external, and in Francis Ford Coppola's *Apocalypse Now,* the horrors of war take on comic book proportions, all gaudy and fantasmagorical. *Platoon,* Oliver Stone's Academy Award winner, gives us war through the eyes of an American foot soldier, and what we see is exhaustion, boredom, tension, bugs, blisters, fear, snakes, rain, oppressive heat, and sudden explosions of searing violence followed by the sight and smell of death.

In these films, war is still a passage to manhood, however, and it is still a contest of good guys versus bad guys. Of course, in the jungle things get murky, and the bad guys can then turn out to be crazy Americans like Colonel Kurtz or Sergeant Barnes, and the good guys are always gripped by angst, but the larger point remains: war is an event in which the forces of good confront (and triumph over) the forces of evil. It's all so neat, so Hollywood.

The problem from an antiwar perspective is that "war is hell" can be read in a variety of ways. It can certainly tap an antiwar impulse, but it can as easily increase our admiration for those who have encountered war—indeed, it can make us long for a similar passage in our own lives. It can focus our collective attention on the human and ecological waste of war, or it can comfortably reinforce a view that Americans should not fight land wars in other countries, that distant wars should be fought from the air and from the sea or by natives armed and supported by American dollars—all minimizing American causalities.

In *Democracy and Education,* John Dewey argued that it was never enough to teach people the horrors of war because that is not reason enough to make peace. He argued for an emphasis on "whatever binds people together in cooperative human pursuits and results." And this is where the "war is hell" motif in these films is completely inadequate. In *All Quiet on the Western Front,* the classic antiwar novel about World War I, and the work from which *Platoon* is at least in part derivative, the pivotal scene occurs when, in the midst of chaos, death, wreckage, and horror, the young German soldier, pinned down for a day in a foxhole, picks through the belongings of the Frenchman he has just killed and realizes that his enemy is just like him, a humble working man with a family, a trade, hopes, and dreams much like his own. He already knows that war is hell; what he discovers is that the young men who fight the wars are blinded to their common pursuits, common problems, and common enemies by mystifications like nationalism and patriotism. Again, from an antiwar viewpoint, failure to make a human connection to the "enemey" is where contemporary American war films prove disastrous.

In virtually every film, Vietnam is portrayed as a kind of hell on earth. Scenes of its color and its lushness are shot from above and afar; its soft and yielding beauty is seductive, but Vietnam sings a siren song, luring the innocent to wreckage, captivity, and death. Up close, Vietnam is heat and dust, and, well, the opening line of *Apocalypse Now* is, "Saigon . . . Shit!" Vietnam is routinely referred to as "the worst place in the world" or "the asshole of the world," a place completely lacking in contour or depth—at best, gratuitous to the three-dimensional Americans and, at worst, an overgrown jungle prison. There is a pervasive sense of American innocence, of Vietnam as a quicksand that seizes and traps the simple misstep and sucks helpless victims into itself.

The Vietnamese are similarly rendered nameless and faceless. They are "gooks" or "slopes" or "Charlies," and they are part of the danger, a background like the rats, the trees, the unmapped roads, the obscure jungle paths.

The Vietnamese are pathetic victims, ridiculous clowns, duplicitous villagers, relentless hordes. Vietnamese women are dangerous booby traps, amoral and inscrutable: in *The Deer Hunter,* for example, a Vietnamese prostitute begs Nick to screw her even though her child is in the room watching; Nick, of course, is revolted and refuses. Nowhere are there Vietnamese who are effectively raising their children, thoughtfully defending their country, or sensibly speaking about their work or their hopes or their dreams. The Vietnamese people are, in fact, central to what makes the place so awful.

All of this leads to a comfortable and appealing rewriting of the history of the war and of Vietnam. In *The Deer Hunter,* history literally stands on its head as Cimino uses the most memorable popular images of the war to tell a different story: here, it is the Vietnamese who put the Americans in tiger cages, who commit the My Lai massacre over American objection, who encourage unwilling Americans to rape and pillage, and who play a deadly game of Russian roulette with life itself. It is, of course, the Vietnamese who regard human life as cheap, who know no constraints, who move with no understandable motives, who are endlessly barbaric, mindless, and manipulatable. One remembers, however, forty-two volumes of the *Pentagon Papers* and the revelations of a bipartisan foreign policy deliberate, willful, and consistent, and a domestic corollary based on manipulation, obfuscation, and lies. One remembers an active, energetic opposition that broke free of the simple-minded hawks-doves debate about technical and legal issues and put forth instead a position that humanized the Vietnamese and opposed imperialist aggression in principal. And one weighs the awful risk of living with a forgotten history, in a place where war is not understandable and therefore not avoidable and in a time when killing lacks contractual knowledge, when everyone both knows and doesn't know, and when every soldier and citizen is a potential war criminal.

It is almost thirty years since the Tet Offensive—the decisive moment in the Vietnam War, the moment when the American defeat was sealed, although there would be years more of killing and destruction to come—and I am walking beside the Vietnam Memorial in Washington. I remember images of Vietnam: a girl burned by napalm running naked down a highway, a suspected Viet Cong being summarily executed in the street, the American CIA fighting to retake the U.S. embassy in downtown Saigon. I focus now on a girl with pigtails here at the memorial, crying. Why? Her mom is about fifty; she is touching a name on the wall, and she is crying, too. Is this her brother? First husband? Childhood sweetheart? What does it mean to the girl in pigtails? There are flowers and notes and artifacts left everywhere along the wall. Two men are making rubbings for a long line of people, solemnly locating a name, holding the delicate white paper to the wall, and transferring the image from wall to paper. The wall is a living drama. It seems to grow out of the ground, and the names of the dead are animated by all the human motion and action taking place around them because of them. It is sad and moving to walk along the wall, to feel the emotions swelling out of that ditch. It goes on and on, and still there are no Vietnamese names here.

Vietnam is the kind of event that shows us to ourselves. Like Hiroshima or the Holocaust or the gulags, it shows us things about being human, some of which we don't want to know and don't want to see. We live now in a post-Vietnam world, as well as in a post-Holocaust, post-Hiroshima world. We live in a world marked by genocidal warfare and irregular warfare, psychological warfare and economic warfare—a world that has known desert warfare, guerrilla warfare, mobile warfare, mountain warfare, naval warfare, aerial warfare, open warfare, position warfare, bacteriological warfare, chemical warfare, underground warfare, nuclear warfare, robotic and "smart" warfare, and so much more. Standing against it all is simply peace. We know something of precariousness, it is true, and something of indifference and narcissism as well; it is our task now to become intensely aware, powerfully related to one another and the space we share, proactive in creating a world without war.

❋   ☮   ❋

Rene Char wrote about his sense of loss in returning to the "opaqueness of private life." He was sad to leave the freely chosen life of resistance, the intensity of facing other people daily as free and authentic (and, yet, without road maps or guarantees), the excitement of a public space. Returning to the ordinary, he said, "We lost our treasure." In the movement, we used to talk of a "freedom high"—a less elegant, but nonetheless similar thought.

Holding on to the treasure is part of what is before us. To hold on is to move toward a public space, a place where people are recognized for their experiences and their capacities, where there is profound respect for the uncommon common people and recognition that the people with the problems are also the people with the solutions—where understanding points directly to action.

Emile di Antonio made a film about the Weather Underground Organization at the height of the resistance. Recently viewing *Underground* with a group of young people, I had two distinct reactions: I thought the politics—the analysis of imperialism, the understanding of racism as a main instrument of division and control, the vision of a world based on justice—held up remarkably well; I was embarrassed by the arrogance, the solipsism, the absolute certainty that only we knew the way. I saw again how the impulse toward community, too, can betray us. We are drawn, then, to "easy belief," to the decisiveness of our dogma. Here is Don DeLillo describing a mass wedding conducted by the Reverend Moon at Yankee Stadium:

> When the Old God leaves the world, what happens to all the unexpended faith? He looks at each sweet, round face, long, wrong, darkish, plain. They are a nation, he supposes, founded on the principle of easy belief. A unit fueled by credulousness. They speak a half language, a set of ready-made terms and empty repetitions. All things, the sum of the knowable, everything true, it all comes down to a few simple formulas copied and memorized and passed on. And here is the drama of mechanical routine played out with living figures. It knocks him back in awe, the loss of scale and intimacy, the way love and sex are multiplied out, the numbers and shaped crowd. This really scares him, a mass of people turned into a sculptured object. It is like a toy with thirteen thousand parts, just tootling along, an innocent and menacing thing. . . . When the Old God goes, they pray to flies and bottletops. The terrible thing is they follow the man because he gives them what they need. He answers their yearning, unburdens them of free will and independent thought. See how happy they look.

In Monty Python's ridiculous *Life of Brian,* a reluctant messiah appears before the eager crowd and proclaims, "I am not the savior."

They respond dutifully, "You are not the savior."

"You are free, . . . you have minds of your own," he shouts.

"We have minds of our own," they cry eagerly.

"Funny," says a stranger in the crowd, turning to those around him. "I don't feel free. I don't think I have a mind of my own."

"Shut up," they shout. "You have a mind of your own."

To think of democracy as participatory, to think of people actually making the decisions that affect their lives, is to notice that although we experience our problems as personal—we can't find adequate child care, perhaps, or our child is not learning as she should in school, or the options for our aging parents are inadequate—they are, indeed, social. It is to move from *me* to *us,* from loneliness to society. It is to move in a different direction.

In a country that claims a large and entirely settled notion of freedom as birthright, it is ironic to find so much human suffering and everyday misery at its heart. But this is precisely the American predicament: massive, gaudy displays of our commodified freedom, the insistent claims of a kind of fixed freedom that is simply there—the blaring brass bands, the smothering folds of flags waving lazily above us, the bombs bursting in air, thrilling, terrifying, suffocating—become themselves obstacles to the accomplishment of actual freedom. Certain that we are free, people become paralyzed in the search for freedom.

When freedom is posited as pageant, when our sense of it follows a script already written, we find ourselves reduced, unnerved, befuddled. When freedom is equated with consumer choice, we become pacified, enervated. The trappings of freedom, oddly, entangle us; they are themselves walls that must be breached in our search for freedom as an achievement of consciousness and action, freedom as a collective accomplishment to overcome what stands in the way of our humanity.

But dogma, again, and the reduction of complex ideas into slogans are not the property of only the bad guys or of only one group. After due thought and consideration, we must undertake every action with both conviction and misgivings. We must act; simultaneously, we must doubt.

Ironically, today most popular commentators on the movements of the sixties (primarily social democrats whose bona fides are established through some form of fighting mano a mano with the lunatic left) have no doubts. They are certain that they—and only they—know the truth of what happened; that truth, not coincidentally, always implies that if they had only been believed and followed, America would have been magically transformed into that City on the Hill. For sure.

My models remain freedom fighters like Ella Baker and Septima Clark, each an activist community educator. They were workers in literacy and voting rights projects, in community organizations and educational institutions. Every project on which they worked was linked to a larger life project of community empowerment for liberation. Each was a teacher, then, in the largest and best sense: a dreamer, a builder, a creator of intellectual space and ethical action, an enabler of individuals, and a midwife of a new society. When history is being rewritten in the interest of a smoother, less troublesome tale, a story more tailored to an era of selfishness and perceived powerlessness, it is well to reaffirm the choices made in troubled times. These teachers remind us that in spite of humiliation and opposition, resistance continues. Though there are periods of quiet and confusion, people always rise again. As Maya Angelou has written, "You may write me down in history / With your bitter, twisted lies, / You may trod me in the very dirt / But still, like dust, I'll rise."

People go on teaching, go on raising children, go on learning, go on hoping, toiling, troubling, and trying. Beaten down by racism, sexism, class exploitation, by the great white whale, the great myth and the great cultural emptiness, as well as by fear of dying, fear of being different, fear of being impolite—still people rise. We rise because we perceive an alternative; we begin to identify the unacceptable. We find free voices that say "No!" to inequities, to the structure of oppression and privilege, to the growing emiseration that we find everywhere. Free minds dare to dream of something different. We find, then, that our bodies move in new ways, that new freedoms demand new actions, and together we reclaim our lives and begin to build our futures. We dare to dream, dare to act. Like Septima Clark and Ella Baker, if we can become brave in our visions and in our actions, the rest will follow. We can perhaps contribute as builders of something new, a world where people can care more, love more fully and more widely, touch each other more, think more clearly, solve more problems, laugh and cry more. A world fit for all children. This was once worth our trouble and still is.

25

Déjà Vu All Over Again

STAUGHTON LYND

From Civil Rights to Vietnam

THE EARLIEST PICTURE in my mind about the war in Vietnam is a scene in Mississippi during the summer of 1964. The place was the site of a burned church in Philadelphia, Mississippi. The church had been offered for use as a freedom school and was burned for that reason in June 1964. As the 1964 Mississippi Summer project was beginning, civil rights workers James Chaney, Andrew Goodman, and Michael Schwerner went to Philadelphia to seek another location for the school. They were arrested, released in the middle of the night, ambushed, and murdered. In my memory, it is late July or early August, the bodies of Chaney, Goodman, and Schwerner had been found a few days before, and I am attending a memorial service in Philadelphia.

Bob Moses of the Student Nonviolent Coordinating Committee (SNCC) stood at the bottom of a slope, at one corner of what had been the church, with the ruined building before him. We who were listening had traveled by car under very tight security to be there. We stood in a semicircle on the hillside, as if in a Greek amphitheater. Moses said that the bodies of the three men had been found just as President Johnson was using the Tonkin Bay incident to obtain congressional authorization for undefined escalation of the war in Vietnam.

Moses spelled out the connection between civil rights and Vietnam at the Berkeley Teach-In the next year.

Before the summer project last summer we watched five Negroes murdered in two counties of Mississippi with no reaction from the country. We couldn't get the news out. Then we saw that when the three civil rights workers [Chaney, Goodman, and Schwerner] were killed, and two of them were white, the whole country reacted, went into motion. There's a deep problem behind that, and I think that if you can begin to understand what that problem is—why you don't move when a Negro is killed the same way you move when a white person is killed—then maybe you can begin to understand this country in relation to Vietnam and the third world, the Congo and Santo Domingo.[1]

I think I can pinpoint the moment when the war took the place of the civil rights movement in my consciousness. It was early in 1965, a few months after Lyndon Johnson's election as president and shortly before the beatings on the bridge in Selma, Alabama, which triggered passage of the 1965 Voting Rights Act. I was on a plane back to New Haven from Selma when I read that the United States had escalated the air war by bombing North Vietnam. I could almost feel my mind and body readjusting themselves, refocusing on what was happening overseas. I suspect that much the same thing happened to many others.

In January 1966, a year before any comparable action by Students for a Democratic Society (SDS), SNCC publicly stated its support for refusing induction. During the months that followed, a number of whites who had been in Mississippi—among them, Mendy Samstein, David Harris, Dennis Sweeney, Dan Wood, Jake Blum, John Wilhelm, and myself—worked to develop a draft resistance movement. We shared the movement concept of "putting your body in the way" and sought a strategy to act in that spirit against the Vietnam War.[2]

Being Driven, Being Effective

There was an intensity about our lives during the years of the Vietnam War that is easy to remember, but hard to put in words. Like others, I over and over again did things that I had no reason to expect to succeed but felt driven to do. Over and over again, what we did proved effective.

Often what we did seemed amateurish, impromptu. In April 1965, I was asked to chair the first march on Washington against the Vietnam War.

Paul Potter, president of SDS, was to deliver the keynote speech. His speech had been mimeographed. As the rally at the Washington Monument was about to begin, we discovered that the mimeographed copies had been left in the local SNCC office. Rennie Davis and I hurried to the office. It was locked, but, jimmying open a window, we slithered inside and retrieved the copies. By then, it was well past the time at which the speeches were to begin. As Rennie and I hurried toward the mall with our arms full of paper, I could only wonder how the rally was proceeding without its chairperson. The rally was doing just fine! Senator Gruening (one of the two senators to vote against the Tonkin Bay resolution), independent journalist I. F. Stone, and of course Paul Potter spoke memorably.

I mention my own experiences only because I know them at firsthand. In May 1965, at the Berkeley Teach-In, I called for an improvised vote of no-confidence in the form of civil disobedience so massive that President Johnson and his advisers would be forced to resign. (Three years later, Secretary of Defense McNamara did in fact leave the government, and President Johnson announced he would not run again.) I was particularly concerned that during the summer of 1965, when students were away from campus, so many U.S. soldiers would be sent to Vietnam that by fall it would be impossible to dissent.

In June 1965, I went to the steps of the Pentagon with a very small group of friends. Within moments of our arrival, we were surrounded by military policemen incredulous that a handful of people would undertake so obviously ineffectual an action. "You don't understand," I replied with all the dignity I could muster, "we are just the first of thousands." (As it turned out, we were.)

In early August 1965, on the twentieth anniversaries of the bombing of Hiroshima and Nagasaki, an Assembly of Unrepresented People convened in Washington. After two days of workshops (in the course of which my wife Alice decided to become a draft counselor),[3] we carried out a plan to march to the steps of the Capitol to declare peace with the people of Vietnam. I was in the front row flanked by David Dellinger and Bob Moses. Red paint was thrown on the three of us as we proceeded slowly from the Washington Monument toward the Capitol. There we encountered several lines of police and were arrested.

In December 1965, I took part in what turned out to be my most publicized act of opposition to the war. Herbert Aptheker, a fellow historian and a member of the Communist Party of the United States, invited me to go to North Vietnam and to take with me another noncommunist active in the peace movement. I first invited Moses. After consultating with others in SNCC, he declined. Only a few weeks before my scheduled departure, Tom Hayden visited us in New Haven. He and I took my two small children sledding. As we were waiting for Barbara and Lee to drag their sleds back up the hill, I asked, "Tom, how would you like to go to Vietnam?" After talking it over with colleagues in SDS, Tom accepted.

My model in making the trip was a Quaker physician named George Logan. During the late 1790s, when the United States was on the verge of war with revolutionary France, Dr. Logan went to Paris and spoke with leaders of the French government. Returning to this country, he reported to President John Adams and apparently contributed to averting a war. (By way of thanks, Congress passed the "Logan Act," which forbids private citizens to conduct diplomacy on behalf of the United States.)

No diplomatic breakthrough occurred as a result of the trip to Hanoi. I see now that this was because, from the beginning, the Vietnamese expected to win their war for independence. Aptheker, Hayden, and I passed through Moscow on the way to Vietnam and talked with Dang Quang Minh, the North Vietnamese ambassador to the Soviet Union. He was a slight, elderly man, who spoke very softly. Some remark of mine alerted him to my assumption that the United States had the military power to destroy the Vietnamese guerrilla movement. "You don't understand, professor," I recall him saying. "We're going to win. The United States has two choices. One, you can withdraw from our country immediately, which, of course, we would prefer. Two, you can send more American soldiers, in which case we will also win because for every United States soldier who lands in Vietnam one more Vietnamese will come to the National Liberation Front."

One result of this mission to Hanoi was that I could no longer find full-time work as a teacher of American history.

Others took resistance much further. In November 1965, Norman Morrison went to the steps of the Pentagon, poured kerosene over himself, and burned himself to death. Norman, a Quaker, was employed by the Stony Run (Baltimore) Friends Meeting, where Alice and I had been married. We knew him slightly, and Alice's parents knew him well: he drove to the Pentagon in a car owned by Alice's mother. When Aptheker, Hayden, and I arrived in Hanoi a few weeks after Norman's death, we found that he was a national hero there.

It seems clear that Norman Morrison's self-immolation was a turning point in Secretary McNamara's private thoughts about the war. According to biographer Deborah Shapley, "In the early evening of November 2, during rush hour, McNamara was in a meeting in his office at the Pentagon. He was told something was happening outside his window. Moving to the big curtains and looking down into the dusk, he saw a knot of agitated people, and ambulances and smoke. Medics were covering something in blankets." Years later, McNamara was barely able to talk about what had happened.[4]

In his autobiography, McNamara goes further. "I reacted," he writes,

> by bottling up my emotions and avoided talking about them with anyone—even my family. I knew Marg and our three children shared many of Morrison's feelings about the war, as did the wives and children of several of my cabinet colleagues. . . . There was much Marg and I and the children should have talked about, yet at moments like this I often turn inward instead—it is a grave weakness. The episode created tension at home that only deepened as dissent and criticism of the war continued to grow.[5]

Norman Morrison's legacy was passed on to Brian Willson, who had been acquainted with Norman in high school. Brian grew up as a very religious, deeply conservative young man, and when he was eighteen, his occupational objective was to join the FBI. In 1966, he volunteered for the air force. Arriving in South Vietnam, he was assigned to travel to villages after they had been bombed by South Vietnamese pilots and to conduct a ground assessment of the "success" of the raids. One day,

> while assessing the "success" of a bombing mission in a small village south of Sa Dec, I looked at the face of a young mother on the ground whose eyes appeared to be open as she held two children in one arm, another child in the other. Upon closer examination I realized she and her children had been killed by bomb fragments. Napalm had apparently burned much of her face, including her eyelids. I stared into her eyes from a close distance, leaning over to do so. Tears streamed down my face.
>
> I looked at that mother's face, what was left of it, and it flashed at that point in my mind that the whole idea of the threat of Communism was ridiculous. Somehow I couldn't see Communism on her face. I remember looking at that woman's face, and thinking, "I wonder what a Communist looks like?" All I saw was the face of a mother no older than twenty hold-

ing her children. All of them were dead. I said, "My God, this bombing, this war, is a lie. I've been living a lie. What does all this mean? These people are just persons, just human beings."[6]

In 1987, Brian sat down in the path of a train carrying munitions for El Salvador and Nicaragua and lost both his legs.

War and the Working Class

In the late 1960s, it was generally supposed by the media (and by many in the movement as well) that White male workers—the "hard hats," as they were known—strongly supported the Vietnam War. It now appears that, in the words of United Auto Workers (UAW) official Paul Schrade,

> workers were moving against the war at a more rapid rate than people in the middle and upper classes. A study by Harlan Hahn that appeared in the late sixties showed that in all the referenda in all parts of the country at that time, the working-class precincts were leading the other precincts in terms of the need for a pullout from and an end to the war in Vietnam. In 1971, according to a Lou Harris poll, sixty-four percent of the labor union membership was in favor of an early pullout from Vietnam. In California, during that period, fifty-nine percent of labor union members favored an early pullout. Another poll showed that fifty-three percent of union members disapproved of the hard-hat approach of beating up demonstrators.[7]

Rank-and-file union members were more prepared to oppose the war than were their leaders. I saw this for myself at a conference on "Labor for Peace" in St. Louis. The gathering was convened by the top officers of certain unions generally considered progressive: the UAW, American Federation of State, County, and Municipal Employees (AFSCME), the Longshoremen and Warehousemen (ILWU), the Furriers, and so on. These gentlemen sat on a platform at the front of the hall and made it clear that what they wanted were resolutions, not direct action. One of the rank-and-file members, a teacher from New Rochelle, made a motion that the conference should call for a single day of protest in workplaces all across the United States. He was not proposing a general strike: he made it clear that in each workplace workers should use their own judgment as to whether they could take an extended lunch break, demonstrate before or after work, or wear antiwar caps and T-shirts on the job. But the proposal frightened the leaders on the platform. Emil Mazey of the UAW, chairperson of that session of the conference, suggested with heavy sarcasm that a straw vote be taken to show what a poor idea the teacher had suggested. When a show of hands was called for, the motion passed overwhelmingly! The officers caucused during the lunch hour and then brought forward the leader with the most radical reputation—Harry Bridges, president of the ILWU—to move successfully for reconsideration.

As the Vietnam War dragged on, the soldiers who more and more resisted it were for the most part workers, White and Black. Official Department of Defense statistics show that between 1965 and 1973 from seventeen thousand to eighteen thousand members of the armed forces applied for noncombatant status or discharge as conscientious objectors.[8] And this was only the tip of the iceberg of military protest: a far greater number refused to fight, deserted, or even sought to kill overzealous officers. For example, one of the so-called Presidio 27—who in October 1968 staged a sit-down strike at the Presidio military base in San Francisco on behalf of an end to the war, opposition to racism, and better treatment in the stockade—recalls that most of the group "were working-class guys."[9]

The Gulf War

During the Gulf War in 1991, my wife Alice and I were living in Youngstown, Ohio. We had moved there fifteen years earlier and were employed as lawyers in a legal services office that gave free legal aid to poor and working-class clients. We had developed bonds of trust with many groups of workers in struggling against arbitrary discharges, plant shutdowns, race and sex discrimination, and the erosion of pension and medical insurance benefits for retirees.

The Youngstown Workers' Solidarity Club (Alice and I among them) called for picketing everyday at noon in the downtown city plaza. Alice and I went to an ad hoc meeting of groups opposed to the war to propose the idea. Another member of the club, a lineman for Ohio Edison, got to the meeting before we did. By the time we walked in, the picketing idea had already been approved.

We began by picketing at the site of a memorial stone on which had been carved the names of Youngstown residents killed in Vietnam. Our presence there upset the members of a veterans' group that had erected the monument, so we talked with them. Greg Yarwick, the lineman, said that the names of three friends with whom he went to high school were on that stone: he didn't want to see the names of anymore dead friends. In the end, we agreed to move our picket line to a location that was just as visible but less offensive to the veterans. It became a regular part of our protests to step out of the picket line and talk with any heckler or obvious opponent. We probably did not change any minds, but at least respectful relationships were established. The hecklers rapidly diminished.

I recall that when we decided to picket—and I was among those who suggested it—I felt, "Well, fifteen years of work in Youngstown may be going down the drain. But we have to do it anyway."

What actually happened surprised me. One very outspoken man looked me in the eye and said, "Lynd, you know I disagree with you about the war." Then everything went on as before. Another retiree came up to me as I was walking with a group of former steelworkers along a sidewalk in Cleveland. "You know I agree with you about the war," he said.

Had the Gulf War lasted more than a few weeks, the numbers of people opposed to what was happening would have increased rapidly. There were two huge demonstrations in Washington as the war was getting underway. Seven busloads from Youngstown went to one of them. Leaving about midnight, we stopped at Breezewood, Pennsylvania, where U.S. 70 takes off from U.S. 76 toward Washington, about 4 A.M. It seemed that every other bus from the Midwest had done the same. I remember especially talking over breakfast with a man from Iowa. He had been a policeman during the Vietnam war. Reflecting on his experience, he had decided that the demonstrators were right. This time around he was determined to be one of them.

Déjà Vu All Over Again

Historians have not done very well in explaining anything about the 1960s. Why did the movement begin? We don't really know. Why did the movement so precipitously come to an end? We don't know that, either. And why was there a Vietnam War? Was it because of oil, markets, manhood, or the desire of the best and brightest in the governing class not to be left out of their World War II? I have not seen an adequate explanation. Vietnam is like a recurrent illness, the cause of which is unexplained but which can be recognized by its symptoms. For example, the U.S. government now specializes in beating up nations much smaller than itself in wars that it can finish quickly. Vietnam was intended to be such a war. The invasions of Grenada and Panama, and the Gulf War, filled the bill.

Such dirty little wars are shameful, and everything about them fills the soul with remorse. I agree with my friend David Harris:

> Our disorder is plain to see: having made lying an accepted government function, our government is now overrun with liars [as in the matter of the exposure of Gulf War servicemen and women to toxic chemicals]; having made our public posture heartless as a matter of policy, we are now unable to bring our heart to public affairs; having made killing a measure of our national efforts, we watch helplessly as killing has become one of our principal cultural currencies; having failed to look our transgressions straight in the face, we have not been straight with one another since; having refused to live up to our values, we are now increasingly without values; having made language into hype, we now have nothing believeable to say.[10]

It might be comforting to suppose that Vietnam was a Great Aberration: that it came once, but will not come again. In my opinion, any such conclusion is irrational. Multinational corporations based in the United States believe they are running the world. The "American Century" projected by Henry Luce—a Pax Americana safeguarded by the U.S. nuclear arsenal—is, from the standpoint of the centurions, finally here. It follows that those who refuse to put a pinch of incense on Caesar's altar or to hang out yellow ribbons on demand have to be prepared for a lifetime of what in the 1960s we called "resistance."

Resistance is halfway between protest and revolution. Resistance means forthrightly refusing to fight in imperialist wars, if it comes to that. It also means more subtle things: for example, choosing a lifestyle that will minimize the tax dollars that we render to the U.S. war machine. At the end of World War II, *Politics* magazine correctly prophesied that the United States would henceforth seek to forestall a repetition of the Great Depression of the 1930s by means of a "permanent war economy." We shall have to project in opposition a permanent resistance on behalf of life.

Actually, why should we complain? It was in mortal combat with the dragons of racism and genocidal war that the movement of the 1960s came into being. Writer after writer in this collection looks back to the 1960s as a time when he or she dared to dream of better things, when brothers and sisters held hands in a circle of love, when we experienced what William James called "the moral equivalent of war." So it can be again. What we valued in the 1960s—nonviolence, participatory democracy, an experiential approach to learning, accompanying rather than manipulating those whom we sought to organize—remains as true today as it was a generation ago.

We were not mindless activists: we had not yet found adequate words for our new experiences. We were not nihilists: we were trying to make real the values we had been taught. We were not elitists: we only asked that people vote their whole lives, not a strip of paper merely.

The movement can be, must be for the sake of this fragile world of ours, a Once and Future Movement.

Notes

Index

Notes

1. Introduction

1. Marvin E. Gettleman et al., eds,. *Vietnam and America* (New York: Grove, 1995).

6. The Responsibility of Intellectuals

1. Such a research project has now been undertaken and published as a "Citizens' White Paper": F. Schurmann, P. D. Scott, R. Zelnik, *The Politics of Escalation in Vietnam* (New York: Fawcett World Library; Boston: Beacon Press, 1966). For further evidence of American rejection of UN initiatives for diplomatic settlement, just prior to the major escalation of February 1965, see Mario Rossi, "The US Rebuff to U Thant," *New York Review of Books* November 17, 1966. There is further documentary evidence of NLF attempts to establish a coalition government and to neutralize the area, all rejected by the United States and its Saigon ally, in Douglas Pike, *Viet Cong* (Cambridge, Mass.: MIT. Press, 1966). In reading material of this latter sort, one must be especially careful to distinguish between the evidence presented and the "conclusions" that are asserted, for reasons noted briefly below (see note 22).

It is interesting to see the first, somewhat oblique, published reactions to *The Politics of Escalation* by those who defend our right to conquer South Vietnam and institute a government of our choice. For example, Robert Scalapino (*New York Times Magazine,* December 11, 1966) argues that the thesis of the book implies that our leaders are "diabolical." Since no right-thinking person can believe this, the thesis is refuted. To assume otherwise would betray "irresponsibilty," in a unique sense of this term, a sense that gives an ironic twist to the title of this essay. He goes on to point out the alleged central weakness in the argument of the book—namely, the failure to perceive that a serious attempt on our part to pursue the possibilities for a diplomatic settlement would have been interpreted by our adversaries as a sign of weakness.

2. At other times, Schlesinger does indeed display admirable scholarly caution. For example, in his introduction to *The Politics of Escalation,* he admits that there may have been "flickers of interest in negotiations" on the part of Hanoi. As to the administration's lies about negotiations and its repeated actions undercutting tentative initiatives towards negotiations, he comments only that the authors may have underestimated military necessity and that future historians may prove them wrong. This caution and detachment must be compared with Schlesinger's attitude toward renewed study of the origins of the Cold War:

in a letter to the *New York Review of Books* (October 20, 1966), he remarks that it is time to "blow the whistle" on revisionist attempts to show that the Cold War may have been the consequence of something more than mere communist belligerence. We are to believe, then, that the relatively straightforward matter of the origins of the Cold War is settled beyond discussion, whereas the much more complex issue of why the United States shies away from a negotiated settlement in Vietnam must be left to future historians to ponder.

It is useful to bear in mind that the United States government itself is on occasion much less diffident in explaining why it refuses to contemplate a meaningful negotiated settlement. As is freely admitted, this solution would leave it without power to control the situation. See, for example, note 26.

3. Arthur M. Schlesinger, Jr., *A Thousand Days: John F. Kennedy in the White House* (Boston: Houghton Mifflin, 1965), p. 421.

4. *The View from the Seventh Floor* (New York: Harper and Row, 1964), p. 149. See also his *United States in the World Arena* (New York: Harper and Row, 1960), p. 244: "Stalin, exploiting the disruption and weakness of the postwar world, pressed out from the expanded base he had won during the second World War in an effort to gain the balance of power in Eurasia . . . turning to the East, to back Mao and to enflame the North Korean and Indochinese Communists."

5. For example, the article by CIA analyst George Carver placed in *Foreign Affairs* (April 1966). See also note 22.

6. See Jean Lacouture, *Vietnam Between Two Truces* (New York: Random House, 1966), p. 21. Diem's analysis of the situation was shared by Western observers at the time. See, for example, the comments of William Henderson, Far Eastern specialist and executive, Council on Foreign Relations, in R. W. Lindholm, ed., *Vietnam: The First Five Years* (East Lansing: Michigan State University Press, 1959). He notes "the growing alienation of the intelligenstsia," "the renewal of armed dissidence in the South," the fact that "security has noticeably deteriorated in the last two years," all as a result of Diem's "grim dictatorship," and predicts "a steady worsening of the political climate in free Vietnam, culminating in unforeseen disasters."

7. See Bernard Fall, "Vietnam in the Balance," *Foreign Affairs* (October 1966).

8. Stalin was neither pleased by the Titoist tendencies inside the Greek Communist Party, nor by the possibility that a Balkan federation might develop under Titoist leadership. It is, nevertheless, conceivable that Stalin supported the Greek guerrillas at some stage of the rebellion, in spite of the difficulty of obtaining firm documentary evidence. Needless to say, no elaborate study is necessary to document the British or American role in this civil conflict, from late 1944. See D. G. Kousoulas, *The Price of Freedom*, (Syracuse, N.Y.: Syracuse University Press, 1953); *Revolution and Defeat* (London and New York: Oxford University Press, 1965), for serious study of these events from a strongly anticommunist point of view.

9. For a detailed account, see James Warburg, *Germany: Key to Peace* (Cambridge, Mass.: Harvard University Press, 1953), p. 189ff. Warburg concludes that apparently "the Kremlin was now prepared to accept the creation of an All-German democracy in the Western sense of that word," whereas the Western powers, in their response, "frankly admitted their plan 'to secure the participation of Germany in a purely defensive European community'" (i.e., NATO).

10. *United States and the World Arena*, pp. 344–45. Incidentally, those who quite rightly deplore the brutal suppression of the East German and Hungarian revolutions would do well

to remember that these scandalous events might have been avoided had the United States been willing to consider proposals for neutralization of Central Europe. Some of George Kennan's recent statements have provided interesting commentary on this matter—for example, his comments on the falsity, from the outset, of the assumption that the USSR intended to attack or intimidate by force the Western half of the continent and that it was deterred by American force, and his remarks on the sterility and general absurdity of the demand for unilateral Soviet withdrawal from Eastern Germany together with "the inclusion of a united Germany as a major component in a Western defense system based primarily on nuclear weaponry." *Pacem in Terris,* edited by E. Reed (New York: Pocket Books, 1965).

It is worth noting that historical fantasy of the sort illustrated in Rostow's remarks has become a regular State Department specialty. Thus, we have Thomas Mann justifying our Dominican intervention as a response to actions of the "Sino-Soviet military bloc." Or, to take a more considered statement, we have William Bundy's analysis of stages of development of Communist ideology in his Pomona College address, February 12, 1966, in which he characterizes the Soviet Union in the 1920s and early 1930s as "in a highly militant and aggressive phase." What is frightening about fantasy, as distinct from outright falsification, is the possibility that it may be sincere and may actually serve as the basis for formation of policy.

11. Subcommittee on the Far East and the Pacific of the Committee on Foreign Affairs, House of Representatives, *United States Policy toward Asia* (Washington, D.C.: U.S. Government Printing Office, 1966).

12. *New York Times Book Review,* November 20, 1966. Such comments call to mind the remarkable spectacle of President Kennedy counseling Cheddi Jagan on the dangers of entering into a trading relationship "which brought a country into a condition of economic dependence." The reference, of course, is to the dangers in commercial relations with the Soviet Union. See Schlesinger, *A Thousand Days,* p. 776.

13. *A Thousand Days,* p. 252.

14. Though this too is imprecise. One must recall the real character of the Trujillo regime to appreciate the full cynicism of Kennedy's "realistic" analysis.

15. W. W. Rostow and R. W. Hatch, *An American Policy in Asia* (New York: Technology Press and John Wiley, 1955).

16. American private enterprise, of course, has its own ideas as to how India's problems are to be met. The *Monitor* reports the insistence of American entrepreneurs "on importing all equipment and machinery when India has a tested capacity to meet some of their requirements. They have insisted on importing liquid ammonia, a basic raw material, rather than using indigenous naphtha which is abundantly available. They have laid down restrictions about pricing, distribution, restriction, profits and management and management control."

A major postwar scandal is developing in India, as the United States, cynically capitalizing on India's current torture, applies its economic power to implement what the *New York Times* calls India's "drift from socialism towards pragmatism" (April 28, 1965).

17. Although, to maintain perspective, we should recall that in his wildest moments, Alfred Rosenberg spoke of the elimination of thirty million Slavs, not the imposition of mass starvation on a quarter of the human race. Incidentally, the analogy drawn here is highly "irresponsible," in the technical sense of this neologism discussed earlier. That is, it is based on the assumption that statements and actions of Americans are subject to the same standards and open to the same interpretations as those of anyone else.

18. *New York Times,* February 6, 1966. Goldberg continues, the United States is not certain that all of these are voluntary adherents. This is not the first such demonstration of communist duplicity. Another example was seen in the year 1962, when according to U.S. government sources fifteen thousand guerrillas suffered thirty thousand casualties. See Arthur Schlesinger, *A Thousand Days,* p. 982.

19. Reprinted in a collection of essays, *The End of Ideology: on the Exhaustion of Political Ideas in the Fifties* (New York: Free Press, 1960). I have no intention here of entering into the full range of issues that have been raised in the discussion of "end of ideology" for the past dozen years. It is difficult to see how a rational person could quarrel with many of the theses that have been put forth—e.g., that at a certain historical moment the "politics of civility" is appropriate and, perhaps, efficacious; that one who advocates action (or inaction) has a responsibility to assess its social cost; that dogmatic fanaticism and "secular religions" should be combated (or if possible, ignored); that technical solutions to problems should be implemented, where possible; that *"le dogmatism ideologique devait disparaitre pour que les idèes reprissent vie"* (Aron), and so on. Because this is sometimes taken to be an expression of an "anti-Marxist" position, it is worth keeping in mind that such sentiments as these have no bearing on non-Bolshevik Marxism as represented, for example, by such figures as Luxembourg, Pannekoek, Korsch, Arthur Rosenberg, and others.

20. The extent to which this "technology" is value-free is hardly very important, given the clear commitments of those who apply it. The problems with which research is concerned are those posed by the Pentagon or the great corporations, not, say, by the revolutionaries of Northeast Brazil or by SNCC. Nor am I aware of a research project devoted to the problem of how poorly armed guerrillas might more effectively resist a brutal and devastating military technology—surely the kind of problem that would have interested the free-floating intellectual who is now hopelessly out of date.

21. In view of the unremitting propaganda barrage on "Chinese Expansion," perhaps a word of comment is in order. Typical of American propaganda on this subject is Adlai Steveson's assessment, shortly before his death (cf. *New York Times Magazine,* March 13, 1966): "So far, the new communist 'dynasty' has been very aggressive. Tibet was swallowed, India attacked, the Malays had to fight 12 years to resist a 'national liberation' they could receive from the British by a more peaceful route. Today, the apparatus of infiltration and aggression is already at work in North Thailand."

As to Malaya, Stevenson is probably confusing ethnic Chinese with the government of China. Those concerned with the actual events would agree with Harry Miller in *Communist Menace in Malaya* (New York: Praeger, 1954) that "Communist China continues to show little interest in the Malayan affair beyond its usual fulminations via Peking Radio." There are various harsh things that one might say about Chinese behavior in what the Sino-Indian Treaty of 1954 refers to as "the Tibet region of China," but it is no more proof of a tendency towards expansionism than is the behavior of the Indian government with regard to the Naga and Mizo tribesmen. As to North Thailand, "the apparatus of infiltration" may well be at work, though there is little reason to suppose it to be Chinese—and it is surely not unrelated to the American use of Thailand as a base of its attack on Vietnam. This reference is the sheerest hypocrisy.

The "attack on India" grew out of a border dispute that began several years after the Chinese had completed a road from Tibet to Sinkiang in an area so remote from Indian control that the Indians learned about this operation only from the Chinese press.

According to American air force maps, the disputed areas is in Chinese territory. Cf. Alastair Lamb, *China Quarterly* (July–September 1965). To this distinguished authority, "it seems unlikely that the Chinese have been working out some master plan . . . to take over the Indian sub-continent lock, stock, and overpopulated barrel." Rather, he thinks it likely that the Chinese were probably unaware that India even claimed the territory through which the road passed. After the Chinese military victory, Chinese troops were, in most areas, withdrawn beyond the McMahon line, a border that the British had attempted to impose on China in 1914 but which has never been recognized by China (Nationalist or Communist), the United States, or any other government. It is remarkable that a person in a responsible position could describe all of this as Chinese expansionism. In fact, it is absurd to debate the hypothetical aggressiveness of a China surrounded by American missiles and a still-expanding network of military bases backed by an enormous American expeditionary force in Southeast Asia. It is conceivable that at some future time a powerful China may be expansionist. We may speculate about such possibilities if we wish, but it is American aggressiveness that is the central fact of current politics.

22. Douglas Pike, *Viet Cong,* p. 110. This book, written by a foreign service officer working at the Center for International Studies at MIT., poses a contrast between our side, which sympathizes with "the usual revolutionary stirrings . . . around the world because they reflect inadequate living standards or oppressive and corrupt governments," and the backers of "revolutionary guerrilla warfare," which "opposes the aspirations of people while apparently furthering them, manipulates the individual by persuading him to manipulate himself." Revolutionary guerrilla warfare is "an imported product, revolution from the outside" (other examples, besides the Viet Cong, are "Stalin's exportation of armed revolution," the Haganah in Palestine, and the Irish Republican Army; see pp. 32–33). The Viet Cong could not be an indigenous movement because it had "a social construction program of such scope and ambition that of necessity it must have been created in Hanoi" (p. 76—but on pages 77–79 we read that "organizational activity had gone on intensively and systematically for several years" before the Lao Dong Party in Hanoi had made its decision "to begin building an organization"). On page 80 we find "such an effort had to be the child of the North," even though elsewhere we read of the prominent role of the Cao Dai (p. 74), "the first major social group to begin actively opposing the Diem government" (p. 222), and of the Hoa Hao sect, "another early and major participant in the NLF" (p. 69). Pike takes it as proof of communist duplicity that in the South, the party insisted it was "Marxist-Leninist," thus "indicating philosophic but not political allegiance," whereas in the North it described itself as a "Marxist-Leninist organization," thus "indicating that it was in the mainstream of the world-wide Communist movement" (p. 150). And so on. Also revealing is the contempt for "Cinderella and all the other fools [who] could still believe there was magic in the mature world if one mumbled the secret incantation: solidarity, union, concord; for the gullible, misled people" who were "turning the countryside into a bedlam toppling one Saigon government after another," for the "mighty force of people" who in their mindless innocence thought that "the meek, at last, were to inherit the earth," that riches would be theirs and all in the name of justice and virtue." One can appreciate the chagrin with which a sophisticated Western political scientist must view this "sad and awesome spectacle."

23. Lacouture, *Vietnam,* p. 188. The same military spokesman goes on, ominously, to say that this is the problem confronting us throughout Asia, Africa, and Latin America, and that we must find the "proper response" to it.

24. William Bundy, in *China and the Peace of Asia,* edited by A. Buchan (New York: Praeger, 1965).

25. Lindholm, *Vietnam.*

21. Visiting Vietnam

1. Proceedings of the Southeast Asian Seminar on Women and Science in Developing Coutries, Hanoi, Vietnam, January 8–10, 1987. Kovalevskaia Fund, 6547 17th Ave., N.E., Seattle, Wash. 98115.

2. Ibid., p. 12.

3. A brief report about Vietnam's high incidence of abnormal pregancies can be found in ibid., pp. 10–11.

25. Déjà Vu All Over Again

1. Louis Menashe, ed., *Berkeley Teach-In: Vietnam,* record album no. FD5765 (Washington, D.C.: Folkways, 1966), quoted in *Nonviolence in America: A Documentary History,* edited by Alice Lynd and Staughton Lynd (Maryknoll, N.Y.: Orbis Books, 1995), pp. xxxiv–xxxv.

2. Michael Ferber and Staughton Lynd, *The Resistance* (Boston: Beacon Press, 1971), chapters 3 and 4.

3. One product of her work was *We Won't Go: Personal Accounts of War Objectors* (Boston: Beacon Press, 1968).

4. Deborah Shapley, *Promise and Power: The Life and Times of Robert McNamara* (Boston: Little, Brown and Company, 1993), pp. 353–55. Paul Hendrickson likewise concludes that "it is clear now from scholarship on the war, and not least from McNamara's own testimony in a New York libel trial, and also from what's tucked between the lines of [McNamara's] 1995 memoir, that the season in which a secretary of defense began to make a turn against all he had made and masterminded" was the same season in which Norman Morrison burned himself to death outside McNamara's office at the Pentagon. Paul Hendrickson, *The Living and the Dead: Robert McNamara and Five Lives of a Lost War* (New York: Alfred A. Knopf, 1996), p. 195; and pp. 181–240.

5. Robert S. McNamara, *In Retrospect: The Tragedy and Lessons of Vietnam* (New York: Times Book, 1995), pp. 216–17.

6. S. Brian Willson, *On Third World Legs,* with an Introduction by Staughton Lynd (Chicago: Charles H. Kerr, 1992), pp. 17–19.

7. *Vietnam Reconsidered: Lessons from a War,* edited by Harrison E. Salisbury (New York: Harper and Row, 1984), pp. 79–80.

8. Charles C. Moskos and John Whiteclay Chambers II, *The New Conscientious Objection: From Sacred to Secular Resistance* (New York: Oxford University Press, 1993), pp. 42–43, and sources cited on pp. 241–42.

9. James W. Tollefson, *The Strength Not to Fight: An Oral History of Conscientious Objectors to the Vietnam War* (Boston: Little, Brown and Company, 1993), p. 183.

10. David Harris, *Our War: What We Did in Vietnam and What It Did to Us* (New York: Times Books, 1996), p. 8.

Index